FLASHBACKS

Books and monographs by Timothy Leary

The Dimensions of Intelligence (M.S. thesis, Washington State University, 1946)

The Social Dimensions of Personality (Ph.D. thesis, University of California, 1950)

The Interpersonal Diagnosis of Personality (John Wiley, 1957)

The Multi-level Assessment of Personality (Psychological Consultation Service, 1957)

The Existential Transaction (Psychological Consultation Service, 1960)

The Psychedelic Experience (with R. Metzner and R. Alpert, University Books, 1964)

The Psychedelic Reader (ed., with G. Weil, University Books, 1965)

Psychedelic Prayers from the Tao Te Ching (University Books, 1967)

High Priest (NAL-World, 1968)

Politics of Ecstasy (Putnam, 1968)

Jail Notes (World-Evergreen, 1971)

Confessions of a Hope Fiend (Bantam, 1973)

Neurologic (with Joanna Leary, Starseed, 1973)

Starseed: A Psy-Phi Comet Tale (Starseed, 1973)

The Curse of the Oval Room (Starseed, 1974)

Terra II (with Joanna Leary and L. W. Benner, Starseed, 1974)

Communication with Higher Intelligence (ed., Spit in the Ocean, 1977)

Changing My Mind-Among Others (Prentice-Hall, 1982)

Future History Series (Peace Press)
Vol. I: *What Does WoMan Want?* (1976)
Vol. II: *Exo-Psychology* (1977)
Vol. III: *Neuropolitics* (1977)
Vol. IV: *Intelligence Agents* (1979)
Vol. V: *The Game of Life* (1979)

FLASHBACKS

An Autobiography

Timothy Leary

J. P. TARCHER, INC.
Los Angeles
Distributed by Houghton Mifflin Company
Boston

Library of Congress Cataloging in Publication Data

Leary, Timothy Francis, 1920–
    Flashbacks, an autobiography.

    1. Leary, Timothy Francis, 1920–
2. Psychologists—United States—Biography. I. Title.
BF109.L43A38 1983   150'.092'4 [B]   82–16915
ISBN 0–87477–177–3
ISBN 0-87477-317-2 (ppbk.)

Jeremy P. Tarcher, Inc.
9110 Sunset Blvd.
Los Angeles, CA 90069

Designed by John Brogna

MANUFACTURED IN THE UNITED STATES OF AMERICA

S 10 9 8 7 6 5 4 3 2

To Barbara and All the Children

Acknowledgments

Jeremy Tarcher is the publisher about whom wistful authors dream. His literary wisdom has guided this project since its beginning. In addition, his editorial comments, witty and withering, added up to a fair-sized manual on how to cure adjectival addiction and other word abuse.

The task of editing and revising several thousand pages of manuscript was miraculously performed by Stephanie Bernstein. Over time our collaboration moved from respectful debate to fond negotiation to reflex feedback to resonant telepathy.

Valuable advice and support came from other friends on the Tarcher staff—Kim Freilich, Leslie Brown, Janice Gallagher, Millie Loeb, Laura Golden, and Robin Raphaelian.

I am grateful to Derek Gallagher, Thom Dower, and Kelley Alexander for their innovative production and design; to Dorothy Schuler, Jon Bradshaw, George Koopman, Arel Lucas, and Karl Stull for literary counsel; to George Milman for legal counsel; and to June Newton (Alice Springs), Lawrence Schiller, and John Loengard for visual support.

To the many valiant souls, named and unnamed, who shared and shaped these adventures go my deepest thanks.

My beloved wife, Barbara, conceived this book and has nurtured it through every stage of growth.

Many conversations in this book have been reconstructed from notes and memories dating back over sixty years. In some cases dialogues that occurred at different times have been compressed into one interaction. Every attempt has been made to retain essence, style, and emotional tone.

Parts of certain chapters (including those on Allen Ginsberg, G. Gordon Liddy, Cary Grant, Charles Manson, Cord Meyer, Jr., William S. Burroughs, Thomas Pynchon, and Eldridge Cleaver) have been paraphrased from previous writings by the author.

In a few instances names have been changed to protect the privacy of persons who are not, and presumably have no wish to be, public figures.

All resemblances between the characters in this book and real people, living or dead, are intentional.

CONTENTS

Prologue

My Conception
of My Conception

I was conceived on a military reservation, West Point, New York, on the night of January 17, 1920. On the preceding day alcohol had become an illegal drug.

Academy records reveal that there was a dance that Saturday night at the Officer's Club. Now that booze was illegal, the ingestion of ethyl alcohol took on glamorous, naughty implications. The Roaring Twenties were about to begin.

My mother, Abigail, often recalled that during her pregnancy the smell of distilling moonshine and bathtub gin hung like a rowdy smog over Officer's Row. My father, Timothy, known as Tote, was about to convert from social drinking to alcohol addiction. In training me for future life he often told me that prohibition was bad but not as bad as no booze at all.

It was a very special night! Dress-blue uniforms, white gloves, long gowns, *Antoine de Paris* mannish shingle bobs. The flirtatious but virtuous Abigail, by all accounts, was the most beautiful woman on the post: jet-black hair, milky-soft white skin, curvy Gibson-Girl figure.

Tote was behaving arrogantly, as usual. Always the sportsman, he stood at the bar—tall, slim, pouring an illegal recreational drug from a silver pocket flask into the glasses of Captain Omar Bradley, Captain Geoffrey Prentice and Lieutenant George Patton.

Abigail, abandoned at a linen-covered, candlelit table, talked to her friend General Douglas MacArthur, Superintendent of the Military Academy, who asked her to dance. The orchestra played "Just a Japanese Sandman." Lt. Patton, a notorious womanizer, cut in.

Afterwards Tote approached Abigail's table. Swaying a bit to the "Missouri Waltz," my father said, "Look at you sitting there as proper as the Virgin Mary. I'm going to take you for a little annunciation."

Abigail, her elegant poise compromised only by the faintest flush, folded her fan, rose gracefully, waved gaily to her companions and walked to the cloak room.

Captain Timothy Leary drove his Packard unsteadily to the house on Officer's Row, humming "Somebody Stole My Gal." My mother retired to the bedroom, changed to her nightgown, knelt beside the bed, and prayed.

HAIL MOTHER, FULL OF GRACE

Tote mixed a drink of distilled gin. Draining his glass, he ascended unsteadily to the bedroom, removed his Army Blue Jacket with the two silver bars, his black shoes, his black silk socks, his white BVDs. He lay down next to Abigail and initiated the prim fertilization ritual typical of his generation.

Roughly two weeks previous, a splendid, once-in-a-lifetime adventurous egg had been selected carefully from the supply of one million ova stored in my mother's body and had slowly, sweetly, oozed down her soft, silky Fallopian Highway until it reached, on the night of January 17, 1920, the predetermined rendezvous.

THE LORD IS WITH THEE

At the moment of climax, Tote deposited over 400 million spermatozoa into my mother's "reproductive tract."

Opinions still vary in scientific circles about what then transpired. According to traditional biological scenarios the 400 million sperm, one of which was carrying half of me, immediately engaged in some Olympic swimming race, jostling, bumping, frantically twisting in Australian crawl or flagellating tail-stroke to win the competition, to rape poor, docile-receptive Miss Egg. Reproduction allegedly occurred when the successful jock-sperm forcibly penetrated the ovum.

I passionately reject this theory of conception. I was not reproduced! I was *created* by an intelligent, teleological process of Natural Election. Disreputable, goofy Lamarck turns out to be right at the important level of RNA. Like you, I was precisely, intelligently re-created to play a role necessary for the evolution of our gene pool. The selection of the fertilizing sperm and the decision about the final chromosome division was made by the Egg. It was the *She* of me that had the final say.

BLESSED ARE THOU AMONG WOMEN

I found myself rocketed into Abigail's re-creational laboratory, exactly where I was supposed to be, in a warm, pink ocean-cave pulsing with perfumed signals and chemical instructions, enjoying the ineffable Bliss oft-described by mystics.

Up ahead, I saw to my astonishment that Miss Egg, far from being a passive, dumb blob with round heels waiting to be knocked up by some first-to-arrive, breathless, sweaty, muscular sperm, was a lumines-cent sun, radiating amused intelligence, surrounded by magnetic fields bristling with phosphorescent radar scanners and laser-defenses.

With this particular Elegant, Educated, Experienced Egg one did not rush in with macho zeal. Laid back, late blooming, I studied her many sensory apertures, trying to decipher the signals she emitted, trying to figure out *What Does WoMan Want?* My career depended on it. Naturally I performed some tricks to attract her attention. They must have worked because soft magnetic attraction floated me gently along the Grand Ovarian Canal, up the Boulevard of Broken Genes, feeling myself measured, treasured and in some giggling way, sought and taught.

AND BLESSED IS THE FRUIT OF THY WOMB

I was eased into this soft, creamy home, my slim, serpent body sputtering with pleasure. The closer I was pulled to this solar-sphere, the more I dissolved in whirlpools of warm intelligence.

Goodbye. Hello!

Part 1

Metamorphosis:
The End of the Old

... the life of the prominent individuals within a generation cannot stand apart from the generation itself. If they are the fish, the gene-pool is the liquid in which they swim. The generational sensitivity they share is far more significant than the things that separate them.

—Landon Y. Jones,
Great Expectations:
America and the Baby Boom
Generation

A new civilization is emerging in our lives, and blind men everywhere are trying to suppress it. This new civilization brings with it new family styles; changed ways of working, loving, and living; new political conflicts; and beyond all this an altered consciousness . . .

The dawn of this new civilization is the single most explosive fact of our lifetimes.

It is the central event—the key to understanding the years immediately ahead. It is an event as profound as that First Wave of change unleashed ten thousand years ago by the invention of agriculture, or the earthshaking Second Wave of change touched off by the industrial revolution. We are children of the next transformation, the Third Wave.

—Alvin Toffler

It ain't bragging if you really done it.

—Dizzy Dean

DANTE ALIGHIERI (1265-1321), Tuscan poet, politician, romantic, psychologist, created one of the great philosophic systems of the Middle Ages. He lived amid controversy. His intellectual life centered on his worship of the female principle (personified by his beloved Beatrice) and on his consistent opposition to organized religion and papal authority. His resistance to the temporal power of Pope Boniface VIII lead to his disgrace and banishment from Florence at the age of thirty-seven.

During his exile Dante wrote *The Divine Comedy*, a long allegorical autobiography, a tale of the poet's journey through the past (Hell) and present (Purgatory) to the future (Heaven). Written in the encyclopedic-epic style, the *Commedia* is a classic portrayal of human evolution. Its theme is the gradual step-by-step understanding by the pilgrim of the stages of personal growth and development.

Dante's message was powerfully expressed through his use of the vernacular in place of the Latin used by the bureaucratic priesthood. His later works included *The New Life,* a treatise on love; the *Convivia*, a dissertation in support of humanistic science; and *De Monarchia*, an eloquent defense on secular as opposed to papal power.

1. Search for the Key

OCTOBER 22, 1955
BERKELEY, CALIFORNIA

Exactly in the middle of the allotted term of this life's journey, my thirty-fifth birthday, I entered a dark place. Marianne, my sweet, loving wife, mother of Susan and Jack, killed herself.

It was a cloudy Saturday morning. We had tickets for the football game between the California Golden Bears and the USC Trojans. I woke with a hangover but sensed at once that Marianne was not beside me. I jumped up, then lugged my leaden stomach around the house shouting, "Marianne."

No answer.

I ran outside. The garage door was closed, but I could hear the motor running inside. I wrenched the redwood door open and smelled the stale breath of exhaust. Marianne lay on the front seat, relaxed and cold. Our two children, Susan (age eight) and Jack (age six), awakened by my shouting, stood in the driveway in their pajamas, eyes bulging.

"Susan," I shouted, "run to the firehouse, and tell them to bring oxygen."

The firemen came. It was too late. Marianne had left us to our own devices.

SPRING 1959
FLORENCE, ITALY

I was living in a penthouse overlooking the domes and towers of this medieval Tuscan city. From the patio I could look down on Dante's slow-moving Arno River. Susan, now twelve, and Jack, now ten, were with me, attending the American school just east of the Old Bridge.

I was almost broke, and employment prospects were dicey. Until the preceding year, I had been a successful psychologist, author of many scientific papers and two well-regarded books on the diagnosis of personality. After sixteen years of research and teaching I had quit my post as Director of Psychological Research at the Kaiser Foundation Hospital, Oakland, California, because I felt confused about my profession. For ten years my research team had been keeping score on the success-rate of psychotherapy. We found that no matter what kind of psychiatric treatment was used, the same discouraging results occurred. One third of the patients got better, one third stayed the same, one third got worse. Control groups receiving no treatment showed the same scores.

For all its efforts, psychology still hadn't developed a way of significantly and predictably changing human behavior. I had found myself practicing a profession that didn't seem to work.

For the last year I'd been in self-imposed European exile, living on a small research grant and cashed-in insurance policies, reading philosophy and thinking. I wouldn't accept the apparent fact that humans, even university-educated humans, couldn't solve the problems of human nature: unhappiness, stupidity, and conflict. This personal and professional malaise spread out to the Cold War and the Bomb. Nothing had really been right since Hiroshima.

I had just finished typing a manuscript called *The Existential Transaction* on an old-fashioned rented Olivetti. This book suggested new, humanist methods for behavior change. For the first time since my thirty-fifth birthday I was feeling some flickers of enthusiasm. I thought I knew how humans could direct their personal evolution. The next step was to find a clinic or university where I could put these ideas to the test.

The penthouse bell rang and there, shaggy, tweedy, his Celtic eyes twinkling with intelligence and rebellion, was Frank Barron, my old friend and drinking companion from graduate school at Berkeley. Since then he had earned a reputation as one of the world's leading authorities on the psychology of creativity. In the course of his studies Frank had become passionate in his belief that only psychology, by effecting a fundamental reprogramming of the human mind, could prevent a nuclear holocaust.

Barron, passing through Europe on sabbatical, was burning to tell me about some unusual experiments he'd performed recently. He said his research on creativity had led him to Mexico, where he interviewed a psychiatrist who had been producing visions and trances using the so-called "magic mushrooms." Frank had taken a bag filled with the mushrooms back to Berkeley and ingested them. At this point Frank lost me with this talk about William Blake revelations, mystical insights, and transcendental perspectives produced by the strange fungi. I was a bit worried about my old friend and warned him against the possibility of losing his scientific credibility if he babbled this way among our colleagues.

Frank left two very practical gifts of friendship. He offered me $500 from his Ford Foundation research grant to go to London and interview Arthur Koestler on creativity.[1] Then he told me that the director of the Harvard Center for Personality Research, Professor David McClelland, was taking his sabbatical leave in Florence. He might help me get a job.

Professor McClelland had read my book *The Interpersonal Diagnosis of Personality* and was eager to talk shop. He invited me for lunch the next day.

The professor was a lanky, Lincolnesque man about 45, married to Mary, a petite, dynamic Quaker. They bubbled with New England academic charm. McClelland and I sat on a patio with a view of the fabled city, hometown of Dante Alighieri, drinking pale chianti and discussing the future of psychology. McClelland examined the title page of my manuscript. He wanted to know what it was all about.

I explained that by *existential* I meant that the psychologist should work with people in real-life situations, like a naturalist in the field, observing behavior in the trenches. "We should treat people as they actually are and not impose the medical model or any other model on them."

McClelland lit a twisted Italian cigar and motioned for me to go on.

"By *transaction* I mean that psychologists shouldn't remain detached from their subjects. They should get involved, engaged in the events they're studying. They should enter each experiment prepared to change as much or more than the subjects being studied."

McClelland raised an eyebrow. "The scientist should change himself?" He picked up my manuscript and flipped through the pages with concentration. I poured more wine and wondered whether I'd ever again be able to make a living in psychology.

McClelland took off his glasses and looked still more solemn. "What you're suggesting in this book is a drastic change in the role of the scientist, teacher, and therapist. Instead of processing subjects, students, and patients by uniform and recognized standards, we should take an egalitarian or information-exchange approach. Is that it?"

"That's what I had in mind."

"I gather you're hoping some unsuspecting educational organization will hire you to set up activist research projects, which will require the institution to change itself."

"That's it," I admitted. I figured it was time to collect my manuscript and pedal Susan's bicycle back down the hill.

McClelland poured us both more wine. He lit another stogie. "Okay, I'm prepared to offer you a job at Harvard."

"Are you serious?"

"I'm intrigued," said Professor McClelland. "There's no question that what you're advocating is going to be the future of American psychology. You're not a lone voice. There are several hotshots in our profession—like Benjamin Spock, Carl Rogers, Abraham Maslow, Harry Stack Sullivan, Milton Gloaming—urging that we emphasize inner potential and personal growth through self-reliance, so patients avoid dependence on authoritarian doctors and dogmas. You're spelling out front-line tactics. You're just what we need to shake things up at Harvard."

WILLIAM JAMES (1842-1920), a philosopher-psychologist, was America's first distinguished brain-drug researcher. Son of a Swedenborgian minister and brother of novelist Henry James, he wrote the classic text *Principles of Psychology* (1890) and established himself as the father of American psychology. In contrast to authoritarian European theories, James' approach stressed the active and self-determining role of the mind in creating individual reality. His hypothesis that we "carve out" our realities from the "jointless continuity of space" became the principle underlying the drug culture of the 1960s.

William James initiated the Harvard tradition of brain-change research, shocking the academic community with his peyote and nitrous oxide experiments. In *The Varieties of Religious Experience* William James demonstrated that important levels of intelligence, hidden behind the narrow-gauged conditioned mind, could be accessed by drugs.

2. Harvard Department of Visionary Experience

JANUARY 1960
CAMBRIDGE, MASSACHUSETTS

Harvard at the beginning of this new decade was a prestigious academic coral reef, a solid accumulation of academic traditions piled up over the centuries, supporting a great variety of shoreline creatures: barnacled full professors, quick-darting lecturers, nervous slippery graduate students, gaily colored tiny undergraduates, who were snapped up by scuttling faculty crabs and occasionally by Kissinger-Schlesinger type killer whales who swept through these sheltered waters on annual migrations to and from Wall Street, Washington, and other feeding grounds.

Upon arriving in Cambridge, Susan and Jack and I moved into a two-bedroom suite at a hotel one block away from the Center for Personality Research. The next day I enrolled them in public school and visited Calvin Pembroke, famed Harvard Square tailor.

"I've just joined the faculty, Mr. Pembroke, and I need a varsity uniform."

Pembroke peered at me over his spectacles, emitted an approving croak, and selected for me the appropriate button-down shirts and tweed jackets with leather elbows. With my horn-rimmed glasses I looked like a caricature of a professor—except for the white tennis shoes, which I wore everywhere.

Dwight D. Eisenhower was finishing his last year of office. Richard Nixon was vice-president. The Cold War heated up with the Castro victory in Cuba and the Chinese invasion of Tibet. Publisher Barney Rossett of Grove Press overthrew a Post Office ban against *Lady Chatterley's Lover. Naked Lunch* by William Burroughs was an underground bestseller. *Hiroshima, Mon Amour, Black Orpheus,* and *Some Like It Hot* were popular movies. An anti-anxiety drug, Librium, became the most widely used mood-changer available to the American public.

I got off to a fast start on the Harvard academic track. There was much student dissatisfaction with the Freudians, whose theories of psychopathology thrived in the damp atmosphere of the Back Bay. The Skinnerian conditioners had alienated many with their clannish, humorless manipulations. The Social Relations Department had just completed a statistical survey of diagnostic systems used in psychology, and my *Interpersonal Diagnosis of Personality* (named the best book in psychotherapy for the year 1957) fared well under this analysis, attracting much interest in its new approaches to behavior change.[1] The graduate students were especially ready for new techniques. They had hoped to find human psychology the most thrilling, lively, and optimistic area of science.

The Center for Personality Research was located in a Puritan-style frame building located, prophetically enough, at 5 Divinity Avenue. I was offered a suite of offices on the third floor but chose a small typist's room near the entrance, because I wanted to be near the center of the action.

My assignment was to teach the advanced graduate seminar in psychotherapy, but first I had to change the field sites for clinical training. Decentralize. Graduate students were normally assigned to Freudian-oriented clinics and hospitals, which encouraged rote-learning of sterile and ineffectual tests like the Rorschach Ink Blots. In speeches to the students, I said, "Let's learn how to deal with problems in skid-rows, ghetto community centers, Catholic orphanages, marriage clinics, jails, and other natural habitats of humans. Let's tackle some steamy, jungle/street-life crises out there, where they happen." The more traditional faculty bridled.

I accompanied the students on interviews with junkies, street cops, and social workers. I arranged conferences with Bill Wilson, founder of the most successful self-help group, Alcoholics Anonymous, and with Bill Dederich, founder of Synanon. Basically I was always asking the same big question: "How do *you* change human behavior?" It seemed obvious that the decentralized, do-it-yourself methods practiced in egalitarian encounter groups and client-centered therapies were pointing in the right direction, encouraging self-reliance and optimism. However, even these methods needed so much time to change human nature, slowly reconditioning habits built up over the years.

Talk therapy was still hot air. Freud had acknowledged fifty years before that talking in the doctor's office couldn't duplicate the power of the original childhood emotional fixation. He suggested that physiological (i.e., chemical) stimuli were needed to loosen neurologic bonds. So far as I knew, no such magic potions had been discovered.

Fortunately there were lots of graduate students and young professors also interested in new methods of behavior change. Professor McClelland had staffed the Center with several maverick instructors who were eager for something exciting to happen.[2]

Down the hall, for example, in a high-prestige corner office, was a most engaging faculty member, someone who was to play a major role in the events to follow. Assistant Professor Richard Alpert was a tall boyish thirty-year-old psychologist, an ambitious academic-politician—engaging, witty, a big tail-wagging puppy dog. A bachelor, Dick was the only other faculty member to keep night office hours.

It was my custom after dinner, when the kids were in bed in our hotel suite, to walk the two blocks past the tiny jewel-box chapel of the Swedenborg church to my office where I read, wrote, drank California white wine from half-gallon bottles, smoked Marlboros, and chatted with graduate students. An endless procession of ill-at-ease young men paraded past my door for after-hour interviews with Dick. Often he joined the group in my office to listen to our discussions. Later we'd catch a beer and a midnight sandwich at Harvard Square.

At this time Dick's father was president of the New York, New Haven and Hartford Railroad, a bankrupt outfit still loaded with prestige and lootable assets. Dick made playful use of his connection to the railroad, enjoying the penthouse apartment the company maintained on Park Avenue, the limousines, and access to the inner sanctums of Grand Central Station. A funloving kid, he was the last person you'd accuse of religious or spiritual potential.

Dick was especially beloved by children. His joking, we're-all-kids-together manner made him popular with the twin sons of Professor McClelland (he was their Godfather) as well as with the offspring of other important professors. I was very grateful to him for the affection he lavished on my two kids.

The prankster in Professor Alpert responded to the anti-establishment flavor of my ideas. Partnership with him came naturally to me because of an attitude fostered in earliest childhood by a subversive book that I almost committed to memory. The two rebellious pals, Tom Sawyer and Huckleberry Finn, were role models. To me they have always represented what America is all about. Like Tom Sawyer I was an avid reader of historical novels and heroic tales. Like Tom I lived mostly in a fantastical mythic adventureland, dodging arrows as I bicycled the Pony Express mail, hiding from my white-skinned parents in a tipi in the back-yard, slipping out the window of my bedroom to sneak across the roof and down the drainpipes on late night sorties, surreptitiously lifting finger-prints of the neighbors, stalking unsuspecting friends on missions for the Detective Bureau.

I sized up Richard Alpert as a potential Huck for my Tom. When I told him that I was planning to spend the summer in Mexico, Dick, a licensed pilot, proposed that he buy an airplane and ferry us on a tour around Mexico and the Caribbean.

Professor McClelland dropped by my office. There was an opening on the faculty for a one-year appointment. Did I have any suggestions?

This was an amazing introduction to power. After six weeks on the job, I was being asked by the Director to recommend staff members for that most coveted post—a Harvard appointment.

It was my chance to repay a favor. I suggested Frank Barron and re-counted his many virtues. McClelland picked up the phone for a trans-continental conference call with Frank and his boss, Donald McKinnon, Director of the Institute of Personality Assessment and Research (IPAR) at Berkeley. Within a couple of days it was arranged that Frank would spend the next year as a visiting professor at the Center. I was amazed by the ease with which this transfer was accomplished.

Later I learned there was a continual flow of researchers between the two personality assessment centers. At the top level everyone seemed to know everyone. I was interested in how these power networks worked, especially when they involved psychology and the government.

When Frank phoned to thank me for the recommendation, we agreed to take a house together when he arrived in the fall. The kids loved Uncle Frank. Frank said he'd stop in to see us during the summer in Mexico. He'd try to locate some magic mushrooms. He suggested that these mushrooms, which stimulated visions and enhanced creativity, were the tools for behavior change we were seeking.

"We'll see, Frank."

MARK TWAIN (1835-1910) was born Samuel Clemens and raised on the American frontier during the peak period of the westward expansion.[1] Like Huckleberry Finn, his greatest literary creation, Mark Twain turned away from formal schooling at an early age and "lit out for the territory," having picaresque adventures and gaining wisdom from his observation of people and places.[2]

His Bohemian days ended in 1870 with his marriage, which put him in contact with a bourgeois society. He moved to an upper-class Connecticut home, raised a family, wrote books, and toured as a lecturer. During the next twenty-five years he created his quintessential characters of adolescent rebellion in Tom Sawyer, Huck Finn, and Puddinhead Wilson. Mark Twain made his works accessible to more people than any previous American writer. Like Dante he spoke directly to the people in language they understood.

Personal tragedy (the loss of his wife and two of his children) and business failures, together with an acute awareness of the materialism and military opportunism that infected the Western frontier after it had been settled, gradually turned the author into a deeply cynical man. His later works of pornography and satire, which foreshadow black comedy, existentialism, and Punk, contrast sharply with his earlier works of optimism and innocence. Many of his anti-establishment writings were suppressed by his surviving daughter in order to save the family from embarrassment.

3. Reunion with Widow Douglas

SPRING 1960
HARVARD UNIVERSITY

The move to Harvard provided many fringe benefits, the greatest of which was the reconciliation with my widowed mother, Abigail. She was living with her sister, Aunt Mae, in the house where she had been born seventy-two years before. Aunt Mae had lived her entire life in this white clapboard farmhouse, built by my great grandfather before the Civil War.

These two genteel ladies inhabited a sedate society of retired schoolteachers, all Irish Catholic and all (with the exception of my mother) spinster-virgins. During their tea parties the chief topic of conversation was families. Poor Abigail had had little good news to report about her only child after Marianne's death. My sudden appearance as a Harvard faculty member changed all that. My mother was very pleased. The first warm weekend of spring, I piled the kids into a rental car and headed west along the Mass Turnpike for a visit.

1920-1930
SPRINGFIELD, MASSACHUSETTS

At the time of my birth, Springfield, my father's hometown, was a pleasant, medium-size industrial city. Known for being the site of Shays' Rebellion, the first armed insurrection against the authority of the American government, Springfield later became a station on the Underground Railroad, a haven for black slaves escaping to freedom.

The Leary family was urban, urbane, well-to-do, and—to me—glamorous. The Boston branch produced several physicians, the most prominent a professor at Tufts University who for years was the medical examiner of Boston. This renowned Dr. Timothy Leary, for whom my father Tote and I were named, published classic works on blood circulation.

The Learys were among the first cadre of Irish immigrants who rose up through crime, manual labor, and politics to join the professional and scientific class on the new continent. Grandfather Leary was considered to be the richest Irish Catholic in western Massachusetts—real estate on Main Street. He collected playbills of the great actresses and actors of the nineteenth century, entertained scholarly guests, and tried to ignore the wild escapades of his family. By the time I reported in for genetic duty, he was retired and spent much of his time in an enormous room walled with books.

My most vivid memory of my grandfather dates to a wintry evening when he found me sitting on the floor of his study reading *Life on the Mississippi*. He questioned me about my reading. When I told him I read eight to ten books a week, he asked what I had learned. Then he motioned me to follow him into his bedroom, a forbidden sanctum to which only the maid was allowed entry. He undressed with such prudish skill that I never caught a glimpse of his body while he put on a long nightgown.

"Nine children, six grandchildren," he mumbled, "all hellraising illiterates. You're the only one who reads."

He lifted his frail body onto the bed and motioned me over.

"How old are you?"

"Ten."

"You're the youngest and the last so I'll give you the best piece of advice I can." He raised himself to a sitting position. "Never do anything like anyone else, boy. Do you understand?"

"I'm not sure, sir."

"Find your own way. Be the only one of a kind. Now do you understand?"

I still wasn't sure, but I said I did.

"Good. Now I'm going to sleep. Turn out the light when you leave."

Those were the only meaningful words he ever spoke to me.

Uncle Arthur was the hub of glamour in the Leary house. Although no one spoke or even thought of homosexuality, it is obvious in retrospect that he was gay. He owned a chain of swanky women's boutiques in Palm Beach, Saratoga, and Springfield, and he went to Paris openings and New York showings accompanied by beautiful models and salesgirls. Arthur always returned with high-fashion gifts for the women—a fur coat for my mom or jewels for Aunt Sarah. Women adored the effeminate bachelor Arthur, who seemed to understand what women wanted.

My dowager Aunt Sarah also lived in the Leary mansion. She was jolly, musical, affectionate. Her son Phil, a handsome, good-natured man with smiling eyes, was 15 years older than I and was my only adult friend. I watched Phil court and marry Anita, a raven-haired stylish beauty who smoked Murad cigarettes in the most elegant fashion, inhaling the smoke from her mouth into her nose. Oh Anita!

There were other Leary aunts and uncles and cousins who dashed in and out making scenes, scandals, strange disappearances. Aunt Frances ran away to Kansas City with a Protestant, and Tote was dispatched by train to bring her back. Cousin Sissy married a prosperous Episcopalian and then—saints, preserve us!—sailed to Paris for a divorce.

Wonderful soap operas accompanied these comings and goings.

The Learys were hot, sassy, and very different from my mother's family, the quiet pious farm-gentry Ferrises, who lived in Indian Orchard, a village six miles east of Springfield.

I never knew my grandparents on the Ferris side. They died in the influenza epidemic of 1918, leaving the diminished acreage and two farm-houses to my Aunt Dudu, a timid, fanatically religious gnome who futilely tried to direct family affairs with Irish-village piety, sitting on a couch all day clicking her false teeth, mumbling prayers, and reading Catholic tracts. As befitted her venerable status as ruler of the household, Aunt Dudu slept in the master bedroom, called "Grandfather's Room" in honor of the doughty little farmer-tyrant who built it.

It was Aunt Dudu's custom to retire early. Once bedded she was brought a nightcap: a glass of whiskey mixed with steaming hot milk. During one period when Mother fled from my alcoholic father to the Ferris house—I was assigned the chore of delivering Dudu's bedtime drug. Sometimes when I carried the drink upstairs I would sniff at the curious udder odor with amazed distaste.

Aunt Mae's eagle eye detected this nasal indulgence. She announced that I was no longer authorized for this mission. The implication was that the scent of the liquor might trigger my Leary nature. The vigilance worked. I have always associated hot milk with funless unhealthy virtue.

None of the farm-bred Ferris amounted to much in the industrial cul-ture. The star of their gene pool was an uncle, Father Michael Cavanaugh, who received his training in Rome and went on to become a monsignor and a member of the Vatican elite. As the pastor of a wealthy church Father Michael lived in baronial style and traveled extensively, driven by a chauffeur. Tall in his black robes, surrounded by Italian art, he gave off an impressive air of feudal arrogance.

The Ferris house, in which I spent much time as a child, was a quaint repository of religious art. On summer vacations my schoolteacher aunts sailed to Europe to visit cathedrals and museums, returning with colored reproductions of Italian and Flemish paintings. By the time I was five I could identify the madonnas, the nativities, the martyrdoms and ascensions, the miracles, and the saintly convocations of Titian, Raphael, Giotto, da Vinci.

I cannot remember one moment of wild merriment in the farm house. The Ferris clan was the most respectable Irish Catholic family in town, and for seventy years they occupied the second pew on the St. Joseph's side of the village church.

In their house there was a distrust of men and sexuality, focused particularly on Tote, who never visited the Ferris house. Aunt Mae was so distressed when Mom and Dad married that she cried for three days and begged Abigail not to leave for the honeymoon. The Jansenist phobia about sex was obsessive. Every action, every book, every movie or play was scoped for erotic nuance.

My early years thus provided two extremely different models. The Ferris clan: traditional, family oriented, suspicious of all things joyous, frivolous, or newfangled. Versus the Learys: sexy, funloving, self-oriented. Each Leary flaunted a unique style.

For a Ferris the village was the unit of existence. Doctrines promulgated by the church and by the neighbors were paramount. The Ferris family condemned the Learys as *selfish*. The Learys hardly bothered to talk about the Ferrises because nothing much ever happened among them. For a Leary it was the individual that mattered, and the more dashing the better.

As a child I naturally gravitated toward the Learys. My cousin Phil served as my Leary model. An eternal teenager, a sportsman, an expert bridge-player, he refused to be angry or upset about the melodramas swirling around him. When I was seven he started courting the luscious woman who eventually became my Aunt Anita. I often found them necking in the cloakroom. They were hot stuff, always together, giggling, stirring up fun. Phil was never ambitious. He took over the boutique after Uncle Arthur died but spent most of his time in the shipping room, placing bets on horses and ballgames. His recurring message to me was: "Be happy." He was pretty avant garde for an Irish Catholic New Englander in 1930.

The polar contrast between the Learys and the Ferrises caused me a certain confusion. I loved Mom and later understood her yearnings to be the respectable wife of a prosperous dentist. But Mother put the clan first. She spent at least an hour a day on the phone with Aunt Mae, holding the black earpiece to the left side of her head, saying "Ay-yah, ay-yah."

My lasting image of Mom originated when I was ten. Around the border of the lawn behind our house, Mom had planted flowers. One day, while playing ball by myself, I heard her sobbing. I ran to the garden. She was sitting in the dirt, weeping because our German shepherd had destroyed a plant. Her skirt was pulled up to her thighs. There was a run in her stocking. Her face was contorted. Even then I sensed something self-indulgent in her sorrow. She looked like a Titian martyr suffering in the garden for the original sin, whatever that might have been.

It must have been at this time that I determined to seek women who were exactly the opposite to Abigail in temperament. Since then I have always sought the wildest, funniest, most high-fashion, big-city girl in town.

FEBRUARY 1960
INDIAN ORCHARD, MASSACHUSETTS

I pulled off the Mass Turnpike at the Ludlow exit and drove across the Chicopee River into my hometown, past the drugstore where I used to buy erection-magazines called *Spicy Detective* and *Spicy Adventure*, past houses on streets where I delivered the Christmas mail when it was twenty below, past the Indian Leap Hotel, past the fields that my mother's family sold off to the Chapman Valve Company. I headed into the driveway leading to the farmhouse.

Mother and Aunt Mae came trotting on little-old-lady feet to greet us. They looked great. Slim, bubbling with pleasure. Yet I felt wary. Even at forty I was on guard, ready to protect myself and the kids from Aunt Mae's fierce moralizing.

There was much personal history to catch up on, and then we talked pleasantly about Florence and the Uffizi Gallery and the Michelangelo statues. The kids told charming anecdotes about European schools and reeled off a few phrases in Italian. Mom and Mae accepted my invitation to have lunch the following week at the Copley Plaza.

We sat down to Sunday dinner, the familiar delicacies: roast chicken, mashed potatoes, cranberry sauce, gravy, peas, salad, and hot rolls. As my mother took off her apron and came to the table, she said, for the thousandth time, "Well, I've eaten in the finest restaurants in New York and Paris, and nothing tastes as good as a home-cooked meal."

Everyone agreed.

At the head of the table Aunt Mae said grace. "Blessed, oh Lord, are these Thy gifts which we are about to receive, through Thy bounty, through Christ our Lord, Amen." I had drilled the kids on this procedure. They dropped their heads and closed their eyes like good little troopers. Both Mother and Aunt Mae watched their performance and nodded in approval.

The dinner was a smash hit. Mother was radiant, and Aunt Mae came close to smiling. Finally, after forty years of worry and disappointment, my mother's dreams were coming true: Her son was a Harvard psychologist, and the family was reunited.

Aunt Mae was positively pleased. She found no signs of immorality. It was her custom to hold a rolled-up newspaper in her right hand like Queen Victoria's scepter. Occasionally, to subdue my mother's garrulous enthusiasm, she said, "Oh, Abby, be quiet," and lightly struck my mother's arm with the paper.

At sunset, as we climbed into our coats to leave, Aunt Mae took me aside.

"You have made your mother very happy today."

"I know. Isn't it wonderful?"

"You have made your mother very unhappy in the past, Timothy."

I nodded.

"Now you're not going to get into trouble at Harvard, are you?"

"Trouble?" I exclaimed. "What trouble?"

"You know what I mean. Expelled from high school. Expelled from Holy Cross. Silenced at West Point. Expelled from the University of Alabama. Marianne's death. Then you running off to Europe. If you get into trouble at Harvard, it will be the end of your mother."

"Harvard's different, Aunt Mae. They're encouraging me to try new things."

"They always love you at first. But then you do something deliberately wild. Promise me that you'll conform, Timothy. Promise me for your mother's sake."

"You can count on me, Aunt Mae," I said.

She was always being the Widow Douglas from Hannibal, Missouri, doing her best to "sivilize" me. This time I thought I might let it happen.

BIOGRAPHY

F **RANK BARRON** (1922-   ), psychologist and philosopher, received his Ph.D. at Berkeley in 1950. Early in his career, because of brilliant publications in the field of creativity, Barron attracted the interest of the Central Intelligence Agency.

He worked for over thirty years at the Berkeley Institute for Personality Assessment and Research, an organization funded and staffed by former OSS-CIA psychologists. On two occasions Barron rejected offers to become director of psychological personnel of the CIA.

Barron was one of the first contemporary psychologists to study the effects of psychedelic plants and drugs and was a co-founder of the Harvard Psychedelic Drug Research (1960-1961).

Barron's contributions to psychology and philosophy appear in his books: *Creativity and Psychological Health, Creativity and Personal Freedom, Scientific Creativity, Creative Person and Creative Process, Artists in the Making, Shaping of Personality.*

4. Sacred Mushrooms of Mexico

SUMMER 1960
CUERNAVACA, MEXICO

In 1960 Cuernavaca was a charming spot, for centuries a retreat for sophisticated Aztecs, corrupt politicians, and wandering scholars. Charles Lindbergh, one of my heroes, courted Anne Morrow there.

In the days of Montezuma this town, called "horn-of-the-cow," was the home of soothsayers, wise men, and magicians. Cuernavaca lies south of a line of volcanic peaks, Popo, Ixtacihuatl, and Toluca. On the slopes of the volcanoes grow the sacred mushrooms of Mexico, divinatory fungi, *teonanacatl*, flesh of the gods.

My son Jack and I scouted the town and leased a villa next to the golf course on the Acapulco road. It was a rambling white stucco house with a scarlet trim, surrounded by grey stone walls. A carriage drive led up to a wide staircase opening onto a long veranda. Next to the upper terrace was a swimming pool and a sloping lawn of thick rough grass, which left welts on your sweaty back. The lower lawn was shaded by lacy *ahuehate* trees. On the walls of the house bougainvillea splashed red, orange, and fuschia against the cloudless blue of the mile-high Morelos sky.

Many lively guests whipped in and out of the villa. There was Ruth Dettering and her semanticist husband Richard, who was usually drunk and declaiming witty philosophy. They brought a friend, Bruce, a bearded logician from Michigan. Professor David McClelland and his family were spending the summer ten miles east in the haunted valley of Tepoztlan. Frank Barron and Dick Alpert were en route. Jack Leary kept busy playing with the maid's son Pepe. My daughter Susan was visiting friends in Berkeley for the summer.

Crystal clear summer days, swimming trunks around the pool before breakfast, cold grapefruit, hot discussions with visiting scholars. Touch football on the grass and the shouts of Jack and Pepe chasing ducks on the lower lawn. The sudden cooling splash of the evening rain, the sky darkening over the volcanoes and the crash of thunder. Margaritas. Candlelit dinners.

A frequent visitor was Gerhart Braun, the anthropologist-historian-linguist from the University of Mexico. Gerhart had been studying the culture of the Aztecs and translating texts written in Nahuatl, their ancient language. He had discovered frequent references in Nahuatl to the use of magic mushrooms. The mushrooms were used by soothsayers to forecast the future and were passed around to everyone on ceremonial occasions. Gerhart's curiosity was aroused. He asked me if I would like to try them.

I remembered Barron's joking prediction that the mushrooms might be the tool for changing the mind that we had been looking for.

"Why don't you see if you can find some," I said.

The following week Gerhart phoned from Mexico City. He had met a *curandera* in the village of San Pedro, near the volcano of Toluca. Away from the tumult of the market, in the shade of a church wall, Juana had shown him a bag of mushrooms. When he asked if they were safe, she popped two in her mouth. He took them home and washed them in cold water. The mushrooms were now resting on the center shelf of his refrigerator.

"See you Saturday," I said.

Gerhart arrived around noon. With him came his girlfriend Joan, her daughter Mandy, and Betty, an English major from Berkeley who wrote poetry, cracked jokes, and played football with the boys.

Gerhart had been talking with University of Mexico botanists. While he sorted the mushrooms, he told us some of the things he had learned: used by the Aztecs, magic mushrooms were banned by the Catholic

Church, so effectively that leading contemporary botanists denied that such a species even existed. Pushed out of history's notice until the last decade, they were rediscovered by botanists Weitlaner and Schultes and by amateur mycologists Valentina and Gordon Wasson. By this time a few scientists, poets, and intellectuals looking for mystical experience had tried the mushrooms. They were supposed to produce wondrous trances.

Gerhart arranged the fungi in two bowls on a table under a huge beach umbrella. He said we should each take six. The effect would begin after an hour. Then he stuffed a big black moldy mushroom in his mouth, made a face, and chewed. I watched his Adam's apple bounce as it went down.

I picked one up. It stank of dampness. The smell was like crumbling logs or certain New England basements, and it tasted worse than it looked. Bitter, stringy. I took a slug of Carta Blanca, jammed the rest in my mouth, and washed it down.

Everyone was listening to her or his own stomach, expecting to be poisoned. Five of us sat on the sunlit terrace in our bathing suits waiting. Waiting. Asking each other: How many did you take? Do you feel anything?

Two people abstained. One was Ruth Dettering, who was pregnant. She had a degree in nursing, so I was glad she would be there as an observer. The other abstainer was Bruce, who said he suffered from nervous fits and feared a reaction. He was wearing bathing trunks over flowered undershorts, green garters, black socks, leather shoes, and a silken robe— so we appointed him official scientist. He was to take detailed notes of our reactions.

I began to feel strange. Like going under dental gas. Mildly nauseous. Detached. Moving away, away from the group in bathing suits on a terrace under the bright Mexican sky. Everything was quivering with life, even inanimate objects.

Dettering said he felt it too.

Bruce busied himself writing, his thin shoulders bent over the notepad like a Viennese psychoanalyst. The scientist! But he had no idea what he was observing. This professional revelation struck me as immensely comic. Laughing. Laughing. Laugh. Couldn't stop laughing.

Everyone looked at me in astonishment. Their wonder increased my amusement. Bruce looked up, his red tongue flicking out from the shrubbery of his beard.

I laughed again at my own everyday pomposity, the narrow arrogance of scholars, the impudence of the rational, the smug naivete of words in contrast to the raw rich ever-changing panoramas that flooded my brain.

I walked into the house, fell on the bed. Dettering followed, watching.
"Do you see it, Dick? Our little minds?"

He nodded. Good, he saw. He began to laugh.

I gave way to delight, as mystics have for centuries when they peeked
through the curtains and discovered that this world—so manifestly real—
was actually a tiny stage set constructed by the mind. There was a sea
of possibilities out there (in there?), other realities, an infinite array of
programs for other futures.

Starting back to the terrace. Hello, my walk had changed to a rubber-leg
slither. The room was apparently filled with invisible liquid. I undulated
over to Poet Betty. Her classic face unfolded like a sunflower. She was
in some place of bliss. There was Ruth Dettering standing by the door.
I swam to her.

"Look Ruth," I said, sounding surprisingly normal, "these mushrooms
are stronger than I expected. I think you should send the kids to the
movies in town and give the maid the afternoon off. Stay close and
keep your eyes on things."

Then I was gone into the fabled optical department. Nile palaces,
Hindu temples, Babylonian boudoirs, Bedouin pleasure tents, gem
flashery, woven silk gowns breathing color, mosaics flaming with Muzo
emeralds, Burma rubies, Ceylon sapphires. Here came those jeweled serpents, those Moorish reptiles sliding, coiling, tumbling down the drain
in the middle of my retina.

Next came a trip through evolution, guaranteed to everyone who signs
up to this Brain Tour. Slipping down the recapitulation tube to those
ancient mid-brain projection rooms: snake-time, fish-time, down-through-
giant-jungle-palm-time, green lacy fern leaf-time.

Calmly observing the first sea thing crawl to shore, I lay with her,
sand rasping under my cheek, then floated down into the deep green
ocean. Hello, I am the first living thing.

IT IS NOW EIGHT O'CLOCK STOP MUSHROOM EATING BEGUN
AT FIVE O'CLOCK STOP EFFECT STARTING TO WEAR OFF STOP
WANT TO STAY HERE STOP RETURNING SOON STOP HAVING MO-
MENTS OF NON-TRANCE CONSCIOUSNESS STOP THEN ENRAP-
TURING VISIONS RETURN DON'T STOP.

The journey lasted a little over four hours. Like almost everyone who
has had the veil drawn, I came back a changed man.

St. John of the Cross, Aldous Huxley, your kid brother, William Blake,
John Lennon, Plato after Eleusis, Lucy in the Sky with Diamonds, and
on and on—they all agree there are extraordinary realms within the brain
for us to explore.

We've all listened to and read our share of breathless reports from trippers, yet for most people this discovery is a glorious surprise. Mystics come back raving about higher levels of perception where one sees realities a hundred times more beautiful and meaningful than the reassuringly familiar scripts of normal life.

For most people it's a life-changing shock to learn that their everyday reality circuit is one among dozens of circuits which, when turned on, are equally real, pulsing with strange forms and mysterious biological signals. Accelerated, amplified some of these alternate realities can be microscopic in exquisite detail, others telescopic.

Since psychedelic drugs expose us to different levels of perception and experience, use of them is ultimately a philosophic enterprise, compelling us to confront the nature of reality and the nature of our fragile, subjective belief systems. The contrast is what triggers the laughter, the terror. We discover abruptly that we have been programmed all these years, that everything we accept as reality is just social fabrication.

In the twenty-one years since eating mushrooms in a garden in Mexico, I have devoted most of my time and energy to the exploration and classification of these circuits of the brain and their implications for evolution, past and future. In four hours by the swimming pool in Cuernavaca I learned more about the mind, the brain, and its structures than I did in the preceding fifteen as a diligent psychologist.

I learned that the brain is an underutilized biocomputer, containing billions of unaccessed neurons. I learned that normal consciousness is one drop in an ocean of intelligence. That consciousness and intelligence can be systematically expanded. That the brain can be reprogrammed. That knowledge of how the brain operates is the most pressing scientific issue of our time. I was beside myself with enthusiasm, convinced that we had found the key we had been looking for.

The days after my first trip were free for introspection and contemplation. This was lucky. A heavy psychedelic experience is upheaval time for anyone. In subsequent manuals and lectures I have always suggested that at least one day free from mundane distraction be set aside so that one can quietly digest what happened.

A few days later I drove to the nearby village of Tepoztlan to share my discoveries with Professor McClelland. In addition to being a gallantly creative psychologist, he had become a Quaker. This transcendental religion was founded upon the wild visionary experiences of George Fox, so I expected that McClelland would be receptive to the idea of trying the mushrooms.

He wasn't. Moreover, he seemed vaguely annoyed by my enthusiastic predictions about the value of altered states for psychological research.

McClelland cared for me, believed in my existential-transactional theories of behavior change, and cherished the hope that we would work together to humanize psychology.

I sketched a proposal for systematic drug experiments at Harvard. As my faculty sponsor he was understandably alarmed at the administrative and political problems he could foresee down the line.

During that meeting with McClelland I realized that it was practically impossible to convey the experience of altered states to someone who hadn't been there. (I remembered my negative reaction to Barron when he tried to relate his mushroom experiences to me.) Even the most supporting friend looked at you with skepticism. So you saw bizarre things? You made yourself crazy for six hours? So? What does this have to do with practical problems of normal life?

I tried to explain to McClelland. The activity of every sense organ was intensified. Colors and shapes were fresh and clear. I became every musical instrument. Everything was alive. Even inanimate objects sent signals, took on meaning.

"Bruce's beard took on meaning? I don't get it," sighed McClelland, glancing at his watch.

Frank arrived and was delighted to learn that I had taken the mushrooms. We spent long hours by the pool drinking another powerful native potion, tequila and tonic, having long discussions about the scientific implications of the multiple-reality phenomenon. When I told him about McClelland's resistance, he warned me about the compulsive tendency to run around explaining to *everyone* about these amazing events and what they meant.

Soon I would find that the world was divided into those who had had the experience (or were eager to have it) and those who had not (and shuddered at the possibility).

In years to come it also became apparent that emotional connections developed between those who had. This sharing of the secret about the potentials of the brain later became a significant and widespread social phenomenon. Hardly a day in my life has gone by without someone— a stranger on the street, a waiter at a restaurant, an airline steward, or a new acquaintance at a party—grabbing my hand with that intense look and pouring out a resume of their first psychedelic experience.

Frank and I agreed to start a research project at Harvard to pursue this further. Frank would concentrate on the creativity aspect, while I would work on using the drugs to accelerate behavior change.

After Frank left, Dick Alpert flew down in his new Cessna, ready to eat the mushrooms. But we couldn't locate any. Our visits to San Pedro to find the *curandera* proved futile. No one had ever heard of Juana!

The summer ended on a high note. Jack and I flew back with Dick, dodging thunderstorms, misplacing airports in the fog, bouncing in to refuel in Michoacan cow pastures—in general learning to trust each other in Tom and Huck adventures.

ALDOUS HUXLEY (1894-1963), educated at Eton and Oxford, was blocked from a career in biology by his poor eyesight. During the 1920s he wrote several ironic novels satirizing the decadence of European intellectual life.

Migrating to California in 1935 Huxley devoted the rest of his life to studying and writing about transcendental philosophy, futurism, and the evolution of intelligence. *Doors of Perception, Heaven and Hell,* and the utopian novel *Island* made him the world's most influential advocate of psychedelic drugs.

Huxley traced his interest in brain-change drugs to his childhood reading about Erasmus Darwin (1731-1802), who anticipated his grandson Charles' work by explaining organic life in terms of evolutionary principles. Erasmus Darwin is also famous for having grown England's first marijuana plant (*cannabis indica*) with Sir Joseph Banks, president of the Royal Society. The plant was eighteen feet tall.

5. Harvard Drug Research

FALL 1960
CAMBRIDGE, MASSACHUSETTS

In early September the kids and I moved to Newton Center, a Boston suburb about five miles from Cambridge. The house was a three-story mansion on a hill with trees, lawns, a four-car garage, a garden gazebo, and 185 stone steps up to the front door. It was luxuriously furnished: wood paneling, thick rugs, plush sofas, Moroccan metalwork lamps. There was a wide staircase winding up from the entrance hall.

The house belonged to a professor taking his sabbatical in the Soviet Union. Having spent most of my professional life as an itinerant researcher I found it cozy being an accepted member in a society of academic privilege. The power network offered plenty of advantages: travel around the world on government-sponsored fellowships, research grants, comfortable homes available to colleagues.

When Frank moved into the east wing, he unpacked a suitcase filled with books about visionary experiences.

"I'd read William James first," he said.

James, the founder of the Harvard Psychology Department, was to my surprise an advocate of brain-change drugs. In *The Will to Believe* (1897) he wrote this about his experiences with nitrous oxide:

> I strongly urge others to repeat the experiment which with pure gas is short and harmless enough. The effects will of course vary with the individual, just as they vary in the same individual from time to time . . . With me,

as with every other person of whom I have heard, the keynote of the experience is the tremendously exciting sense of an intense metaphysical illumination. Truth lies open to the view in depth beneath depth of almost blinding evidence.

After James, Frank showed me the writings of Morton Prince, the Harvard psychologist for whom our center was named, another pioneer American psychologist who recognized the importance of altered states of consciousness.

Next Frank took me around to meet Harry Murray, the wizard of personality assessment who, as OSS chief psychologist, had monitored military experiments on brainwashing and sodium amytal interrogation. Murray expressed great interest in our drug-research project and offered his support.

At One Divinity Avenue, the entrance to Harvard Yard, we wandered in the Swedenborgian Chapel where William James listened to his father preach on transcendental-scientific visions.

By this time I felt like I was being initiated into a secret order of Cambridge Illuminati. Frank smiled at the idea.

On the day I checked in for the fall semester I ran into George Litwin, considered one of the brightest graduate students in the department. During the preceding spring, when he had told me of some mescaline experiments he had performed on himself and others, I had voiced disapproval. At the time it sounded like chemical meddling.

I pulled him into my office and poured out the story of the mushroom session in Mexico. Litwin was delighted that my interest in altered states had been awakened. He agreed to join the research project. In a few days several other graduate students came around to volunteer their services.

The seeds of our political troubles with other faculty were sown during the initial meetings of the group, when we decided to make our research existential-transactional. Our experiments would not follow the medical model of giving drugs to others and then observing only external results. First we would teach ourselves how to use the drugs, how to run sessions. Since we were using a new kind of microscope, one which made visible an extraordinary range of new perceptions, our first task was to develop experimental manuals on how to focus the new tools. The scientists we trained could then use the drugs precisely and safely, on themselves and others, to study any and all aspects of psychology, aesthetics, philosophy, religion, life.

First we had to obtain the drugs. Litwin said that Sandoz Laboratories, the Swiss firm that discovered LSD, had synthesized the active ingredient of the mushrooms and that their branch office in New Jersey would send it to qualified researchers. I dictated a letter on Harvard stationery requesting a supply of psilocybin.

In the interim George introduced me to Aldous Huxley's books on mescaline and LSD. Huxley entranced me with his uncanny ability to relate the sometimes chaotic events in an activated brain to the perennial issues of aesthetics and ontology.

Back at our luxurious house things were progressing nicely. A Harvard football player and his wife moved in to act as housekeepers. They had a baby of their own and enjoyed my kids, so a cozy domestic scene unfolded. The big modern kitchen was the center of family life. Susan and Jack were happy in the Newton Center school system and delighted to have Uncle Frank around. Slowly the wounds from Marianne's death were healing.

After the eventful summer vacation it was time to visit Mother and Aunt Mae. Abigail was ecstatic telling her tea-party pals success stories about her son and grandchildren. Family approval made me feel closer to them than ever before. I sent Uncle Phil money to buy and deliver a television set: the two elderly ladies, with New England frugality and suspicion of novelty, had kept themselves aloof from the new electronic fad.

It was a crackling bright Indian summer day as the kids and I drove along under the blue sky, leaves exploding around us in flamboyant colors. Since my mushroom session I was much more aware of the exuberance of nature. For the first time I was seeing colors and forms as things in themselves. The glimpse of a maple tree flaming yellow and red reminded me vividly of the drug state. This phenomenon was later called a "flashback"—a brief but intense reliving of a memory, a sudden re-entry into highly charged rooms in the brain. To me the flashbacks were a positive indication that once new circuits of the brain were accessed by drugs, one could learn how to re-activate the experience without drugs.

1923-1935
Springfield, Massachusetts

As a member of the landed gentry, married into a wealthy town-family, Abigail disdained trade, commerce and financial shrewdness. Her attitude and style in daily life rested on the expectation that she would be rich when Grandfather Leary died.

My father was even more contemptuous of those who worked for the system. He practiced dentistry sporadically, as a gentlemanly hobby. He also was waiting for his inheritance to assume his rightful aristocratic role.

In later years, while his dental practice in Springfield was crumbling, Tote used to invite Mother and me to sit on the living room couch late at night while he drunkenly recited Shakespeare, Keats, Poe, Swinburne, Coleridge. Tote inherited a love of theater from his father, who had entertained Edwin Booth and John Barrymore in his book-walled study. Tote passed down to me the Celtic flair for intoxicated poetry, the bardic fever, the tradition of declamation.

Everyone in the Leary clan believed the wonderful myth that we would all be rich when The Old Man died. Naturally he lived. Grandmother died. Aunts and uncles dropped like flies. But grandfather endured until 1934.

I stood at the top of the stairs. Below, Mother was sobbing on the phone. Grandfather had passed away. Where was Tote? Disappeared on a three-day bender. Uncles were dispatched to country clubs, saloons, and downtown bars to locate the prodigal son and sober him up for the funeral, which turned out to be a noisy family reunion with the elegant Boston Learys.

Then came the great day, the reading of Grandfather's will. I was playing my special brand of solitary baseball in front of the house. Tote rushed out of a taxi, which stayed at the curb with its motor running. He stopped on his way in to hand me, his only son and heir, a hundred-dollar bill, then walked rapidly into the house, where he told Abigail the bad news. The estate was depleted: the stock market crash, the years of mismanagement, the large loans to Uncle Arthur's boutiques, the large loans to Tote, now called in, left just a few thousand dollars. Tote handed Abigail a thousand, announced his plan to go to New York on business, and jumped back in the cab.

By midnight, after getting royally drunk at the Astor Bar, Tote had been rolled of every last cent of the inheritance he had anticipated for forty-five years. I did not see my father again for twenty-three years.

What pride! Tote never returned to his hometown, never faced the burghers he had once looked down on with pity. He just disappeared, invented a new life. He worked as a contract dentist in Boston, on construction crews in South America, as a steward on transatlantic steamers. Now and again Uncle Phil would get drunken phone calls. Occasionally a Springfield resident, sailing first class to Southampton, would answer the knock at the cabin door and there would be the exile, nattily uniformed, with a complimentary bottle of wine, come to chat up hometown news. During World War II he served as a steward on convoys making the dangerous North Atlantic run to Murmansk.

I have always felt warmth and respect for this distant male-man who special-delivered me. During the thirteen years we lived together he never stunted me with expectations. (My sorrow at his abandonment of me emerged later during a drug session with Jack Kerouac.)

Dad remained for me a model of the loner, a disdainer of the conventional way. Tote dropped out, followed the ancient Hibernian practice of getting in the wind, escaping the priest-run village, heading for the far-off land, like one of the Wild Geese of Irish legend.

OCTOBER 1960
INDIAN ORCHARD, MASSACHUSETTS

Mother and Aunt Mae were raking leaves when we drove up. They fluttered over to the kids and hugged and kissed them.

On the lawn we sipped cold (non-alcoholic) drinks. I took the kids up the lawn to the enormous cavity where the barn once stood. The red sandstone ground walls still remained, creating the effect of an archeological excavation. Finding a broom handle I showed the kids how I used to spend hours hitting pebbles smoked in by Bob Feller and Dizzy Dean.

Aunt Mae was beside herself to hear the kids identify the painters of the Madonnas in the living room and stairway. Titian, Raphael, and Leo . . . Leo . . . Nardo!

Susan proudly showed the medal she received for low-board diving during the summer. Jack told the tale of our odyssey from Mexico in Dick Alpert's plane, savoring the part about how we smuggled his iguana across the border.

Mother and Aunt Mae recounted their summer adventures, which included a trip to New York to see Broadway plays. Two were wonderful. One was off-color. They enjoyed a splendid bus tour to Lake Champlain sponsored by the retired teachers' association.

And how was your summer, Timothy?

I launched into a dramatic account of my mushroom revelations. The kids were bored. They'd heard too much of this already. Mother tried to go along, nodding and saying, "How interesting." Aunt Mae held a rolled newspaper tightly in her hand. When I announced that we were starting a large research project to give these vegetables to subjects at Harvard, she could contain herself no longer. "Timothy, you must be careful. This sounds very unusual. I've never, never heard of such a thing."[1]

I tried to reassure her with facts and figures.

"I have never heard of such a thing in my life. Are you sure this is legal? It sounds dangerous. Or worse."

There was no stopping me. I said that no drugs should be illegal, and that Aldous Huxley, Henry Luce, and Father Murray, the Jesuit philosopher, had all endorsed experimental-chemical mysticism.

My dear mother tried to protect me. "Now Mae," she said, "we know science has progressed from what we were taught in Teacher's College. Things have changed since 1906. As long as Harvard University backs what Timothy is doing—"

Aunt Mae whacked my mother with her paper scepter. "Be quiet, Abby," she said. "This drug business is going to cause trouble. I can feel it in my bones. More Leary foolishness."

"You *will* be nice and careful, won't you, son?"

Aunt Mae was sure I wouldn't, and when we were alone she told me so. "Why must you continue to break your mother's heart? Why can't you be normal? Why can't you conform? Look what happened to your father."

I promised to be careful. I swore that I would make an important contribution to society.

Monday morning brought another of those synchronicities that always seem to happen when you're open for new information. Someone at a faculty cocktail party told me that Aldous Huxley was spending the semester in Cambridge as visiting professor at MIT. I wrote him a long letter describing our research plans. Two days later he telephoned me at the office, even more excited than I was. He volunteered to participate in our experiments. We set up a lunch for the very next day.

Huxley was staying in a new MIT faculty housing complex overlooking the Charles River. I rang the bell and he appeared at the door—towering, frail, friendly. I drove him to the Harvard Faculty Club, talking all the way about my mushroom visions.

Through his magnifying glass, he examined the menu as though it were a scientific specimen. "It seems to be pre-ordained that we order the soup," he said.

"Good. What kind is it?"

"Mushroom." He burst into high laughter, which I came to recognize as characteristic of him.

Aldous Huxley was exactly the person you'd cast as a British philosopher—a serene Buddha with an encyclopedic mind. His elegant Oxford voice bubbled, except in moments of amused indignation when its pitch rose at the arrogance of the power-holders who labeled altered states of consciousness as disease.

I was thrilled by his immediate understanding and approval of the existential-transactional design for the research.[2]

During October of 1960 we held regular meetings to plan our experiments. Aldous listened with eyes closed in meditation. His detachment was a bit unnerving at first, but then Aldous would open his eyes and utter a diamond-pure comment. He made many practical suggestions about how to create an aesthetic environment for the upcoming sessions.

Just before Thanksgiving a cardboard box with four small brown bottles arrived. Printed on the label was the exciting admonition: NOT TO BE SOLD: FOR RESEARCH INVESTIGATION. Under the plastic stopper there was a wad of cotton in the neck of the bottle. I shook out a few of the pills, which glistened like pink pearls in my hand. We stared at them, thinking solemn thoughts. The lives of all of us would be transformed by these tabs.

The next few weeks were devoted to experimental sessions with the drug. It was a naive romantic time. We were excited by the notion that we humans could fly, cut loose the synaptic cords that held us to low levels of mentation, soar into uncharted realms of the brain. It was Wright Brothers season as each novice took off, sometimes wobbly and then sailing out beyond normal consciousness. Hey Wilbur, watch that tree! Orville, how are you doing? One by one we flight trainees would fly out beyond our radars, get lost within, and then swoop back for landings with wondrous tales.

We were on our own. Western psychological literature had almost no guides, no maps, no texts that even recognized the existence of altered states. We had no rituals, traditions, or comforting routines to fall back on. In line with our existential-transactional theories we avoided the sterility of the laboratory and the sick-man atmosphere of the hospital. We conducted the experiments in faculty homes, in front of comforting fireplaces, with candles instead of electric lights, and evocative music.

To guide us in these experimental rituals Aldous Huxley brought over a description by Theophile Gautier of the techniques used by Baudelaire and the Hashish Club of Paris one hundred years earlier:

> It is understood, then, if one wishes to enjoy to the full the magic hashish, it is necessary to prepare in advance and furnish in some way the *motif* to its extravagant variations and disorderly fantasies. It is important to be in a tranquil frame of mind and body, to have on this day neither anxiety, duty, nor fixed time, and to find oneself in such an apartment as Baudelaire and Edgar Poe loved, a room furnished with poetical comfort, bizarre luxury, and mysterious elegance; a private and hidden retreat . . . .
>
> In such circumstances, it is probable, and even almost certain, that the naturally agreeable sensations turn into ravishing blessings, ecstasies, ineffable pleasure, much superior to the coarse joys promised to the faithful in the paradise of Mahomet . . . .

Without these precautions the ecstasy is like to turn into nightmare. Pleasure changes to suffering, joy to terror; a terrible anguish seizes one by the heart and breaks one with its fantastically enormous weight . . . . At other times an icy cold is felt making the victim seem like marble up to the hips . . . .

After six weeks we had run sessions for fifteen staff members. We learned a lot about dosage and the importance of setting—the tone of the environment, which included the people attending a session. We soon discovered that strong bonds developed among those who shared a session. They seemed to need to see each other, be close to each other for the week after the experience. For this reason we decided that each explorer should be allowed to invite family members and close friends to participate.

Our excitement naturally provoked concern among other faculty members. Almost all of the graduate students at the Center signed up for brain-drug training, which caused a predictable jealousy. According to ancient custom every student was apprenticed to assist the research of a senior faculty member. The swarming of students to the drug project became a hot in-house political issue. Frank Barron and I talked to our faculty colleagues and offered to set up sessions for them, but most declined the experience. They had no paradigms by which to understand this new phenomenon, so they weren't interested. They simply wanted their allotment of graduate students back.

Inevitably we mushroom researchers began to hang out together, enjoying the deep attachments and enthusiasms that pioneers always share, meanwhile drifting away from former friends. The trip was so powerful, so different, so shattering to one's illusion of a single reality that the people who had experienced it inevitably formed an in-group. The differences between those who wanted to explore new brain terrain and those who reflexively avoided the challenge foreshadowed the bitter cultural conflict that raged everywhere in the decade to come.

The question that haunted our work in those early days was: how could we introduce these methods for mind expansion to society?

I raised this issue with Huxley one day at the Faculty Club.

"Why don't I come over to your place tonight," he said. "We'll take the drug and ask our expanded brains that question."

Around sunset I built a fire while Aldous stacked the books he had brought with him on a coffee table, then stretched himself out on the couch. We each took psilocybin. For the next three hours we listened to music—Bach, Mozart, African drums, Indian chants, Ravi Shankar. Occasionally we waved reassurance to each other or murmured of bliss.

Aldous sat up, lanky legs crossed, and looked at me quizzically. "So you don't know what to do with this bloody philosopher's stone we have stumbled onto? In the past this powerful knowledge has been guarded in privacy, passed on in the subdued, metaphorical obscurantism of scholars, mystics, and artists."

"But society needs this information," I said, passionately. My anti-elitist button had been pushed.

"These are evolutionary matters. They cannot be rushed. Work privately. Initiate artists, writers, poets, jazz musicians, elegant courtesans, painters, rich bohemians. And they'll initiate the intelligent rich. That's how everything of culture and beauty and philosophic freedom has been passed on."

We fell into silence. The fireplace threw dancing colors around the room, a meadow of serenity. Huxley's eyes were closed. A beatific smile played around his thin mouth.

Suddenly he clapped his hands against his bony leg. "Your role is quite simple. Become a cheerleader for evolution. That's what I did and my grandfather before me. These brain-drugs, mass-produced in the laboratories, will bring about vast changes in society. This will happen with or without you or me. All we can do is spread the word. The obstacle to this evolution, Timothy, is the Bible."

"I don't remember any discussion of brain-change drugs in the Bible."

"Timothy, have you forgotten the very first chapters of Genesis? Jehovah says to Adam and Eve, 'I've built you this wonderful resort eastward of Eden. You can do anything you want, except you are forbidden to eat the fruit of the Tree of Knowledge.' "

"The first controlled substances."

"Exactly. The Bible begins with Food and Drug prohibitions."

"So the Fall and Original Sin were caused by the taking of illegal drugs."

By this time Aldous was chuckling away very pleased with himself, and I was rolling on the floor with laughter.

"Timothy, you must expect opposition. There are people in this society who will do everything within their considerable power to stop our research."

"You're telling me it ain't gonna be easy."

"That's precisely what I'm saying," Huxley replied. "The managers of consciousness, from the Vatican to Harvard, have been in this business for a long time, and they're not about to give up their monopoly. And, after all, they're the experts and we're the amateurs. They're the pros and we're just the lovers."

I said it again. "It ain't gonna be easy."

ALLEN GINSBERG (1926-), one of the most influential American poets of the mid-twentieth century, was born in Patterson, New Jersey and graduated from Columbia in 1949. He was chief spokesman for the Beat Generation, a movement that flourished in New York and San Francisco during the 1950s. Essentially anarchic, Ginsberg and the Beats rejected conventional cultural and artistic forms. They sought altered and intensified states of consciousness, novel experiences, and mystical perceptions through drugs and oriental yogic techniques, especially Zen.

Continually "on the road," usually accompanied by Peter Orlovsky, his companion for thirty years, Ginsberg traveled the world preaching a Buddhist quietist philosophy layered with socialist anger and a pagan celebration of life. During this era his stance was anti-scientific, anti-technological, anti-future, non-evolutionary. In the 1980s Allen Ginsberg functions as a genial poet laureate, meeting regularly in international conferences with his "opposite numbers" in China, the Soviet Union, and the Third World.

6. Politics of Ecstasy

DECEMBER 1960
HARVARD UNIVERSITY

By this time we had become aware of an international network of scientists and scholars experimenting with psychedelic drugs like psilocybin, LSD, and mescaline. They varied widely in age and temperament and held widely differing ideas about how the drugs should be used. One powerful premise was common to all: these plants and drugs, as expanders of human consciousness, could revolutionize psychology and philosophy.

Many of these men and women were psychiatrists who had personally experienced one or more of the drugs and hoped to fit them into the medical-treatment model. Our group was in contact with Humphry Osmond, the witty learned Briton who coined the word "psychedelic." He was using LSD in psychotherapy at the University of Saskatchewan. In Los Angeles Sidney Cohen and Keith Ditman were treating neurosis and alcoholism with the drug. Abram Hofer and Nick Chewelos were using LSD with mental hospital patients in Canada.[1]

The experimenters involved in therapeutic applications urged us to work within the system. Their message was: "Society has assigned the administration of drugs to the medical profession for healing disease. Any non-doctor who gives or takes drugs is a dope fiend. Play ball with the system. Capture the medical profession the way Freud did." Willis Harman, a prestigious Stanford professor, later a University of California regent, himself a mystic philosopher, warned that any non-medical use of psychedelic drugs would provoke an hysterical prohibition, as with marijuana, and set back the research.

The philosophers and scholars in the movement saw that the promise of the drugs went beyond medical treatment. They realized we were using drugs to restate in modern psychological terms the platonic-pagan-gnostic vision of a world *within* containing blueprints that would enable us to understand, harmonize, and collaborate with the physical laws of the external world.

In the tradition of the esoteric schools of antiquity these sage scholars also advised us to keep the movement scholarly, elitist, apart from politics and public.

Our project was being contacted and visited by many from this extraordinary network of prominent people, all aware of the potency of Harvard's name. The message was clear. Let's keep this knowledge to ourselves. Don't go public or you'll bring down the wrath of the custodians of society. Aunt Mae and Abigail were somewhere in my head nodding agreement.

Frank and I found all this concerned attention exhilarating, educational, and quite confusing. Our personalities and our training were American: democratic with a dash of the frontier spirit. We couldn't see ourselves as part of a select priestly class following models that belonged to the Old World. We realized that we were approaching a crossroads.

Then came a hand-scrawled letter from Allen Ginsberg. He wrote that he was a long-time student of altered states. He had heard about our experiments from a New York psychiatrist and wondered if he could come up to learn more about our research. I wrote back in the affirmative. A few days later I met Allen at the Boston railroad station. With him was his boyfriend Peter Orlovsky, a tousle-haired handsome fellow with a mischievous Bohemian presence.

It was late afternoon when we reached the house in Newton Center. I showed the poets to a bedroom and then they joined Frank and me and the kids in the kitchen.

Allen hunched over a teacup, peering out through black-rimmed glasses with a fractured left lens, telling of his experiences with Ayahuasca, the visionary vine of the Peruvian jungles. He had retraced the steps of Bill Burroughs in quest of the elixir of wisdom, studying with medicine men.

Frank and I asked many questions about these *curanderos* or shamans. We wanted to learn the rituals, to find out how other cultures handled the visionary business. Speaking of his fear and sickness whenever he took drugs, Allen described the solace and comforting strength of the *curandero*. It was good to have someone with you who knew, who had been to those far regions of the mind and could tell you by a look, by a touch, by a puff of smoke—"All right, go ahead. Explore the strange world. It's all right, you'll come back." He'll take you up. He'll bring you down. He'll put your feet back on the ground.

Allen told us about the training of *curanderos*. The candidate goes off in the mountains for weeks with an old witch doctor, who gives him the drug day after day, night after night, and he explores all the corners and caves and hidden inlets of the visionary world—the terrain of heavens and hells, the joys, the horrors, the peaks and black-burning swamps, the angels and devil-snakes—until he has been all the way to the far antipodes of consciousness. Then he is equipped to act as *curandero*, to guide other visionary travelers through the jungles of their own brains.

Frank and I hung on these words, which confirmed our growing intuition that the intelligent use of psychedelic drugs required a new professional, unfamiliar to the western world—the brain guide. The multiple-reality coach.

For thousands of years, Allen said, pre-industrial societies taught that personal growth involved visionary experiences. A guru, a shaman, had always been necessary to pilot one through the confusing realms within. In all the eastern yogic texts it was strongly emphasized that the release of internal (i.e., neurological) energies could result in confusion unless a master was on hand.

We had learned by this time that when one of our trainees launched from normal reality into the immensity of hyper-brain consciousness, there was simply no way of knowing what the voyager was experiencing. Rational commands by the guide were often irrelevant and confusing. The task of the guide was not to follow the wildly accelerating imagery of the tripper but to remain available as a secure reference base, a reassuring presence to which the voyager could return.

That evening Frank got out the little brown bottle and gave eighteen magic mushroom pills to Allen Ginsberg and Peter Orlovsky.

Sometime later I went up to check on the lads. Allen was lying on top of the blanket. His glasses were off and his pupils were completely dilated.

His eyes were patiently searching, he was working with the drug—actively, voluntarily—pushing himself into panics and fears, into nausea, trying to learn something, trying to find meaning. Peter lay next to him, sleeping or listening to music.

Allen asked me what I thought of him. I leaned over and looked down into the black eyes, fawn's eyes, man's eyes, and told him that he was a great man and that it was good to know him. He reached up his hand.

On the way downstairs I checked Susan's room. She was curled up on the floor with her books scattered around her, reading in the shadows.

I scolded her for ruining her eyes and flicked on the wall switch.

I went to check on Allen and Peter again after a half hour. Jack was standing sleepy-eyed and cheerful at the head of the stairs. I wanted to hug him, remembering my father.

1932
SPRINGFIELD, MASSACHUSETTS

The sound of my mother weeping outside my door woke me. She was in her nightgown wringing her hands. "Your father is drunk and carrying on downstairs."

I walked to the head of the stairs and flicked the light on and off to get his attention. "Hey. We're trying to sleep up here."

This enraged him.

"Please let us sleep. I have school in the morning."

"I'll teach you a thing or two right now," he said. He started toward me, holding onto the bannister with his right hand and pushing away from the wall with his left. His threatening face came level with my knees. I leaned down and pushed his forehead gently. Very gently. He tumbled back, in slow motion, against the bannister, then head over heels down the stairs, crashing into the telephone stand. His glasses broke.

He pulled himself up slowly and glared at me. "I'll get you for that." He started toward me again.

I felt horrified about knocking him down. But also scared. I pulled open the hall window and escaped onto the roof as I had a thousand times in my Tom Sawyer escapades.

I was sure-footed on the sanded-tar surface. There were several routes to safety. Up the steep gabled roof. Down the drainpipe. I hid behind the chimney. Tote poked his head out the window, cursing me. Then he slammed the window shut and locked it.

I stayed on the roof, feeling sad and guilty about Dad but exulting in my freedom until Mother waved through the window that he had fallen asleep.

DECEMBER 1960
NEWTON CENTER

Frank and I were in the study when Allen and Peter came in looking like medieval hermits. Both stark naked. Well, not quite. Allen was wearing his glasses. He raised his finger with a mad holy gleam in his eye.

"I'm the Messiah. I've come down to preach love to the world. We're going to walk through the streets and teach people to stop hating."

"That sounds like a good idea," said Frank. But he didn't leap from his chair to begin the crusade.

"Come on," Allen said, "we're going out to the city streets to tell the people about peace and love. And then we'll get lots of important leaders on a big telephone to settle all this about the Bomb once and for all."

"Fine," said Frank, "but why not do the telephone bit first."

"Who we gonna call?" asked Peter.

"Well, we'll call Kerouac on Long Island and Kennedy and Khrushchev and Bill Burroughs in Paris and Norman Mailer."

"Who we gonna call first?" asked Peter.

"Let's start with Khrushchev," said Allen.

"Why don't you start with Kerouac," said Frank.

Allen dialed "Operator." The two thin figures leaned forward, rapt in holy fervor to spread peace. They looked as though they had just stepped out of a quattrocento canvas—apostles, martyrs, prophets.

Allen said, "Hello, operator, this is God. G-O-D. I want to talk to Kerouac. Try CApitol 7-0563. Northport, Long Island."

A pause. We were all listening hard.

"No such number? Oh, right. That's the house in New Jersey where I was born. Look, operator, I'll have to go upstairs to get the number. Then I'll call back."

Allen looked at us sheepishly and hopped out of the room, returning in a moment with his address book.

The two saints stood gaunt by the desk. Allen shouted into the phone to Jack Kerouac. He wanted Jack to come up to Cambridge. And Jack's mother too. And Jack apparently had a lot to say, because Allen held the phone for long spaces. Kerouac agreed to take psilocybin as soon as we could arrange a session. Frank sat behind the desk, smiling.

Allen and Peter went to the big couch in the living room, where Allen started describing his visions, and how much it meant to him that I said he was a great man, and how this mushroom episode had opened the door to women and heterosexuality. He said he could see a womanly body and family life ahead. Peter's hand meanwhile was moving back and forth on Allen's naked shoulder. Peter was looking at Allen the way Betty from Berkeley looked at me during and after the Mexican session.

As a good *curandero* I asked if they wanted anything to eat or drink.

"How about some hot tea?"

Allen and Peter put on robes upstairs. I poured some water in a kettle, and soon we were talking around the kitchen table about the world we hoped to create. World peace. Nuclear disarmament. The end to ignorance, conformity, and unhappiness.

It seemed to us that wars, class conflicts, racial tensions, economic exploitation, religious strife, ignorance, and prejudice were all caused by narrow social conditioning. Political problems were manifestations of psychological problems, which at bottom seemed to be neurological-hormonal-chemical. If we could help people plug into the empathy circuits of the brain, then positive social change could occur.

It was then that we started plotting the neurological revolution, moving beyond scientific detachment to social activism. We would no longer be psychologists collecting data. We would create data.

Allen, the quintessential egalitarian, wanted everyone to have the option of taking mind-expanding drugs. It was the fifth freedom—the right to manage your own nervous system. The Grand Plan seemed quite logical. First we would initiate and train influential Americans in consciousness expansion. They would help us generate a wave of public opinion to support massive research programs, licensing procedures, training centers in the intelligent use of drugs. It was at this moment that we rejected Huxley's elitist perspective and adopted the American egalitarian open-to-the-public approach. And thereby hangs the tale.

NEAL CASSADY (1920-1968), although less renowned than Allen Ginsberg and Jack Kerouac, is generally considered to have been the inspiration of the Beat Movement in American literature and popular culture. Born in Denver, the child of a broken home, Cassady went "on the road" in his teens. He was known as the "Johnny Appleseed of Dope," because he introduced friends and strangers during his cross-continental peregrinations to the pleasures of marijuana and other mind-changing drugs.

Cassady and his partner Jack Kerouac roared around the country, ingesting large amounts of methedrine, peyote, grass, and alcohol, jabbering endless streams of anecdote and philosophic observation.

During the last years of his life he continued his wild search for acceleration, fueled by speed, downers, and alcohol. He died of exposure on some railroad tracks in Mexico in 1968.

7. Secrets of the Beatniks

DECEMBER 1960
HARVARD UNIVERSITY

Because of Allen Ginsberg the existence of our drug research project came to the attention of the Beatnik network. The first ambassador from Bohemia was a swaggering cowboy of medium height with close-cropped hair and insolent blue eyes. Dressed in jeans, string tie, Texas boots, he had come to find out what those square Harvard professors were up to.

"Professor Leary!" Country-western voice. "What a flash, a smash, a gas to meet you. What a long-stemmed, long-remembered honor. I cannot begin to tell you what a chilling thrill to press your flesh and look into your merry Irish eyes and pinch myself to ascertain I'm not dreaming. After all I've heard about you, you understand, from coast to coast across this great land and what you are doing for the cosmological illumination of America, you understand, not to mention the world. So permit me to introduce myself.

"I am Neal Cassady. While some have called me beatnik, you understand, I prefer to identify as wandering poet, amateur philosopher, autopilot outlaw, sent here by destiny and the advice of good friends to gobble down everything you are learning about these wonderful magical mystical drugs."

"I'm afraid you have the wrong idea," I replied, cautious. "We're scientists here, performing experiments in consciousness alteration and self-induced brain-change."

"What is this research?" asked Cassady.

"We are giving drugs to volunteers under a variety of sets and settings to chart the range of reactions."

"Which drugs?" said my visitor, brightening up.

"Psilocybin."

"Groovy, man. Now let me tell you. I've done the Magic Mushroom in Oaxaca, you understand, and felt the rainbow peacock tail brush my eyeballs. And I've done peyote with the Navaho in Arizona, in a *hogan*, you understand, with the fire carefully guarded through the long, wolf-howling desert night and the chanting and the drums and the feathered scepter. But psilocybin is new to me. Can you lay some on me?"

"We don't work that way," I said. "We spend considerable time before the drug session training our subjects, alerting them to what they can expect. We've found that with adequate preparation, subjects have little trouble and can master the fears involved."

Cassady shook his head dubiously. "Why are you making it sound so dangerous?"

"The social atmosphere, even in an enlightened place like Harvard, reeks with fear of the strange and the new, particularly when the word *drug* is involved. So we've had to deal with that reality. We've had to build up the aura of safeguards and guidance to counteract the dread. Otherwise no one would want the experience."

At this my visitor hooted with laugher. "Dread! Not want the experience! Man, what are you talking about? I should think you'd be driving away candidates with sticks."

"The undergraduates are eager for the experience," I said, "but we've agreed not to use them as subjects. Unfortunately, the older the subject, the more fear seems to exist. It's my guess they're afraid of losing something that the young haven't gotten attached to."

"You gotta stop this pedantic nonsense," said Cassady. "You're defiling and corrupting something, you understand, that is beautiful and free and wild and spontaneous. Why, you're running a defloration clinic where people can lose their virginity in a sanitized mental health situation."

"If we weren't doing it this way, it wouldn't be done at all. No one knows anything about this kind of Experimental Mysticism. We're doing our best. We've read everything that's been written in the last four thousand years on the subject."

"You're cracking me up, man. There are no books written by scientists about ecstasy and cosmic orgasms. It's oral history and poetry. The history books are about meaningless public events like wars and elections and revolutions. The only important things happen in the bodies and brains of individuals, you understand. That's the great secret of human life that scientists never talk about."

"Is that right," I said.

"You do know that the English romantic poetry of the nineteenth century was almost entirely drug inspired? Shelley, Keats, Robert Louis Stevenson, Coleridge, Byron. Even Charles Darwin dug his inspiration from the opium bottle. Not to mention our own home-grown dopers like Edgar Allan Poe, Samuel Clemens, Jack London. Dope inspired the mainstream of French poetry for the last two centuries. Don't you know that the great minds of the last generation—Freud, Joyce, Gurdjieff, Crowley—got their wisdom from drugs? My God, man, don't you know that there are hundreds of hip human beings hanging around New York City right now ready to help with your research?"

"That's interesting," I said.

"Interesting!" he shouted. "Don't you want to get out of the Ivy Tower and see what's really happening?"

Cassady scribbled on a piece of paper. "Here's an address in New York. We'll meet you next Sunday night around eight o'clock."

The door to Cassady's apartment was opened by a young woman in tight blue jeans and a tight sweater. "I'm Salinas. I've heard of you from Neal and Betty."

"Betty from Berkeley?"

"She was my roommate at UC last year. She talked about you all the time." She led me into the living room.

"Where's Neal?"

Salinas motioned to an open door. "He's in there balling Patty-Belle. Go in and tell them that you're here."

I walked to the bedroom. Two naked bodies were writhing and bumping on a single bed, dog-fashion. The girl was blond, her pretty face jerking back and forth in rhythm. She smiled at me and waved her hand. Cassady was on his knees pumping away. He waved cheerfully. I was embarrassed, transfixed. I was forty years old and this was the first time I'd ever watched two people copulate.

"Hello Timothy," gasped Cassady breathlessly. "Please . . . ah . . . please excuse us for a moment. This . . . is . . . Patty-Belle . . . and if she doesn't get her juicy streamline chassis overhauled every day, you understand, she gets . . . pouty." Cassady closed his eyes to narrate. "So I gotta grind her sweet soft valves, lubricate her tubes, fire her spark plugs, you understand, lay down some tire-tracks across her rumble-seat, oil her transmission, grease her gearbox, you understand, tune up her soft li'l cylinders, and jam her throttle to the floor."

I beat a nervous retreat back to Salinas, who said, "I can't wait to start."

"Did Cassady tell you about the experimental contract?" I asked, thinking there must have been a less stuffy way of saying the same thing.

"I provide you with the drugs. You take them and tell me what you experience. I'm particularly interested in how psilocybin measures relative to other drugs you've taken. Psychopharmacologists haven't yet been able to collect this kind of comparative phenomenological data."

"You mean, man, you want us to get high on your drug and then compare it with other stuff we've done?"

"Yes, that's right."

"Weird."

I took the vial from my pocket and spilled out a few dozen pink pills on the coffee table. Salinas leaned forward wetting her lips. Cassady, wearing blue jeans but naked to the waist, knelt in front of the table and poked the pills with his finger. His dark eyes glittered. Patty-Belle, dressed in shorts and a carelessly buttoned man's shirt, sat cross-legged, her blue eyes bulging.

"How much is a dose?" Cassady asked.

"Two is what most experimenters have used. Six is what we have found to be a moderate dose. Ten is an intense experience."

"What's the most anyone has taken?" asked Salinas.

"Twelve."

"Who took twelve?"

"I did."

"Then I want twelve," she said.

"Body weight is a factor," I added. "I'd say twelve for me would be eight for you."

"You mean you'll turn on with us?" Salinas let her surprise show. Suddenly I felt more comfortable.

"Yes. I want my brain to be operating at the same speed and elevation as yours."

As the pills were passed around, I was fascinated to witness the calm devotion, the almost religious commitment of the beatniks to the moment of ingestion. Used to the giggling nervousness, the uneasy rationalization, the tightfaced panic with which Harvardites approached the drug, I found Salinas, Neal, and Patty-Belle serious, hopeful, and wise. They were connoisseurs, experienced space-travelers approaching a promising new planet.

For three hours the room remained silent. Salinas curled in the corner of the couch, occasionally scanning the room. Neal folded his body into an oriental meditation posture and seemed to be concentrating on his breathing. Patty-Belle lay motionless on the rug.

We hovered effortlessly in the supernatural quiet, in that silent serene bubble of communication where people need say nothing because everything is understood. Or so one thinks.

Neal leaped to his feet and began pacing the room. His face was flushed, radiating beneficence.

"This stuff is incredible! Are you sure it's legal?"

I nodded.

Salinas opened her sloe-eyes and smiled enigmatically. "It does seem too heavenly to be true. Admit it, man, it's addictive."

I shook my head.

"You wanted a report on this experience?" asked Neal.

I nodded.

"Well, I'll give you one expert's opinion. This combines the good sides of every other drug with none of the bad. This is the ultimate luxury, the flawless wisdom-pleasure hit. More mellow and cozy than heroin, but you don't nod out. I feel more alive and wired and energetic than with speed, but not jangly. It's got the blast of cocaine, but it lasted ten times longer."

"It must cost a fortune," said Salinas.

"It's spacey like the best hashish," continued Cassady, "but also light and bouncy."

"I've never been so horny in my life," said Patty-Belle.

"It's philosophical," added Cassady. "I could write a book about the cosmic thoughts I had. This is the Rolls Royce of dope. The ultimate high."

Waves of affection rippled around the room.

At dawn Salinas untwined herself from the couch, "Man, I don't have a clue as to what you're all about. When I first heard about you, I thought you might be looking for a little girl to play Dr. John with. What *do* you want?"

"I want to thank you for teaching me so much last night."

"What did we teach you? How psilocybin is different from other drugs?"

"Don't you see, Salinas?" interjected Cassady. "The professor has never seen anyone getting righteously high before last night. Right?"

"Right," I agreed. "You're not afraid of altered states. You seem to thrive on them. Our experience last night confirms that mental set and setting are what's important. The drug has very few specific predictable effects. It frees your mind to go anywhere you are ready to go."

During the drive back to Cambridge I reviewed what had been learned from this unusual experiment. The four of us had reached a place where we were momentarily beyond social roles, beyond normal strivings. We had apparently tapped some meditative overview circuit of our brains that allowed us to share a moment of philosophic understanding, linking an Ivy League intellectual and three very earthy and very free spirits.

The ability of the drug to connect diverse people in empathetic bonds suggested exciting social applications. Once people learned to share others' perceptions, a higher level of human communication might be possible.

BIOGRAPHY

ARTHUR KOESTLER (1905-1983), European philosopher, was born in Budapest. Living in Berlin during the 1930s he attracted notice as a science writer and political activist. He became a Communist in 1931 but left the Party because of the Stalin purge trials. During the Spanish Civil War he was imprisoned by Franco and spent weeks on a "death row," where he experienced a life-changing vision. After the German conquest of France he was held in a concentration camp, from which he escaped in 1940.

Darkness at Noon (1941), a powerful portrayal of the repressive nature of communism, described the purge of a veteran Bolshevik for his defense of the individual. After World War II Koestler wrote several novels, two volumes of autobiography, and a series of philosophic-scientific texts. *Janus* (1978) explored the technologies and strategies of evolution and presented a good critique of the Darwinian theory of blind natural selection.

Koestler was an intellectual hero of the twentieth century, who probed deeply into the subjects essential to human nature, such as humor, creativity, epistemology, genetics, and telepathy, as well as providing a glamorous model of the "engaged sage."

8. Getting High on Toil and Suffering

FALL 1960
HARVARD UNIVERSITY

Soon after the psilocybin project got underway, I wrote an enthusiastic letter to Arthur Koestler in London, summarizing our work and inviting him to join us. His writings had prepared me for the "mystic experience," and I wanted to repay him for changing my life. I heard from him straight away. He was coming to America for a neurological conference and would be interested in trying the mushrooms.

I had a few reservations about Arthur as a subject. He was so rational and controlled, with little sense of humor. He seemed tormented by an ancient European pessimism.

A few days before his scheduled arrival Arthur phoned from Michigan to say he had been given psilocybin there and it was the worst experience of his life. He was cancelling the visit to Cambridge. No thanks.

After I promised that we would serve him nothing stronger than good French wine, he agreed to come anyway.

He looked terrible when I picked him up at the airport. It seemed an English psychiatrist at Ann Arbor named Pointsman, learning that

Arthur was scheduled to take psilocybin with me, had suggested that he run a session for Arthur instead.[1]

By the time we settled into the *Blanc de Blanc*, Arthur was rolling along with his narrative.

"It started off very well. I lay down on the couch and soon began to experience the kind of phenomena that mescaline mystics have reported. Luminous patterns of great beauty. If I had allowed myself, I probably could have shared the vision of the prophet Elijah as he was swept up to heaven. But I felt this was buying one's visions on the cheap, so I forced my eyes open. No easy paths for me. I congratulated myself on my sober self-control. Mine was a rational mind, not to be fooled by little pills."

"That's an invitation to disaster," I told him, "trying to master your brain."

"By now," he continued, "even with open eyes the room looked different. The colors were not only more luminous and phosphorescent, they were different in quality from any color previously seen. To describe them I would have to invent new terms—the curtains were breen, the walls darsh, the sky outside the window emerdeen. But my mind was not to be lulled by this tinsel hallucination. Suddenly the intermittent reflection from the tape spool became meaningful, ominous. When Dr. Pointsman entered the room, he had undergone an incredible transformation. His face was a sickly yellow. It was split in two like a cell dividing. A small scar on the doctor's neck, which I had not noticed before, was gaping wide, trying to swallow the flesh of his bulbous chin. One ear had shrunk. The other had grown by several inches. He looked like a smirking, vicious devil.

"I suppose I took the mushrooms in the wrong state of mind, and they awakened memories of past experiences as a political prisoner, memories of torture, brainwashing, and extorted confessions."

"That's a shame," I sympathized. "While you are here, let me arrange for you to observe a session run in a supportive context. I assure you it's quite different."

"Agreed. So long as I don't have to participate."

The next day Koestler accompanied me to the Harvard campus, where his presence caused quite a stir. We lunched with B. F. Skinner and conferred with Jerome Bruner, the famous cognitive psychologist.

On the second day I phoned over to the Massachusetts Mental Health Institute to arrange a meeting between Koestler and Dr. Max Rinkel, a renowned drug authority. Rinkel had never heard of Koestler, and I joshed him for his illiteracy. It was arranged that we meet at the Ritz bar for cocktails.

Crossing the Charles River to Boston Arthur fell to reminiscing about two dear friends of his who had researched mescaline in Berlin in the twenties. Their psychedelic sessions opened realms of shared experience and revelation. They tried to tell others about their discoveries, but neither friends nor colleagues nor even their families would listen. Finally the alienation became so great that they cracked under the strain. One went to Mexico, where he died within a short time. The other went to Munich to be treated, or mistreated, by a famous psychiatrist who failed to understand the creative transcendental nature of his experience. Quitting treatment in despair he returned to Berlin and killed himself.

Rinkel was waiting at his special table. Within minutes the two European-trained men sank into boozy argument. Rinkel seemed irritated that Koestler, without a medical degree, claimed knowledge of the nervous system; Rinkel was offended in spite of, or perhaps because of, the fact that Arthur had just returned from a prestigious scientific conference on the brain, where he delivered a keynote address. Pressed by Koestler's logic Rinkel slipped behind an undergrowth of swizzle sticks. Rising from behind an island of potato chips he denied there was such a thing as the midbrain. Koestler triumphantly swallowed an olive and lobbed a glance of resignation my way.

Suddenly Koestler's face grew tense.

"Max," Koestler murmured thoughtfully. "Did you ever practice psychotherapy at the Reichsklinik in Munich? Do you remember treating a psychiatrist from Berlin named Dr. Moses?"

Rinkel remembered no Dr. Moses.

Moving in like a cross-examiner Koestler sketched in more details about his friend. "He had been experimenting with mescaline."

Recognition dawned. "Oh, yes, now that you refresh my memory, I do seem to remember treating the case. Such a long time ago."

"Do you have any idea what became of him?"

"No. I was about to ask you if you knew his whereabouts."

Arthur sighed and shook his head. "As a matter of fact he killed himself in Berlin a few weeks after you discharged him."

Silence spread around the table like a spilled drink. Rinkel, not happy with the implied rebuke, puffed at his cigar, motioning to the waitress for the check. Arthur and I rose, bowed formally, and left.[2]

Outside the air coming off the Boston Common was clear and fresh. We felt good getting away from the unpleasant encounter. We drove merrily to the North End to meet Frank Barron and the new woman in his life, the beautiful Nancy. Our plan was to dine and then return home, where Arthur could observe a mushroom session with Charles Olson, the legendary bard of Gloucester.

Our dinner with Frank and Nancy at the Steel Helmet was festive.
When we arrived at the house, Charles Olson was in the kitchen, talking
to young Jack. The group assembled in the study. From a recess in
the wall I took a quaint oriental box inlaid with different colored woods.
The pills were counted out for each tripper. Arthur reached for some,
much to my amazement. "Let me go along too." He took ten tablets,
a good sized dose, and washed them down with his highball.

We listened to Bach. There was giggly sporadic conversation. The soft
peace of the mushroom descended. Jangled racing minds purred slowly.
We grew lighter and more serene. A candle flame on the table flickered.
Nancy and Frank looked into each other's eyes. Nancy laughed saucily,
did a whirling dance, and they were gone.

Arthur's face was transfigured.

"This is perfection," he murmured. "Everyone, everything is so beautiful. I've never heard music like this before." He closed his eyes, leaving
only his Cheshire smile. The peace continued for hours. Then, with
Mozart shimmering in the room, I looked up to see Arthur's face red
and tortured, his eyes expressing the sorrows of the ages.

His voice rose in woeful counterpoint to the concerto. "This is wonderful, no doubt," he said. "But it is fake, ersatz. Instant mysticism. There
is no quick and easy path to wisdom. Sweat and toil are the price of
knowledge.

"I remember in the beloved Austrian mountains of my school days,
it took us six hours to climb a 7,000-foot peak. Today, these peaks can
be reached in a few minutes by motor car or ski lift."

"What did he say?" asked Olson from a million miles away.

"Something about sweat and toil," I said.

"Yet still today," Arthur continued, "you see thousands of schoolboys,
middle-aged couples, and even elderly men puffing and panting up the
steep path, groaning under the load of their knapsacks."

"Did he say groaning?" asked Olson.

"When they arrive at the Alpine refuge near the summit, streaming
with sweat, they shout for their reward—a glass of schnapps. Then they
look at the view.

"My point is not the virtue of toil and suffering. My point is that,
although the view is the same, their vision is different from those who
arrive by motor car." At this he burst into cheerful chuckling.

"Have some schnapps, Arthur," cried Olson heartily.

"The rational mind and sober self-control," shouted Arthur, grinning
ear to ear in spite of himself. "This pressure-cooker mysticism is the
ultimate profanation." With that Arthur burst into laughter, waved to
us cheerily, and hiked out of the room.

Fearing a return of the Michigan paranoia I knocked at his door. Barron's merry voice shouted for me to enter. He and Nancy were cuddled under the covers.

"Where's Arthur?"

"We didn't know this was his room. We just fell into the first bed we saw. He popped in a minute ago. He was full of apologies."

I checked the guest rooms down the hallway. "Arthur. Arthur."

"Tim? Is it you?"

Arthur was cuddled up under the blankets, clutching a pillow to his chest and grinning madly, high as a balloon. Relieved to have my charge safely stowed away I went downstairs. I watched the fire and smoked cigarettes late into the night.

1932
SPRINGFIELD, MASSACHUSETTS

I lay in bed practicing my inhaling style with an imaginary cigarette, trying to decide which brand I would select when I became sixteen. There was no reservation in my mind about addicting myself to nicotine. Every movie star flaunted the vice as a necessary adjunct to glamour. Bette Davis, Claudette Colbert, and Katherine Hepburn nervously puffed away as they paced around their penthouses. Cary Grant, Clark Gable, and Humphrey Bogart dangled butts from their mouths with sexy unconcern as they performed heroic deeds. FDR, the ultimate authority figure, was always appearing in photographs with his jaunty cigarette holder tilted upwards. Senators and sports stars shouted the praises of their favorite brands. They'd walk a mile for a Camel. Old Golds promised not a cough in a carload. Lucky Strikes implied good fortune with every hit. New Yorker ads portrayed elegant upper-class figures calming their nerves (the butler dropped soup in the duchess' lap!) by lighting up a Murad.

I was tempted to choose Kentucky Winners because they sponsored the Red Sox games on the radio. Every time Joe Cronin or Jimmy Foxx slugged a homer, they won cartons of this rich tasty smoke. But Chesterfields were my ultimate favorite. I liked the white and gold package.

My bedroom door slammed shut. As a private eye I had looped a string through a pulley above the door so that I could open or close it while lying in bed. I pulled the cord to open the door. There was Tote, tipsy, looking puzzled. "Son, I'm going to make love to your mother, and I want this door closed."

He slammed it again.

Feigning sleep I pulled the cord and the door swung open.

"Goddamn it, what's wrong with that door?" muttered Tote. He slammed it again. I opened it again.

In a few minutes Tote returned with a hammer and nailed my door shut. I wasn't worried. I knew the escape routes.

FALL 1960
HARVARD UNIVERSITY

The next morning when I woke him for another round of Harvard appointments, Arthur sat up in bed still grinning. "Those pills last night didn't affect me at all. I have a strong mind."

"You surely do," I replied.

On the way home from our day on the campus Arthur bought two bottles of *Pouilly Fuissé* and a bottle of scotch whiskey. In the study we began on the whiskey. Arthur held up his glass and shook it with an icy tinkle.

"I'll stick to my drug. Alcohol is a social stimulant. It warms one and brings one closer to people. Mushrooms whirl you inside, too close to yourself. They produce a temporary therapeutic psychosis. I never felt better. But there's no wisdom there. I solved the secret of the universe last night, but this morning I forgot what it was."

The next day I dropped by Frank Barron's office. Like a worried parent I asked, "Where did we fail with Arthur? He said he found the secret of the universe but forgot it."

"Maybe it's just as well," said Frank. "But perhaps there's a lesson in that. William James was not above taking notes on his own experiences as they came to him under the influence of nitrous oxide. After one session he found that he had written: 'The secret of the universe is the smell of burned almonds.' The universe can keep its secrets as far as I'm concerned, but I'd like to have a record of what people are experiencing under unusual conditions."

"So the solution," I said, "is for us to take lots of notes. And to record the external circumstances at the time. The smell of burned almonds is not bad for starters. With a nitrous oxide hose over your nose it's understandable that the portal to the gates of mystery would be nasal."

"Very understandable."

"But why," I asked, "does Koestler reject the ecstasy if it doesn't involve toil and suffering? Sounds like the Luddite rejection of technology."

"What's that?"

"Ned Ludd was a half-witted Leicestershire workman who persuaded nineteenth-century English weavers to destroy labor-saving looms. You know—if it's new and pleasurable and saves time, then it must be bad. Arthur's flogging himself with the Biblical guilt trip."

Frank shook his head. "I'm not sure it's all that simple. The idea of revelation after trial and suffering is one of the oldest in philosophy.

Hard work versus technological shortcuts. Drugs are shortcuts. But they also give us added options. Ski lifts and motor cars are alternatives to walking. I agree with Aldous. It's not a case of either/or, it's both/and. If you want, you can sweat and suffer hiking up today, *and* you can choose to zoom up tomorrow using technology."

"Arthur is saying that those who hike up see a different view from those who get there through technology."

"Who can doubt it," Frank said. "Well-earned sore feet always improve the view. And self-sacrifice, if it doesn't go on too long, makes piety easier. But it's inaccurate to imply that shortcuts are easy. It takes plenty of disciplined, inventive, and risky work to construct a ski-lift or to run one of our drug sessions."

"Come to think about it," I added, "all the secrets of life are shortcuts. I'm a scientist. Rejecting drugs as a tool would be like rejecting the microscope because it makes seeing too easy. I think people deserve every revelation they can get."

"I just want to know one thing," Frank said wryly. "Did Arthur walk, huffing and puffing, back to New York?"

"No. He took an Eastern Airlines shortcut with a bottle of schnapps in his luggage."

JACK KEROUAC (1922-1969), American novelist, was born in Lowell, Massachusetts and educated at Columbia. In 1957 he wrote *On the Road*, a picaresque account of his adventures with Neal Cassady. This novel became the bible of the Beat movement. Kerouac's writing used the freestyle rhythms and improvisational flourishes of jazz.

Though he was identified in the public eye with the Beats, Kerouac in his later years remained aloof from and critical of the drug-culture lifestyle. His opinions, probably stimulated by alcohol abuse, became extremely conservative.

Other autobiographical novels include *The Subterraneans* (1968), *The Dharma Bums* (1958), *Big Sur* (1962), and *Desolation Angels* (1965).

9. Literary Elites and Black Hope

FALL 1960
NEW YORK CITY

Allen Ginsberg phoned from New York, eager to begin our campaign for the politics of ecstasy. He had lined up mushroom sessions for Jack Kerouac, Robert Lowell, and Barney Rossett, famed avant-garde publisher.

Allen and Peter lived in a terminally dingy apartment on the Lower East Side. I had never seen such domestic disrepair, but Allen's cheery-abbess bustling made me feel at home.

Jack Kerouac sat at the kitchen table, drinking red wine and unleashing a non-stop stream-of-consciousness monologue about the hinge in the middle of Allen's penis and about barracuda Buddhas, etc., etc. Between the word games, puns, boastful teasing, and locker-room jokes, we fell to discussing sports. It turned out that, like me, Kerouac had developed a game of baseball-solitaire with rosters of imaginary players whose statistics—hits, runs, errors—he recorded.

1926-1930
INDIAN ORCHARD, MASSACHUSETTS

I grew up lonely, immersed in tales of heroism, history, romance, and exploration. And sports. Excellence was my preoccupation.

Unlike my Catholic schoolmates, who were encouraged to imitate sorrowful saints, virtuous virgins, masochistic martyrs, I modeled myself after legendary heroes and lovers. Each week I lugged home ten do-it-yourself glory manuals from the library, plunging into the worlds of King Arthur, Robin Hood, Ulysses, Jeb Stuart, Socrates, and Horatio at the Bridge.

After reading about Indian life, I built and—to my mother's distress— inhabited a small tipi in the backyard. Later I was busted by the fork-tongues for carving the wooden clothesline supports into totem poles.

Given a chemistry set for Christmas I became Tom Swift working to produce a drug, "Idicton," which would save humanity. During my Sherlock Holmes phase I assembled a homemade burglar kit with a mask and gloves. I paid surreptitious visits to neighborhood homes, looking for evidence of insidious attacks on American freedom.

I stalked like a safari hunter through the woods near the Ferris farmhouse, tracking rabbits with my BB gun. On summer days I rode my bike across the Chicopee River bridge, beyond the steaming jute mills to fresh farm meadows and down sylvan paths to a creek. Roping two discarded barn doors together, I constructed a raft, dangling a fishing pole over the stream, wickedly smoking corn tassels in a corncob pipe.

I was not muscled for competition but had good coordination. I perfected athletic skills in games that I invented. By fourteen I had worked out solitary versions of several sports. I played baseball on the street with a golf ball, which could be thrown to hit the curb and bounce back as a sharp grounder, a high fly, or a slashing line drive, depending on the angle of impact. Pedestrians would stop to watch me hurl the ball, run to field a grounder, wheel to start the double play, and jerk up the umpire's thumb—you're out!

My radio was propped out my bedroom window so I could follow the play-by-play broadcast of Red Sox games. Even when the announcer's voice wasn't audible, I could tell what was happening at Fenway Park by listening to the crowd noises. The sounds of the collective brain at an athletic event have always intrigued me. To this day I can reconstruct the play-by-play at Dodger Stadium while waiting in the hot dog line out of sight of the field.

I have always based my professional life on an athletic model: players, coaches, teams, leagues. My work as psychologist and philosopher was organized on the same principles: try all the life games, find the ones you want to learn. Infield, outfield—select the positions you wish to master. Get the best coaching available. Practice, practice, practice. Improve. Excel. Keep changing the game. Winning is a short-range concept, suspect and often irrelevant. The aim is to move on to more complex games.

My wide-eyed reading of the sports page taught me the basic American truisms: Percentages are important. You win some, you lose some. Everyone has slumps and hot streaks. Be graceful and sportsmanlike in both victory and defeat. Take each game as it comes. Play it clean because today's rivals may be traded to your team next season.

This combination of dedication and detachment—the attitude of the pro—and my avoidance of those hot heads who get so involved they forget it's just a game, have led some people to see me as cold and uncaring, when I have seen myself as standing calmly on the pitcher's mound, sweating moderately, thinking about my next pitch.

FALL 1960
NEW YORK CITY

Having spent most of my early life in the chambers of romantic invention I felt a bond with the introverted drunken novelist. But Jack Kerouac was scary. Behind the dark good looks of a burly lumberjack was a New England mill-town sullenness, a Canuck-Catholic soggy distrust. This is one unhappy kid, I thought.

"So what are you up to, Doctor Leary, running around with this communist faggot Ginsberg and your bag of pills? Can your drugs absolve the mortal and venial sins which our beloved savior, Jesus Christ, the only Son of God, came down and sacrificed his life upon the cross to wash away?" He was teasing, and yet he wasn't.

"Why don't we find out?" said Ginsberg quietly.

I produced the bottle, counted out the pills, and we all launched off.

Kerouac continued to drink and rant like a sailor in a port-town bar, striding around the room, jumping on chairs, declaiming funny, poetic gibberish. He leaped on the couch. "I'm King of the Beatniks. I'm François Villon, vagabond poet-rogue of the open highway. Listen while I play you hot-lick, spiral improvisations from my tenor typewriter." It was charming, witty, and lovable, but when the drug started to expose my tender tissues, the noise became jarring. I longed for the familiar mushroom silence.

By this time I had shared voyages with over a hundred persons, but no one had tried to control, dominate, overwhelm the experience like Kerouac. He was imposing his saloon style on it, and for me it was simply too much.

I walked into the dark bedroom and flopped on the bed. Kerouac continued to shout and guffaw with alcoholic exuberance. I fell into depression. Kerouac had propelled me into my first negative trip. Maybe it was the drabness of the slum, so different from our carefully prepared session rooms. Perhaps it was jittery New York itself, never a town for serene philosophers. Or was it Kerouac's French-Catholic gloom? Anyway, down I went.

No kidding around, the world was a dismal dreary place. Aunt Mae and Kerouac were right. It *was* folly trying to change human nature. Who was I to eliminate suffering when now, from my own soul, oozed a pus of despair. Yes, the Catholic nuns were right. This world was a vale of suffering. My life was a fraud. Behind my cheerful facade I was a miserable child, abandoned by my father, breaking my mother's heart, driving my wife to suicide, incapable of true love and levity. Alone and lonely.

My father had never paid much attention to me. I remembered that terrible day when I came home from school and Mother told me that Dad had wanted to take me to Lake Congamond for the afternoon. Since I wasn't home, he just left without me. I ran down the three flights of stairs to the apartment parking lot. Dad's car was pulling out the driveway. I ran shouting. "Dad, wait for me." He didn't hear me, he drove off.

Was it possible for him or me really to love anyone?

Mother and Aunt Mae waited year by fearful year for me to break their hearts again.

I was always driving off, leaving dear ones in the lurch. Marianne, sweet lost bride. My poor abandoned children, Susan and Jack.

I rode to the hospital with Marianne's motionless body. They rolled her into the emergency room. A young doctor, short, black-haired, bent over her for a moment. Then he threw the sheet over her face.

Allen found me curled into a fetal ball on the bed.

"Oh no," he exclaimed, "this time *you're* the cosmic worrier. Are you all right? We miss you."

He was reminding me of his first mushroom trip, when he had come safely through a painful moment with my help: it was exactly the right thing to say. I felt better, reassured by Allen's loving eyes.

With the aid of these drugs I was exposing myself to the most intense emotions available to the human nervous system. Having dealt now with session crises from both sides I was learning that it was possible to control and modulate emotions. Consciousness could flick in and out of any imaginable happy/horror chamber. The trick was not to get caught, not to freeze the flow of reality.[1] Then one could securely say: no emotion is alien to me, no single emotion can trap me.

Kerouac was still in his barroom reality so I joined in, drinking red wine, smoking cigarettes, and exchanging stories. At one point Allen and I tried to talk to Kerouac about the cultural value of drug-sessions and the philosophic implications of altered states. He dampened our pagan enthusiasm with the gloomy Catholic koan: "Walking on water wasn't made in a day."

By dawn we had run out of nicotine. Kerouac and I volunteered to walk to the corner. We gasped in pleasure—a gentle blanket of pure white snow covered the grimy tenement streets. Kerouac's response was instinctual; he rolled and flung a snowball at me, zing, just missing my head. I ducked and fired back. We whooped down the East Side like schoolboys. The corner saloon was just opening so we sat at the wooden bar, downed some beers, and played the jukebox. At the store we bought a loaf of oval-shaped Italian bread and ran back to Allen's, lofting spiral passes to each other.

After a breakfast of steaming coffee with milk and sugar and toast with jam Allen announced it was time for us to move uptown to turn on Robert Lowell. We parted with Kerouac in front of the apartment. Jack embraced me and headed off alone, shoulders hunched. Before he reached the corner, I shouted, "Jack," and threw him a snowball, a long arching football pass. Kerouac jumped up, caught it, and we all cheered.

As Kerouac disappeared from view, I thought over the session. It had been fun and instructive but had fallen short of the philosophic trips produced at Harvard. Throughout the night Kerouac remained unmovably the Catholic carouser, an old-style Bohemian without a hippie bone in his body. Jack Kerouac opened the neural doors to the future, looked ahead, and didn't see his place in it. Not for him the utopian pluralist optimism of the sixties.

Allen, Peter, and I took the subway uptown. Peter, with typical beatnik directness, asked me childlike questions about my sexual habits. Did I like to fuck girls? Yes. What kind of girls? Smart, sexy ones. Did I have a girlfriend now? No, not at the moment. Did I like to suck pussy? I needed more practice. Did I like to suck cocks? Never tried.

Meanwhile Allen was outlining the task at hand. "Robert Lowell is this old-line Brahmin. His poetry is intense, personal, gloomy. The problem is that he tends to flip out every once in a while and has to be hospitalized. We're not dealing here with a Dionysian funlover. He's a good guy with a psycho streak. We should be cautious about the dose."

"Why *are* we giving psilocybin to Lowell?" Peter asked.

"We hope to loosen him up, make him happier. And on the political front, if Pulitzer Prize-winner Robert Lowell has a great session, his product endorsement will influence lots of intellectuals."

Lowell and Elizabeth Hardwick, his wife, lived in a spacious bright apartment overlooking the Hudson River. I laid down a brief rap about the experience, and Allen chimed in with insightful asides. We gave Lowell about half the dose I gave to Salinas.

Peter and I talked quietly with Elizabeth in the kitchen. After three hours Allen said everything was cool and we could go. Lowell, always the gentleman, took me aside and wrung my hand in gratitude.

"Now I know what Blake and St. John of the Cross were talking about," he said. "This experience is what I was seeking when I became a Catholic."

I wasn't sure whether I believed him or not. For most people the dose would have been too low to produce transcendental effects.

On the way downtown I said to Allen, "Well, that all went placidly. But what did it prove?"

"That a brilliant but unstable genius who's suffered nervous breakdowns can take psychedelics safely, if the setting is secure."

"Yeah, but I don't think we changed his life," I said. "Maybe we should have given him the option to have a heavy-dose experience and go all the way."

"That could have been more risky for us," said Allen. "I wouldn't want to be known as the guy who put America's leading poet around the bend."

"Yes, but I still feel a bit disappointed. My take with Kerouac and Lowell is that we're batting zero for two in the Life-Change Revelation League."

"Now we face an even stiffer challenge," laughed Allen. "Barney Rossett has been through several psychiatrists. He is the Mickey Mantle of introspective intellectuals."

"Why are we turning on Rossett?" asked Peter. "Why don't we pick up some pizza and have a party?"

"Rossett is one of the most influential publishers in America. If we can turn him on, we can illuminate New York and London."

We arrived at Barney Rossett's elegant townhouse just as he was finishing dinner. With him was Zelda, a languorous woman with chocolate-colored skin. We moved upstairs to the lush living room for the experiment. Of the psilocybin, there remained only enough for two doses. I suggested that Allen and Barney use the mushrooms. Zelda, Peter, and I would take mescaline, which was freely available by mail order from several New York pharmaceutical houses. As soon as the mushrooms started happening, Barney motioned to Allen, and they retired to the study to examine the universe.

We Three Mescaleros lay on the carpet, which began to pulse and grow like a field of green hay. The effects on my vision were spectacular. The colors on the wall radiated with a jewely sheen. Pigment stuck out of the paintings at least twelve inches, forming valleys and mountains of raw, furrowed, gleaming color. No point in further breathless descriptions here: in *Doors of Perception* and *Heaven and Hell*, Aldous Huxley, a man nearly blind, gave us the classic descriptions and analysis of these archetypal inner visions.

In the deep green grass Zelda, Peter, and I grinned adoringly at each other, linked by a special sharing.

Zelda lifted her head. "You know, this sort of thing can solve the problem."

I knew what problem she was talking about.

"No more black and white up here," she mumbled.

Allen walked in with a harried expression on his face. Looking at us he brightened up. "I see you three are feeling no cosmic angst."

"How's Barney?"

"He seems to be in the gloomy thought department. He's been writing obituaries about his life, his career, his family, politics, religion, complaining that he pays his analyst $75 an hour to help him avoid this sort of thing."

Toward dawn Zelda replaced Allen in Barney's bedroom.

Allen, Peter, and I cleaned up the living room, stacked the records, turned off the lights, and walked out to the winter streets. Sunrise tinted pink the snow-covered city canyon. A cluster of remarkable trash cans by the curb hailed us, "Good morning." Their metal sides and their contents sparkled like diamonds and rubies. They were earnestly giving me an amusing wordless lecture on the Hindu theory of It-ness, animate, vibrating.

"Come along now, no more of that," joshed Allen, pulling me by the arm. "I know that nothing in the galaxy is as beautiful as a well-used trashcan. But we have work to do."

At Allen's flat we tallied up the score on our weekend of experiments. We had administered psychedelic drugs to three middle-aged intellectuals and one young black woman. The three men fought to control the experience, clung to their personal realities, and emerged (in our observation) relatively unchanged. Credit them for curiosity. Considering their knowledge of their own neuroses, praise them for courage. But there was no wild hunger for meaning, no passion for transformation.

Their holding back presented us with a moral paradox. What were our responsibilities as to dosage? On this neurological frontier no code of ethics had yet been articulated. Nowhere in history books was there an account of philosophers facing our dilemmas—the ready availability of chemicals capable of transforming people as far as they were willing to go.

Robert Lowell was an intelligent but tormented man whose creative peak was behind him. Should I have challenged him to change, offered him the risky choice? "Look, if you take a large enough dose of these mushrooms, you'll have a deep mystical experience, you might even be flung into the deepest part of that hell you have been struggling to escape. Chances are you'll come back reborn, refreshed, ready to start anew."

Over time we were to realize that some people were more attracted to personal mutation than others. We had scores of reports describing how voyagers felt their lives had changed for the better. Most of our Harvard subjects came back from their experience ready to make expanded consciousness part of their careers, their lives—eager to learn how to run sessions for others.

Why did some people turn away from the experience, while others like Zelda, immediately understood its purpose? Was it because she was young? To our chagrin youth was becoming a consistent indication in our research. The older the person, the more fear of visionary experience. Race, religion, and caste were also important predictors. The more the person had to lose, the less willingness to go joyously beyond the Judeo-Christian linear mental structure.

Zelda's positive response to the drug suggested that women might be more receptive to multiple realities and more tolerant of the pluralism and relativity of Nature. The possibility of male-female differences went on the agenda for future study.

Another thought-provoking result followed this session: Zelda's bond to her boyfriend Barney seemed to have weakened. In a few days I got a flustered letter from Allen saying that Zelda had taken to hanging out at his house and wanted to marry him! Thus, a new and titillating development in Allen's sex life.

Then I got a call from Zelda. Could she come up to Newton to see me? As soon as she arrived, the connection from our session lit up again. She moved in as though we had been lovers for years.

Zelda taught me a lot about enjoying life. She was astonished that we, who had stumbled upon these effective hedonic instruments, were dallying with intellectual research rather than pursuing sensual pleasure.

In many ways Zelda was too advanced for me. I was caught up in the middle-class mission of achievement and responsibility, feeling that evolution wouldn't happen if I didn't throw all of my energies into the task.

We never reattained the tender union we had shared in New York. When a friend offered her a job modeling in Hollywood, I urged her to take it. At the airport she looked at me with bewilderment. "I don't know why I'm leaving you," she said. I understood it somewhat better myself. I still hadn't gotten over Marianne's death.

BIOGRAPHY

RICHARD ALPERT (1931-), American psychologist and philosopher, took his doctorate at Stanford. In 1953 he was appointed assistant professor at Harvard University, and three years later he succeeded Frank Barron as co-director of the Harvard Psychedelic Drug Research Project.

In 1967, during a pilgrimage to India, Alpert became a devotee of Neem Karoli Baba, a Hindu guru, who changed Alpert's name to Baba Ram Dass. His lecture tours and his books, especially *Be Here Now,* introduced the American public to Eastern practices of meditation and inner development.

Alpert's enormous influence as a spiritual teacher was due to personal charisma and his ability to translate Eastern philosophical concepts into language of simplicity and humor. His modesty, his frankness, and his ability to evolve inspired the millions who shared his voyage of discovery.

10. Partner in Time

WINTER-SPRING 1961
HARVARD UNIVERSITY

After four months our research project had introduced over a hundred subjects to psilocybin. Apart from occasional moments of fear and confusion the sessions had been positive, stimulating, thought-provoking. Caught up in the excitement we began to think that we had discovered the long-sought after philosopher's stone, the key to increased intelligence.[1]

Training centers like ours, we believed, could be set up in any medical school, in any divinity school, in the psychology, philosophy, anthropology, sociology departments of every college in the land. In another year or two anyone with philosophic ambitions and a thoughtful desire to increase intelligence could learn how to use drugs effectively. The context would be educational. Freshman courses in college curricula could train students to activate their own nervous systems according to instructions of the manufacturers.

1936-38
SPRINGFIELD, MASSACHUSETTS

My desire to fashion new educational methods based on the imprinting capacities of the brain was undoubtedly due to my own unfortunate educational experiences in high school and my first two colleges.

In 1935, Classical High School was an imposing institution, reputed to be one of the best "college prep" schools in New England. Approaching the wide stairs one expected to see Plato, Aristotle, Andrew Carnegie, and Herbert Hoover, all of them dressed in togas, bearing the tablets of wisdom. To me, this Protestant Mind Factory was a bewildering place, populated with superior creatures. Girls in bobby sox, saddle shoes, and bulging soft sweaters dazzled me with their Episcopalian glamour. The older boys were all huge swaggering jocks being groomed for Harvard, Princeton, Dartmouth. I was intimidated.

The principal of Classical High, William C. Hill, was a towering man with a Supreme Court Justice shock of white hair. It was his custom to assemble incoming freshmen classes and explain the motto of the school—the Kantian Categorical Imperative—"No one has a right to do that which if everyone did would destroy society." When escorting adult visitors the principal would stop students in the hallway to have us parrot this totalitarian doctrine.

For two years I was withdrawn socially and confused academically. I commuted from outlying Indian Orchard, carrying my peasant paper-bag lunch. I studied diligently but without comprehension, especially in Latin class, where I was alternately aroused and irritated by hotshot goody-goody girls from snooty Longmeadow suburbs who could decline nouns with precision. I tried out for athletic teams, but my scrawny body and pipestem limbs proved inadequate. In my eagerness to excel I joined the debating team, the traffic squad, the glee club, and the school paper. But it was all kid stuff.

Then I encountered a gene-pool that was to play a central role in my future life. I started hanging out with a group of Jewish students. Before high school I had never known anyone Jewish. In the New England of the 1930s one's friends came from one's own religious and economic grouping.

I was delighted to encounter these strange kids, so different from WASPs and Catholics, smart, brash, funny, worldly, earthy, and playful. Probably because I admired and liked them for the right reasons, they adopted me as the only Christian in their set. We played poker and tennis and discussed sports and girls. They showed me that the world was bigger, wilder and more delightfully varied than my insular background had led me to believe. From them I learned to look beyond the conventional.

My sexual immaturity was glaringly obvious to my new friends. I listened in awe to their tales of the female anatomy. We were all obsessed with fleetingly seen breasts and flashing thighs. "Her dress was up to her neck and I could see what she had for breakfast" was a phrase used at least three times a day.

My new friends contributed further to my education by lending me dirty comic books, in which Jiggs turned Maggie from nagging wife to enraptured concubine with his three-foot-long member and Olive Oyl threw silken panties to the wind, screaming with pleasure at the ministrations of the equally endowed Popeye.

At sixteen I obtained a driver's license. With it came a job as a delivery boy for Uncle Arthur's boutique. I had mobility, I had money—and sitting at the desk in front of mine was Rosalind, the wildest sexiest girl in the school. After classes I would walk to the store, package dresses to be home-delivered, pick up Rosalind at her house, and zoom around the exclusive sections of the city, stopping on deserted streets to smooch with my sophisticated girlfriend.

One night she led me into her family's sun porch, lay down on the couch, and held her arms out to me. I lay on top of her. We kissed madly. Rosalind moved her hips and guided me into my first fuck.

With my hormones activated, I changed from a shy, reserved youth to a brash, confident extrovert. Rosalind and I became high school steadies and popular stars in the adolescent social life. Within six months I became president of the school senate and editor of the paper.

Rosalind's sophistication gave me a wordly perspective that made high school activities seem childishly simple. We shared that delicious sense of sexual complicity that gave us courage to innovate. Rosalind brought a playful style to the school paper, contributing to a racy, funny gossip column full of innuendos that the kids loved and the teachers puzzled over. We ran several comical exposes. We put out a special program issue for the big football game with *Tech*. At year's end our paper swept the competition and was named the outstanding high school publication in western Massachusetts.

But in spite of our success I got in deep trouble with Principal Hill. I was called into his office after writing a particularly fiery editorial suggesting that the Categorical Imperative was totalitarian and un-American in glorifying the welfare of the state over the rights of the individual.

Mr. Hill stood stiffly behind his desk holding in his hand my attendance record, incontrovertible evidence that I had been playing hooky with some regularity. "Do you realize that you have skipped school more than any other student in your class? I suppose your absences were caused by your editorial duties?"

"There's a lot of running around involved in the job, sir."

Mr. Hill turned his back on me and looked out the window onto State Street and St. Michael's Cathedral.

"I could and I should expel you," he said, "but I won't. I have known your family for a long time and I know how this would crush them."

"Thank you, sir," I said.

"One final thing. Are you considering asking me to write you a letter of recommendation for college entrance?"

I nodded.

"My advice to you is: don't. Do you understand?"

"Yes sir," I said.

Principal William C. Hill made good his threat.

My applications were turned down by the prestigious WASP colleges. So Abigail called on Monsignor Michael to use his feudal influence as distinguished alumnus to arrange for my admission to Holy Cross. Abigail wanted me to spend a year or two at this Jesuit institution as preparation for taking the competitive examination to West Point.

For the first semester I was a dean's-list academic star and a model of deportment, which is saying a lot, given my genes and the nature of the institution. Catholic colleges were radically liberalized in the ensuing years, but in 1938 Holy Cross was run like a monastery. Compulsory chapel at 7 a.m.; prayers before each class; no elective subjects, everyone following the narrow quadrivium set down by St. Ignatius Loyola 400 years before: Greek, Latin, rhetoric, religion. Except for some rudimentary chemistry and mathematics courses which had just been introduced as a daring novelty for premedical students, there was no science—physical or social.

The professors were aloof, mysterious, black-robed creatures who taught like martinets. The students, sturdy sons of New England Irish-Catholic businessmen, docilely accepted the curriculum. There was an obsessive emphasis on athletics, but little concern for ideas or intellectual matters.

The student body was, with few exceptions, virginal. There was some nervous college-boy banter about sex, but no pin-ups, indeed no social events on campus except football rallies. Girls, except with visiting families, were never seen on campus.

I enjoyed Latin, translating Cicero, Virgil, Tacitus, the odes of Horace (with the sexy parts omitted), but I continued to wonder. Why were these good-hearted, Irish lads preparing for their jobs as small businessmen and politicians by performing ill-comprehended rote translations of Roman satirists? Later it became clear. They were being trained to defend their faith against science, secularism and free thought.

By the second semester I had located another restless outsider, Angelo, a clever premedical student from New Haven whose father was a Mafia don. We started a bookmaking ring—taking bets on stake races and sports events. By running a continuous poker game I won enough money to buy a second-hand Model A Ford and the two of us began going over the wall after Aunt Polly's bed check, to hang out at workingmen's bars and pick up shop girls.

During the summer vacation Abigail arranged for me to take the competitive examinations to the service academies sponsored by the local Congressman. I got the highest score and the option of choosing Annapolis or West Point. I wanted to go Navy, but family tradition won out and I signed up for the Military Academy. During the ten months before entrance I intended to get a job in New York, but Abigail, sensing escape, remanded me back to Holy Cross. It was not such a hot idea. Since the simple-minded classwork was now doubly irrelevant, I spent most of my time in classical schoolboy mischief.

Neither the Jesuits nor I wept when I packed my bag of books and headed for West Point.

JANUARY 1961
NEWTON CENTER, MASSACHUSETTS

During the fall semester Richard Alpert was in Berkeley, a visiting professor at the University of California. I kept him informed as to our progress.

His return coincided with the biggest blizzard of the winter. Snow fell for eighteen hours; drifts outside the house piled up three feet high. Jack and I lugged in silver-birch logs for fires in the living room and study. After dinner I was working. Jack ran into the room. "Guess who's here!"

I could hear Susan yipping in pleasure. There was Richard with an arctic coat and fur gloves and boots plastered with snow, hugging the kids and filling the house with good feeling. As a professional wanderer, a perennial house guest, warm entries were one of Dick's endearing skills.

We trooped into the kitchen and stood him on a chair. Sue broomed off his trousers. Dick shouted, "No, Jack, don't use the toilet brush."

We were all laughing our heads off. Later Dick and I sat at the table drinking beer and talking about the sacred mushrooms. Dick was fascinated by the psychedelic research and eager to join. The first step, of course, was to start his training. "When?"

"Here and now. Are you ready?"

It was a jolly loving session with much joking. The stories I told about our research adventures imprinted on his receptive brain the romance, adventure, idealism, and excitement in store if he joined us.

Q. Behind the merriment, did deep changes occur in the subject?

A. Richard Alpert in talk and print has described this first experience with psilocybin with extravagant eloquence. "Turning point in my life. Saw beyond my social identity. Discovered that an 'I' existed independent of social ego. Realized the existence of multiple realities.

Learned that everything can be here now. Entire new realms of possibility opened up."

Q. How did the session end?

A. At dawn, Dick put on his boots, but continued rapping and laughing for another hour. At the front door we gazed at the snow-covered lawn, crystal clean and glittering, and at the trees heavy with white like Christmas cards. Dick gave a big shout and a big jump and bounded down the slope. When he reached the road, he waved up and I waved back. He returned to his parents' house, shoveled snow from the front walk, and chopped firewood.

Dick's arrival coincided with another change. Frank Barron married Nancy in January and decided to devote his energies to connubial bliss. Frank's participation in the project would be curtailed. He turned over most of his functions to Richard.

Dick and I flew in his Cessna to Long Island to run a session for Dorothy Norman, prominent orientalist and confidante of Nehru. She wrote about our work to the prime minister, who replied with an invitation to set up a research center in India. Two weeks later we flew down to Durham, North Carolina to activate the staff of J. B. Rhine's parapsychology project. After the session we flew, dodging thunderstorms, back to La Guardia and cabbed to the New Haven railway's suite on Park Avenue. We ordered champagne from room service to toast our victory. We had safely introduced eight important psychologists to psilocybin in one interstate house call.

Encouraged by our successes, Dick and I continued our educational program. We gave lectures, workshops, seminars. We swept through dozens of cocktail parties and dinners, touting mind expansion through chemicals to prominent intellectuals and artists. We drove to Sandoz Laboratories in New Jersey to tell them of our ideas for disseminating psilocybin. We went on to Washington with the idea of convincing the head of the federal prison system to introduce psilocybin therapy into his penitentiaries.

We were an effective team—two attractive well-brought up Harvard psychologists, poised, cheerful, clean-cut, blithely using our all-American enthusiasm to generate support for the drug research project.

Between ourselves we enjoyed the trust and confidence that comes from all-out team play. Ten years older I was the ideological leader, writing the scripts. Dick, an exceptionally talented salesman and diplomat, spoke the lines with the wonderful seriousness of high camp. He encouraged my Gaelic goofiness, my wild intoxicated strobes into the future, reserving for himself the part of protector and ground control. In later days of communal living Dick worried about what neighbors would think, fussed over the kids, balanced the checkbook, managed the kitchen—a domestic partnership that continued for four momentous years.

Genially we divided the labor. I kept busy directing the many drug-research experiments being performed by our team of twenty-five scientists. Dick concentrated on diplomacy. He was wonderful with faculty wives and children. When a prominent professor's son was killed in an automobile accident, it was Dick who organized the memorial fund. When a dean's son ran wild with rebellion, it was Uncle Dick who counseled and joked the crisis back to ground.

Psychedelic drugs gave Dick the power and confidence to change, to find himself, and later to defy the system openly. Dick was born to cut loose. He was basically an outsider, a deep-cover spy within the system. His Jewishness and his homosexuality gave him that precious alien perspective.

In 1961, blissfully ignorant of the colorful future that lay ahead, Dick and I enjoyed that most wondrous bond: a loving brotherhood, a Sundance-Butch Cassidy alliance of psychological outlaws working to market and merchandise expanded consciousness.

R ALPH METZNER (1935-   ) was born in Germany. His father was German, his mother British. He graduated from Oxford with First Class Honors in psychology in 1958 and received a doctorate in Clinical Psychology and Personality from Harvard in 1962. In 1963 he was a post-doctoral fellow on Psychopharmacology at Harvard Medical School.

In 1960 Metzner joined the Harvard Psychedelic Drug Project and the subsequent Divinity School research. In 1963 he became editor of the *Psychedelic Review,* the authoritative source of scientific and scholarly information about drugs and consciousness.

From 1963 to 1967 he was a director of the International Foundation for Internal Freedom (IFIF) and the Castalia Foundation, helping to develop programmed settings for brain-change sessions.

Metzner's prolific writings on the subject of consciousness became classics in this new and rapidly growing field. His ability to combine current scientific findings with classic philosophic theories helped bridge the gap between Eastern metaphysics and Western psychology.

His books include *The Psychedelic Experience* (1964), *The Ecstatic Adventure* (1968), *Maps of Consciousness* (1971), and *Know Your Type: Maps of Identity* (1979).

11. Prisoners to Prophets

MARCH 1961
HARVARD UNIVERSITY

By spring we had given psychedelic drugs to over 200 subjects and had learned a lot about how to run sessions. Eighty-five percent of our subjects were reporting that the experience was the most educational of their lives. These testimonials were pleasing because most therapies, including psychoanalysis, traditionally reported around thirty-three percent positive change.

As scientists we were still dissatisfied. We were faced with the unavoidable problem in the field of psychiatry. How do you demonstrate that someone has improved? Self-appraisals are an important index but inconclusive; heroin addicts and born-again Christians claim to feel better but others might disagree. There didn't seem to be an objective way to keep score on life changes. Half of the people coached might have loosened up and half might have gotten their lives more tightly organized, and for any or all of them the changes might have been a genuine improvement. Half might have increased the intimacy and closeness of their marriages, and half might have left their spouses. Some might have benefited by making more money, some by making less. We needed clear statistical indices, like batting averages, for the game of life.

About this time a call came from two officials of the Massachusetts prison system, requesting that Harvard graduate-interns be assigned for research and training. They expected a quick turn-down. Just as prison guards were the bottom of the law-enforcement hierarchy, prison work was at that time the pits of psychology. Criminals simply didn't change.

Much to their surprise I invited the prison officials over for lunch at the Faculty Club. I welcomed the chance to get into a prison and initiate a volunteer rehabilitation program. I had two purposes in mind: first, if we could change the behavior of violent criminals with our drugs, we'd demonstrate that our methods and theories worked where nothing else did. Second, prison rehabilitation would provide us with the behavioral scientist's dream, an iron-clad objective index of improvement— the recidivism rate.

The return-rate in Massachusetts prisons was running seventy percent. I felt we could decimate that percentage. What a boon to society—converting violent criminals to law-abiding citizens! If we could teach the most unregenerate how to wash their own brains, then it would be a cinch to coach non-criminals to change their lives for the better.

A deal was made over lunch. I agreed to send Harvard graduate-interns into the prisons; the officials agreed to get clearances from the wardens and correctional psychiatrists for us to give drugs to convicts.

A week later I drove out to the prison. I wore my Ivy League tweed uniform. I even wore leather shoes for this occasion. Warden Tom Grennan, a fellow Irishman, was impressed and pleased. A Harvard psychologist had never come around before.

Next I had to get the approval of the prison psychiatrist. This could have meant trouble. Shrinks didn't usually like programs of head expansion, and medics liked to preserve their monopoly on drugs.

I walked nervously down the hallway to the metal cage that opened into a prison cellblock. Rang a bell. A slot opened. A guard looked out, nodded, and opened up a second metal door. I walked through the prison with a sense of foreboding. And precapitulation. I'd been here before and I'd be here again.

AUGUST 1940
WEST POINT, NEW YORK

"YOU MAN, HALT! DROP THAT SUITCASE!" Three upper-class cadets approached.

"Hello," I said, flashing a cheery civilian smile. I dropped the suitcase. Not fast enough. The three cadets were infuriated.

"STAND UP STRAIGHT AND TALL. CRAAAAACK THOSE PUNY SHOULDERS BACK."

I obeyed clumsily, looking to my tormentors for approval. This was a mistake.

"EYES FRONT, MISTER. YOU WILL SPEAK ONLY WHEN SPOKEN TO. GOT THAT, DUMBCROW?"

"Gotcha," I replied, facing forward stiffly.

"AND YOU SAY 'SIR' EVERY TIME YOU SPEAK TO AN UPPERCLASSMAN. GOT IT?"

"Yes, sir."

"ROLL UP THOSE PANT LEGS, MISTER."

I rolled my sport trousers to my knees.

"PICK UP YOUR BAG."

I did, keeping my shoulders wrenched backwards and my eyes idiotically frontwards.

"DROP THAT BAG."

I did.

"PICK IT UP."

I did. They marched me to an enormous granite-Gothic quad filled with other plebes, similarly harassed, similarly pant-legged. The upperclassmen were dressed in uniform splendor: starched white trousers, blue-gray jackets, gray caps with mirrorlike patent-leather visors, gleaming black shoes. We plebes were a ragged rabble with hairy calves and colored socks. Our civilian individuality was clearly unauthorized and ridiculous.

Every step was by the numbers. Stand in line. Pick up a mattress. Stagger to barracks room. Muscles weeping, eyes pounding, heart sweating, ATTENTION! Confused, disoriented, we were surrounded by cool smart upperclassmen barking orders. A merciless barber cut my hair to skin. New uniforms: not crisp whites but heavy, wrinkled factory-smelling drabs.

"Beast Barracks" at West Point lasted six weeks, a total assault on the adolescent nervous system. Familiar hometown habits of dress, grooming, posture, gait, and language were drilled out and military bearing was drilled in. Far from regretting my loss of individuality I was delighted at being admitted to this masculine elite. I found myself using the cadet jargon in letters home. I marveled that my sexual drive had been turned off by military discipline.

Beast Barracks ended with our transfer to the summer campground where the Corps was in residence. Our graduation ceremony was a parade, presenting us to the Corps. We were issued white trousers so starched that the legs had to be peeled open with a bayonet. We stood at attention as our masters circled like gray sharks. We were about to become Cadets, goddamn it, and we were expected to look and act the part.

The warm summer air crackled with commands. The band played martial music. Talk about technicolor romance, this was what I joined for! Two hundred legs scissored in unison. Flags flew. Officers' sabers flashed, and our company moved with massed precision along the elm-shaded road to the parade ground hallowed by the footsteps of Lee, Grant, MacArthur. A thousand spectators ringed the field.

"ORDER ARMS!"

A hushed silence fell over the history-drenched plain. The band played "Retreat." At mid-point the dramatic pause . . .

Boom!

The sunset cannon roared from Lookout Point, its blast rumbling like a bowling ball down Rip Van Winkle's Hudson Valley.

This was no Boy Scout caper. This was no campus ROTC march-around. This was the real thing: the military, an exclusive club within and yet apart from America, with its own special rituals, roles, goals, rules, territories, plus a cabalistic conviction of superiority. This elite ran every country in the world by force of arms, either openly or covertly, and I was now a part of it.

My disillusion wasn't long in coming. Within a matter of weeks I realized that we cadets were not being groomed for battlefield strategies, not for innovative thinking, nor scientific logic but to fit, unquestioningly, into an enormous gray bureaucracy.

The cadet hierarchy prepared us for the regimented life ahead. Freshmen were fourth-classmen, or plebes; sophomores were third-classmen, yearlings; juniors were second-classmen, cows; seniors, first-classmen, were exalted creatures who served as cadet officers. The term upperclassmen referred to everyone except the plebes. The only people lower than plebes were civilians.

I had just spent two years with the Jesuits and the medieval quadrivium. However outdated the curriculum, at least the fathers were dedicated to a life of study and teaching. At West Point in 1940 the teachers—career officers enjoying a soft four-year assignment—conveyed no interest in knowledge. It was learning by rote. Forty years later I can still recite the definition of "leather":

"Sir, if the fresh skin of an animal cleaned and divested of all hair, fat, and other extraneous matter be immersed in a dilute solution of tannic acid, a chemical combination ensues. The gelatinous tissues . . . blah . . . blah . . . blah . . . . This, sir, is leather."

My tenure at West Point occurred during a most creative period in military history. The Germans were overthrowing the theory of trench warfare and standing armies. The Luftwaffe and the RAF were developing new tactics of aerial warfare. These radical developments, however, were never mentioned by our lethargic officers. I can recall a professor of mathematics who in the spring of 1941, when Rommel was overrunning

North Africa, scolded the class for poor penmanship. "Listen," he said,
"I don't care whether you learn or not. In twenty years I'll retire as
a colonel, so it doesn't make any difference to me."

The physical fitness courses, however, were wonderful, and for them
I shall always be in the debt of Colonel Thayer. Every morning we
spent two hours at the gym being trained in the neuromuscular skills
required by an eighteenth-century cavalry officer. We learned fencing,
both saber and rapier, from a wizened teacher of French aristocrats. A
grizzled one-eyed wrestling coach, formerly a world champion, bearishly
prepared us for hand-to-hand encounters in any port town bordello. We
learned boxing, gymnastics, and the escapist skills I had signed up to
master: rope-climbing, daredevil multi-flip tumbling, and high-rings. And
running, of course, a skill obviously necessary for the successful soldier.
The coaches, by the way, were the only staff who ever mentioned the
war.

The atmosphere was gloomy. The discipline was petty and nagging.
Smiling and laughing were taboo. The most damning accusation that
could be made against a cadet was that he didn't take this nonsense
seriously. We had to show in every gesture and response that we were
running scared: eager, on-the-ball, straining to conform. A two-degree
slouch of the straining shoulders, half-an-inch of slackness in cracking
back your chin, any slight suspicion of a smile would bring the wrathful
accusation barked into your ear: "MISTER, ARE YOU INDIFFER-
ENT?" Indifference was the kiss of death.

The malaise that hung over the academy was probably just old-
fashioned sexual frustration. During the first two years cadets had less
contact with girls than the inmates of a maximum security prison. The
worldly first-classmen were allowed only occasional weekends off post, and
this was a new and risque innovation. Even the most docile cadets complained. We looked forward to summer vacations and graduation the way
prisoners anticipated the end of their sentence.

I did the best I could under the circumstances, shinnying down the
lightning rod after taps to pick up girls in Newburgh or Highland Falls.
By day, during off hours, I read the lives of the philosophers, ransacking
the meager library stacks for intellectual fare.

During the gray autumn the only streaks of color in academy life were
football trips. The Corps would march to special troop trains, roll to
New York or Princeton, march to the stadium, and shriek cheers in
deafening unison. After the game cadets would scatter free for a few
hours and reassemble at the train station around midnight.

The Army-Navy game in Memorial Stadium, Philadelphia was the
last trip of the season. With ten months of Trappist isolation looming

ahead I felt compelled to shop for all the experience that could be had in six hours. After the game, with my friend Fitzgerald in tow, I tried to debrief a cab driver outside the stadium. He refused to advise.

A second cab driver grinned and drove us to a residential section. He stopped and phoned ahead. The door to the apartment was opened by a giggling housewife wearing a black negligee. Her hair was waved, her body round, and the air was electric with fun and games. Our hostess—Bubbles was her name—put on a record and mixed drinks. Her robe fell open. Her legs were creamy white. While Fitzgerald dallied with Daisy, Bubbles and I danced and smooched, and she led me to the bedroom. This was the warrior's life, *mon capitain.*

En route back to the station I bought four half-pints of whiskey, stuffing two bottles in each sleeve. I stood at attention during report, arms held stiffly to my sides, then found a seat on the troop train and slid into a delicious Hemingway reverie about the day.

Fitzgerald pulled at my shoulder. He asked me to give him one of the bottles, explaining that some first-classmen assembled in the toilet wanted to party. I slid him a bottle. He returned all too soon for another. I figured it was a payoff and complied. Again he returned. The first-classmen wanted me to join them, an offer no plebe could refuse.

The first-classmen were silly drunk and out of control. I produced a bottle, drank a hefty swig, and passed it around. We exploded after months of repression into a barroom revel, old and powerful. The fourth bottle soon followed.

When the train pulled into West Point, I strode out with regal confidence. Did I really smoke a cigarette in ranks as we marched to the barracks?

MARCH 1961
CONCORD STATE PRISON

I walked through the first tall cellblock, across the prison yard to the hospital. Bell, peephole, metal hinges creaking. Entered the hospital. Knocked on the door of the prison psychiatrist. It opened and facing me was good news. The prison psychiatrist was black and definitely avantgarde. Hurray! Philosopher Thomas Kuhn said that when you wish to introduce change-technology to a culture, you'll find your best allies among the outsiders, those whose alienation from the establishment makes them more open to change.

Aside from being a black psychiatrist Dr. Jefferson Monroe stood out in the primitive period of 1961 as another kind of rarity—a sophisticated psychiatrist. Impeccable, graceful, hip. He had a twinkle in his eye and a wise, cool way of looking at you. He was definitely ready for something new.

A few days later Dr. Monroe paid a return call at the Faculty Club and then came to a staff meeting at the Center. We put him on the Harvard payroll as a consultant. The following Sunday he brought his wife over for cocktails.

"Your plan to teach prisoners to brainwash themselves is simply delicious. There's even a slight chance you can pull it off. Do you know what that might mean?"

"A great boon to society," I suggested.

Dr. Monroe crossed his legs gracefully and laughed. "My dear, you don't really understand what you're getting into, do you? Sooner or later you're going to discover that law enforcement people and prison administrators have no desire to cut crime. They want more crime and more money to fight it. I'll cover you from the medical and psychiatric end, but sooner or later, if your methods work they'll start coming down on you. Reporters, bureaucrats, officials. 'Harvard Gives Drugs to Prisoners!' And you're going to have to do the impossible. Cure prisoners with your left hand while you try to hold off the entire bureaucracy with your right."

"So what? If it works."

"Being human, sooner or later you'll make a teeny little mistake. One of your subjects will revert. 'Harvard Drug Parolee Robs Bank.' "

"As long as we do everything out front, no secrets," I said, "we can make a few honest mistakes."

"Maybe," said Monroe. "Look, here's the deal. I'll back you all-out, until you goof. When they start coming down on you, exactly at that point I'll have to protect my own pretty black ass. 'Cause, I'm not you. I'm not the new Freud. So I'll win with you, but I can't afford to lose with you."

On that basis we agreed on a plan: Monroe would line up volunteers in the prison population for the drug project and I'd line up Harvard graduate students willing to put their nervous systems on the line taking drugs with maximum security prisoners.

A few days later I was visited by a graduate student named Ralph Metzner. Metzner had a reputation for being one of the most rigorously experimental students in the department. He wanted to work on the prison project.

My first reaction was that Metzner was too academic, too dainty-British, too ivory tower to walk into a prison and take drugs with hoodlums. But Metzner said he wanted to learn how. So I guided a training session for Metzner, his girlfriend, Dr. Monroe and his wife, and graduate student Gunther Weil and his wife. This was the fifty-second time I had taken psilocybin.

My study was the site of this experiment. Since this was an exploratory training session, I told the participants to relax, have a good time, and learn what they could. After a few hours of silent serenity, Jefferson took over spontaneously as guide. His joking and warm earthiness created a benign atmosphere. Ralph turned out to be a natural inner explorer.

A few days later Ralph, Gunther, and I, feeling a sense of camaraderie as a result of the session, drove out to the Concord prison to meet the six candidates Jefferson had selected from the pool of volunteers. Two murderers. Two armed robbers. One embezzler. One black heroin pusher.

In a dreary hospital room—gray walls, black asphalt floor, barred windows—we told the six suspicious men about an experience that could change their lives. We brought books for them to read, reports by other subjects, articles that described the ecstasies as well as the possible terrors. We spent most of the time describing our own experiences and answering questions. We made it clear to the prisoners that this was nothing *we* were doing to them. There was no doctor-patient game going here. We would take the drugs along with them. We were doing nothing to them that we weren't happily doing to ourselves.

We also made a transactional research contract with the prisoners. We said something like this: "We want to find out how and how much you change during this experience. For this reason we want you to take a battery of psychological tests before you eat the mushroom pills. After three or four sessions we'll give you the tests again. After you've taken the post-tests, we'll go over the results with you. Nothing in this project is going to be a secret." To the bored prisoners this sounded like a good deal, so the following week each was administered a complicated battery of psychological tests.

The prison project extended our research into a number of new areas. We were dealing with a very different population from the professionals and high-status subjects in the early research. Second, we were switching from questionnaires and subjective reports to objective measurements of personality change. And third, we had to move from naturalistic settings to the most controlled and least inspirational environment imaginable— the hospital of a maximum security prison.

Six prisoners and three Harvard psychologists met for the first drug session. During the morning I was to turn on with three convicts. The three other prisoners and the two graduate students would act as observers. Then in the afternoon Gunther and Ralph and the three observing prisoners would take the drug, and the first group would act as guides. We brought a record player, tape recorder, and several books of classical art with us. Otherwise the room was bleak: four beds, a large table, and a few chairs. The bowl of pills was placed in the center of the table. To establish trust I was the first to ingest. Then the bowl was passed among the three prisoners, who each took twenty milligrams. After a half hour the effect started coming on: the loosening of thought, the humming pressure in my head, the sharp, brilliant, and then brutal intensification of the senses.

I felt terrible.

What a place to be—locked in a penitentiary, out of light, out of mind. I turned my brain towards the man next to me, a Polish bank robber from Worcester. I could see him much too clearly, every pore in his face, every blemish, the hairs in his nose, the horrid green-yellow enamel of his decaying teeth, the glistening of his frightened eyes, every hair on his head looking big as a tree-branch. What am I doing here?

"How ya doing, John?" I asked with a weak grin.

"I feel fine," he answered, but I didn't believe him.

"How *you* doing, Doc?"

I was about to reply in a reassuring professional tone, but I couldn't. It's hard to lie when you're in the power of the mushrooms. "I feel lousy."

John drew back his purple-pink lips. "What's the matter, Doc?"

Inside his eyes I could see a yellow spider-web of retinal fibers, optical veins shiny and pulsing. "I'm afraid of you," I said.

John's eyes enlarged, and then he began to laugh. I could see in his mouth, swollen red tissues, gums, tongue, throat. I was ready to be swallowed.

"Well, that's funny, Doc, 'cause I'm afraid of you."

We were both smiling at this point, leaning forward.

"Why are you afraid of me?"

"Because you're a criminal. Why are you afraid of me?"

"I'm afraid of you 'cause you're a fucking mad scientist."

Then our eyes locked and we both laughed.

Voila. There it was. We had made a connection. The sun came out in the room. For a while.

One of the prisoners, the heroin pusher, moaned and tossed on his cot.

"Are you all right, Willy?" I asked, apprehensive about a potential threat to our newfound sense of security. Everyone in the room watched, anxiously wondering if the prison setting was just irretrievably wrong, if this was to be one of those dreaded "bad trips."

Willy lifted his head and gave a big grin. "Man, am I all right? I'm in heaven looking down on this funny little planet and I'm a million years old and there's a million things to enjoy—and it's all happening in prison. And you ask me, man, am I all right?"

When Willy laughed, we were all high and happy.

Jefferson checked in every now and then, walked around the room like a dainty, graceful cat not saying much but taking it all in.

At six o'clock, as the afternoon session was winding down, there was a bang on the door, and the guards came in. "Time is up, men. Back to the ward." Ralph, Gunther, and I went with the six prisoners back to the lockup part of the hospital, where we smoked and laughed and compared notes on what we'd seen and where we'd been.

Then it was time for us to go. We shook hands and promised to return the next day for a follow-up. Ralph, Gunther, and I walked out of the hospital, across the dark prison yard, rang the bell, and waited until the iron doors opened into the guardroom. We went through two metal doors, down metal stairs, past the clanking steaming radiators, and outside the prison.

We laughed in triumph. All of us, Harvardites and convicts, had passed a crucial test. We had put our faith in human nature and the drug experience on the line. A bit of pagan magic had occurred, and none of us would ever forget that brief day of grace. It was a heroic moment in our lives.

The morning after the session, driving back to the prison was like returning to some comfortable place in my skull. Strong bonds of empathy had developed. We had been through the adventure together. We had gone beyond the roles of Harvard psychologist and convict, faced fear together, had trusted and laugh.

This time I felt at home in the prison. It always works this way after a good trip. Your old reality fades a bit, and you incorporate a new reality. This identification is not metaphorical. It is neurological. In scientific papers we called this process re-imprinting.

This first session changed our status in the prison. As word went out through the grapevine, prisoners approached us in the yard to ask if they could sign up for the project. Guards and parole officers stopped us to request that a favorite prisoner be admitted to the group.

We spent the next two weeks discussing the prisoners' reactions. Then we ran a second session for the group. This time the prisoners were more sophisticated. There was no sitting around on chairs in nervous anticipation. As soon as the energy began to radiate through their bodies, they headed for the cots and closed their eyes. For the next two or three hours they lay engulfed in the visions, occasionally sitting up to smile or make some quiet comment.

After the third session the convicts repeated the personality tests to measure changes. We brought the test results into the hospital room and handed them to the inmates. No secrets. We explained what the tests measure and what the results meant.

They had changed on the objective indices so dear to the heart of the psychologist. They showed less depression, hostility, anti-social tendencies; more energy, responsibility, cooperation. Their personality scores had swung dramatically and significantly in the direction of improved mental health.

By handing over and explaining their test results we were training the prisoners in psychodiagnostics. The prisoners were becoming their own psychologists. They loved it. There were fierce discussions about personality characteristics as the cons played the psychiatric game.

We planned the next phase of the research. The convicts were to select new recruits for the group. They would learn how to administer the psychological tests. They would give the orientation lectures. They would take over the project.

The prison became a training center. New graduate students were assigned to experienced inmates for orientation and guidance. In session after session the inmates guided the Harvards, and the Harvards guided the convicts.

The energy generated by the sessions was felt beyond the prison walls. The penitentiary session room became a showplace. Whenever visitors came to Cambridge inquiring about psychedelic drugs, we took them out to the prison. The convicts spoke about their mystical experiences to Gerald Heard, Alan Watts, and William Burroughs, Aldous Huxley, and the ex-king of Sarawak, as well as to coveys of visiting psychiatrists. Our strategy here was to do everything possible to enhance their pride and sense of accomplishment. Every power we could turn over to the convicts became a fiber in the body of self-esteem.

By fall 1962 we had over thirty-five convicts and fifteen Harvards in the group. The men started being paroled at the rate of two and three a month, so we started Project CONTACT. The ex-cons and the Harvards were paired up in buddy-system teams, with the Harvards visiting the ex-cons in their homes. There was a twenty-four-hour telephone to rush help in case of emergencies.

We sobered them up, praised them to the parole officers, cooled out angry bosses. In short we did what a family does for its confused members. We kept them out of jail.

Soon our circus had grown into a three-ring extravaganza. There was the in-prison group. There was the outside CONTACT project. And there was the equally important task of keeping the state administrators and officials happy. We sent out a steady flow of memoranda and progress reports to the myriad departments that had a jealous interest in the work of rehabilitating criminals. Following Jefferson's sage advice we never let a week go by without contacting the bureaucrats, making them a part of the action.

One morning in the second year of the project I came into Warden Grennan's office to report the most recent statistics. We had kept ninety percent of our convicts out of jail.

He listened politely but kept glancing behind me. When I finished, he clapped me on the back and led me to the corner. "Look at that, Timmy," he said proudly.

It was an architect's color drawing of a super-prison. "Look. Two football fields. This wing is for admitting and orientation. Two more cell blocks. Mess halls double in size. We'll have capacity for twice as many inmates, and we can double the staff all the way down the line."

His face was glowing. This was his fantasy coming true. A huge prison and an organizational table twice as big to go with it! Bureaucrat Heaven.

"That's wonderful, Bill," I said. "But have you forgotten? You're not going to need a larger prison."

His face registered surprise.

"Why not?"

"Because we're cutting your return-rate from seventy percent to ten percent. If you let us continue our project, you won't need half the cells you have right now."

The warden laughed, in spite of himself. "I can't argue with you, Timmy. You have kept these men straight, although I'll be damned if I know how you did it."[1]

We were trying to figure this out ourselves. It seemed that two major factors were bringing about changes in the convicts: first, the perception of new realities helped them recognize that they had alternatives beyond the cops and robbers game; then, the empathetic bonding of group members helped them sustain their choice of a new life.

Similar kinds of sudden behavior change had been observed in other species. Konrad Lorenz, the German ethologist, and Nico Tinbergen, the Dutch naturalist, were the first to describe *imprinting*, a form of permanent learning assimilated in one shot, as opposed to step-by-step, painstaking and often painful, punishment-reward conditioning, which traditional psychologists and educators believed to be the basis of change. Lorenz discovered the imprinting phenomenon one day when goose eggs hatched in an incubator in his laboratory. In the absence of the mother the goslings followed him around, apparently because he was the only warm moving object on the scene. The baby birds continued to focus on him, ignoring their mother when she was brought to them.

Hundreds of experiments by Lorenz and others have demonstrated that this immediate learning, which requires no reward or punishment, occurs only during a critical period, shortly after birth or metamorphoses. During this critical period the organism, rather than acquiring behavior *from* the environment, hooks up an innate behavior pattern *to* the environment. The nervous systems of mammals and fowl respond to the first available stimulus, usually the mother, activating and binding instinctual behavior. Birds, for example, have been known to seek mothering from ping pong balls. Baby giraffes have imprinted the jeep of the hunter who shot the mother.

Psychologists were at first reluctant to apply the imprinting principle to human behavior, probably because of the challenge it posed to our notion of free will. However, the dramatic changes in behavior that followed our prison experiments seemed to be best explained by these concepts. The drugs appeared to suspend previous imprints of reality (in this case, the prison mentality) inducing a critical period during which new imprints could be made.

People tended to form powerful positive attachments to those present during a trip, sometimes following one another around like Lorenz's goslings. It was also true that I was becoming attached to those present during *my* sessions.

Even more important than the bonding was the re-imprinting of new belief systems and attitudes about others and society that occurred during the sessions. In a positive, supportive environment, new non-criminal realities were being imprinted. (And in some weird and ominous way, I may have been re-imprinting a prison mentality, a reality which I was forced to inhabit between 1970 and 1976.)

Everything that I have learned in the subsequent twenty years of drug research has strengthened my conviction that psychedelic re-imprinting ranks with DNA deciphering as one of the most significant discoveries of the century.[2]

Unfortunately the subsequent controversy about drugs overshadowed scientific implications of this experiment. Though we had dramatically cut the crime rate, teaching prisoners to clear their own brains of old programs and create new ones, the prison project was shut down after Alpert and I were driven from Harvard. Our ex-cons formed their own group, with the help of our colleague Professor Walter Houston Clark. They continued to operate the Self-Help program for fifteen years on their own.

Scientific tradition requires that important findings be replicated: disproved or verified. There were and still are hundreds of psychologists eager to perform experiments of this sort. The government remains steadfast in its curtailment of meaningful psychedelic research, though every other form of criminal rehabilitation has failed and thousands are recruited into the cycle of recidivism each year.

ROBERT GORDON WASSON (1903-), born in Montana, grew up in Newark, New Jersey. A banker by profession, Wasson climbed the corporate ladder to become vice president of J.P. Morgan & Co. Working with his wife, Valentina, Wasson also gained recognition as an ethnobotanist specializing in the role of hallucinatory mushrooms in the history of culture.

In 1955 Wasson became the first white in recorded history to eat "sacred mushrooms," which were administered to him by Maria Sabina, the renowned Oaxacan shaman. His are probably the most poetically moving and philosophically convincing accounts of drug-induced experiences ever published. *Mushrooms, Russia and History* (1957) was the first of several books by Wasson that traced the origins of many world religions to psychedelic mushroom or lysergic acid cults.

Wasson's research in mind-altering plants led him to Mexico, Japan, India, New Guinea, and Afghanistan. He served as Honorary Research Fellow at the Botanical Museum of Harvard University and as Honorary Research Associate and Life Manager at the New York Botanical Garden.

12. Drugs Are the Origin of Religion and Philosophy

SPRING 1961
HARVARD UNIVERSITY

Around the corner from our Center for Personality Research was the Harvard Botanical Museum, lair of the world's leading ethnobotanist, Professor Richard Evans Schultes. His specialty: psychoactive plants. Professor Schultes had spent years up the Amazon during and after World War II, scouting rubber sources for the American government. To while away long nights in the field the diligent botanist experimented with various mind-altering herbs, roots, vines used by the natives. He reported that for eight years he chewed coca leaves on a daily basis for energy and euphoria.

Considering his openly expressed right-wing political views and the continual government sponsorship of his work, few were surprised to learn (in *The C.I.A. and the Acid Generation* by Lee and Schlaen) that his reports were used by the CIA in its brainwashing experiments during the 1950s and 60s.

As novices in the visionary field of psychobotany we in the Drug Project viewed Professor Schultes with the respect due to an intrepid scholar. It was our custom to drop by the museum to ogle the specimens displayed discreetly in glass cases. Schultes was always cordial to us but distant. We felt like natives whose drug habits he was observing.

One day we received a call from Schultes' office at the museum. On the line was Robert Gordon Wasson, made famous by a long article in *Life* magazine that described his treks to Mexico and his discovery of psychedelic mushrooms. Before Wasson most mycologists had denied the existence of the magic mushrooms. Wasson proved them wrong. The dignified Manhattan banker had taken the mushrooms, lain down on the mud floor of an Oaxacan shaman's hut, and experienced profound philosophic visions.

Wasson made subsequent trips to Mexico with Roger Heim, distinguished French mycologist. They sent specimens to the drug laboratories of Sandoz, where Albert Hofmann synthesized the active ingredient. So we owed our psilocybin supply to the diligence of a New York banker and the craft of a Basel chemist.

Wasson asked if he could come around to visit. We arranged a high-tea ceremony in the Center conference room.

Banker Wasson was a good-looking guy with a serious manner.

We listened as he told us about his first psychedelic experience and the hypothesis that led him to seek it out.

"I do not recall," said Mr. Wasson, "which of us—my wife or I—first dared to put into words, back in the forties, the surmise that our remote ancestors, perhaps 4,000 years ago, worshipped a mushroom. In the fall of 1952 we learned that the sixteenth-century writers describing the Indian cultures of Mexico had recorded that certain mushrooms played a divine role in the religion of the natives. The so-called mushroom stones [found in Mexico] really did represent mushrooms. They were the symbol of a religion, like the cross in the Christian religion or the star of Judea or the crescent of the Moslems. Thus we find a mushroom in the center of the cult with perhaps the longest continuous history in the world."

Cheerful glances criss-crossed the room as we heard our psychological research being linked with an impressive historical precedent. This was the sort of pep-talk we hungered for.

"The advantage of the mushroom is that it puts many, if not everyone, within reach of a visionary state without having to suffer the mortifications of Blake and St. John. It permits you to see vistas beyond the horizons of this life. To travel backwards and forwards in time. To enter other planes of existence. Even, as the Indians say, to know God.

"All that you see during this night has a pristine quality: the landscapes, the edifices, the carvings, the animals—they look as though they had come straight from the Maker's workshop. The newness of everything—it is as if the world had just dawned—overwhelms you and melts you with its beauty."

Dick, seeing how our credit rating would rise with this Morgan Bank testimonial, told Wasson about the content analyses we were making of the writings of visionaries and philosophic drug users. He mentioned our plans to develop a scientific classification model of the levels or circuits of the nervous system and our plans for an Experiential Typewriter (subjects could press appropriate symbol-keys instead of struggling for words.)

But Wasson hadn't come to listen. He'd come to tell us about his first drug trip.

Wasson was playing gentleman pedant to the hilt, savoring his position as Honorary Associate at the Harvard Museum as only a civilian could, delighting in the recitation of the scientific names for plants. Peyote was *Lophophora williamsii*, a synonym for *Anhalonium lewinii*, named to honor Lewis Lewin. Lysergic acid turned up as *Rivea corymbosa*, the morning glory seed. Junkies were addicted to *Papaver somniferum*, and that white powder Hollywood producers and Wall Street bankers stuffed up their noses was *Erythroxylon coca*.

It was somewhat disappointing. Wasson had safaried down his cerebellum and had come back, like most khaki-clad nineteenth-century explorers, expecting to stake *the* claim on these undiscovered regions. He didn't want to hear that we had ventured into this same territory. They were *his* fucking mushrooms controlled from *his* Maker's Board Room. He seemed to view us as rivals. I made a mental note to phone Aldous about how to deal with colonial competition.

Wasson suggested that every major world religion had originated in the botanical hallucinations of some early visionary. He recited and then translated the ancient names for mushrooms in various Middle Eastern and oriental languages, proposing that they all implied a religious experience—food of the gods, flesh of the gods. Even the name of Jesus Christ in Aramaic, he claimed, was derived from the word for psychedelic mushroom.

But Wasson was opposed to any current use of the mushrooms. Although these fungi had produced all of the great philosophic visions of antiquity, he proclaimed, they had no relevance to the modern world. During our conversations Wasson made it clear he was the only one capable of explaining the mushrooms, and he was proud that he published his reports in respectable journals and magazines like *Life*. He was particularly upset that mushroom visions had been published in "vulgar" magazines. He expressed approval of police raids on "oddballs"—young people who used the psychedelic mushrooms for personal growth and spiritual discovery.

Ironically, his writings inspired numbers of young people to descend on such villages as Huautla to share the experiences he so eloquently described. Wasson's possessiveness puzzled me. He approved of raids by the *federales* on these youthful searchers, and he made no protest when Maria Sabina was arrested soon after.[1]

Insisting that the shamans ought to remain silent about their work, he then expressed guilt that he had broken the secret circle and publicized its ceremonies. He said airing the cult secrets destroyed their power.

We were soon to prove him wrong.

WILLIAM SEWARD BUR-ROUGHS (1914-) was born in St. Louis, a descendant of the family made rich and famous by the manufacture of calculating machines. He graduated from Harvard in 1936. In 1944 Burroughs started a life of experimentation with drugs, including a long period of heroin addiction. He traveled extensively in civilized and primitive countries, studying patterns of drug usage and experiencing a wide range of psychoactive botanicals, many of which had never been taken by non-natives.

In 1953, under the name William Lee, he wrote *Junkie*, an unsparing account of the low-life. In 1959 *Naked Lunch* established Burroughs as a major American writer and cult hero.

Other works by Burroughs include *Nova Express* (1964), *Soft Machine* (1966), *The Ticket That Exploded* (1967), *Exterminator* (1973), and *The Last Words of Dutch Schultz* (1978). *Cities of the Red Night* (1981) is generally regarded as William Burroughs' magnum opus.

13. Hostile Territories

SUMMER 1961
HARVARD UNIVERSITY

"You've got to write a big, enthusiastic letter to Burroughs," said Allen Ginsberg, "and get him interested in taking psilocybin. He knows more about drugs than anyone alive."

I wrote Burroughs asking if he would participate in an American Psychological Association symposium on psychedelic drugs in September and then spend some time in Cambridge working with us. The answer came back yes along with an invitation to visit him in Tangier during the summer, which I did in August.

The taxi climbed the winding street to the Tangier hotel where Allen had reserved rooms for me at two dollars a night. Allen was out. Into the lobby shuffled a thin stooped man wearing glasses and a grey fedora. I recognized Burroughs from book jacket photographs. Two handsome British boys about nineteen years old accompanied him.

"Let's have a drink while we wait for Allen," I suggested.

We sat in the outdoor garden of a restaurant and downed several gins while reviewing the APA and Harvard plans. Back at the hotel we had dinner with Allen, Gregory Corso, and another beat poet, Alan Ansen, and then went to Burroughs' room. Dark. Big bed. Desk littered with papers. Three off-tuned radios blaring static.

We all took psilocybin. Burroughs lay on the bed. The English boys watched him. The rest of us walked out to the garden wall and looked down on Tangier Harbor. Allen was depressed over the departure of his companion Peter.

The Royal Fair was in town. The King's picture was draped over wires at every intersection. We could see the fairground ablaze with lights, and we heard pipes and drums. The night was warm and clear as we stood in the garden above North Africa's port, Moorish music drifting up to us. We looked at each other, breathing in deeply. Allen Ansen and Gregory were grinning.

Burroughs wanted some quiet, so we left him and floated down the steps to Allen's hotel then up to the patio in front of his room. The city beneath us was a glittering carpet. Lanterns shone from the rigging of ships in the harbor, and the carnival rollicked by the water's edge.

We were all in the highest and most loving of moods. Ansen couldn't believe it. He kept laughing and shaking his head. It was his first mushroom experience and out came the familiar: "This can't be true. So beautiful. Heaven. But where is the devil's price? Anything this great must have a terrible flaw in it. It can't be this good."

Later we decided to pick up Burroughs for a visit to the fair. Allen climbed part way up the wall of Burroughs' hotel and called: "Bill BUH-rows. Bill BUH-rows."

We waited by the door. It creaked open, and there was Bill, collapsed against the jamb. His face was haggard and sweating. He stared out like a man caught in the power of Sammy the Butcher.

"Bill, how are you doing?" I asked.

"I'm not feeling too well. I was struck by juxtaposition of purple fire mushroomed from the Pain Banks. Urgent Warning. There are many hostile territories in the cerebral hemispheres. I think I'll stay here in this shriveling envelope of larval flesh. I'm going to take some apomorphine."

He heaved but nothing came up.

"One of the nastiest cases ever processed by this department," I said to Ginsberg, quoting Dr. Benway from *Naked Lunch*.

NOVEMBER 1940
WEST POINT, NEW YORK

Boom.

The wake-up cannon fired once. *Boom, boom, boom*—the echoes reverberated in concrete quads and around the granite buildings of the U.S. Military Academy. A bugle sounded reveille.

Baynes and Barnes, my roommates, jumped out of their beds and started dressing feverishly. Ten minutes to reveille formation. Plebes had to report in five minutes.

I slept.

"Hey, wake up," said Baynes.

"I'm not feeling too well," I mumbled.

The drum-and-bugle squad marching through the yard below played stirring variations on the reveille tune.

I can't get 'em up
I can't get 'em up
I can't get 'em up
In the morn-ing.

"REVEILLE FORMATION! THE UNIFORM FOR TODAY IS OVERCOATS. FIVE MINUTES TO GO," shouted the plebe at the foot of the stairs.

"You better get dressed for reveille," said Barnes, worried.

I leaned my head out of bed and heaved, but nothing came up.

"We gotta go," said Baynes. "Move your ass or you'll be late."

"You fellows go," I mumbled. "I'm too sick."

Baynes and Barnes ran down the stairs.

"REVEILLE FORMATION! THE UNIFORM FOR TODAY IS OVERCOATS. TWO MINUTES TO GO."

Dum da da dum da da da: "The Captain's worst of all," sang the bugles.

Down in the quad the plebes were braced in ranks while upperclassmen sauntered into formation. It was dark, just before dawn.

"REVEILLE FORMATION! THE UNIFORM FOR TODAY IS OVERCOATS. ONE MINUTE TO GO," shouted the plebe at the foot of the stairs.

A buzzer rang out. The bugler sounded "Assembly," very slowly, allowing stragglers a few extra seconds to make the formation.

There's a monkey in the grass
With a bullet up his ass
Pull it out
Pull it out
Pull it out
Pull
It
O u . . . . t

"Company, atten-shun!" bawled the Captain. "*Re* -port!"

"First Platoon present-accounted for, *sir*."

"Second Platoon present-accounted for, *sir*."

"Third Platoon. Cadet Leary absent, *sir*." A stir of wordless amazement.

Baynes was shaking me.

"You missed reveille," he said. His face was solemn at the mention of this unheard-of violation. "And today's the first day that demerits count against furlough."

"I'm never getting up." I fell back on the pillow and moaned.

A first-class officer entered, bashing the door almost off its hinges. "Leary."

I opened two red crab-eyes.

"You will report to the Captain's room in five minutes."

Baynes and Barnes helped me dress. I wobbled downstairs to the cadet officer's room. It was filled with first-classmen looking very grim.

"THERE ARE FIVE MINUTES UNTIL BREAKFAST FORMA-TION!" shouted the plebe outside.

"Leary, did you get drunk on the troop train last night?"

"Yes, sir."

"Where?"

"In the toilet, sir."

"With Robbins and Hawkins?"

"Yes, sir."

"Did they order you to join them?"

"No, sir. I would say that they invited me."

Disapproval swept the room. Fraternization with untouchable plebes offended the Brahmin First Caste.

The following week I was called from my room during study hours by an order to report to the Honor Committee, an officially sanctioned clique, self-chosen on the basis of piety. My roommates looked at me with alarm. An honor infraction was lethal to a West Pointer. The committee could force a cadet to resign.

I was accused of having lied to the Company Commander and the first-classmen who questioned me the morning after the Army-Navy game.

"Cadet Leary, did you bring liquor onto the troop train and give it to the first-classmen?"

"Yes, sir."

"This is not what you said during your interrogation."

"No, sir."

"You lied then."

"No, sir."

"Why do you say you didn't lie?"

"Because they never asked me where the liquor came from."

A silence fell. It hadn't occurred to my earlier interrogators that a lowly plebe would have supplied the forbidden drug. Now the fact was confirmed. Whether I lied was no longer the issue. There was the Company Commander's loss of face to consider.

"You knew you were being questioned about drinking on the train.

And you withheld information the cadet officers were looking for."

"Yes, sir. If that's a violation of the honor code, then I'm guilty."

"Good. Then we must ask you to resign from the Corps of Cadets. Will you do so?"

"I'd like to think it over."

The next day I refused to resign. I wouldn't have minded leaving West Point, but I knew my resignation would have been a cruel disappointment to my mother. And it was a matter of pride, bearing up under the pressure. The next move was theirs.

A few days later the disciplinary busts for the liquor were announced in the mess hall. All four troop train revelers were ordered to walk punishment tours for six months. A week later the cadet adjutant announced a special meeting for every company in the basement sinks immediately after supper. A ripple of wonder followed. As I entered the barracks, the Company Commander called me aside. "Leary, you are excused from attending this meeting."

I sat alone in my room, nervously smoking Chesterfields. Half an hour later the footsteps of the company rumbled in the stairs. There was no chatter. My roommates entered, in tears.

"You've been silenced," said Baynes.

"We can't talk to you any more. We gotta move out of this room tonight."

"It's all for the best," said Baynes. "In a month they'll court martial you and then you can leave this hellhole and start again at a coed college. You aren't an army type anyway."

By the next morning I had become a non-person, completely ignored. At the mess hall the two seats on either side of me were empty. I was given a pad and pencil to write down my requests for food. I refused to comply. A silent protocol of leaving pitchers and trays within my reach evolved.

Part of me watched with amazement, enjoying this astonishing turn of events, realizing that something important was happening. But I slept fitfully, had bad dreams, and came down with head colds that wouldn't go away.

Then came the court martial. I was assigned a judge-advocate lawyer, a nice round little captain named Turnipseed. He liked me, but assumed from the outset that no defense could win against the cadet committee and the line of witnesses they had against me.

HARVARD UNIVERSITY
SEPTEMBER 1961

Burroughs' plane cleared to land at Logan Airport. He made it through customs clean as a whistle, taking no chances.

It was Indian summer in Newton. Burroughs worked on his paper for the APA convention: *Points of Distinction Among Psychoactive Drugs.* His approach would be scholarly.

We went on to Manhattan for the symposium on consciousness-expanding drugs. Other papers to be presented included *Set-and-Setting* by Timothy Leary, *Unusual Realization and Alterations in Consciousness* by Frank Barron, and *Ecstatogenic Comments* by philosopher Gerald Heard. Everything about the symposium was an historic first.

Attendance was unexpectedly large. The room was not big enough. Hundreds crammed into the room, standing ten-deep in the hallway, sitting around the speaker's table, sprawling on the floor. Burroughs lectured dryly from his manuscript, his voice low and non-committal.

After the convention Burroughs took up residence in my house. Under his gray fedora Burroughs sat cynical and alone in his third-floor room, surrounded by cut-up photos. Evenings he slumped unsmiling against the kitchen table, drinking gin tonics between Hassan-i-Sabbah monologues. He was increasingly bitter and paranoid, always brilliant.

One night Bill Burroughs and Jefferson Monroe, two masters of high camp, squared off at the kitchen table and pushed each other to extremes of funky decadence.

Bill snarled in his low nasal mutter, "Anyone who wouldn't enjoy fucking a twelve-year-old Arab boy is either insane or lying."

Monroe screamed in a high falsetto, flicking his wrists in mock disdain. "You're so middle-class, my dear. Have you ever fucked a . . ."

We Harvardites listened to this with jaws gaping. We were simply too square, too straight. Burroughs was too far out for us. In almost twenty years of experimenting with drugs, he had been through the Andes, and he had lounged on flophouse beds in every North African city listening to poetic drug raps by cocaine freaks, opium dreamers, amphetamine tap dancers, and hashishines. He had heard addicts rave about each new morphine derivative invented by "a fiendish German chemist," and brigades of wide-eyed peyotists chanting praises of the magic button. Don't talk to Burroughs about the cub scout god you just found in your hallucinatory baby carriage, man. He had seen them all.

Burroughs was disappointed to find us not scientific enough. He hadn't come to Harvard to run psychedelic encounter sessions or listen to our blatherings about love and cosmic unity. He saw me as a Notre Dame coach of consciousness, giving my players locker-room pep talks about internal freedom.

"Computers, man. Precise pinpointing of the hostile and friendly realms of the brain. Neurological implants. Brain wave generators. Bio-feedback."

He was right, of course. He was far ahead of us.

BIOGRAPHY

WALTER H. CLARK (1902-), Professor Emeritus in the Psychology of Religion at Andover-Newton Theological School, is a graduate of Williams College and Harvard University. In *The Oxford Group* and *The Psychology of Religion* Clark approached the subject of religious experience in the tradition of William James.

In 1962 he joined the Harvard Psychedelic Drug Project. Later he worked at the Worcester Foundation for Experimental Biology and at the Maryland Psychiatric Research Center at Spring Grove State Hospital investigating the effects of psyche-delics in a hospital setting. His findings were published in many scholarly articles, reviews, and research reports in the fields of psychology, education, and religion, including *Chemical Ecstasy* (Sheed & Ward), "Pharmacological Cults" (*Encyclopedia Britannica*), and *Religious Experience* (C. C. Thomas).

Clark was a co-founder and twice president of the Society for the Scientific Study of Religion. In 1961 he received the American Psychological Association's William James Memorial Award for his contributions to the psychology of religion.

14. Miracle of Good Friday

SPRING 1962
HARVARD UNIVERSITY

During the summer and fall of 1961 considerable interest in psychedelic drugs developed among the Cambridge religious community. It started when Frank and I ran a training session for Professor Houston Smith, Chairman of the MIT Philosophy Department. In the subsequent months Smith ran psilocybin sessions for MIT undergraduates and graduate students as laboratory exercises for his seminars on mysticism. How elegant and civilized! This was exactly how we thought education should operate.

Dr. Walter Clark, a sixty-two-year-old professor at Andover-Newton Seminary and visiting scholar at Harvard, dropped in several times asking to have the experience. He was a distinguished figure, awesomely respectable. He didn't drink or smoke but was eager to take our powerful drugs. To tell the truth I felt Professor Clark might be too academic and conservative. But he kept insisting. As usual my apprehensions were unfounded. Clark had been searching for mystic experience for most of his life. After his session he became a committed project member.

Another religious visitor who came around to see us was Walter Pahnke, a fresh-faced gee-whiz enthusiast with solid-gold credentials—a ministerial degree, an M.D., and now a D.D. candidate in the Harvard Divinity School. Dr. Pahnke wanted to do his doctoral thesis on psychedelic experience: a medically supervised, double-blind pre- and post-tested, scientifically controlled, up-to-date experiment on the production of religious ecstasy as described by Christian visionaries and measured by questionnaires, checklists, and interviews. This was just what we had been waiting for.

"How many subjects, Pahnke?" I asked.

"Thirty in the control group and thirty in the experimental group. They'll take the drug—or a placebo—in church on Good Friday with organ music and a sermon and the whole ritual going full blast. He added with boy-scout sincerity, "I've read your comments about set and setting."

"You want to turn on thirty people at the same time in a public place?"

"Yup. In the Boston University Cathedral. I've already spoken with Dean Thurmond, and he'll let us use the small chapel."

"Pahnke, that is the most reckless suggestion I've heard in weeks. Turning on thirty inexperienced people at once. You don't understand what you are dealing with. A psychedelic experience is intimate. It's intense. You laugh at cosmic jokes. You moan in cosmic terror. You may end up on the floor wrestling with God and the devil. The first session must take place in protected, quiet, secure surroundings."

"It'll be secure," Pahnke said defensively. "I've got a medical degree. I'll have tranquilizers on hand and I'll do psychiatric interviews to screen out pre-psychotics."

"You don't get the point. What you are proposing may be psychiatrically safe, but it's indecent. You've never had a session, have you? I like your idea of a systematic study of the mystic experience, but you must have several sessions yourself before you even begin to think about a research study. You must know what is involved."

No, he couldn't do that. He anticipated opposition to his study—from Harvard, from the Divinity School, from the medical people. He didn't want to be accused of bias. Therefore he must preserve his psychedelic virginity. He had to be able to say that he had never taken the drug until after his thesis was accepted.

The more time I spent with the indefatigable Dr. Pahnke, the more impressed I became. Behind his facade there was an inner dedication, an unruffled optimism, a deep belief in the religious experience and power of psychedelics to produce it. He thus won me over.

An informal religious seminar evolved at the Center. Our aim was to generate faculty support for Pahnke's project. We began meeting on

Sunday nights at Professor Houston Smith's house: Walter Clark and Dr. Pahnke, professors and students from the Divinity School, and visiting theologians. I described the religious aspects of the psychedelic sessions we had been running and answered questions. Smith, Clark, and Pahnke discussed the role of sacred drugs in history.

Lively interest developed. We ran training sessions for members of this group and gradually built up a staff of session guides for Pahnke's research.

FEBRUARY 1941
WEST POINT, NEW YORK

The courtroom scene, my first, was impressive. At ten in the morning seven elegant officers convened my court-martial in an oak-paneled conference room, their sabers laid on the table. Shades of Dreyfus. The evidence did sound bad. I was being nailed for possession of dangerous drugs. Two Honor Committee members testified that I had admitted my guilt.

I took the stand and denied the charges. I swore that the question about whose booze it was had never been asked. Then my drinking companion took the stand. Fitzgerald sheepishly told how he had badgered me for the liquor on the troop train and how the first-classmen "invited" me to join the party.

Then Baynes testified in my defense.

"On the Sunday morning in question," asked Captain Turnipseed, "what was your first contact with Cadet Leary?"

"He wasn't getting up for reveille, sir. So I shook him and tried to awaken him."

"What did Cadet Leary say?"

"He said he was dying and would never be able to make reveille again in his whole life."

"Did he seem ill to you, Cadet Baynes?"

"Well, he seemed to be suffering from what my father used to call a 175-and-a-half howitzer hangover."

At this, the stern board of officers smiled. The court took two minutes to acquit me.

My moment of victory was not long. That night the Corps was again ordered to the sinks for company meetings, and it was explained that even though legally innocent I was still guilty of defiance. The silencing would continue. Since there was no cause for my dismissal from the service, a new plan was devised by the Honor Committee. I would be demerited out.

At every formation cadet officers swarmed around me, examining my grooming with microscopic care. I was written up for "untrimmed hairs in nostrils." A shaving cut was cited as "careless injury to government property." Without notice my assignment in ranks was changed, and for lining up in the old slot I was gigged for "incorrect formation."

I resolved to stick it out. In some strange way I believed that this was what I was supposed to do, survive a training ordeal. The young hero stands up alone against the oppressive system. I saw it all as valuable preparation for more important experiences ahead. Ironically, I was right about that.

I was protected to a certain extent by minority factions and outsiders hiding within the system. The Catholic chaplain called me to the chapel to offer his support.

The black cadets were on my side, all two of them. The "Negroes," who had received nominations from congressmen in the early years of the New Deal, were silenced from their first day of admission. When we met crossing the yard, they would wink and march on. In the commissary line or in gym they would whisper, "Go get 'em, baby," and continue about their business without cracking their expressions. I thus became the "white nigger" in the Corps.

I had another vector of support. General Eichleberger, the Superintendent, felt the silencing was wrong. He summoned me to his office once a week for friendly talks. He said the army shouldn't be run by pious preaching types and he was going to recommend that the institution of silencing be abolished. Despite this encouragement my situation was a dreary one. Days without talking to a single person. Reading, writing, walking punishment tours. In spite of the drama I was bored. The classes were unchallenging, the routine relentless. I longed for the joys of college life.

The two activities that kept me going during this period of alienation were philosophy and sports. I read *The Story of Philosophy* by Will Durant, a popular survey of the great sages of history relating their personal lives to their theories. I next read the works of Plato, Aristotle, Kant, and Schopenhauer, and in the spring of 1941 I wrote my first book—a pedantic adolescent essay after Schopenhauer attempting to prove that everything in the world, animal, vegetable, mineral, existed as an expression of intelligent energy.

The only recreations allowed cadets on restriction were athletics, and so I spent every free hour in the gymnasium. During compulsory athletic classes my comrades were forced to accept me as a teammate, though they never spoke a word. It gave me a perverse delight to play first base on our company baseball team, watching my silencers cheer in spite of themselves when I got a hit. I took particular pleasure in winning the long-distance run for plebes (even though in my nervousness I had become a chain smoker).

Finally, the time awaited by all plebes, June week, the end of the year of torment. The Corps moved from the barracks to summer camp in preparation for the Graduation Parade and "recognition" for the plebes. Old graduates returned. The walkways were crowded with proud families, girls in flowered dresses, thousands of tourists.

Our company was by this time a magnificent marching assemblage, having practiced this lawn ballet for ten months. Each line stepped in perfect unison so that the spectator saw just one white trouser-flash. Into this last hour of hazing the upperclassmen poured their most passionate contempt, bearing down with their final insults.

From the moment of "recognition" in June, the plebe was accepted into a life-long fraternity of West Pointers. The elite club. The upperclassmen and no-longer-plebes shook hands, laughing, embracing each other, pounding backs, whooping in delight.

A storm of brotherly acceptance swept through ranks, around me. Alone, invisible, ignored, I was jostled and pushed by the embracing cadets. I hurried to the northeast corner of Central Barracks and stood facing the rough granite wall weeping in self-pity. When the company began to re-form, I returned to ranks and marched to summer camp, my spirits rising in the sophomore's freedom to let my shoulders swing free. Solitary in my tent I listened with envy to the exultant horseplay of the other new third-classmen as the sun set over green mountains and bugles sounded.

With the former first-classmen gone a new Honor Committee took over my delicate moral problem. First they tried a crackdown to get me to resign. More demerit harassment. I was continually observed and questioned about petty infractions.

A few cadets, however, began to acknowledge the unfairness of the situation and spoke to me. In August 1941, when the new plebes moved from Beast Barracks to summer camp, the silencing started to crumble in another way, very threatening to the Honor Committee. The new generation of plebes talked to me.

In general no social relations existed between upperclassmen and plebes. However, any upperclassman could "recognize" a plebe by means of a ceremonial handshake. Thereafter the plebe could address that upperclassman on equal terms. This suspension of the rules occurred rarely, usually among cadets who knew each other before entering the Academy.

But I existed outside the caste system (my tent was located at the end of the company street), so I could talk to anyone I damn well pleased. The first night the plebes were in summer camp a few dropped by out of curiosity. It was a thrill for them to find an upperclassman who would speak to them. I answered their questions about camp routine, joked, and thus gave them a rare friendly contact with a veteran cadet. When stern warnings were issued, the plebes started sneaking in after taps. My outsider status had put me in a powerful position with the younger generation.

One night, after taps had sounded the mournful homesick soldier blues, I saw a flashlight bobbing down the company street, approaching my tent. Two top cadet officers, not members of the Honor Committee, called my name. I pulled the mosquito netting aside and motioned them to sit down. The Battalion commander spoke first.

"The Superintendent and most of the faculty think your situation deplorable. We're getting letters from graduates attacking us and the honor code. Most of the upperclassmen now feel that the Honor Committee made some bad mistakes last year. We're your backers, if you want to call us that. We have enough strength to force the new Honor Committee to absolve you.

"Then there are the new plebes. They keep asking why you are silenced. Dammit, you know if they question the system during the first weeks here they'll get off to the wrong start and they'll never absorb the spirit.

"You've been silenced for nine months," said the Regimental Captain. "You can't remain silenced for four years or you'll infect seven classes of cadets. We can't have that."

The two clean-cut men stared levelly at me.

"Will you make a deal to leave?"

"Maybe," I said.

"Be specific. What are your terms for leaving?"

I felt a flash of elation.

"I want a written statement from the Honor Committee that I'm innocent, and I want it read in the mess hall."

The cadet officers rose, nodded.

"Right. The next step is to see if the guardians of virtue buy it. We'll be back in a day or two."

We shook hands solemnly.

They came back the following night. The deal was agreed to. The Superintendent called me in to be sure there was no coercion. He promised that no cadet would ever be silenced again if he had anything to do with it.

The capitulation of the Honor Committee was announced at lunch. The Cadet Adjutant bellowed the mess hall to silence, read some routine announcements, paused, and stated the terms. "IN THE CASE OF CADET LEARY, THE HONOR COMMITTEE AGREES TO ABIDE BY THE DECISION OF THE COURT-MARTIAL. NOT GUILTY."

Stunned shock and scattered bursts of clapping. The braver of my tablemates shook my hand. From neighboring tables, waves of congratulation.

After lunch I got a jeep from the post garage, drove into summer camp, and parked in front of my tent. As I loaded my footlocker and duffle bags, a friendly swarm descended. Many apologized for not having spoken up. It was impossible to get away. The narrow company street was jammed with well-wishers shaking my hand.

I drove the jeep past the riding hall, down the railroad station by the river, unloaded my bags on the platform. I looked up at the turrets and gargoyled towers of the United States Military Academy. They seemed antiquated, fuedal. Nothing good for America could come from those grey gothic piles.

SPRING 1962
HARVARD UNIVERSITY

Dr. Walter Pahnke and Professor Walter Clark proceeded diligently with the plans for the Good Friday experiment. Pahnke was unstoppable—a master politician in the art of the feasible. Professor Clark's wise, dignified support persuaded the administration of the Andover-Newton Seminary to allow students to participate. In accomplishing this feat of diplomacy Clark and I ran sessions for two deans, both past presidents of the Northern Baptist Church.

Pahnke agreed to change his research design. He would not march a crowd of stoned out subjects around. The new plan was to divide the sample into five small groups. In each group there would be four divinity students: two would be given psilocybin and the other two a placebo. Each group would be monitored by two trained guides.

No one, not even Pahnke or Clark, would know who got the sacrament and who who drew the inactive pill.

Pahnke balked at the guides taking the drug. Observer involvement was one of the main objections leveled at our work.

But Professor Clark and I insisted. Selected by lot, one guide would be straight and one would be high. The guides would seek the same thing as the subjects—a deep spiritual experience on Good Friday.

During the Lenten weeks we divided into groups. The guides met with the four students in their group for a period of orientation, getting to know each other's concerns and aspirations and ignorances.

We assembled at ten on the morning of Good Friday. Five rooms in the basement of the Boston University chapel were reserved for us. Panke arrived with coded envelopes. After an opening prayer we each opened our envelopes and took the pill.

We waited to discover what we had taken. The students were reading their Bibles, but I was sure they weren't concentrating on the words. After a while I felt something changing. Good! I got the psilocybin. I waited. My skin became pink and flushed. Hello. That's odd. Never felt like this from the mushrooms. Soon my body was radiating heat, but my consciousness was unchanged. I realized Pahnke had given us a placebo with a somatic kick. (It was a form of the vitamin niacin.)

I saw that two students had flushed faces. They were squirming with pleased expressions. One of them winked at the other. He rose and said he was going to the toilet. The other red-faced student joined him. As guide I trailed along. Inside the john they exulted like happy conspirators.

While we stood there, the door banged open. A third student walked in. He looked neither left nor right. His eyes were glowing and he was smiling. He walked to the window and stood for a long time looking out.

"God is everywhere," he cried. "Oh, the Glory!"

The two red-faced students shrugged, hopes dashed.

The ridiculousness of running a double-blind study of psychedelic drugs was apparent. After thirty minutes everyone knew who had taken the pill.

Ten of the students sat attentively facing the altar like good worshipers. Silent. The visionary ten were less conventional. Some lay on the benches. One lay on the floor. Some wandered around the chapel murmuring in prayer and wonderment. One chanted a hymn. Another wandered to the altar and held his hands aloft. One played weird exciting chords on the organ.

By five o'clock the group was pretty well out of visionary terrain. Pahnke and Clark were conscientiously collecting interviews on a tape recorder.

The plan was to go to my home after the session for a communion supper. The scene there was gentle and radiant. The trippers were still too high to do much except shake their heads, saying "Wow!"

I was in the kitchen having a celebration beer. Pahnke and Clark bustled in. We grinned and shook hands. It was like the first session at the prison. We had seen once again that good will, trust, and courage were the basic drug research tools.

During the next few weeks Pahnke had teams of psychologists who knew nothing about the study rate the student descriptions on scales of religious experience. The questionnaires and interviews revealed that the participants who ate the mushrooms had mystic religious experiences and the control group didn't. The statistical results were clear cut. Our administration of the sacred mushrooms in a religious setting to people who were religiously motivated provided a scientific demonstration that spiritual ecstasy, religious revelation, and union with God were now directly accessible. Mystical experience could be produced for and by those who sought it.

Time magazine published a long and very favorable account of Pahnke's research, supported by quotes from leading theologians. Thus word of the Good Friday Experiment got out to the nation. We expected that every priest, minister, rabbi, theologian, philosopher, scholar, and just plain God-seeking man, woman, and child in the country would follow up the implications of the study. But this was not to happen. A tide of disapproval greeted the good news.

The trustees of the Divinity School put pressure on Walter Clark to dissociate himself from our research. This gentle thoughtful man consulted his conscience and refused to back off. But follow-up studies at the Seminary were stopped, and the enthusiasm of the divinity students was officially discouraged.

Walter Pahnke got his Harvard thesis uneasily approved. He wasn't allowed to continue this work. His subsequent requests for government funds to repeat his studies were denied. A man named Goddard, a medical administrator who ran the Food and Drug Administration, derided the reports that psychedelics could produce psychological benefits, calling our results "Pure bunk."

We remembered Huxley's observation that the original sin was ingestion of a brain-change fruit in the Garden. There was not much chance that the bureaucrats of Christian America were going to accept our research results, no matter how objective.

We had run up against the Judeo-Christian commitment to one God, one religion, one reality that has cursed Europe for centuries and America since our founding days. Drugs that open the mind to multiple realities inevitably lead to a polytheistic view of the universe. We sensed that the time for a new humanist religion based on intelligent good-natured pluralism and scientific paganism had arrived.[1]

BIOGRAPHY

MAYNARD FERGUSON (1928-), born in Montreal, was recognized in his pre-teens as a musical prodigy. During the 1950s he performed as a trumpet soloist for Stan Kenton and later formed his own "big band." Generally regarded as one of the top trumpet players in the world, Ferguson's technical virtuosity has probably never been rivaled in the history of the instrument.

During the 1960s Maynard and his wife Flora Lu hosted salons in New York and Millbrook, where illustrious artists, musicians, and scientists met to discuss philosophic matters. Much of the high style of the early drug culture was inspired by Flora Lu Ferguson's experiments in combining Asian design with modern fashion.

15. The Ultimate Aphrodisiac

SPRING 1962
NEWTON CENTER, MASSACHUSETTS

Along the Charles River toward Boston a sickle moon hung low in the cloudless sky. I arrived at Logan Airport just in time to see the New York shuttle taxi in.

In two minutes I caught sight of my visitors: Salinas, in jeans, and with her a smartly-dressed blond woman about thirty—creamy skin, a full mouth, and enormous dark blue eyes. She wore no makeup, and her small face exuded worldliness and poise. Flora Lu looked me over, her eyes flashing with intelligence. "Well," she said, "you look like an earthling. After what Salinas told me, I was expecting an extraterrestrial of some sort."

At the curb was a middle-aged man with a serious case of slumping shoulders.

"Poor guy," murmured Flora Lu. "He doesn't look happy."

On second glance I recognized a friend. "Abe!"

Abe Maslow smiled back.

"Can we give you a lift?"

"No, don't bother. I'm waiting for a cab."

"Come along. We're going to Newton Center. No problem to drop you off."

With Flora Lu and Salinas in the back seat, Abe in front, I drove through the tunnel, around the dock area of Boston, and along the

Charles River. Abe and I kept up a running tour-guide commentary on historical spots for the visitors.

"What do you do, Abe?" asked Flora Lu.

"Abe is one of the most important psychologists of our times," I said. "Almost single-handedly he overthrew the Freudian notion that the human unconscious is a primitive homicidal swamp. Abe introduced the term *peak experience,* and he's convinced a lot of people that the human psyche is filled with wonderful potentials waiting to be awakened and used."

"What's a peak experience?" Flora Lu asked.

"That's what we're going to have tonight," drawled Salinas, "if the professor is good to us. Want to come to our session, Dr. Maslow?"

"I'd love to," replied Abe, "but I'm afraid I'm not feeling too cheerful."

"Wouldn't that be exactly the time to have a peak experience?" asked Flora Lu.

"I wouldn't know," Abe said softly, "because I never had one. It's the old philosopher's paradox. Those who theorize about it are often the last to do it. Freud taught us that."

Our group that evening included a psychiatrist and his wife, two graduate students, and the two elegant ladies from Manhattan. Salinas dominated the session with her fast needle-sharp hipster mind.

In the morning I was up early. I made scrambled eggs and bacon for myself, Susan, and Jack. Salinas and Flora Lu were still asleep. I drove Susan to the home of a friend, where she was planning to spend the day, and Jack to a nearby baseball park, where I acted as assistant manager of a Little League baseball team. Jack was the only one who played every inning of the game, because he was a catcher and there was no other boy with his consistency at this difficult position. Jack hit a double and a triple. In the last inning he leaped high in the air to catch a throw from the outfield and tagged the runner at home plate, which saved the game. The coach said, "That Jack Leary is a rock."

When I returned home, Salinas and Flora Lu were chatting at the kitchen table.

"Where have you been?" asked Salinas.

"Out and about. Did you have breakfast?"

"Yes. But it was pretty strange to wake up and find the house empty. We thought we had hallucinated everything." I poured myself a cup of coffee.

"We've been talking about you," said Flora Lu smiling.

"We decided you may be a hotshot psychologist but you need some help in the little down-to-earth things, like how to dress. And how to cut your hair—"

"—and what music to listen to and how to make these sessions more aesthetic than this faculty-club atmosphere you've got going here. So I'd be honored," Flora Lu continued, "if you'd come to my house next weekend. I could arrange experiments with some interesting subjects and show you what life is like in the first-class lounge."

Flora Lu told me to meet her at Birdland, the Manhattan nightclub where top jazz musicians like her husband played and hung out.

Sitting with Flora Lu was a black-haired spellbinder. We listened to music for a while and talked to the musicians who came by the table. The woman was named Malaca, from Morocco. Now a model—her picture on the cover of *Holiday* magazine—she had been married to a member of the royal family of Iran, who had given her a lot of money and treated her badly. She was looking for new meaning in her changed life. Flora Lu had told her about our drugs. But Flora Lu had also told her that I might be an extraterrestrial, so she watched me closely with her mouth half open. I found her overwhelmingly attractive, and was grateful to Flora Lu for arranging such interesting companionship for the upcoming neurological experiments.

Then Maynard took the stage, your basic young-man-with-a-horn, standing with legs apart, body arched, blasting, screeching, soaring higher and higher.

Around midnight we piled into a black limousine parked in front of the cabaret, rolled along the West Side Highway, and thirty minutes later pulled into some woods and up a gravel driveway to a large Tudor house. There were two Jaguars in front.

"Let me show you your new laboratory," said Flora.

The living room was enormous and plushly carpeted. A huge U-shaped couch, deep and soft, framed the giant fireplace. Rubbed-wood paneling and bookshelves made the flashy non-objective paintings stand out. One wall was lined with electronic sound equipment and yards of record albums.

What impressed me about the luxury of this room was the sure erotic intelligence with which each detail had been arranged.

"Come, I'll show you your room."

Flora Lu opened a door off the long upstairs hallway. "I hope you'll be comfortable here." The floor and the huge bed were covered with furs, splashed with pink silk pillows. Wood and velvet. Mirrors.

"Would you like to see our room?" she asked.

The master bedroom was a soft cave of lace, tassels, drapes, and furs. Reubenesque paintings and Tantric yantras. It was a delightful introduction to hedonic consciousness. Indeed the very existence of pleasure as a way of life had been unknown to me.

I had lived much of my adult life amid the usual upper-middle-class comforts, the habitation-functional machines used by professional people in this era.

But these were more than convenient quarters. Flora Lu had designed a temple to seduce each sense into rapture, to entice the body into a harem embrace. In this bordello baroque shrine my hedonic education was initiated.

I was at that time a successful robot—respected at Harvard, clean-cut, witty, and, in that inert culture, unusually creative. Though I had attained the highest ambition of the young American intellectual, I was totally cut off from body and senses. My clothes had been obediently selected to fit the young professional image. Even after one hundred drug sessions I routinely listened to pop music, drank martinis, ate what was put before me.

I had "appreciated" art by pushing my body around to "sacred places," but this tourism had nothing to do with direct aesthetic sensation. My nervous system was cocooned in symbols; the event was always second-hand. Art was an academic concept, an institution. The idea that one should live one's life as a work of art had never occurred to me.

After we took psilocybin, I sat on the couch in Flora Lu's Elysian chamber, letting my right cerebral hemisphere slowly open up to direct sensual reception. Flora Lu and Maynard started teaching me eroticism—the yoga of attention. Each moment was examined for sensual possibility. The delicious grace of moving one's hand, not as part of a learned survival sequence, but for kinesthetic joy.

I was wearing the silk shirt and velvet trousers that Flora Lu, true to her promise to be my fashion coordinator, had left on my bed while I showered. Flora Lu was wearing light blue silk. Maynard was a Florentine noble garbed in tight-fitting velvet pants. In a Moroccan caftan Malaca was soft, touchable.

A fire burned gently in the hearth. The air was scented with incense. His sensitized ears now as big as the Arecibo Dish, Maynard swayed with pleasure. Flora Lu floated around the room, her face transfigured with delight. Malaca blossomed into a flower of great beauty, her classic features now stylized with the dignity of an Egyptian frieze.

My eyes connected with hers. We rose as one and walked to the sun porch. She turned, came to me, entwined her arms around my neck.

We were two sea creatures. The mating process in this universe began with the fusion of moist lips producing a soft-electric rapture, which irradiated the entire body. We found no problem maneuvering the limbs, tentacles, and delightful protuberances with which we were miraculously equipped in the transparent honey-liquid zero-gravity atmosphere that surrounded, bathed, and sustained us.

This was my first sexual experience under the influence of psychedelics. It startled me to learn that in addition to being instruments of philosophic revelation, mystical unity and evolutionary insight, psychedelic drugs were very powerful aphrodisiacs.

Malaca was upstairs taking a bubble bath. Maynard dozed on the sofa. I stood by the glass doors in the dawn, aware that my sunrise-watching index had risen dramatically since initiating this research into brain-change.

Flora Lu carried in a tray containing a silver coffee pot, a silver pitcher of cream, two porcelain cups, and a bowl of apples, bananas, and shiny green grapes.

She placed the tray on a low table and rode gravity down to a sitting position on the rug. "I want to continue the discussion we were having last night."

I felt a flush of warmth in my body, as my face muscles softened into a smile. "Yes, I remember." The secret-of-the-universe business.

We had been sitting harmoniously in front of the fire when Flora Lu leaned towards me. "It's all Sex, don't you see?"

It had all become clear. Black jazz combos playing the boogie. Swedish blondes disrobing on a tropical beach. Tanned slim Israeli boys belly dancing to frenzied drums. Soft laughter from dark corners and behind bushes. The real secret of the universe was that everyone knew it but me.

A few days after this session I asked Aldous Huxley what he thought about the erotogenic nature of psychedelic drugs. His immediate reaction was agitation. "Of course this is true, Timothy, but we've stirred up enough trouble suggesting that drugs can stimulate aesthetic and religious experiences. I strongly urge you not to let the sexual cat out of the bag."

My first reaction to the aphrodisiac revelation was to have a good laugh at my own expense. We had been running around the land offering mystic visions and instant personality-change to priests, prisoners, and professors, and all the time we were unwittingly administering the key (if used in the right circumstances) to enhanced sex. What an inhibited square I had been. Why did it take so long for me to stumble on this fact? We had long recognized that these drugs tremendously intensified bodily sensations—taste, smell, touch, colors, sounds, motion, breathing. And we knew that in the right setting strong empathetic connections formed between people. By programming set and setting toward the philosophic, spiritual, or scientific, we had steered ourselves perversely away from an otherwise inevitable heightening of sensuality and affection.

Huxley was unrealistic about one thing. It simply wasn't possible to censor everybody's experience as we had censored our own. About this time we learned to our dismay that hip pleasure-seekers in Las Vegas, Beverly Hills, and Aspen were saying that LSD (a psychedelic drug none of us had yet tried) meant "Let's Strip Down." These discoveries came as a delicious shock to our prudish academic minds.

It had never occurred to us that this experience, which we treated with such deference and awe, could become a popular party item. (Except for that rascal Dick, who was already researching this area with cooperative Harvard undergraduates.) It was that night's experience with Malaca that alerted me to the certainty that our G-rated philosophic drugs would eventually be used recreationally.

Since this sexual awakening at the Fergusons' house I have found myself duty-bound as a scientist-philosopher to pass on the information that psychedelic drugs, with appropriate set and setting, can be intensely aphrodisiac. This statement—perhaps more than any other—makes antidrug people furious.

It seemed natural somehow that Malaca and I would stay together. When I drove back to Newton Sunday night, we dropped by her place for some of her belongings and she set up residence in my house.

It was hard for her to adjust to my domestic scene—two noisy kids, crowds of graduate students and researchers always talking shop. After a week I still saw Malaca as a temple dancer-divinity from the thirty-third dynasty. But it soon became obvious that up here in the middle-class twentieth century she was out of place, turning into a petulant spoiled Arabian girl. The image from the drug session was slowly fading.

RALPH WALDO EMERSON (1803-1882), born in Boston, was educated at Harvard College and Harvard Divinity School. In 1832 his refusal to preach dogmatism led to his resigning from the Second Unitarian Church of Boston, his only pulpit.

During a visit to Europe Emerson became an intimate of the English transcendentalists Carlyle, Wordsworth, and Coleridge, who were using nitrous oxide, hashish, and opium as sources of inspiration and revelation. His awakened interest in inner exploration and personal development led to his studies of yoga, neo-Platonism, and gnosticism.

In 1838 Emerson's lecture at the Harvard Divinity School, in which he urged his audience to find God within, develop inner potential, and drop out of organized Christianity, caused him to be banned from Harvard, an ostracism that lasted twenty-eight years. In 1866 Harvard belatedly awarded him the LL.D.

Emerson published several volumes of poetry and philosophy but attained his greatest fame as a touring lecturer. In spite of being rejected by the academic establishment, Emerson championed a system of ideas—individuality, inner growth, self-reliance, rejection of authority—that established him as one of America's most influential philosophers.

16. Ambushed by the Harvard Squares

SPRING 1962
HARVARD UNIVERSITY

There now arrived on the scene a most enigmatic agent who was to change the lives of all our crew, Michael Hollingshead.

Sporting an Oxford professorial accent he phoned me with greetings from his alleged mentor, the distinguished British philosopher G. E. Moore. I took the bait and invited Hollingshead to the Faculty Club for lunch. He was in his mid-thirties, medium height, balding, and he had a whimsical style, spinning witty multi-reality tales. On the basis of his claim to have ingested more LSD than anyone in the world I invited him to stay at our house and act as a project consultant.

Apparently he and a New York doctor had obtained 10,000 doses of lysergic acid from Sandoz to study the effects on the web-spinning of spiders. They mixed the stuff with moist powdered sugar, which they shoveled into a laboratory flask on the theory that spiders would go for the sweets. Just as an afterthought they licked the spoon. Since they knew nothing about human dosage, they were unaware of the fact that they had absorbed about a hundred times more than anyone in the recorded history of pharmacology.

According to Hollingshead the two diligent scientists sat immobilized in the laboratory for hours, transfixed by what was happening inside their brains. They became mystics on the spot, dedicated crusaders for the cause of altered states. Hollingshead packed half of the sugar paste into a mayonnaise bottle, said goodbye to the spiders, and set out to turn on the world. His first stop on the mission was our project.

Michael bounded around my house with this Venusian expression, jar in hand, offering anyone and everyone the inter-galactic trip. Initially there were no takers since we had decided to restrict our research to psilocybin. I had imposed a prohibition against even harmless little marijuana, wishing to keep our project free of any connection to notorious drugs. Because it had been used in chemical warfare research and by psychiatrists trying to induce psychosis, LSD had a dubious reputation.

Hollingshead tried our cozy know-thyself psilocybin and scornfully dismissed it as just pretty colors compared to the philosophic detonations of lysergic acid.

Enter Maynard and Flo Ferguson, intrepid ontologists visiting me for the weekend. They were easily persuaded to follow Hollingshead out where no other humans had been before. Docilely they swallowed a heaping tablespoon out of the famous mayonnaise jar. Thirty minutes postlaunch, Flora Lu's face radiated that glow you see in Giotto paintings.

"You gotta try this," she whispered.

Well, what could I do? I did.

It took about a half hour to hit. And it came suddenly and irresistibly. Tumbling and spinning, down soft fibrous avenues of light that were emitted from some central point. Merged with its pulsing ray I could look out and see the entire cosmic drama. Past and future. All forms, all structures, all organisms, all events were television productions pulsing out from the central eye. Everything that I had ever experienced and read about was bubble-dancing before me like a nineteenth-century vaudeville show. My illusions, the comic costumes, the strange ever-changing stage props of trees and bodies and theater sets.

After several billion years I found myself on my feet moving through the puppet show of reality. The thought of my kids led me upstairs to my daughter's room. Susan was sitting in bed, the very picture of a thirteen-year-old with her hair up in curlers, frowning at the school book in her lap while rock-and-roll music blasted through the room. It was pure *Saturday Evening Post*. "Hi, Dad." She was biting a pencil. I slumped against the wall, amazed at this marionette stranger from assembly-line America. She glanced up at me. "Dad, what would you like for Christmas?" She went on biting the pencil, frowning at the book, waving slightly at the beat of the music. In a minute she looked up again. "Dad, I love you."

A shock of terror. This was my daughter and this was the father-daughter game. A shallow superficial stereotyped meaningless exchange of Hi, Dad, Hi Sue, How are you Dad? How's school? What do you want for Christmas? Have you done your homework? The plastic doll father and the plastic doll daughter both mounted on little wheels, rolling past each other, around and around on fixed tracks. A complete vulgarization of the real situation: two complex trillion-cell clusters, rooted in an eternity of evolution, sharing for a flicker this unique configuration of space/time. Offered this chance to merge souls and bring out the divinity in the other, we exchanged Hi-Dad-Hi-Susan squeaks.

I looked at her beseechingly, straining for real contact. I was stunned with guilt.

Slowly I walked downstairs out to the lawn. Snow, trees, starlight. Everything was etched, sharp, magnified. I stood there listening for the answer. Where is the center? What can we do? Then rapidly, I recapitulated every solution that the human mind had attempted. Society, migrations, groupings, tribal wanderings, invasions, the planting of crops, the building of cities, the restless searching for possibility and meaning, the moral codes, the taboos and kinships. What to do and where to go? I could foresee the outcome of any action I should begin. Then, like a string being reeled back I retraced my steps to that central spot in front of the fire where the session had begun.

My previous psychedelic sessions had opened up sensory awareness, pushed consciousness out to the membranes. Psilocybin had sucked me down into nerve nets, into body organs, heart pulse, and air breath; had let me spiral down the DNA ladder of evolution to the beginning of life on this planet.

But LSD was something different. Michael's heaping spoonful had flipped my consciousness into a dance of energy, where nothing existed except whirring vibrations and each illusory form was simply a different frequency.

It was the most shattering experience of my life. And through it all, sitting with his head cradled in his knees, was the architect of this enlightenment, the magician who had flicked the switch to this alchemical show, Michael, the trickster.

The effects of the drug began to wear off by dawn. I was still higher than ever before, but some structure was coming back. The flow of electronic vibrations was slowing, and I felt myself freezing into a mold of plastic. There was a terrible sense of loss, of nostalgia for the radiant core of meaning.

I walked up to the Fergusons' room. They were feeling the same despair, ejected from paradise. I knelt before Flo with my head in her lap. Tears came down her eyes, and I found myself shaking with sobs. Why had we lost it? Why were we being reborn in these silly leather bodies with these trivial chessboard minds?

For the rest of the morning I was in a daze, stunned by what had happened, trying to figure out what to do with these revelations, what to do with life routines that were completely artificial.

I remember driving to my office in Cambridge the next day, still feeling a strange electric noise in my brain. Why did I return? Where had I lost the flow? Was it the result of fear, greed, past stupidities? And would I ever again break through to that other illusion, dance at the center of the great vibration dance? Then I realized what I was doing. I was imposing a pre-acid mental game on the revealed mystery of life. It all had to do with trust and acceptance.

It has been twenty years since that first LSD trip with Michael Hollingshead. I have never forgotten it. Nor has it been possible for me to return to the life I was leading before that session. I have never recovered from that ontological confrontation. I have never been able to take myself, my mind, or the social world quite so seriously. Since that time I have been acutely aware that everything I perceive, everything within and around me, is a creation of my own consciousness. And that everyone lives in a neural cocoon of private reality. From that day I have never lost the sense that I am an actor, surrounded by characters, props, and sets for the comic drama being written in my brain.

After the session a new relationship with Michael developed. My LSD-charged brain portrayed Michael as an agent for some higher intelligence, a wise alien who could spin through a million realities a minute. He was some sort of a god. A raffish sad clown of a god but unmistakably divine.

I watched his every move, seeking clues about the meaning of the space/time scenarios that he juggled so knowingly. I felt sheepish that I had not recognized Michael's extraordinary powers before the session and tried to make up for my neglect.

This picture of Michael as a superior alien gradually diminished. The effect of the session seemed to last about seven days.

Michael accompanied me to the prison, where the convicts adored his stoned-out nonchalance and the various officials were impressed by his haughty upperclass demeanor.

Those of us who had participated in the acid session felt a strong bond. Since Dick had not been exposed to the powerful LSD imprint, he did not share my awe of eccentric charming Michael.

Everyone in our network was intrigued and a bit scared by my post-LSD reaction. I had the blank look of someone who is seeing too much. Dick was upset and understandably so. He was ready to deal with psilocybin, the nice friendly love drug, but he sensed that LSD spelled the downfall of our plans to win Nobel Prizes and full-professor posts at Harvard. Just when the ontological complexity was becoming almost manageable, LSD propelled us into a dissipative chaos. New circuits of the brain were open, and there was no going back. Everyone in the research project heaved a sigh, bade fond farewell to picturesque psilocybin, and bravely signed up for the new level of exploration.

The introduction of LSD couldn't have come at a more delicate time in our political ballet with Harvard administrators.

The prison project and the Good Friday session had provided hard experimental evidence that psilocybin used according to our methods was safe and life-changing; we hoped that fellow scientists and administrators, recognizing the power of drugs to change behavior, would support our work. The opposite reaction developed. The Semmelweis effect.[1] The more successful our research, the more grumbling from the bureaucrats of science.

This resistance was based on a belief, held by many psychologists and psychiatrists, that personality was built up over years by conditioning and that change was slow and painful. These were deep-seated philosophic-religious convictions—Christian, Darwinian, conservative. Then we came along. If we could change convicts, divinity students, *and ourselves*, then it followed that psychologists would have to change their beliefs and methods. The suggestion that drugs could do what conventional therapeutics could not do was insufferable.

The fact that psychoanalysis didn't help most patients was irrelevant. Social systems, including the mental health establishment, are designed to benefit those who control them. Like Communism and Christianity, psychoanalysis was a revered orthodoxy that brought respectability and fortune to an elite.

We received support from other fields. In academia radical revisions can be tolerated in a neighboring discipline. The Divinity School professors, intrigued that we secular scientists were producing religious-philosophic experiences in their students, felt no threat from us.

A number of MIT physicists and astronomers were using our drugs to experience multiple realities and relativistic perspectives, as were Herman Kahn and many staff members at the Hudson Institute. We also heard from physiologists around the country who were involved in drug research of their own. Among the most interesting results was Karl Pribram's holographic theory of the brain.

Graduate students, not yet committed to a system, were lining up at our office doors for neurological fieldwork. Following our contract with the University we excluded undergraduates, who were the most interested group of all. Drugs were becoming ultra-trendy. Every weekend the Harvard resident houses were transformed into spaceships floating miles above the Yard.

At this point the opposition made its first move.

Professor Herbert Kelman stormed into the office of director McClelland, voicing serious complaints about our project. McClelland decided to convene a staff meeting to air the grievances. Graduate students were to be invited—most unusual.

The reason for Kelman's annoyance was apparent. Fewer students were coming to his office to assist on his tame questionnaire projects. We had tried to get him to take the drug or at least observe what we were doing at the prison, but he declined.

Kelman was a formidable rival. He had undeniable clout in Washington, as demonstrated by an uncanny facility for obtaining annual grants, fellowships, and visiting professorships in foreign countries. Actually no one could explain why he was in the Center for Personality Research since his field was social and political psychology.

Richard and I knew that Kelman was preparing an ambush. We discussed bringing in heavy-hitters from other departments to defend us but decided to play it low key, avoid confrontation. We felt no need to convince anyone of anything.

Such a large crowd showed up that the staff meeting had to be moved to a basement auditorium. Professor Kelman read a list of accusations: with our egalitarian approach we were violating the traditional apprentice relationship between professor and student; we were corrupting students by encouraging enthusiasm; we were failing to maintain all the proper forms of objectivity in our research; other departments in the University were talking about our Center with disdain; we were threatening faculty harmony, dividing the Center into two competing groups.

When Kelman finished, another ambitious professor stood up to continue the assault, Brendan Maher, a dour rat-lab experimentalist known for his rigid insistence on teaching students exactly the way he had been taught in medieval English universities. Maher quoted from psychiatric journals stating that psilocybin and LSD were dangerous drugs that should be administered by physicians in a medical setting.

Sitting in the front row, surrounded by our staff members, I rather enjoyed the show. It was a good ventilation of feelings by outraged authorities, similar to the lectures I had heard from school principals and West Point moralists. But then it got impolite. Standing before me like a prosecuting attorney with the journal articles in hand, Maher demanded that I respond. "Have you bothered to read the literature in your own field?" he asked.

"Yes. I've read those papers," I said.

"Then how can you continue administering these drugs outside a mental hospital?"

"I don't believe those results," I replied. "They are impressionistic subjective judgments by psychiatrists who don't understand set and setting, who substitute the mystique of an M.D. for experimental methodology. Who don't prepare their subjects. Who use no objective methods, not even patient reports, to evaluate what happens. In light of our own results do you really expect us to believe this psychiatric gossip?"

"In other words you dismiss the reports of recognized authorities in this field?"

"Indeed I do," I replied. "I take anything said by a psychiatrist with a grain of salt. That's the first thing we teach our students in clinical training here in America."

At this point Dick walked to the front of the room, radiating genial poise. He was imitating his lawyer father. As attorney for the defense Richard passionately refuted the charges and praised our research as a courageous and productive demonstration of new methods for behavior change. After both sides had aired their views, a committee was formed to look into the matter, and the meeting ended on a note of civilized coexistence. We were satisfied.

The next day, to our alarm, the Harvard *Crimson* ran a lurid account of scandal and dissension in the Center for Personality Research. Drug Profs Attacked by Colleagues!

The meeting was supposed to have been limited to staff members and graduate students, but someone had arranged for an unfriendly reporter to be present. The following day the story was picked up by the Boston papers and the wire services. Drug scandal at Harvard! There were, of course, no specific charges of wrongdoing. A large majority of the faculty and students backed our position. But it sounded bad in the press. Friendly faculty members who checked around reported that the confrontation was a political move by Maher and Kelman to embarrass McClelland, who came off looking like a bumbling administrator. These new developments left us with an uneasy feeling.

Was I in trouble with the Honor Committee once again for using dangerous drugs? I hoped that Abigail and Aunt Mae wouldn't read the Boston papers.

AUGUST 1941
INDIAN ORCHARD, MASSACHUSETTS

My homecoming from West Point was received as a disappointment but not a total disgrace. Throughout the silencing Abigail and Mae had been in close communication with my friend Father Murdoch, the cadet chaplain. In spite of their distress that my military career was over, they were mollified by the priest's high regard for my potential as a civilian.

The second day after my arrival I borrowed Mae's 1940 Chevrolet (her cars were always black) and drove to the Springfield Public Library, an imposing marble-granite temple built with Carnegie money. I was tracking down a book, unavailable in the West Point library, that I hoped would change my life. I consulted the author index. On the card, in shocking red letters, were the words: RESTRICTED CIRCULATION: CONSULT STAFF. The librarian, a sweet gray-haired lady, appeared unsettled by my request for this dangerous text. After I explained that I was a college student writing an assigned term paper, she opened a drawer, took out a key, ceremoniously opened a room behind the desk, and returned with the volume.

I sped the Chevrolet up the State Street hill, past the Springfield Armory, where the Garand automatic rifle had been invented; past the weatherbeaten sandstone marker celebrating Shays' Rebellion against the federal government; past the Indian Motorcycle factory, a red-brick fortress of industrialization; past St. Michael's cemetery, and the Ferris and Leary family plots (I'll never be buried there). I barreled along Wilbraham Road to the farmhouse, kissed Abigail and Mae, walked up the lawn and beyond the well, and sat on the grass. The August sun was hot, and the moist New England summer amplified the sound of insects.

I opened the cover, scanned the preface by Morris Ernst and the court decision by Judge Woolsley, which allowed this dangerous book to be printed in America. Then I turned to the first page. *Ulysses*. "Stately, plump Buck Mulligan . . ."

The enormous letter S warned the reader with a headline shout that this book was going to explode our understanding of what words could do. Joyce wittily, recklessly fissioned the structure of language. Change in the structure of thought would inevitably follow. My brain was permanently damaged that hot August afternoon on the lawn under the maple trees. Joyce's playfulness made it impossible from then on to take seriously the corseted limits of grammar and linear thought. In the two decades to come I spent much time analyzing how Joyce stripped words from their prudish structures and let them spin like charged particles. It was in part the long training with Joycean relativity that prepared me for the psychedelic experience.

After a week with my two eyes buried in *Ulysses* I responded to Abigail's insistence and dispatched forty-eight letters to every state university in alphabetical order. Abigail and Mae had their hearts set on a fancy Ivy League mens' college, but not me. One thing I had learned with the Jesuits and at the Military Academy—I was resolved to go to a coeducational country club.

The University of Alabama, just starting its campaign of expansion, was the first to accept my application.

Aunt Mae was distressed. All she knew about the University of Alabama was that Huey Long, the non-conformist governor, had created some scandal there. When other relatives criticized my new *alma mater* as a play school, I smiled with lustful anticipation. After four years in monastic cells it couldn't be too coed for me.

The migration sunward involved a dusty sooty train to Birmingham—in those days a dark smoking city with the Vulcan armpit smell of coal smoke and racial smoldering—then a bus to Tuscaloosa.

The university gymnasium was the site of registration. I joined a long line of students seeking to major in philosophy. At the booth next to PHIL was PSYCH. Behind the PSYCH desk was a pleasant-looking baldheaded man who waved and beckoned. He introduced himself as Dr. Dee, Chairman of the Psychology Department. He seemed delighted to find that I was from Massachusetts. He had taken his doctorate at Harvard.

"Why in the world," asked Dr. Dee, "are you standing in the Philosophy line? There is no philosophy department at this university. Professor Lang is the Protestant chaplain. His classes are called 'custard courses.' Dumb coeds and football players are the only ones who sign up. If you are searching for intellectual stimulation, you should major in psychology. I'm just building the department here and need bright students."

I was impressed by Dr. Dee. He spoke with a polished self-confident New England accent, and the way he said "bright" sounded super-professional. This was the first time in my life I had ever heard anyone imply that intelligence was a desirable trait. Up to this moment being smart always got me in trouble. Conformity was the virtue I was used to hearing about.

On the basis of this casual conversation I began the study of human behavior.

This was also my first encounter with the "gay network," which has always played such a crucial role in human history. Dr. Dee first tried to seduce me, then adopted me as surrogate son. By the semester's end I was the amazed recipient of Dee's intimate steamy confidences. Ours was not a sexual relationship. Dr. Dee was the paternal figure I had always missed, and over the years I probably became the son-friend he wished for.

I was a top student. The liberty to take elective classes in biology, physics, and psychology, courses in which the aim was not to defend the faith or master the jargon but to learn, to frivolously ingest information, thrilled me the way psychedelic drugs did later.

My favorite classes were in biology, taught by Professor Waldheim, another gay New England academician who had migrated southward. (I later learned that many of the best professors on the campus were northern academic stars who flocked to Alabama because of its gay infrastructure.) Professor Waldheim was an impish plump middle-aged bachelor who spoke with magnificent Shakespearean diction. He made the story of evolution come alive. He possessed an uncanny skill for drawing on the blackboard, organic forms, tiny boneless creatures, and the inner organs of beast and fowl. Professor Waldheim's love for his wiggly subject matter, his joy in sharing the scandalous intelligent patterns developed by lower species to solve the problems of eating, drinking, transporting themselves, defending, attacking, and reproducing was virulently contagious. Biology became my paramount interest. Accordingly I changed my major to girls.

SPRING 1962
HARVARD UNIVERSITY

The press coverage of the debate with Kelman brought us to the attention of the Massachusetts State Narcotic Bureau. The agent sent over to investigate was an Irishman named O'Connell, a wiry fellow who knew my family. He remembered that my great-uncle, also Timothy Leary, had been a professor at Tufts Medical School, medical examiner for Boston, and the first local Irish-Catholic to make it big in the field of science. Inspector O'Connell was proud that another Timothy Leary had now made it to Harvard. He naturally suspected a Protestant plot against the long-suppressed Irish race. I took him to lunch at the Faculty Club, and he left agreeing to keep us informed about any further developments.

With the Harvard community, however, it was not that easy. A committee was formed to oversee our work. It was a sticky situation all around. Everyone knew that our experiments were sound. Over 300 drug experiments had been conducted and there had not been one bad trip. That was not the issue. Our staff included the brightest graduate students. We had a solid phalanx of support throughout the faculty.

I felt a certain sympathy for the University. The sensational nature of our work and the infectiousness of our success placed the administrators in a tough position. After much discussion among ourselves we decided to avoid further confrontation.

We told McClelland that in the next academic year we would try to find outside sponsorship for our project, thus taking Harvard off the hook. And we would move the project to Mexico for the summer.

At this propitious moment the outside support for the next stage of our research appeared in the glamorous person of a twenty-eight-year-old blond heiress. Pretty Peggy Hitchcock was an international jet-setter, renowned as the colorful patroness of the livelier arts and confidante of jazz musicians, race car drivers, writers, movie stars. Stylish, with a wry sense of humor, Peggy was considered the most innovative and artistic of the Andrew Mellon family, a tough-minded prudish North Ireland clan that had in its largesse sponsored the Bollingen Foundation, publisher of scholarly esoteric books including the works of Carl Jung and that bible of acid-trippers, the I Ching. Peggy was easily bored, intellectually ambitious, and looking for a project capable of absorbing her whirlwind energy. And that was us. Thus Peggy continued the Mellon sponsorship of visionary research.

I was extremely attracted to Peggy, but when Richard announced that she was the first woman in his life to turn him on romantically, I restrained my ardor and played best friend. According to his anguished play-by-play descriptions nothing at all happened, and soon we were hanging out as a trio. Dick and I had found our Becky Thatcher.

We flew to Mexico to look for a quiet beach village for our summer center. It was like a Spanish sexual comedy. In Mexico City, Taxco, and Acapulco, Dick and Peggy would end up in one bedroom both thinking about me while I, next door, simmered with desire for Peggy. The tension grew to the amusement of us all.

On the map we fingered a fishing village a hundred miles north of Acapulco called Zijuatanejo. It turned out to be idyllic. The rundown airstrip and the unpaved highway kept all but the most daring travelers away. Since Zijuatanejo was not scheduled to be built up until the 1980s, the Mexican government deliberately steered tourists to the well-known resorts.

The village was small and sleepy. A bumpy dirt road curved along sea cliffs, deadending at the Hotel Catalina, a complex of terraced one-story cottages overlooking the magnificent deserted bay with its mile-long private beach. The stone staircases zig-zagging down to the shore were bordered by insanely colorful tropical flowers. Painted birds chirped shamelessly from lush trees. At night the stairs, the cottages, and the open-air bar/dining area were lit by strings of rainbow lights.

It was a Peter Max fantasyland. The owner, a German named Oscar, bored and going broke, was very happy to have Harvard faculty renting his hotel for the slack summer season. I allowed him to continue in the misconception that I was Tom Lehrer, the Harvard mathematician much beloved for his satirical songs. There was no mention of drugs.

Everyone back in Cambridge seemed pleased. In May, after my classes were finished, I was to fly first to the West Coast, to consult with some well-known LSD researchers in Hollywood, and then down to Mexico to set up the Summer Training Camp. Dick, Susan, Jack, Peggy and a group of our staff members would join me there.

A week or so before my departure for the Pacific Coast an urgent phone call came from my friend O'Connell, the state narcotics agent. O'Connell seemed a bit nervous as he walked into my office. He glanced around the room and suggested that we take a walk. We strolled through Harvard Yard, crossing the Charles River at the Business School Bridge. O'Connell pointed to the football stadium. He told me how he had once staked out some college kids suspected of smoking marijuana by lying on the lawn next to the stadium hidden under his black coat. I didn't think this was as funny as he did.

"I had a chance to look over some of our files, Timmy, and talked to some of my friends in the Feds. I ran across some heavy stuff. You may be getting in over your head here. I wouldn't want a nice Catholic lad like you to get into any trouble."

"Tell me about it."

O'Connell looked at me seriously. "I'm here not as a cop," he said, "but as a friend who wants to help you. Can I ask you some questions?"

"Sure."

"First, tell me, why do you think this Professor Kelman set up that meeting to attack you?"

I shrugged. "Normal conservative professor reaction. He's upset because we're trying something new. He's jealous because the graduate students are more interested in our work than his."

"I see," said O'Connell in an unconvinced tone of voice. "Well, tell me this. How much money have you received from the government for this research project you're running?"

"Not a cent. Our application to the National Institute of Mental Health got turned down—which was kind of surprising because we had glowing letters of recommendation from the Director of the Prison System, the Head of the Parole Board, and Warden Grennan. Plus lots of support from Harvard big wheels."

"So how do you run a project with over twenty-five people?"

"Except for $5,000 from the Uris Foundation for secretarial help all our workers are volunteer."

"Okay, one more question. What are you doing this for?"

"To expand knowledge about human nature. Find out how the brain can be changed by drugs. To help people improve their lives."

O'Connell shot me that parental look—patient, patronizing, protective. "Timothy, I don't know what we're going to do with you. Maybe you've been smoking too much of that funny stuff. You're living in a dream."

"What do you mean?"

"Let me give you some facts about what's happening in the real world. Suppose I told you that there are some people in the government who've spent $25 million to research these drugs of yours. Secretly. A lot of it right here in the Harvard medical school."[2]

O'Connell brushed away my objections. "Now this is between you and me and the Pope, you understand, but some very powerful people in Washington have sponsored all this drug research, and they are behind your recent troubles here. They want to stop you."

"Why?"

"Well, for starters this fellow Professor Kelman who brought the press down on you is not just jealous of you personally. He's funded by a CIA front called the Ecology Fund."

I remembered Kelman's international junkets and federal support.[3]

"That's the way it is," replied O'Connell soberly. "These guys in Washington are good patriotic Americans, and they have to do things under the table now and then, like anyone else. They're our team against the Russkies, Timmy, and they play for keeps in that league. There's nothing wrong with sending smart fellows like this Kelman to foreign universities to protect our interests. So I hope a word to the wise is sufficient. Why don't you give up this drug work? Let the CIA play with drugs. You've got a fine career going for you here at Harvard. You could become state superintendent of mental health—as long as you don't step on toes that you shouldn't be stepping on. If you see what I mean."

I thanked O'Connell and reassured him.

"Good luck, Timmy," said O'Connell. "Keep your nose clean. And don't forget what I'm telling you. There are some important people in Washington very interested in what you're doing. And they'll be watching your next moves."

Hardly a week had passed before the complications suggested by Inspector O'Connell took on a curious twist. While sitting at my desk I looked up to see a woman leaning against the door post, hip tilted provocatively, studying me with a bold stare. She appeared to be in her late thirties. Good looking. Flamboyant eyebrows, piercing green-blue eyes, fine-boned face. Amused, arrogant, aristocratic. "Dr. Leary," she said coolly: "I've got to talk to you."

She took a few steps forward and held out her hand. "I'm Mary Pinchot. I've come from Washington to discuss something very important. I want to learn how to run an LSD session."

"That's our specialty here. Would you like to tell me what you have in mind?"

"I have this friend who's a very important man. He's impressed by what I've told him about my own LSD experiences and what other people have told him. He wants to try it himself. So I'm here to learn how to do it. I mean, I don't want to goof up or something."

"Why don't you have your important friend come here with you to look over our project for a couple of days. Then if it makes sense to all concerned, we'll run a session for him."

"Out of the question. My friend is a public figure. It's just not possible."

"People involved in power usually don't make the best subjects."

"Look," said Mary Pinchot, "I've heard Allen Ginsberg on radio and TV shows saying that if Khrushchev and Kennedy would take LSD together they'd end world conflict. Isn't that the idea—to get powerful men to turn on?"

"Allen says that, but I've never agreed. Premier Khrushchev should turn on with his wife in the comfort and security of his Kremlin bedroom. Same for Kennedy."

"Don't you think that if a powerful person were to turn on with his wife or girlfriend it would be good for the world?"

"Nothing that involves brain-change is certain. But in general we believe that for anyone who's reasonably healthy and happy, the intelligent thing to do is to take advantage of the multiple realities available to the human brain."

"Do you think that the world would be a better place if men in power had LSD experiences?"

"Look at the world," I said. "Nuclear bombs proliferating. More and more countries run by military dictators. No political creativity. It's time to try something, anything new and promising."

I offered her some California sherry from a half gallon jug, but she made a cute little face and invited me out for champagne. She continued asking me questions as we sat in the cocktail lounge. When I rose to go back to my office, she invited me to have dinner. I suggested that she come along to Newton Center to eat at my house, where the kids were waiting. When we walked in, Malaca flashed a hostile glance at Mary, then recovered and greeted her with French-accented charm.

We never got to eat. Michael Hollingshead mixed drinks, got a bit tipsy, and started lecturing about brain drugs. Mary helped Malaca and me prepare dinner for the kids, and later we four took a low dose of mushrooms and sat around the fire. Michael was in top form, acting out high-spots of former sessions. Behind his wild comedy he was teaching Mary about the problems of inner navigation: how to deal with them, how to center yourself, how to avoid panic, how to locate handholds of comforting reality.

Then I saw her face go tense.

"You poor things," she murmured. "You have no idea what you've gotten into. You don't really understand what's happening in Washington with drugs, do you?"

"We've heard some rumors about the military," I said.

"It's time you learned more. The guys who run things—I mean the guys who *really* run things in Washington—are very interested in psychology, and drugs in particular. These people play hardball, Timothy. They want to use drugs for warfare, for espionage, for brainwashing, for control."

"Yes," I said. "We've heard about that."

"But there are people like me who want to use drugs for peace, not for war, to make people's lives better. Will you help us?"

"How?"

"I told you. Teach us how to run sessions, use drugs to do good."

Even though we were glowing with that pleasant conspiratorial feeling of those who are sharing a psychedelic session, imprinting each other with positive feelings, I felt uneasy. There was something calculated about Mary, that tough hit you get from people who live in the hard political world.

I asked once again, "Who are these friends of yours who want to use drugs for peace?"

"Women," she said laughing. "Washington, like every other capital city in the world, is run by men. These men conspiring for power can only be changed by women. And you're going to help us."

I drove Mary to the airport the next day and loaded her with books and papers about our research.

"I don't think you're quite ready to start running sessions," I told her.

"I agree. I'll be back soon for more practice. And don't forget," she said. "The only hope for the world is intelligent women."

Malaca was subdued after this session. She told me that during the evening she had seen the three of us, Mary, Michael, and me, as alien Christians, very distant from her culture. "These drugs make you see too much," she said thoughtfully.

A few days later Malaca flew to New York, then to Puerto Rico for a modeling assignment. When she returned to New York, she took to phoning me late at night. She longed to return to the mushroom world. It was the only place where she had found happiness. I saw her at Flo's from time to time, but we never got together again. Apparently the Christian-Moslem imprint from the session endured.

OSCAR JANIGER (1918-) received an M.A. in cell physiology from Columbia, and an M.D. from the University of California School of Medicine at Irvine, where he is now Associate Clinical Professor of Psychology.

During the period 1954-1970 Janiger was the central figure among a group of physicians, psychologists, and philosophers in the Los Angeles area who were researching drug experiences. In the course of their studies of personal and spiritual growth they introduced LSD to a number of influential and famous people, including several movie stars.

Ironically, while psychedelic drug activity in San Francisco and on the East Coast attracted sensational headlines, the quiet and meticulous Janiger group remained unpublicized, following the tradition of "mystery" sects that has kept the transcendental spirit flourishing throughout human history.

17. The Hollywood Connection

MAY 1962
HOLLYWOOD, CALIFORNIA

When I walked off the plane at Los Angeles, there waiting were my hosts—Max, a stocky man of forty, deeply tanned, and his wife Veronica, a stemmy blond. As we waited for my luggage, Veronica filled me in. More than a dozen prominent psychiatrists here were using LSD in their practices, the most influential being Oscar Janiger. Janiger had given LSD to a number of people, some of whom were in the entertainment business. Cary Grant, Jimmy Coburn, Jack Nicholson. "They're all becoming mystics," Veronica told me. "Kubrick's going crazy."

"That's interesting," I said. I preferred to wait and see.

Max and Veronica lived in a chrome and glass house overlooking the majestic expanse of Los Angeles, shimmering with rectangles of light. The bar, the library, the living room, all opened through glass doors to wide impeccable lawns and the blue-tiled swimming pool, lit by gas torches. Southern California.

My hosts led me along the pool terrace to the guest quarters, a one-bedroom mini-edition of the main house—glass, books, fireplace.

"Join us pool-side after you freshen up," said Veronica. Breezy sleek Southern California, so different from the sophistication of eastern hedonists like the Fergusons.

The next morning Veronica, red fingernails hooked lightly over the wheel of the Mercedes, swung down a narrow road that curled around houses covered with flowering vines, dove through tunnels of palms and Italian cypress. I concentrated on not spilling the mug of steaming *cafe au lait*. Veronica wheeled into a parking lot next to a house converted into a medical complex. As we entered, Dr. Oscar Janiger bounced up to meet us. Veronica was right; he *was* a powerhouse. Solid athletic build, gray hair, strong tanned face, merry eyes.

Down a long hallway hung with psychedelic watercolors, Janiger's study contained a remarkable private collection of volumes about brain-drugs— seventeenth-century first editions of opium studies, classic German texts on altered states, an exhaustive bibliography of scientific papers. It reawakened the feeling I had when Frank Barron began my schooling in psychedelics: there was a long and distinguished tradition of conscious- ness exploration, yet it was known to so few. I asked him how he got started in LSD research.

Janiger was happy to talk.

"It was the philosopher Gerald Heard who introduced me to psychedelics. He told me that the emergence of LSD in the twentieth century was simply God's way of giving us the gift of consciousness. He believed that LSD was a device for saving humanity from Arma- geddon.

"My first experience was in 1954. I won't bore you with details. It was not a uniformly beautiful experience. There were elements of it that were totally and remarkably transforming, and elements of nightmarish quality. So I got the whole treatment, the heaven and the hell. There were parts of it that were just so bad that I wanted out. And there were parts of it that were so astonishingly marvelous that I never wanted out.

"So by next morning, I was just stunned. And then I began to think about the experience, and, from that moment on, my mind didn't stop for one minute. I learned that there were other workers in the vineyard. And nothing would please me more than to get in touch with them right away.

"In those days, when you made contact, it was like two people looking at each other from across the room, and with a sort of nod of the head that acknowledged that 'you too.' It was so different then, you know, like 'Welcome, brother, you have now entered the Mysteries.' That was your ticket of admission. Nothing else. That knowing look, and from then on you were part of a sort of strange fraternity. We saw ourselves as current members of a consciousness clan that goes back through history to Eleusis and the Sufis and the Vedic Hindus. Welcome to the club."

Janiger took us on a tour of the clinic. The place was a revelation factory. The session rooms were naturalistic, comfortable, attractive. Sev- eral subjects would take the drug on a session day and trip for eight hours, accompanied by a "baby-sitter"—a person with LSD experience who was trained by Janiger to provide a supportive environment.

The purpose of the research was to study how LSD could be used for personal growth. For over six years Janiger had accumulated reports and test results on large groups of people from every walk of life, many of whom report life-changing illumination. In one experiment artists drew designs before and during the experience, providing a valuable body of data on how LSD changes perception. Janiger had conducted studies on LSD as an anaesthetic. He also studied patients suffering from depression, who received minimal doses each morning and then went about their daily schedule—reporting happier lives.

Janiger led me into his data room, jammed with file cabinets full of reports and questionnaires. From sophisticated psychological tests and stacks of notes his assistants had abstracted a list of the typical reactions to LSD. This particularly interested me.

"The most frequent reaction, checked by almost every LSD subject, was: 'Everything is alive.' The second most frequent reaction: 'It comes in waves.' "

I laughed, "Waves. Your tests confirm an observation we've made at Harvard—that the activated human brain experiences the world the way it is described by the equations of Einstein and quantum mechanics."

Janiger invited me to share his data, to collaborate. He radiated an attitude of trust and companionship, rare in the world of science. I had been associated with psychologists and psychiatrists for over fifteen years and this enthusiasm, this straight-arrow scientific zeal, this dedication to a utopian vision contrasted sharply with the usual competitiveness and secrecy.

Janiger spoke about the psychology of migration, and the evolution of culture—neurogeography. "It's no accident," he said, "that there's so much acceptance of altered states in Southern California. This is a special place. For the last twenty years there's been a movement of brilliant thinkers to Los Angeles. Thomas Mann. Schoenberg. Huxley. Isherwood. Notice how their thinking has changed. More philosophic, more visionary. Change is in the atmosphere out here. A new physics seems to be happening at Cal Tech and up the coast at Stanford and Berkeley. People here encourage each other to innovate. We're getting support from our local community because it's geared for the new. We've watched Harvard and the East Coast establishment react against you, and we understand why. The East is not the place where the changes will happen. The FDA is already threatening to close down all LSD experiments. Too much enthusiasm. Maybe it's time to take inventory."

Janiger and I agreed to stay in touch as we moved into the complex and conflicted days to come.

Veronica said it was time to get in the wind for lunch with Cary Grant. We flew along the flatlands, up La Cienega past Melrose, Santa Monica Boulevard, Sunset Boulevard, Hollywood Boulevard, magical names slipping by—jewels on a string of dreams. Like any East Coast tourist I was thrilled to be en route to a movie studio to meet a famous film star.

But to me Grant was more than just another pretty face. He was legendary among LSD enthusiasts for his eloquent endorsements of the product. Many Americans learned about LSD from his interviews in the mass media.

The security officer at the studio gate waved us through. We located a pleasant cottage surrounded by a small lawn and flowers. Waiting to greet us was the handsome man with the charisma and relaxed charm. Cary Grant kissed Veronica on the cheek and shook my hand warmly.

"What a pleasure. I've been looking forward to meeting you."

I was awed, tongue-tied. He waved us to the sofa. I blurted out, "Nice place you have here."

Cary Grant smiled happily. "It *is* comfortable, isn't it? Do you think it would be a good place to take LSD?"

"Really should have a fireplace," I said.

"You're absolutely right," Grant said. "We'll have to do something about that."

He picked up the phone and told some studio official that he wanted a fireplace put in his cottage at once.

His questions about our research at Harvard made it clear the man had done his homework. I was impressed by his grasp of the unique complications of LSD research. He seemed fascinated by the prison project and hooted with delight when I described scenes from the Good Friday experiment.

"What a movie this would make," he said. "Professors and prisoners. Sinners and saints. Jails and chapels. It's crying to be filmed."

I told Cary that all of us who were performing LSD research throughout the country were most grateful to him for his courageous and precise descriptions of what LSD had done for him.

"Not at all," said Cary. "I'm eternally grateful for this experience. LSD changed my life. I've lived more, felt more, enjoyed life more in the last few years than I had dreamed possible. My relationship with my mother, my love for my mother is the greatest gift that LSD gave me. For years I had little contact with her. Didn't talk about her, didn't like to think about her. She was living in a home for the aged in England. Since my LSD revelations I've been over to see her regularly. She's in her eighties and still a lively intelligent wonderful person. LSD gave me that treasure."

"What about the movie?" asked Veronica.

Cary said there was nothing he would rather do than a movie about LSD. He could see himself in the part of a Harvard professor discovering the key to the universe. The only problem was that we needed a script.

"In Hollywood, Shakespeare's advice still holds. 'The play's the thing.' Put on paper the grandeur and the splendor and the romance and the revelation of LSD, and then I'll be begging for a part in the movie."

During the drive back to Veronica's I was still glowing. "That's really exciting that he wants to make an LSD movie."

"He certainly has had a lot of experience in dealing with film ideas," replied Veronica cryptically.

It would take me twenty years to come up with the script.

The party chez Max and Veronica provided another pleasant introduction to Southern California culture and the psychedelic vanguard. There were lots of young movie people, like Peter Fonda and Dennis Hopper, and several LA medics who looked like movie producers—suave, hip, casual-but-rich. A dermatologist said grass was good for music and sex but only acid and peyote could get you past the receptionist, through to God on the phone. There were several orange-garbed swamis surrounded by disciples.

Then there were the successful dope dealers, confident with their lawyers at their side and, adding an ominous note, their bail-bondsmen.

Jennifer Jones sat on the patio looking beautiful. She was concerned about her son Bobby Walker, who was one of the most flamboyant hippies in Hollywood. She asked me several questions about LSD and its effects.

I met a delegation of athletic blond men, surfers from Laguna Beach. Their leader, a vibrant intense lad named John Griggs, took me aside to tell me a story.

He and four of his friends, Orange County high school drop-outs, formed a gang, financing their life of surfing with larceny and dope dealing. One day John's wife read a magazine article about a group of Harvard professors, who openly used drugs that produced ecstasy. She showed the magazine to John, who was astounded. How come these hotshot professors could get high legally and boast about it to the press when his buddies were getting five years in the slammer for possession of a little harmless weed? John and his gang decided to move in on this scene. When they asked around the dope underground, they were told that LSD wasn't for sale. Only a few doctors had access to the drug.

John got an address, and one Saturday night the gang drove to a house in the Hollywood Hills. They found a party in full swing. Pulling out their guns John and the gang ordered everyone to lie on the floor. The host offered to give them money.

"We don't want your bread, man, we want the LSD."

"LSD! You want to steal LSD!" The host was laughing his head off.

"No problem. Be my guest. It's in the white box on the top shelf of the refrigerator."

The gang popped down a double dose and headed for the beach.

At this point I started to laugh in horror and amazement.

"I don't have to tell you what happened," John continued. "By the time we hit the ocean, we were really ripped. The first thing we did was throw our guns into the sea. We became religious mystics on the spot. The next day we called your office and got copies of your books and papers about how to program drug trips. We've been running group sessions once a week ever since."

"Group sessions," I said in surprise, remembering the Good Friday experiment. "That's a tricky business unless your people are well prepared. How many are in a group?"

"From 50 to 200 people. Each week we go to a different place out in nature. Mt. Palomar. A quiet beach. The desert around Joshua Tree. Warner Hot Springs."

"Did you say 200?"

"That was Easter Sunday. Normally we get around 100."

"How many of these are first-timers?"

"About half. Everyone who gets turned on wants to bring their family and friends to the next one. We get lots of parents and even some grand-parents. They lie on the grass and love God. Every now and then some-one shouts 'Thank you God' or 'I love you God.'"

"What do you do if anyone has a bad time?"

"We get bummers now and then, but it's hard to stay on a bad trip when you got all these beautiful people around you."

"You use no doctors or professional guides?"

"Some doctors come around. My dentist is a regular tripper. The guides are mainly us. We're going to start a religion, the Brotherhood of Eternal Love. We're going to open a shop in Laguna Beach to sell books, paint-ings, health food, and hand-made clothes. You gotta come down to Laguna sometime and visit."

I said I would.

When the party was over, I fell into bed. I was sliding down that luscious slope between waking and sleep when I heard the door open quietly.

Peeping through lidded eyes, I saw a curvaceous blonde in a white sleeveless dress.

"Hello," she whispered. "I gotta talk to you."

"Sorry, no house calls," I murmured.

I pulled the pillow over my head. I had had enough stimulation for one day.

FALL 1942
TUSCALOOSA, ALABAMA

The wildest, sexiest girl on the Alabama campus was Betty Harlow, the daughter of an army general. She zeroed in on me with unerring accuracy and I surrendered instantly. She loved to fuck.

My partner was Don, a party-time kid from Illinois who owned a 1941 Buick. Don was short, which made it perfect because Betty's younger sister, Anne, was a tiny bouncing lass who loved fun as much as her sister. On Saturday afternoons the four of us would drive to the next county, hang out at low-ceilinged roadhouses, drink beer, dance to the juke box playing "I'll Be With You in Apple-Blossom Time," walk in the woods, roll on blankets.

One warm Saturday night I found myself talking to Betty through the screen window of her dormitory room. She was on restriction for staying out too late. We flirted through the fragile wire mesh. As I tugged playfully at the corner of the screen, Betty's eyes locked with mine, and she laughed. I tugged some more, and the wanton screen let go its fastenings. I climbed into Betty's honeysuckle chamber. Don, talking to Anne at the next window, followed.

At sunrise Don and I returned to our frat house. I was awakened at noon and told that the Dean of men wished to see me in his office. At once. Don, already inside the dean's sanctum, came out with a stricken look on his face. The dean waved a finger coldly at me to enter. "I have been informed that you spent the night in the girl's dormitory."

I said it was true. The dean wanted more details. Had I been copulating with other coeds? No. Did I use a contraceptive? Yes. Did I engage in oral copulation? Not yet.

The dean shouted that this scandalous behavior had no precedent in the long history of the University. I had sullied the honor of southern womanhood.

I referred to my good scholastic standing.

Oh, yes, the dean knew all about that. He had already received phone calls from Professors Dee and Waldheim. (The gay network, much amused, sprang to my defense.) Yes, the dean was impressed with my good academic record. He was also impressed by my candor, which contrasted with Don's attempts to lie. But there was no recourse. I was expelled. When I called the girls' dormitory, I was told that Betty and her sister had already been bundled off to their home in Washington, D.C.

The expulsion was more than an academic setback. I lost my draft deferment.

The homecoming to Indian Orchard was less than triumphant. Aunt Mae wouldn't say a word. She just shook her head at this new demonstration of Leary wildness. My mother cried a bit but tried to look on the bright side. She read the letter from the dean out loud to Mae. He wrote that I was a fine young man at heart and that my attitude was Christ-like! Mae was not impressed. Jesus would never spend the night in a girls' dormitory.

MAY 1962
HOLLYWOOD, CALIFORNIA

The voluptuous intruder upon my sleep slid her hand under the pillow and rumpled my hair.

"Come on," she whispered. "Just let me have a look at you."

I sat up, my face six inches from hers.

"So you're Timothy Leary."

"And you're Marilyn Monroe," I presume.

She held my hand. "Listen, you've got to turn me on. I've never let anyone into my brain."

"How come?" I asked. "There are lots of great acid doctors right here at this party. Or ask Cary Grant."

"I don't want to do it with anyone else," she said.

I walked to the little bar and opened a bottle of Moet. She followed me into the living room and curled up on the couch.

"You have people hitting on you all the time to get turned on, don't you?"

I nodded.

"So you never know whether people really like you for yourself. Do you feel used?"

"It gets routine, after a while," I admitted. This seemed to be too big an issue to deal with at the time.

I sat on a chair across from her. She studied me intently.

"You go around turning people on, right? But now that I've met you I think that it's *you* who need to be turned on. Isn't that a laugh?"

"Okay," I replied. "We've diagnosed my problem. Now what?"

"Well, I've got some magic pills of my own. Have you ever done Mandys?"

"What are they?"

"Randy-Mandys. They turn off your mind and turn on your body."

"No. Where do they come from?"

"I dunno. London. France. I get them from a Mexican friend. Here, take one. On second thought take two."

"Ah, thanks," I said, swishing the pills down with champagne. How could anyone say no?

"Feel anything?"

"What am I supposed to feel?"

"You're supposed to feel warm and friendly."

I opened my eyes and looked into hers. My body felt like a balloon filled with warm honey.

"You never felt this way before, huh?"

"No. It's fantastic. Where do we get more of this drug?"

She kissed my cheek.

"What drug?"

"But I never felt . . . my body never . . ."

"You just took two aspirins."

She was laughing so hard that I had to laugh myself. She buried her head in my shoulder. "Okay?"

"Perfect. Except that I'm thirsty. I'll get the champagne."

"Are you sure you want to?"

I stood up, took two steps, and watched curiously as my rubber legs bowed under me and I sank into the soft carpet. I giggled. I tried to stand, but my tentacles buckled and coiled. I tried to crawl, but it was too much trouble. I could hear her giggling from the bed. I fell into voluptuous sleep, slump, bump, lying on the carpet.

Next stop, summer camp.

HASSAN-I-SABBAH (d. 1124), a.k.a. the Old Man of the Mountain, figures in a curious saga of sex, drugs, and political intrigue that was brought to the West by Marco Polo.

According to legend, Hassan-i-Sabbah ran drug sessions at his 10,000-foot mountain fortress at Alamaut ("Eagle's Nest" or "Eagle's Teaching"), training undercover agents to use "a certain potion" (probably a mixture of opium and hashish) for brainwashing. These sessions reputedly occurred in a fabulous garden, where subjects were guarded "by the most beautiful damsels in the world, who could play on all manner of instruments, and sing most sweetly, and dance in a manner that it was charming to behold." Hassan's "garden of delights" was fashioned after the one described by Mohammed in the Koran as an image of paradise, wherein "wide-eyed Houris" would satisfy every desire.

According to Polo, these highly motivated agents, both male and female, would risk death to perform political missions for the cult. The legends seem to agree that most of Hassan's training operatives were women skilled in mind manipulation.[1]

18. Psychedelic Summer Camp

SUMMER 1962
ZIHUATANEJO, MEXICO

The two goals of our summer camp were to collect firsthand data in the form of observations, checklists, and written reports and to experiment with methods of guiding drug sessions. In particular we wanted to test the setting theory. We were convinced that drug effects were almost entirely determined by what people around the tripper did. If the environment radiated safety, beauty, wisdom, then even neurotic subjects would have experiences that were safe, aesthetic, and revelatory. The theory held that all "bad trips" could be converted to "good trips" if the environment was intelligently managed to provide support.

I arrived a week early to prepare the hotel staff. I divided my spare time between lying on the golden sand and translating the *Tibetan Book of the Dead*, from Anglo-Buddhist to American psychedelic. This remarkable work describes the stages of consciousness that are said to occur during the forty-nine days after death. It outlines archetypal visions and mental states, some scary, some pleasant. It also presents techniques to be remembered by the voyager or spoken in reminder by a guide as the soul progresses through the various levels, called *bardos*. The psychedelic implications of this oriental text were called to my attention by Salinas.

Our group numbered around thirty: several graduate students, a few academics, including Metzner, Weil and Alpert, two psychiatrists with their families, and some Cambridge hippies. Peggy Hitchcock, her brother Tommy, and some jet-setters breezed in and out.

The daily summer camp schedule called for one-third of the company to be taking psychedelics, another third to be guiding the trippers, and the remaining third to be resting from their previous day's voyage, writing reports, and interviewing with the research team.

Since psilocybin was becoming more and more difficult to obtain in large quantities, we used LSD, which we referred to as "Morning Glory" (M.G.) or "Heavenly Blue" (because lysergic acid was present in seeds packaged and sold under that name). Perhaps if these terms had been used in later years instead of the word *acid*, a more pastoral and harmonious set would have prevailed.

Every day there were trippers walking along the beach, body surfing, meditating, or lazing in hammocks strung along the terrace. At night the grounds were alive with color, fires burned in the sand, guitars and flutes filled the air. Small groups clustered together discussing previous voyages.

We felt that we were involved in a fascinating historical event—the first research project in which experimentally induced mystical experiences were being woven into the fabric of daily work and play. We saw ourselves as pioneers developing modern versions of the traditional techniques for philosophic inquiry and personal growth.

Sometimes I would stand on the top terrace and look down with pride at the magic we had wrought. I felt like Ignatius Loyola, reformer, leader of a dedicated band, author of a new regime of meditation and inner discovery. I also felt like a neurological Knute Rockne. I was a scholar from the greatest university in the greatest country, moving the adventurous search for human knowledge forward. I was following the advice of my grandfather Leary to do what no one else had done. The moon was new and the air rich with flowers and laughter. At these moments I counted myself fortunate to be a member of that long line of visionaries who throughout history have sought peaceful nature-shrines to carry on the search for self-knowledge.

This first Zihuatanejo experiment was a success. Hundreds of morning glory sessions. No problems beyond a few moments of terror, easily talked back to clarity and calm by the guides. We were developing more confidence in our abilities to guide ourselves and others in these awe-inspiring expeditions.

We were re-demonstrating that self-discovery could be pleasurable, that philosophy was fun, that science could be a pagan love of life, that revelation was joyful. We were incubating the positive spirit of the 1960s.

The Saturday night before our departure we held a farewell party. Most of our group took LSD. Mariachis came up from the village, along with the mayor and some other officials. The hotel staff joined us to drink and dance. At midnight we built bonfires on the beach and frolicked till dawn.

The next day we remembered that we had agreed to play a Sunday baseball game with a team from the village. At noon we piled into the VW buses and drove down to the diamond near the airport. Much to our surprise we discovered hundreds of fans assembled to watch the contest. Local papers up and down the coast had billed it as a game between the Harvard University varsity and the official semi-pro state team. Farmers bused in from miles around. Taco, soft-drink, and beer stands had been set up. And it was clear that some serious betting was taking place.

I explained to the coach of the opposition that we were amateurs. As a fellow sportsman he agreed to lend us a substitute pitcher and catcher. I did not tell him that some members of our squad were still hallucinating, including me.

We had four good players: Dr. Allen Cohen, who later became a Meher Baba follower and a member of Governor Ronald Reagan's anti-drug commission, had once played American Legion ball. Even when hallucinating he performed brilliantly. Lowell, the ex-dope dealer, who later died in a Moroccan prison, sparkled at second base. Tommy Hitchcock roamed the outfield with rangy grace. I played first better than I did at West Point. Dick excelled as chief cheerleader.

In the first inning the opposing pitcher walked our first three batters. The fact that they stood with the bats on their shoulders, staring at the pitcher with dilated eyeballs in other-worldly detachment, may have contributed to his control problems. Plus much of the crowd, considering us to be the home team, was on our side.

Tommy hit a home run. Suddenly all of our hitters were slashing singles, looping doubles.

The acid distorted our perception of time. Everything moved slowly. When the ball left the pitcher's hand, it seemed to float toward the plate, allowing plenty of time to count the stitches, examine the Wilson label, speculate about the history of competitive sports since the Greek Olympics, and feel the muscles contract reflexively to hit the ball. It's the busy worrying mind, after all, that keeps us from performing with animal grace. In their relaxed state our hitters could swing the bat exactly the way it's supposed to be swung, effortlessly.

Our pitcher, stimulated by the large cheering crowd and the big lead, hurled his heart out, and when the ball came our way we were equally impressive in the field.

We had agreed to play for seven innings. After six it became clear that we were in trouble. The score was 8-0 in our favor, and the other team was getting surly. The mood of the crowd was swinging back to support the Latin team.

I approached our pitcher, and glancing significantly at the crowd, "I think it would be very sympathetic if you let them hit, Manuel," I said in Spanish. He nodded. As an added precaution I pulled our best players, substituting four graduate students so unathletic they didn't know that the glove went on the non-throwing hand. Our pitcher fed the ball slowly, the opponents connected and ran the bases furiously. Our fielders ran around aimlessly. They threw to the wrong base, misjudged flies, and on several occasions actually threw their gloves on the ground, the better to run after the ball. The crowd went wild when the village team, in a heroic comeback, tied the score. No one was in a mood for extra innings. We all cheered, embraced, and drank beer and tequila. The party spread throughout the town.

Everyone urged us to come back next year. And we planned to. The six weeks at Zihuatanejo had given us a glimpse of utopia.

JANUARY 1943
FORT EUSTIS, VIRGINIA

My draft deferment was cancelled, and orders came right after Christmas. I was to report for basic training in the Coast Artillery.

If there ever existed an anti-utopian sinus-hollow swampier than Fort Eustis, Virginia, then military intelligence has overlooked it. Having already had two and a half years of officer training—more spit-and-polish elite service than most of the young officers on the post—I went in with few illusions about the romance and glory to be attained by service in arms. I had recently read two instructive books: *The Enormous Room*, e.e. cummings' account of his internment in a noisy French barracks, and the story of T. E. Lawrence, after his exploits in Arabia, enlisting in the RAF as a private. I decided to follow a new campaign tactic: lay low.

I spent three catarrhal months in chilly basic training as an invisible presence. My only objective was to survive. The barracks sounded like a TB ward. (These were the days before antibiotics, so there was nothing to do but cough and retch as foot soldiers had done for several thousand years.) The combination of chronic bronchitis and proximity to artillery concussions left many recruits partially deaf, a malady which was corrected in my case many years later.

My branch of the service was anti-aircraft artillery. Our battery was armed with several enormous ninety-millimeter cannon, which I learned to dismount, set up, load, and fire at luckier or smarter people flying high above. The shells were yard-long babies. The sky-scanning weapon was aimed by an ultra-secret black wizard box. Later I realized that we were using an early version of the analog computer.

I remained detached. Occasionally, when it paid off, I would flash my prowess in the manual of arms. I particularly dreaded pounding those frosty nocturnal rounds on sentry duty, so when we lined up for inspection of the guard, I would slap-crack rifle moves with West Point flair and win the honor of spending the night as clerk in battalion headquarters, a warm cozy spot to read.

I was selected for Officer's Training. Again. But the military, realizing that psychologists were needed to win the war and preserve the peace, was offering soldiers with college majors in psychology the opportunity to complete their degrees. I turned down the officer's bars and went for three months' study at Georgetown University, six months' classwork at Ohio State (where females outnumbered males a hundred to one), and a winter of sunning and reading at an Air Corps center in Miami Beach.

Then in the summer of 1944 I was transferred as a psychological consultant to the Troop Carrier Command, slated for the South Pacific. The Troop Carrier Command was staffed by commercial airline personnel. The planes were transports, totally unarmed. Their mission: to ferry parachute troops and to pull gliders that would be cut loose above Japanese home islands, where our boys would be silently and inexpensively crash-landed. It was, in short, a suicide command, whose main mission, as far as I could see, was to eliminate the entire civilian branch of American aviation from post-war rivalry.

Meanwhile Dr. Dee had managed to obtain the position of chief psychologist at an army hospital in central Pennsylvania. We met in Buffalo, and I listened to his poignant tales of love affairs with brilliant young Harvard psychologists and medical officers. He was riding high in the military. He vowed that his "friends" in the War Department would arrange a transfer for me to his command.

I was pessimistic, because a freeze had been imposed on transfers out of the war-bound Troop Carrier Command. But sure enough, within a week, a telegram arrived ordering me to the Army Medical Corps hospital in Butler, Pennsylvania.

The train arrived in Butler at dawn. I took a cab to the Army Hospital with high hopes. I had been promoted to corporal and was eager to start my training as a clinical psychologist assigned to the Acoustic Clinic.

The first person I met was Marianne, an audio technician with jet-black hair, soft brown eyes, and creamy skin. I fell in love on the spot.

She asked me if I had come for a hearing test. Naturally I said yes. Whatever.

She put me in a soundproof room with earphones. My heart was beating madly. She closed the door behind her, and then her voice filled my head with soft-sweet murmured spondees. Sunshine. Moonglow. Snowfall. Roommate. Lovesick. Discovering a mild hearing loss, she was gently fitting me with a hearing aid before I told her I was a new staff member.

During the lunch hour the younger staff sat around the music room of the hearing clinic. There I listened to Marianne playing the piano and singing musical comedy songs in a jazzy rich coloratura soprano. She had a master's degree from Northwestern and came from a wealthy Catholic family in Oregon. I asked her a lot of questions. She radiated excellence, intelligence, and much heat.

She invited me to dinner that night. We had several drinks and started kissing. Nothing like booze to wash away schoolboy inhibitions.

"I never felt this way before," she said.

We fell into bed like it was always meant to be.

Not long after, we rented a small funky apartment in the mill section of Butler and set up housekeeping. Every detail of the domestic arrangements was thrilling. It was achingly pleasant to be sharing life with a woman. We bought dishes and pillowcases and towels, and we stocked the refrigerator. We shared the bathroom. The nesting circuits of our brains were activated. It was the first time for us both, experiencing that most wondrous human pleasure: all-out fucking-for-fusion, secure and safe in our very own bed.

My mother and Aunt Mae and Marianne's parents were all staunch papists, so Marianne and I were married in the post Catholic chapel on April 12, 1944. I was twenty-three; she was twenty-two.

We honeymooned in Manhattan's Hotel St. Moritz, where a disturbing event occurred. While dressing for dinner we drank a joyous bottle of champagne, which spun Marianne into some secret alcohol room in her head. She was decked out in her classy big-city dress with a patent-leather box-hat. After tight-roping through the lobby she slipped in the revolving door and sprawled there, giggling at my futile efforts to extract her. Trapped outside the glass doors I could, neither by push nor pull, extricate her.

Each morning Dr. Dee drove Marianne and me to the post. One day when we came out to the car, we found him staring into space, hands clutching the steering wheel.

"What's wrong," I said in alarm.

Dr. Dee pointed to a newspaper lying on the front seat. A headline shouted that America had just exploded a new super-bomb over a Japanese city called Hiroshima.

My first reaction was relief. This new show of force might shorten the war.

But Dr. Dee felt nothing like relief. "Eighty thousand killed in one explosion. This is the worst thing that we have ever done."

Within days the war ended. A few weeks later I was promoted to sergeant. My five years of honorable service made me eligible for an early discharge.

From the demobilization camp in Indiantown Gap, Pennsylvania Marianne and I boarded a coach railway car for a four-day train trip to Portland. Marianne's family lived in Oregon City, a few miles up the Willamette River.

Her parents were German Catholics, hard-working, thrifty, dour. Her mother was perpetually gloomy. Her father was the caricature of a small-town businessman: his furniture store made a fortune because of wartime shortages. The day after our arrival her father took me downtown, pointed to his real-estate holdings on Main Street, conducted a tour of the store. Then he confided his life's sorrow: he had no son to inherit his empire. He inquired scornfully about the salary of a psychologist. With touching solemnity, he proposed that all this could be mine after a few years of apprenticeship. I politely but firmly declined.

Marianne and I spent the spring and summer of 1946 at Washington State University, where I received a master's degree in psychology. My thesis was a statistical study of the dimensions of intelligence.

In September I was accepted as a doctoral student in psychology at Berkeley.

When Marianne and I crossed the border from Oregon, suddenly the sun began to shine. Towering redwoods shouted hello. Billboards urged every traveler to visit the wineries for free chablis, free cheese. Welcome to California! We rolled south through Marin County, sped through the Sausalito tunnel, and saw . . . the Bay. The Golden Gate Bridge. And across the water the white towers of San Francisco. I've been a Californian ever since.

We found a tiny apartment in the Berkeley Hills near the university. Marianne got a teaching job in the speech department, and I enrolled as a doctoral candidate in what was reputed to be the best psychology department in the world.

For the first few weeks Marianne and I hung out with new graduate students. This was the first post-war class, a bumper crop of war veterans, several years older and more worldly-wise than the usual graduate students. How did these elite young scholars plan to use their training to make it a better world?

Well, they couldn't have cared less about the crisis of human affairs. They had taken the basic courses in philosophy, psychology, and scientific method. They had been taught Socrates and Voltaire and William James. And they identified not with the heroes but with the teachers of the courses about the heroes. They were there to learn how to be professors. Neither were the professors very engaged in the social applications of psychology. They were genial cultured men, serenely performing little experiments in animal learning and enjoying the easy life of post-war California.

I found myself trapped once again in another gray bureaucracy. If I had wanted a comfortable career, I could have remained at West Point or signed up for law or business administration. I felt a return of that ancient Celtic dissatisfaction, a lust for metamorphosis, for something new and more splendid. Another graduate student, himself a half-crazed Irishman, Frank Barron, seemed to share my restlessness. We hung out together, playing tennis and drinking and talking about the poetry of psychology.

A LAN WATTS (1915-1973) came to the United States from his native England in 1938. Over the course of his professional life he was an Anglican priest, teacher, editor, and author of many books on oriental religion and the psychology of consciousness. Beginning with his first book *The Spirit of Zen,* written when he was twenty, Watts eloquently explained Buddhism to western audiences, reaching large numbers of listeners through his radio shows and public lectures.

His deep understanding of Eastern philosophic concepts, his wit, and his forthrightness made him a seminal force in humanistic psychology and the consciousness movement. During the late fifties and early sixties Watts became an enthusiastic adept in the spiritual use of psychedelic drugs. In *The Joyous Cosmology* he wrote a brilliant description of drug-induced mysticism.

His later works include *The Wisdom of Insecurity, The Supreme Identity, Nature, Man and Woman,* and *Psychotherapy East and West.*

19. Farewell to Harvard

FALL 1962-WINTER 1963
HARVARD UNIVERSITY

At Harvard we moved into a three-story six-bedroom house, which Richard Alpert purchased one afternoon. It was in Newton Center, a few blocks from the house which had served as our headquarters the preceding year. In the tradition of Brook Farm we tried something that seemed natural to us but turned out to be a declaration of cultural deviance. We lived as a multi-family community, twelve in all: Dick, myself and my two kids, Ralph Metzner and his new bride Susan, Frazier, a handsome undergraduate with whom Richard had fallen in love, plus his family of three, and Lowell, the black ex-dope dealer, who was with us down in Zihuatanejo. Peggy Hitchcock shuttled back and forth from New York. Our summer school romance had blossomed into a love affair and, eventually, a lifelong friendship.

Trouble immediately raised its head. Some of our neighbors filed a suit with the city, claiming that we were in violation of the zoning laws that limited occupancy to single families. We were ordered to appear at a formal eviction hearing in front of the city council.

"Not to worry," said Dick as he picked up the phone. Our case was represented at the hearing by none other than George Alpert, president of the New York, New Haven and Hartford Railroad, flanked by several company attorneys. Dick's father presented a masterful summary, citing the Bible, the Mayflower Compact, and several Amendments to the Constitution. There were headlines in the paper when our extended household was officially designated a single family.

An intentional multi-family community was a powerful *psychlotron*, a place where passive imprints and involuntary social conditionings can be dissolved. We were free to experience, study, rethink exactly how we wanted to live at which stages in our life.

If your philosophy is one of change, growth, metamorphosis, mutation, migration; if your concept of "real estate" is neurological rather than mammalian, then your habitat defines your launching pad. Your "home" represents a cocoon stage you are passing through. The intentional community can be a life-boat in which a few percipient, adventurous souls leave the ship of previous generations and push off seeking the next open frontier.

Our kitchen became a busy intersection of philosophic and scientific traffic. Alan Watts and Jano, his wife, lived in Cambridge that fall and came by evenings. The wizard held court, drinking heavily, spinning out tales about fabled consciousness expanders of the past. Here was the oral tradition of education in action.

Alan told stories about the great mystics of history, such as the Russian occultist Madame Blavatsky, who studied with spiritual masters in Tibet and started the Theosophist movement in the late nineteenth century; Annie Besant, teacher of Hindu mysticism and the so-called Secret Doctrines; Krishnamurti, a handsome young Brahmin who was selected by Besant to be the next messiah and who, at the height of his popularity, had the common sense to renounce the dubious honor. I was fascinated by but skeptical of those occultists, who claimed magic and miracle, loved secrecy, relied on gullibility, and seemed to avoid science.

Alan didn't talk much about Hindu gurus and swamis. He felt they were humorless, authoritarian. He imitated the pompous Anglo-Indian parrot-talk of the swamis, tilting his head sideways in that self-pleased motion: "Ashram without Guru is like ship without rudder."

Most fascinating to me were the stories Alan recounted of G.I. Gurdjieff, the Russian-Armenian Sufi mystic who taught a lusty good-humored mental science. Gurdjieff encouraged searchers to study the way of the meditative, the yogi, the fakir, but he taught that the most efficient way to increase intelligence and brain-control was the Fourth Way: drugs.

Alan was most instructive in another sense. He gave us a model of the gentleman-philosopher who belonged to no bureaucracy or academic institution. He had published more influential books than any orientalist of our time. Although he could teach rings around any tenured professor, he had avoided faculty status, remaining a wandering independent sage, supporting himself with the immediate fruits of his plentiful brain. He was a full-time all-out philosopher in his words and in his actions.

Watts taught us to divide mystics into two groups—the lugubrious and the witty. Ever since then I have remained unenthusiastic about pious teachers who set up schools, hierarchies, and special rituals that mimic organized religions. The western scientific yoga, which we would help create, would avoid secrecy, bureaucracy, masters, followers, dogma, and fixed ritual, and it would use the experimental method to make accessible to everyone what had for centuries been shrouded in occultism.

1947
BERKELEY, CALIFORNIA

Our first baby was born on September 25, 1947. I was by Marianne's side at the hospital to comfort her as she went through a wild period of distress and disorientation, finally muffled by medication. She was wheeled into the delivery room.

A half hour later the doctor walked up with a big smile. Congratulations! You have a beautiful baby girl.

He took me to the nursery. Behind a glass window, in the nurse's arms, was this tiny new being, looking at me *with my own eyes.*

After Marianne and Susan came home, an agonizing problem showed itself. When mother offered the breast, baby took one sip of milk and let out a fearful shriek.

After a week of this torture I went out and bought the formula "works." Susan took to the bottle greedily. Marianne was never the same. The funloving, competent young woman changed with the motherhood imprint into a duplicate of her mother, worried, introverted, increasingly dependent. I became an industrious father robot, dutifully getting juicy worms for the nest.

Two years after Susan was born came our strong handsome son. We named him John Busch Leary, in a vain attempt to please Marianne's father. This time we were alert to the nursing problem. When Jack recoiled from the breast, we immediately put him on the bottle.

Susan was jealous of her new brother, and right from the start a tension developed between the two children that has caused me sorrow over the years.

After Hiroshima there was much fear about atomic warfare. Marianne continually worried that the nuclear holocaust would come while I was at work and we would not be together at the moment of death. Sometimes she would phone me at the clinic and beg me to come home.

Marianne's withdrawal from the outside world gradually increased. We were no longer inseparable. Two or three nights a week I was busy with meetings. Marianne stayed at home. Weekends there were heavy drinking parties with our friends.

I was going through the motions of graduate studies and clinical internships, but most of my time was devoted to liberal politics. I became a leader of the American Veterans Committee, an organization committed to integration, peace, and economic justice. We started an inter-racial veterans clubhouse, a liberal newspaper, an interracial softball team, and lobbied fervently for the liberal causes of the day. My enthusiasm was recognized by the national leaders of the AVC, Ivy League types like Franklin Delano Roosevelt, Jr., Gilbert Harrison, Michael Straight, Charles Bolte, and Cord Meyer, Jr. They sent us emissaries, including Richard Bolling, later a Congressman from Missouri, who confided to me that the main task of AVC leaders was not to work for veterans' benefits and liberal programs but to unmask and expel the "reds" who had infiltrated the organization. Their fears of a Communist takeover were not unfounded. I had been approached by leftists who wanted me to help unmask and expel the "red-baiters" from the organization. It was a dippy period in American history. Many well educated and intelligent Americans did throw their energies briefly into the pro-Soviet cause. And many sincere idealists and intellectuals did become fanatically obsessed with Cold War paranoias. I was repelled by both groups, who obediently imitated the older politicians, both left and right, issuing grandiose resolutions on global policy, all designed to please their mentors.

Once Cord Meyer and his clique reduced liberal idealism into factional wrangling, I threw myself into psychological research. As a graduate-intern I was required to spend four years in clinics and hospitals. Here was another disillusion. Most diagnostic and therapeutic routines seemed calculated to make the disturbed patient feel even more helpless.

The high point of the psychiatric process was a ritual called the staff meeting, in which the officiants assembled along a rectangular table. At the head sat the ranking psychiatrist, chairman of the board, surrounded by executive M.D.s. Next came the Ph.D. psychologists. At the end of the table were the social workers, usually female.

The social worker would present case history data and gossip about the patient. The psychologists would summarize the results of diagnostic tests. The psychiatrists would finalize the decision about the patient's fate. The commodity being processed, of course, was barred from this exchange of information.

These assessments were extremely unscientific, completely lacking in objectivity: each clinician tended to repeat favored diagnostic epithets. One doctor, for example, found latent homosexuality in everyone; another seemed engrossed with repressed incest feelings. These Star Chamber procedures were demeaning and unhelpful to the patient. I couldn't understand why clinical judgments were kept from the person who had the real need-to-know.

The pudding hit the fan when I suggested that patients should have access to their own files.

"That would be very confusing and dangerous," sputtered one medic.

"The solution, then," I said, "is to write nothing about the patient that isn't factual and constructive. Even if you believe the patient is very sick . . . surely the patient, of all people, should know this. To withhold such vital information breeds the very paranoia you are diagnosing."

I wanted psychology to be an objective discipline, like physics, dealing with specific measurable movements of elements within space/time. A few days in the physics library presented a solution to me. I realized that each unit of human behavior—each gesture, each idea, each word—could be defined as a particle with direction, velocity, force. So, during my third year of graduate studies, I started looking around for an environment where human interactions could be measured like nuclear particles colliding with each other. In physics a place where particles are accelerated, stripped free from their atomic structure, and measured by their paths is called a cyclotron. I saw a need for a *psychlotron*—a place where human elements could be freed, accelerated to higher states of intensity, and recorded.

I did not know how to generate the required intensity in human beings, usually trapped in inhibiting social situations. Group therapy was popping up on the fringes of the profession but was considered radical, reckless, possibly a violation of the sacred doctor-patient relationship. To allow neurotic patients to assemble in groups to discuss their problems made as much sense to a medically-trained analyst in 1948 as allowing surgical patients to gather around and operate on each other. But I felt it was possible that group therapy might create a *psychlotron* effect, giving me the opportunity to study the collisions of human interaction. My plan was to record group therapy sessions, transcribe the verbal interactions, and develop a scheme for classifying the units of human behavior, just as Mendeleev did for the chemical elements.

The plan ran into all kinds of bureaucratic objections. For starters, no respectable clinic would allow graduate students to run group therapy sessions, much less record them. This problem was solved, as such problems often are, when I went to an "outsider" organization, in this case the Unitarian Church of Berkeley, pastored by an intelligent feisty minister, J. Raymond Cope. When presented with the challenge, Cope said he would recruit students from his flock.

To pull off such a project required additional help. Two other graduate students, Mervin Freedman and Abel Ossorio, agreed to join me in a group doctoral dissertation, violating yet another academic taboo. Ph.D.

dissertations were supposed to be individual exercises closely supervised by a faculty sponsor, not group enterprises conducted in a church. The department heavies were not impressed by the argument that in physics dozens of graduate students write theses using data from one reactor.

Help eventually came from two professors, "outsiders" within the psychology department: Hugh Coffey, the resident radical, and Jean Walker McFarlane, the only woman on the scene with any political power.

The lessons learned in this graduate school research were useful in the later Harvard drug studies. Rule number one: work with influential officials on the fringes of the system. Rule number two: use the prestige of the institution while remaining as far as possible from its center. Rule number three: find closet individualists within the system to protect you.

WINTER 1962-1963
HARVARD UNIVERSITY

While homelife blossomed in our multi-family household, things at the office were not as cheerful. Most of our colleagues in the psychology department still couldn't take the brain-change work seriously. It wasn't a question of professional credibility. Our group, all Ph.D.s, had mastered the puritan tradition of American education. We had played the game of academic degrees, had honored the traditional subject matter. Personally they liked and respected us. But they couldn't admit that our new subject matter even existed. Moreover, the professional language we had in common lacked concepts for the types of data our experiments were producing. Altered states of consciousness simply didn't exist as a category in the psychology of that time. It was the familiar tunnel vision that has always narrowed the academic mind.

It probably didn't help our image that the project began attracting adepts and teachers of the more esoteric disciplines. One of our guests, Swami Vishnudananda, conducted a magnificent demonstration of hatha yoga and psychomotor efficiency in the seminar room at the Center for Personality Research, performing a headstand on the conference table while clad in a loincloth. Probably a first for Harvard. Gayatri Devi, the Vedanta guru, dropped by periodically to exchange *darshan*, sometimes bringing along a few of her wealthy Back Bay devotees, who seemed as titillated by our breezy brand of experimental yoga as our conservative colleagues were aghast.

While most of the faculty did their best to take no notice, a number of federally-funded psychiatrists were interested in checking us out. Stanley Krippner, student of altered states, took his first drug sessions with us. He later became America's expert on psychic phenomena behind the Iron Curtain. Martin Orne, a brilliant CIA-funded consciousness researcher, was sometimes to be seen in our kitchen drinking coffee and

asking intelligent questions about the relationship of drug states to hypnosis.

One fall afternoon I received a phone call from Mary Pinchot, my
mysterious visitor from Washington. "Can you meet me right away in
Room 717, Ritz Hotel?"

At the door I paused to smooth my shirt in my trousers and hand-brush
my hair. Enchanting as before, she motioned to a silver ice bucket with
a bottle of Dom Perignon tilting out. "I'm here to celebrate," she said.

I twisted the bottle to make the cork pop gently. "Your hush-hush
love affair is going well?"

"Oh yes. Everything is going beautifully. On all fronts in fact. I can't
give details, of course. But *top* people in Washington are turning on.
You'd be amazed at the sophistication of some of our leaders. And their
wives. We're getting a little group together, people who are interested
in learning how to turn on."

"Really. I thought politicians were too power-oriented."

"You must realize, implausible as it may seem, there are a lot of very
smart people in Washington. Especially now with this administration.
Power *is* important to them. And these drugs do give a certain power.
That's what it's all about. Freeing the mind."

She held out her glass for more champagne. "Until very recently control
of American consciousness was a simple matter for the guys in charge.
The schools instilled docility. The radio and TV networks poured out
conformity."

"No doubt about it," I agreed.

"You may not know that dissident organizations in academia are also
controlled. The CIA creates the radical journals and student organizations
and runs them with deep-cover agents."

"Oh come on, Mary," I said. "That sounds pretty paranoid to me."

Mary sipped at her glass and shook her head. "I hate to be the one
to break the news to you. Do you remember the American Veterans
Committee, that liberal GI group you belonged to after the war? The
CIA started that. Just like Teddy Roosevelt started the American Legion
after the first World War. Remember your liberal friend Gilbert Harrison?
He ran the radicals out of AVC. And later he bought the *New Republic*—
that so-called progressive magazine—from Michael Straight, your hero.
Do you know why Michael Straight backed Henry Wallace for president
in 1948? To siphon liberal votes away from Truman?"

"How do you know all this? How did you know I knew Michael
Straight?"

"I knocked you with those facts to get your attention. It's a standard
intelligence trick. I could tell you hundreds of little stories like that."

She held out her glass again. I filled it, drained and refilled my own.
My head was spinning.

"And guess what these guys are most interested in right now?"

"Drugs, I suppose."

"You got it. A few years ago they became absolutely obsessed with the notion that the Soviets and the Chinese were persuading our POWs in Korea to defect by brainwashing them with LSD and mescaline."

"That's certainly possible. With what we've discovered about set and setting, we know that almost anyone's mind can be changed in any direction."

"Any direction?"

"With a minimum of information about the subject's personal life and two or three LSD sessions, you could get the most conventional person to do outrageous things."

"Suppose the person wanted to be brainwashed in a certain direction . . . wanted to change himself?"

"Easier yet. Our research is conclusive on this. Changing your mind, developing a new reality-fix, is a simple and straightforward proposition. Of course, altering your mind is one thing. Changing the outside world to conform to your new vision remains the difficult problem for us . . ." I struggled for a word. "Utopiates."

Mary clapped her hands together like a birthday girl. "Utopiates! Beautiful. That's what it's all about, isn't it? Make it a better world." She sat down next to me and held my hand.

"Let's make a deal, as one utopiate to another. I'll tell you some things about yourself that are very important and then you'll tell me the same."

"What do you want to know?"

She laughed. "Let me start off. Since drug research is of vital importance to the intelligence agencies of this country, you'll be allowed to go on with your experiments as long as you keep it quiet. You are doing exploratory work the CIA tried to do in the 1950s. So they're more than happy to have you do their research for them. As long as it doesn't get out of hand."

"What do you mean, 'out of hand'?"

"Timothy, think. You're involved in the Big Game here. Mind-change is the key to power. They'll deal with you about the same way the Soviets would handle a nuclear physicist with liberal, libertarian ideals. They'll indulge your utopian fantasies. They know that creative scientists tend to be free-thinkers. They'll run you with a loose silken cord as long as you don't stir up the masses."

"Okay, I'll try not to stir up the masses. And what can I do for you?"

"I told you the first time we met. I want to learn how to brainwash."

"That doesn't sound very ladylike."

At this she burst into laughter. "If I can teach the use of utopiates to the wives and mistresses of important people in our government, then we can . . . well shit, Timothy, don't you see what we can do?"

"What?"

"We can do on a bigger scale what you are already doing with your students—use these drugs to free people. For peace, not war. We can turn on the Cabinet. Turn on the Senate. The Supreme Court. Do I have to explain further?"

Her proposal was scary. But come to think of it, it was close to what we Harvardites in our session rooms, lazily architecturing hopeful futures, had spelled out as the goal of psychedelic research.

I looked at myself in the reflection of the window: a forty-two-year-old man, being lured into a feminist plot to turn on the leaders of the United States government to the idea of world peace. She lay on the bed, pleased with herself, awaiting my reaction, knowing I was going to agree.

"Okay. What do you want from me? The drugs?"

"Just a little bit to get started. With our connections we'll be able to get all the supplies we want. And all you need too. Mainly I want advice about how to run sessions. And how to handle any problems that come up."

We spent the next four hours in a cram course on psychedelic sessions. Set and setting. Centering. Room service brought more champagne and then dinner. I drove her to Logan to get a night plane back to Washington. The next day I mailed off a stack of session reports. Since she had sworn me to secrecy, I told no one except Michael Hollingshead.

That winter the major research tasks were analyzing the reports from our summer studies, continuing the prison project, training new graduate students to run sessions, and bringing into full operation the Experiential Typewriter. The purpose of the E.T. was to deal with the "words cannot express" aspects of accelerated-brain experience. Subjects could indicate any of various levels of consciousness that they were unable to describe at the moment by pressing the appropriate buttons on the typewriter. This signal was recorded on a revolving drum, much the way temperatures are graphed in meteorological stations. After the session, when consciousness was operating at slower speeds, the subject would have leisure to examine the recorded data and describe the sequence of events fully and precisely.

To identify the levels of consciousness (i.e. develop the new software) we had to address a number of questions about the brain as a biocomputer: how is it programmed? what are the circuits that can be accessed? how do these circuits configure the realities we inhabit? Since my first mushroom experience, answering these questions has been my persistent philosophic task.

We identified eight levels of consciousness: stuporous, emotional, symbolic, somatic, sensory, cellular, molecular, and out-of-body. Each level needed a vocabulary. For the emotional and symbolic levels, which lent themselves to verbal description, we were able to use the variables developed during my research in Berkeley. The sensory, cellular, and molecular visions required a non-verbal language. So we collected biology slides and film-strips and overlaid them to create multiple images. We commissioned photographers to make enlargements of cellular activity. The walls of our offices and our living room oozed and dripped with technicolored bacterial pulsations and protozoan encounters.

The auditory vocabularies were the most novel. We assembled a tape library of heartbeats, sound-amplified brain waves, electronic tones, capillary flows, avalanches, heavy breathing, erotic moans, cheering (supportive), cheering (aroused), mob hostility (in twenty-four languages), cash registers, firecrackers, football scrimmages, high tides, whale whistles. We were producing, however crudely, a language for externalizing the aural panoramas that are experienced during moments of transcendence.

These new linguistic devices had an intense effect on visitors. Almost everyone got a bit high in one way or another when exposed to the feedback of bodily images. Many sober types confronted with unfamiliar yet very personal sensory and neural data had to be helped staggering and retching from the room.

We devoted much of our energy to creating environments that would guide consciousness away from the mundane-local into new dimensions. With this in mind we constructed the Time Chamber.

Adjacent to one of our living rooms was a medium-sized study. We sealed off the door and repapered the wall on the living room side so that the existence of the room was hidden. I climbed through a window into the hidden study and used a power saw to slice out a yard-square opening in the hardwood floor. In the cellar we constructed a dark tunnel that led up a ladder and into the enclosed room, now covered, walls and ceiling, with Hindu paisley prints of cellular design. Red velvet cushions covered the floor. At the far end, illuminated by candles in ornate holders, sat a smiling bronze Buddha, which Peggy Mellon Hitchcock generously provided. In this secret chamber, a modern version of Tom Sawyer's clubhouse, it was easy to forget, on drugs or straight, where you were in the house or indeed on the planet. It was an early isolation tank.

The Time Chamber experiments did not work for everyone. Charlie Mingus frequently boomed up to our front door, lugging his bass and full of delightful paranoias. Pounding out jazz improvisations on the piano, he would want to time travel. But heave and push as we might, his ponderous form would not fit through the entrance of the Chamber.

A more lithe visitor was Jean Houston. Fresh from winning off-Broadway dramatic prizes and a Ph.D. in anthropology she was eager to share her thoughts about altered states. She stalked regally through our house, acting out historical monologues—Alexander the Great at the pyramids, on the wine dark sea to Crete, down the yellow-mud Nile to the city that bears his name. She stiffly imitated Egyptian bas-reliefs, chanted mystic poetry, took us hiking through the moors on full-moon nights to Stonehenge. She gave us our first view of the new breed of liberated woman. She presented herself as a philosopher-queen, and we adored her.

Unlike the philosophers telling us to keep our brain-drugs elitist and private Jean believed that science, not religion, was the social institution that could domesticate the use of psychedelics. Not for her these old-time cabals and secret men's clubs. She urged us to go respectably public, rejecting the quiescence and anti-scientific bias of Eastern religions. "What's all this talk about brotherly love, quasi-Eastern mysticism. Galloping *agape!* Male scholars taking drugs and sitting in the lotus position looking wise at each other."

Jean's plan was to get more respectable scientists and psychotherapists involved in the use of brain-drugs. Her tough-minded American common sense brought us back to the tradition of William James. Western logic, western optimism, western empiricism, western drugs.

Jean Houston never joined our project. We were too raffish, too ready for anything. But we were much influenced by her.

Meanwhile our researches were doing fine. We were busy publishing articles in scientific journals, delivering papers at scientific conferences. Experimenters from around the world were coming to observe our work.

The drug enthusiasm of Harvard undergraduates continued to haunt us. In this, the third year of our research, the Yard was seething with drug consciousness. If we prudishly refused to turn them on, no big deal. They scored supplies from Boston or New York. Several enterprising chemistry students constructed home labs to make the stuff themselves. For the most part the drug epidemic sweeping Cambridge seemed benign. Hundreds of Harvard students expanded their minds, had visions, read mystical literature, and wrote intelligent essays about their experiences. It seemed to us they were benefiting.

Inevitably the occasional mishaps caught the attention of the authorities. A few fellows ran to the psychiatric clinic to gasp about their trips. Their flamboyant stories about altered states shocked the inexperienced medics.

"You felt your body dissolve into a pool of honey? Psychotic thinking."

Some students quit school and pilgrimaged eastward to study yoga on the banks of the Ganges: not necessarily a bad development from our point of view but understandably upsetting to parents, who did not send their kids to Harvard to become buddhas. The worst problems arose from the chronic tendency of students to tell everyone *everything*. Dozens of bright youths phoned home to announce that they'd found God and discovered the secret of the universe. The deans became edgy about complaints from parents.

The Harvard administration was caught in a bind. They were solidly in support of our research, which was winning international attention, but they were hard pressed to defend us against the anti-drug backlash. The deans honestly shared their dilemma with Dick and me. We understood their concerns and resumed our search for less restrictive surroundings.

There were other problems. Our graduate students and young instructors were picking up an ominous signal from the more conservative faculty members that their careers would be ruined if they remained associated with our research. Since the academic profession operates on old-boy networks and reference letters, this threat was serious. Professor Brendan Maher, our old rival, spelled it out in conversations with some of our graduate students. "This drug-taking is a campus fad like goldfish-swallowing. Can you really expect to be recommended for a good job if your research here involves schoolboy pranks?"

Under the old-boy tenure system graduate students who didn't fall in line, who manifested interest in non-approved frontier questions, were quickly labeled "flaky." As Kuhn pointed out in the *The Structure of Scientific Revolutions*, almost all intellectual breakthroughs have been produced by mavericks pushed out of and operating independently of establishment knowledge systems.[1]

The older members of our group—Alan Watts, Houston Smith, Walter Clark, Dick, and I—were disturbed by this threat to our younger friends. We called a meeting of everyone involved in the research, families included. More than thirty crowded into the big kitchen at our house. People sat on the stove, the refrigerator, the counters, the floor. Dick outlined the problem. We agreed that as much as we loved and respected the University, this finishing school for Fortune 500 executives was not the place for the philosophic activists bent on changing practically everything.

The honorable thing to do was to dissociate from Harvard and form a new organization. Dick would stay on at Harvard. He had skillfully wangled a joint appointment in the Education Department, which kept the door open for a permanent tenure post.

I felt little emotion at leaving beyond a nostalgic regret. Exits were becoming one of my areas of expertise. I remained on friendly terms with Professor McClelland, and we were both pleased that my departure would be courteous and dignified.

We chose a name for the new drug research project: International Foundation for Internal Freedom, shortened to the wry acronym IFIF. The aim was to set up research centers across America to conduct psychedelic drug training sessions. Each local center would have medical, psychological, and legal advisors on staff to teach members to explore their internal geography. Artists, writers, religious folk, and searchers for meaning would be welcome. Neurotics and those seeking psychiatric treatment would be referred out to doctors. The national headquarters would publish a scholarly journal (the *Psychedelic Review* edited by Ralph Metzner), help locals to obtain good-quality drugs, and coordinate summer workshops in Mexico. The drugs we were researching—psilocybin, mescaline, and LSD—were still legal at this time.

Dick and I wrote a letter to the Harvard *Crimson* outlining our plans. The Boston papers picked up the story, which then went out on the wire services: Harvard Profs Announce Plans for Nation-Wide Chain of Drug Centers. The publicity stirred up considerable response. Within a few weeks over a thousand people sent in ten dollars each to join, and we were avalanched with inquiries. By May 1963 we received over 500 applications for the summer program, and of these aspiring neuronauts 300 were accepted.

Mexico, once again, seemed like the ideal spot for a temporary hegira. The leading Mexican industrial psychologist Elliot Danzig and his wife Dolores, who had both been turned on by George Litwin, were eager to offer their influence in local affairs. My contacts with Mexican psychiatrists, built up over the years, promised solid medical support. There were adequate funds to put several psychiatrists on the payroll as consultants.

In April we had received a letter from a Dr. Bill Brunell, an organic chemist who worked for a Milwaukee brewery. Having researched the chemistry of brain-change drugs for several years, he was anxious for a chance to apply his knowledge. We flew him into Boston straightaway, spending two days with him and colleagues in the Harvard Business School. Brunell knew how to make LSD, psilocybin, mescaline in commercial quantities. In addition, he had experience synthesizing other exotic psychobotanicals. Brunell was eager to obtain a laboratory and the commercial backing to manufacture them.

The plan called for me to fly to Mexico and organize the legal, medical, political backing. I was also to make a deal with a top Mexican pharmaceutical firm to bring Brunell down and put him to work. IFIF would become sponsor of the world's largest organization for research and production of mind-change drugs. Our business administration consultants predicted that in five years we could become one of the largest drug manufacturers in the world. Since IFIF was non-profit, all the revenues would be ploughed back into research and education.

We knew that our program to teach the intelligent use of drugs was as threatening in 1963 as the notion of sex education had been a generation before. We were convinced that society would eventually come to terms with this responsibility, just as it had, out of common sense, with sex education. It was only logical that people would ultimately demand instruction in how to use drugs intelligently. In the next decade billions would be spent in futile enforcement and anti-drug disinformation programs. We knew even then that training in responsible use is the only way to prevent abuse.

As the time for my departure from Harvard approached, it seemed only right to leave a farewell note in the *Harvard Review*, a classy journal edited by undergraduates. The editors had decided to publish a school-end issue devoted to *Drugs and the Mind*. The co-editor was Andrew Weil, who later was to become a world authority on consciousness-altering plants.

Entitled "The Politics of Consciousness Expansion," our article included these section headlines: "Expansion and Contraction is the Rhythm of the Universe," "The Ancient Game: Visionary vs Cop," "The Hippy vs Square Argument is a Bore," "The Next Lunge Forward: Internal Freedom," "Cortical Vitamins: Turn On or Bail Out," "The Visionary Automobile," "Who Controls the Instruments of Freedom?" and "The Fifth Freedom: To Change Your own Consciousness." I have often wondered how many of the sponsors of the *Harvard Review* read this article. It included the following paragraph:

> Can you imagine a language without such words as convertible, accelerator, transmission, General Motors, U.A.W., Standard Oil, super-highway, parking ticket, traffic court? These commonplace terms in our present culture were mystical images three generations. . . .
>
> It is possible that in 20 years our psychological and experiential language (pitifully small in English) will have multiplied to cover realms of experience and forms of thinking now unknown. In 20 years every social institution will have been transformed by new insights provided by consciousness expanding experiences. Many new social institutions will have developed to handle the expression of the potentiated nervous system.

A few days before my departure for Mexico a phone call came from Mary Pinchot. I hadn't talked to her in several weeks. Could I meet her again at the Ritz? She sounded tense.

She was. When I walked in the room there was no bubbling champagne, no happy smiles. "I had to see you. Things are getting more complicated. I got exposed publicly."

"The drug experiments?" I asked, in mild alarm.

"No. Everything there is going fine. It's my love affair." She walked to the phone. "Let's order something. Are you hungry?"

"No, just coffee. Tell me what happened."

"Oh God, where to begin. Well, there's a tremendous power struggle going on in Washington. A friend of mine was losing the battle, a really bloody one. He got drunk and told a room full of reporters about me and my boyfriend."

"Your boyfriend's married, I gather."

Hollow laugh. "To say the least."

"Was there much publicity? I didn't read anything about a big Washington scandal."

"No, here's the scary part. Not a word printed about it."

"That's scary," I said.

"It's really scary. You wouldn't believe how well-connected some of these people are, and nobody picked it up."

There came a sharp knock on the door. We both jumped, then looked at each other and laughed. After the room service waiter left, Mary came over and hugged me.

"Don't let me get you alarmed. There's nothing really new in what I've been telling you. I've seen it a hundred times in media politics. The manipulation of news, cover ups, misinformation, dirty tricks. Because of the drugs I can now step back and see what's going on and the horror of it. Now I see that it doesn't have to be that way. America doesn't have to be run by these cold-war guys. They're crazy, they really are. They don't listen. They don't learn. They're completely caught up in planning World War III. They can't enjoy anything except power and control."

"But that's where you're supposed to come in," I said. "You're going to loosen them up."

Mary stopped pacing.

"You're so right. Thank you. You restore my hope. I guess that's why I came to see you."

"Why don't you come to Mexico this summer and get some intensive training. You'll become the best brainwasher since Cleopatra."

"Don't get carried away," she said dryly. "I'm too exposed already. And you should be careful too. Things are getting edgy in Washington. As we start loosening things up, there's bound to be a reaction. Keep doing what you're doing, but try to keep it low key. If you stir up too many waves, they'll shut you down." She paused for effect. "Or worse."

"How can I get in touch with you?"

"I don't trust the phones or the mail," she said. "I'll stay in touch with you. And do be careful."[2]

C **ARLOS CASTANEDA** was born either in Brazil (1935) or in Peru (1925). Conflicting stories leave his early years a mystery. As a graduate student in anthropology at UCLA he visited Mexico to study with shamans, real or imaginary, who used hallucinogenic plants.

In 1968 he published *The Teachings of Don Juan,* a gripping account of his experiences with peyote and psilocybin under the guidance of a pedantic, rather paranoid Yaqui trickster-teacher named don Juan Matus. Subsequent popular books include *A Separate Reality* and *Journey to Ixtlan,* which was accepted as his doctoral dissertation.

Castaneda's theories about altered states of consciousness may have come from a Yaqui sorcerer, although there is no evidence that Don Juan exists. Even skeptics have applauded Castaneda's sorcerer skill in acquainting millions of readers with the existence of separate realities.

In *The Eagle's Gift* (1981) Castaneda claims to have attained sorcerer status. Most observers would agree. He seems to have pulled off one of the most flamboyant and successful literary hoaxes of the twentieth century, a Zen-master demonstration of the power of the detached warrior to construct his own profitable universe.[1]

20. Earthly Paradise

MAY 1963
MEXICO

I arrived in Mexico City loaded with IFIF money, ready to activate our plans. Step One: I found a lawyer who specialized in handling the affairs of chemical companies. Step Two: I met with Dr. Carl Djarassi, Stanford biochemist, who was using a Mexican chemical laboratory to manufacture his controversial, and successful, contraception pill. Djarassi gave me useful advice. Step Three: Dr. Brunell and I spent several days visiting large pharmaceutical companies. Brunell, who knew his stuff, knocked the socks off the local drug experts. The factory owners were even more impressed with the forecasted profit of our proposals, which indeed looked dazzling. (As it turned out, our projections were extremely conservative, just a fraction of the eighty billion dollars that the non-addictive revelation-recreation drugs would generate annually by 1982.)

The basic strategy, we kept repeating, was responsible distribution. Only doctors trained at IFIF centers could prescribe the new drugs and only to IFIF members. Our prudence was all the more virtuous since in 1963 psychedelic drugs were legal—anyone could buy unlimited quantities.

Mexico City was ringed with American and Swiss pharmaceutical firms manufacturing amphetamines and narcotics.

In these discussions with Mexican psychiatrists, politicians, and businessmen we pointed out that Mexico could become the next Switzerland, the first country to produce psychedelics on a large scale. We presented documents listing top scientists and intellectuals who had agreed to come to our training centers. Brunell and I signed a contract with a drug company in which we agreed to order the base materials, and the special equipment. The lawyers drew up details of the partnership. We lunched with a top government official, who was to be a paid consultant. We kept repeating the need for careful selection, responsible distribution.

We hired a suite of offices near the University of Mexico. Brunell flew back to Milwaukee to settle his affairs; he was to return in a month to set up for production.

Oscar, the owner of the Hotel Catalina, agreed to stay around long enough to teach me the operation, and then we would be on our own for the summer. Within a few days students and staff began arriving, and we started the training routine.

One afternoon a jeep raced into the compound driven by the captain of the port. It seemed that I was being called on shortwave radio from Mexico City. Urgent. He drove me to his office, and there crackling with static came the voice of a *Newsweek* reporter saying that Richard Alpert and I had been fired by Harvard University. Did I have any comments? I said something brash to the effect that I was honored and it couldn't have happened to two nicer guys.

The captain, a handsome athletic fellow in a yachtsman cap, drove me back to the hotel. "Good news, Senor Teem?" he asked me in Spanish.

I shrugged and flipped my hand in that Latin non-committal gesture.

I changed into trunks and swam out to the motor boat moored in the bay. As I lay in the sun listening to the waves lap against the hull, I tried to sort out my feelings.

My first reaction: my mother would be very upset. Second: why had they fired me when I had already left for good? Professor McClelland was away from the campus, and our old rival Brendan Maher was in charge. Apparently he meant to discredit us. Remembering the conversations with Inspector O'Connell and Mary Pinchot I felt a flicker of fear about the security of our Mexican project.

A telegram came from Dick the next day confirming the news. He was not coming to Mexico but would stay in Boston to administer the affairs of IFIF, which were booming. Our firing attracted wide coverage, much of it sympathetic. The media announced that it was the first time in 300 years that Harvard had fired faculty members. They didn't recall that a similar fate had befallen Ralph Waldo Emerson.

The official reason for my sacking was that I failed to show up for classes. A phony rap: I had completed all my course work.

Dick was ousted for something more romantic. He got caught in the middle of a love triangle involving an editor on the Harvard *Crimson* staff. It seemed that Dick had been turning on a brilliant and handsome student (heir to a famous American fortune) whose friend, racked by jealousy, denounced Dick in a fiery editorial. Dick's violation of our promise not to give drugs to undergraduates was thus brought to the attention of the authorities.

It's against the rules of the Association of College Professors to fire a faculty member without a hearing. Although civil liberties groups and the Association expressed a willingness to file suit against Harvard, we didn't want to waste time on litigation. I didn't want to be a professor anyway.

The Harvard firing was painful for me because of my mother. She claimed it wasn't the disgrace of the firing that hurt her but the fact that I hadn't told her myself. She learned the news from neighbors. This distressing event marked the end of our forty-three-year-old friendship. She had always supported me in my escapades and rejoiced in my comebacks. But the Harvard firing and the scandals that followed just couldn't be explained away to her circle of retired Irish-Catholic schoolteachers. During the last decade of her life, when the ladies gathered for tea to gossip about their families, no one ever mentioned the name of her son the doctor. Aunt Mae's worst expectations of the Leary family were now confirmed.

My concern with the Harvard firing was swept away by the rapid influx of guests. Within a few days we realized that we were developing the ultimate-destination resort. Hotel Nirvana. No one wanted to leave. Folks who came down for a week or two started signing up for the whole summer.

We built a twenty-five-foot meditation tower on the beach. Each day at noon a volunteer scrambled up the rope ladder, dropped acid, and spent the next twenty-four hours aloft, coming down for earth-side adventures when that promised more fun. Because the tower could be seen from every point on the grounds, it provided a sense of unity. We told the Mexican staff it was a lifeguard station.

We were a varied group of adventurers—two psychiatrists, a Hasidic rabbi, three businessmen (one kicking a booze habit), and lots of graduate students and young college instructors and families. The editor of *Gourmet* Magazine struck up a fast friendship with our chef. The Hollywood contingent and the Yale Divinity School group were scheduled to arrive in July, as well as psychiatrists and philosophy professors from Europe and observers from the Mexican Psychiatric Association. We were approached by hotel owners from all over Mexico inquiring about franchises.

Back in Cambridge the IFIF offices were humming. International publicity. The Zihuatanejo experiment was an irresistible media event, a resort scene where people got high safely and respectably. As a matter of policy we booked guests from the same city at the same time so they could work together and then return to set up local chapters.

The rhythm of life at the hotel was blissful. Nights the dining patio was candlelit. We gathered in small groups, playing chess, strumming guitars, listening to talks on the brain or the history of mysticism, assimilating the wonderful pagan knack of just hanging out. Guests took acid once a week and spent the rest of the time contemplating, playing, and discussing their trips.

In addition to the routine of one acid trip a week I was very busy with mundane affairs, managing a hotel with twenty-four employees and forty-five guests. I paid the wages, issued supplies, sweated in the jungle with the engineer repairing the pump and the generator, attended weddings and christenings of our village, chatted up the mayor and the captain of the port, kept the night watchman out of the liquor, arbitrated the domestic problems of employees.

Everyone was having the time of their lives. But Eden was not without its serpents. The publicity brought groups of hippies—broke, unkempt, begging for food, shelter, and cosmic illumination. At first we established a hospitality ritual of allowing these pilgrims to stay for twenty-four hours, but this policy didn't work because they spent the time wheeling and dealing to stay longer. So we arranged a shuttle boat to take them immediately across the bay to a public beach where they could camp out. Some of the hippies became outraged when asked to leave, and a few returned to Mexico City and told lurid tales about us to Americans residing in the capital.

The most colorful and persistent of these uninvited guests appeared one afternoon while I was lying on a hammock in front of my cottage, listening to the birds and the rumbling of the surf. Manuel the bartender came down to tell me that a visitor had arrived for Dr. Alpert, who was still in Cambridge.

The visitor appeared to be Mexican. Dressed in a dark suit he approached me with combined eagerness and deference. "Dr. Alpert, I am so glad to meet you. My name is Arana, a journalist from Peru. I have traveled all this way to observe your work here."

"Thanks for your interest, Mr. Arana, but we do not allow observers."

"Dr. Alpert, I beg you to listen. We are twins, soul-brothers. My father, like yours, is the president of a railroad in Peru. And I am Jewish like yourself. Isn't that amazing?"

"Mr. Arana, I'm not Dr. Alpert, and we have a policy of no visitors. I'll be glad to give you copies of our papers."

The hotel station wagon was being loaded up for a run to the village, so I popped Arana aboard, shook his hand, and went back to my hammock.

The next morning Raphael the hotel engineer met me with a solemn face. His aunt Theresa, a medicine woman, had come to him with an ominous story. She had been visited the previous night by a Latin American named Arana, who said he was a professor in a big University in California. This professor claimed that he was studying to be a "warrior of the soul" and needed Theresa's assistance in sorcery. He said his powers were being blocked by a certain person, a *norte americano* who possessed great magic stolen from the Mexican Indians. Arana wanted her to help steal the magic back so that he, a Latino, could protect the Mexican people.

"Who is this *norte americano* who stole the magic?"

"You, Senor Timoteo. This man Arana says that the name of our hotel, 'La Catalina,' is the name of a bad witch-woman who is his enemy. He didn't know that all of Theresa's family work here at the hotel."

"What did Theresa do?"

"She told him that you were a good man under her protection. He got very upset and left, swearing he would not rest until he had stolen your magic."

The next day Arana showed up again, wreathed in smiles. He was accompanied by a sweet-faced American hippy wearing a native dress.

"Dr. Leary, I have come to apologize. It was stupid of me to confuse you with Dr. Alpert. I was so nervous about being here that I forgot to tell you an important message from Maria Sabina. She sent me with a personal gift for you."

Maria Sabina, the *curandera* who had turned on mycologist Robert Wasson, was a great cultural heroine to me.

"Maria wants you to visit her, and she sent you these candles and this power object."

Arana handed me two ordinary church candles and a nondescript leather bag. When I shook it open, some yellow crystals the size of walnuts rolled out. They gave off a pungent odor.

"That is copal, the sacred incense of the Mazatecs. Burn it during your drug sessions."

"You called this a power object," I said. "I thought Maria Sabina was a healer."

Arana laughed scornfully. "There are many things people think about Maria Sabina, but the truth can only be told from her lips. She asked me to share some of her secrets with you."

"What kind of secrets?"

"How to become a man of knowledge, *hombre de conocimientos*. A sorcerer."

"What exactly do you want from me?" I asked.

"To share your knowledge. I want to follow in your footsteps. I have learned much from the Indians of Oaxaca and Peru and northern Mexico. I can share their magic with you. We can both become stronger."

"I'm sorry, Mr. Arana, you're mistaken. I'm not a sorcerer and have no desire to become one. I'm a scientist."

"I too am trying to be a scientist," replied Arana. "Like you I was thrown out of my university for experimenting with mushrooms. My stories about these primitive Indians like Maria Sabina are for your information. I too detest methods of trickery. That is why I'm here, a poor student, to learn from you about the western way of scientific knowledge."

"I'm sorry I can't invite you to stay. Registration for our summer courses has to be made in Boston."

"But I have no place to sleep. I have borrowed money to come visit you."

"Don't worry. Across the bay at Los Gatos beach there's a man named Manolo who runs a campground. Here's ten dollars. You can stay there a couple of days. There are lots of American pilgrims and searchers like yourself. I'm sure you'll learn a lot from them. I'll have the boat take you across."

I excused myself and went to look for the boatman. I ran into Arana's companion in the bar. Her name was Linda. "We can't stay here, right?"

"You can camp out across the bay. I'd like you to do me a favor."

"What favor?"

"Stop by here on your way back. I'd like to find out what's happening over there."

1930-1935
CAMP NORWICH, BERKSHIRE HILLS

The experience of dealing with altered states of human evolution in a pastoral setting was not new to me.

During my tenth to fifteenth years I attended a summer camp in the Berkshires. We lived in lodges named after Indian tribes: Seneca, Mohican, Iroquois. The morning wake-up gun boomed over the lake. The bugle sounded reveille. After my second year I became the one who pulled the cord on the cannon. At sunrise the lake, misting slightly, was warmer to the naked skin than the morning air.

We fished the west shore in skiffs and found secret caves for our clubs. We learned forest lore, identifying trees and mushrooms, and while the counselor slept, we tracked the wildcat to his lair. We chased bulls in Farmer McKinney's pastures. The sun was hot on our tanned hides, except when sudden New England lightning storms crashed around the hills and blew chill raindrops against the canvas tent walls.

Oh the pageantry! Cookouts, ghost-stories, treasure hunts, overnight hikes. The main camp-wide competition, interestingly enough, was based on the adventurous traffic in drugs made illegal during Prohibition. The camp was divided into Smugglers and Coast Guard. The bootlegger team tried to smuggle empty gallon cans across the lake and through the woods to the baseball diamond. When captured, smugglers were imprisoned on the basketball court—until rescued in daring raids by fellow bootleggers. By a toss of the coin I was assigned to the Smugglers.

During my third summer a lumbering mental defective, eighteen years old, whose wealthy family contributed heavily to the foundation that ran the camp, arrived in our lodge. The counselor asked me to look out for the monster, as he was called.

Edgar sat on his trunk the first afternoon, muttering and giggling. The rest of us avoided him. Suddenly he uttered a strange cry and fell to his knees, cooing to a caterpillar on the floor.

"Ooooh. Hello, little friend. Isn't she cute!"

I was stunned. Any of the average little brutes in the lodge would have crushed the insect or popped it into a buddy's bunk.

Each lodge had to come up with a skit to be acted out in front of the entire camp. I suggested that our lodge act out a play about Sherlock Holmes. There was great rivalry for the role of the master detective, but I insisted that the monster be the star. The drama was rehearsed casually. Dominating the boards as the aristocratic detective was the lumbering Edgar, triumphantly stuttering, leering, and scowling cheerfully as he declaimed his lines. I played the faithful Dr. Watson. Whenever Edgar missed a cue Dr. Watson would pull a paper from his pocket and study it intently: Holmes' great bushy head would lean down to examine the paper also, and I would whisper the lines half-audibly to him. The play was a super-hit. Edgar and I were invited to perform at camp reunions during the winter season.

The popularity of our show influenced my later thinking. My natural tendency to look for the unusual, the risky, the reversal of stereotypes, thus early rewarded, re-emerged in my practice as a clinical psychologist, where I tended to approach a patient, however disturbed, as I did Edgar—as a friend and collaborator. Edgar taught me how to befriend the monster that coils within the cells of us all.

MAY 1963
MEXICO

The next day, on the boat bringing fresh fish and buckets of shrimp from Los Gatos, Linda returned.

"How did it go?" I asked.

"Well Arana walked into this camp of hippies across the bay with a big shit-eating grin on his face, and he said, 'Hi, friends! I'm Carlos from Los Angeles, and I'm here to get zonked out!' That entrance didn't go over. I mean, everyone else was being mellow, and in comes this Mexican guy dressed like a narc. Then he starts putting down your whole scene. He said you guys were crazy. That your drugs just rearranged the old glosses. What's a gloss?"

"Your karma."

"Anyway he was so uncool no one would have anything to do with him. At one point he was showing off some magic tricks and pulled a banana out of his trousers. Finally a couple of guys took him aside and told him to get lost."

"So he left?"

"Yeah, he went on the boat and that was the end of him."

"Let's hope he catches on somewhere down the line."

Meanwhile the global publicity continued. *Life* arranged to send a reporter and photographer in July. CBS, NBC, and the BBC, as well as several European networks, planned stories on us. We were turning on the world to something new.

One thing that didn't happen was the visit from Mary Pinchot. I received a short cryptic note, postmarked Washington, D.C., typed and unsigned.

PROGRAM GOING VERY WELL HERE. EXTREMELY WELL!!! HOW-EVER, I WON'T BE JOINING YOU. TOO MUCH PUBLICITY. YOUR SUMMER CAMP IS IN SERIOUS JEOPARDY. I'LL CONTACT YOU AFTER YOU RETURN TO USA.

Then we received a new variety of uninvited guest: two agents of the federal police. *Buenos Dias, Comandantes!* Jorge Garcia was youngish, good-looking, and amused. The other was older and sour-faced, Juan Blicero.

They sat down in the dining area and summoned me to a meeting. They didn't waste words. We were being closed down by the federales. Why? Because we were besmirching the name of Mexico with all this bad publicity. Juan pulled out a Mexico City newspaper. The headline: Harvard Drug Orgy Blamed for Decomposing Body.

"What decomposing body?" I gasped.

A corpse had been found in a village a hundred miles away.

"What does that have to do with us?"

"Why it's very clear. The press blames you, and that sort of public scandal is intolerable."

They showed me another newspaper article, based on reports from hippies we had turned away. They accused us of marijuana orgies, hairy women, black magic, venereal disease, and profiteering.

"Ask anyone here—the staff, the mayor, the local police. We are good people."

"Yes, Doctor, we have heard that too," said Jorge Garcia, the younger policeman. "The formal reason you must go is that you have tourist visas and are not authorized to run a business in Mexico."

The expulsion order would take effect in a week, which gave me time to fly up to the capital to see what could be done. I was stunned but hopeful that the order could be changed. Since the next plane left in two days, the policemen had to stay over. I invited them to be our guests.

During the next day and a half Jorge looked over our place and the people in it. He talked at length with the help. Toward sunset he asked me to walk with him on the beach. We spoke in Spanish.

"Listen, Doctor Leary. I have learned a lot about you. You are what we call a *philosophico loco*. I have talked to the Mexicans here, and what they told me makes me want to take your drug. But you are foolish because you are not practical enough. For example, you charge $300 a month for your guests. My friend, everyone in the world wants what you are offering. But they should pay a fair price. Now listen. My brother is the governor of the State of Michoacan. Let them close you down here. Then you come to my state, and we'll open two or maybe three hotels like this. And we'll charge what the average Acapulco hotel gets: $2,000 a month. You have no objection to being rich, do you?"

For the first time in two days I felt a flicker of optimism.

It was agreed that Jorge would pull strings in the capital to allow me to remain in Mexico. He would arrange a banquet at a fine restaurant where I could meet and talk to the backers he lined up.

On arriving in Mexico City I phoned Dick in Cambridge. It was the first time we had talked since our expulsion from Harvard. He said that some friends were en route to Mexico City with a big-shot Mexican wheeler-dealer, who guaranteed he could bribe us back into the country.

I spent the next day with my lawyer, both of us cooling our heels in the office of the Minister of Health, a pompous fellow who talked about his training at the Menninger Clinic. We hoped to persuade him to rescind the deportation order. He professed himself insulted that we thought we could get away with tricks of this sort in his country.

I pointed out the many wonderful advantages of beginning the intelligence explosion in Mexico and making his land the Switzerland of North America. He wasn't buying it. Many conversations with American authorities had convinced him that I was an undesirable.

That night at the banquet arranged by Jorge I was *mucho* desirable. The Governor of Michoacan sent a top aide to encourage me to move to his state. Having scheduled a meeting with the president the following day they expected easy approval. The president owed the governor many favors. We drank numerous toasts to the future of science and money.

Jorge came by my hotel the next day, brokenhearted. No go. The president himself was handling this matter so there would be no delay in my expulsion. He had received personal calls from the American ambassador, from the CIA, and from Justice Department officials. It was impossible to fix.

The wheeler-dealer checked in with the same story.

When I returned to the hotel, full of the bad tidings, there was more gloomy news waiting. One of the guests, Duane Marvy, an engineer from Boston, had tripped and failed to return to normality after twelve hours. This was our first encounter with an extended "bad trip." I found him sitting on the patio, silent, unresponsive, staring at the sky. Every now and then he jumped up and tried to run away, shouting in a loud voice that we were all Communists and he was going to report us to the CIA. Of course, I thought, the arrival of police had polluted the setting. We should have suspended all sessions. I hoped that he'd snap out of it by the next day, when we were scheduled to leave.

That night we held a final family dinner, everyone much subdued. After dessert Dr. Fred Payne, a gray-haired psychologist who had just arrived from California, begged to have a trip. A psychiatric nurse from Menlo Park and Jack Downing, the psychiatrist, volunteered to guide him. They were so persistent I reluctantly agreed.

An hour later, while I was sitting on the patio watching the moon, a medium-sized gorilla with the smooth skin of a naked man shuffled in, leapt on a table, beat its chest, bounded to another table, uttered a cry, and swung over the ledge into the shrubbery below.

A second later Dr. Downing comes running up the steps, followed by the nurse, who was out of breath. "Did you happen to see Dr. Payne come this way?" the nurse inquired sheepishly.

"I just saw a 170-pound ape-man go through here. See if you can talk him down. And try not to play run-and-catch with him because you are no match for a simian his size."

Swinging through trees, dropping down on roofs, scampering up and down the stairs Dr. Payne led them a merry chase. When they cornered him at the kitchen door, he climbed up a drain pipe and disappeared somewhere on the upper level. The nurse and the psychiatrist came back for help. I found Dr. Payne sitting on a stone staircase, covered with blood from superficial scratches and bruises. He was sucking his toe happily.

"Hi there, Fred. You're having a wild acid trip, aren't you?"

He stared at me in animal curiosity.

"You're going to be high for another hour or so, and then you start to come down. There's nothing to worry about. It's just a wild and woolly adventure you're having."

He jerked his head and sniffed the air suspiciously.

"How about a smoke, Fred?" I offered him a pack of Pall Malls. He moved toward me. Panicking, I rolled over and bumped down a few stairs. My head and my elbow were bleeding. Turning he ran back to the upper level.

Now began one of the silliest scenes of my life. We formed a posse of six men, armed with pillows and blankets. One carried a canvas tarp and a rope. Jack Downing had a syringe loaded with tranquilizer. We approached each cabin cautiously, flung open the door, stuck a flashlight in, strobed the blackness inside. Then one of us leapt in to turn on the wall switch. Cabin after cabin. None of us big-shot experts bothered to ask what exactly we were afraid of.

Finally we saw Dr. Payne crouching on the porch in front of his own cabin. At my command all six of us fell upon the unfortunate fellow with our pillows. He struggled a bit, but we pinned him down. Then Jack Downing stuck him with a triple dose of tranquilizer. With the weight of our bodies, we held him down, rolled him in the tarp, wound a heavy fish net around him for good measure, and then roped him head to toe. He looked terrible, his face bleeding, his eyes rolling wildly. As I crouched over him I happened to look up. On the roof observing us impassively, a bottle of tequila in his hand, sat Pancho the night security man. I felt like a foolish gringo.

We took turns sitting by Dr. Payne's side all night, but there wasn't a peep out of him.

Thinking it over I realized that once again it was the people in the setting and not the tripper who caused the problem. Dr. Payne had not touched anyone. Indeed his every move was meant to avoid hurt rather than cause it. The only blood shed was his own, and mine when I panicked.

He was lucid but very groggy next morning. Dr. Downing agreed to stay with him until they both reached San Francisco.

"We must talk about this some day," Payne mumbled to me as we bundled him off to the airport.

Duane Marvy, the spaced-out engineer, remained unresponsive. He followed me docilely to the VW bus taking us to the airport. We were too many for the Aeronaves plane so the Mexican government sent a large transport. I sat next to Marvy. He seemed to like it when I held his hand.

When we landed in Mexico City, two secret police operatives waited with a back-up squad of uniformed *federales*. It was some scene. I bought Marvy a ticket to Boston and arranged for IFIF people to taxi him home to the suburbs. When it came time to board, we tried to walk him through the gate. It didn't work. The boarding clerk took one look at the catatonic Marvy and refused to let him on the plane.

I phoned one of my Mexican psychiatrist friends, who arranged to meet Marvy at a mental hospital in town. Checking Marvy into the hospital I found that his wallet contained several US government cards attesting to high-level security clearances.

I sent a wire to the Defense Department: "Your agent Duane Marvy is in the Chapultepec Mental Hospital, Mexico City."

In subsequent weeks I kept in close touch with Dr. Payne. He wrote me a long letter about his session, saying it was the most profound experience of his life. Six years later, at a conference sponsored by the University of California Medical School in San Francisco, I heard him give a rousing speech praising LSD.

Duane Marvy worried me more. We phoned his family on arriving in Newton and were relieved to learn that he was already on his way home to Boston. When we talked later by phone, he reported that he was no worse for his scare.

About a year later Marvy came to visit us at our Millbrook center. In his subdued way he was friendly, expressing gratitude for his experience with LSD. He had lost his security ratings and eventually his government job as a result of the episode. He never disclosed the name of his agency or the nature of his assignment, but he claimed to be much happier with his new job as a well-paid engineer. It seemed he had been scared more by losing his security clearance than he had by the LSD session. When I asked him if he wanted to take LSD again, he said that he'd think it over and let me know.

Payne and Marvy represented the two worst LSD experiences I had witnessed up to that time. Their temporary psychotic episodes directly confronted us with evidence that LSD could be a dangerous drug. We were more convinced than ever of the importance of screening, preparation, and supportive setting. In later years, when millions of unwitting Americans took psychedelic drugs, these issues returned to haunt us all.[2]

WILHELM REICH (1897-1956) was one of the most brilliant and iconoclastic members of the early Vienna-based Freudian psychoanalysts, a circle from which he was eventually expelled. His concept of "muscular armor" and his theories about sexuality and the body later became the basis for a number of therapies, including bioenergetics and Gestalt therapy, whose founders were once his students. His classic treatises *The Sexual Revolution* (he coined the phrase) and *The Function of the Orgasm,* written in the early 1930s, were epochal statements. Ironically, he personally disapproved of playful erotic behavior.

An M.D. at heart Reich was mostly interested in the medical aspects of orgone, the lack of which he believed resulted in cancer and destructive tendencies. Reich designed a container in which a person could sit and absorb the healing energy. His work was scorned by the American medical establishment, which considered him dangerous. He went on with his experiments, attempting to comply with restrictions placed on him by the Food and Drug Administration. Finally he was jailed for selling orgone boxes. He died in prison, unsupported by the psychiatric establishment, persecuted by federal agents who confiscated and burned his books. These books later became standard texts in sociology and psychology.

21. Islands in the Sun

JUNE 1963
NEWTON CENTER, MASSACHUSETTS

The retreat to Newton Center from Zihuatanejo was an inglorious rout. Dick and I had suddenly become notorious. The expulsion from Harvard and the deportation from Mexico resulted in our becoming "disgraced," our reputations and credibility forfeited. Suddenly we were outcasts. It was lonely on the frontier. Like everyone else I hungered for acceptance.

Walking around Harvard Yard, surrounded by the stately monuments of hive tradition, I felt a deep distress, realizing that the trajectory of my life was pushing me irrevocably to a position where I could never receive the comfort of normal social approval, the security of institutional support. This sorrow often returned. But never lasted very long.[1]

1953
BERKELEY, CALIFORNIA

Every weekend Marianne and I went to parties with couples our age: psychologists, psychiatrists, university people, Berkeley intellectuals. These were wild drinking bouts with much tipsy necking and lascivious dancing. Our crowd was curiously virtuous about actual fucking. The child-centered ethic kept the suburban mothers in check.

At this time a woman named Delsey came to work at my research project. She was thirty-two, an Audrey Hepburn twin, playful, funny. Delsey was married to Rollo, a talented interior decorator. They had no children.

Delsey and I started hanging out together at parties, flirting, joking. Gradually we fell in love.

It became our habit to stop at bars three afternoons a week after work. Marianne and Rollo knew we were seeing each other but considered the friendship chaste. It *was* innocent for a long time, all four of us being inexperienced and fearful of complications.

But it happened.

When it did, I rented a small apartment on Telegraph Avenue, and for two years Delsey and I met three or four times a week—brief encounters. Waiting by the kitchen window I would watch her park her car and trip in high heels through the parking lot. There was no furniture in the apartment except the bed. She sat on the shoulder-high refrigerator, drinking dry vermouth while I stood in front of her caressing her slim body, both of us talking madly. We really liked each other, enjoyed the play of minds, those long funny passionate conversations of lovers. And then down the hall she would tap in high heels to the bathroom, emerging in a diaphanous blue robe, which she tossed from her naked shoulders as she came to bed.

Lust is such a powerful thing. You forget how compelling it is. The torment! I loved Marianne and Susan and Jack. There was no question of leaving them.

The affair and the uneasy patience of Rollo and Marianne continued so long because everyone involved was afraid to change. Everyone felt that the delicate status quo—skiing trips, camping trips, parties every weekend—was preferable to the terrible fissions that could follow just one word. Marianne suffered the most. Her drinking increased. She started seeing a psychiatrist.

Our continued alcohol abuse made everything worse. Everyone in our set drank enormous amounts of hard liquor, emulating Hemingway, Fitzgerald, Faulkner. People who didn't drink were considered prudes, afraid of the flamboyant impulses that alcohol allowed us to express.

My life—personal, professional, private, and public—has been influenced throughout by drugs and drug abuse. I have had considerable experience with every well-known brain-change substance. Of these alcohol has caused the most damaging incidents in my life. Booze ruined my father's life, smashed his marriage, eroded the lives of four uncles. Marianne's suicide and thus the endless sorrows of my children were due to booze. Most of my fractured friendships have unraveled under the influence of liquor. Ninety percent of the eruptions of vulgarity, insensitivity, or aggression in my history have been triggered by mild-to-moderate doses of booze. (The remaining ten percent have been performed sober.)

In the last twenty years I have ingested enormous quantities of psychedelic drugs (mainly cannabis and LSD). I find that these chemicals stimulate quiet, serene, humorous, sensual, reflective responses. They make me a better person. I have never done anything I regret while under the influence of these substances.

I have spent long hours sorrowfully contemplating how different things would have been if psychedelic drugs had been available sooner. If Marianne and I could have sat in front of the fire discussing our marital problems while smoking giggly marijuana instead of downing pitchers of stupefying martinis . . . If only my father had had LSD to fuel his wild Irish restlessness . . .

JUNE 1963
NEWTON CENTER, MASSACHUSETTS

The phone call from Mary Pinchot came a week after our return. She was at the Boston airport. She could spend only the afternoon. We met at a seafood restaurant downtown.

"Oh, you reckless Irishman. You got yourself in trouble again. It's magnificent, these headlong cavalry charges of yours. *Mais ce n'est pas la guerre.*"

"What'd I do wrong?"

"Publicity. I told you they'd let you do anything you want as long as you kept it quiet. The IFIF plan was ingenious from all sides. They would have infiltrated every chapter to get some of their people trained. But they're not going to let CBS film you drugging people on a lovely Mexican beach. You could destroy both capitalism and socialism in one month with that sort of thing."

I was struck again by the brittleness this aristocratic woman had picked up from those stern-eyed business-suited WASPs who shuttle from home to office in limousines—the information brokers, editors, board members, executive branch officials—youngish men with oldish eyes (faces you used to see around Harvard Square or in the Yale quad), initiated early into the Calvinist conspiracy, sworn to be forever reliable, working for Wild Bill Donovan in Zurich, for Allen Dulles in Washington, for Henry Luce as bureau chiefs and then shuffling from *Newsweek* to the *Post*, manipulators of secret documents, facts, rumors, estimates, arms inventories, stock margins, voting blocs, industrial secrets, gossip about the sexual and drug preferences of every member of Congress, trained to grab and maintain what they can, all loyal to the Protestant belief that the Planet Earth sucks.

"Never mind all that," said Mary. "While you've been goofing around, I've been working hard. My friends and I have been turning on some of the most important people in Washington. It's about time we had our own psychedelic cell on the Potomac, don't you think?"

"So you need more drugs? That's going to be a problem. My plans for chemical plants in Mexico got wiped out."

Mary laughed. "Oh that's no problem. I can give you a contact in England. They'll sell you everything you need. And if things go the way I hope," she said emphatically, "we'll be seeing lots of good drugs produced here at home."

I pressed her, but she declined to say more.

OCTOBER 21, 1955
BERKELEY, CALIFORNIA

I came home one Friday night to find Marianne filled with new enthusiasm. Her eyes, so long sorrowful, were sparkling. She had a plan.

I mixed a pitcher of martinis and we sat at the bar, full of high spirits, like in the old days. Marianne realized that she had become too dependent, too withdrawn, too gloomy. She knew she needed a jolt, something to shake her loose from introverted habits. So she and the kids would go away for a while. She had total confidence that our love would blossom once again.

Her closest friend from college, married to a diplomat stationed in Switzerland, inspired Marianne with letters about the social life there, the skiing, the good schools.

So Marianne would take off for a few months. Get a house in the Alps, learn to ski, put the kids in school, stand on her own feet for a while. I would come over and visit.

But we would need some financial help from her parents.

She dialed Oregon City and outlined her plan. Then she listened. Her face fell. She held the phone, staring blankly at the wall. I could hear the dial tone.

Her father had spoken only one sentence. "You must be out of your mind to leave your home and husband to traipse around Europe."

I put my arms around her and held her close.

"We'll do it anyway," I said. "We can do anything we want."

"Yes, we can," she said. "Let's celebrate. How about a drink." I mixed more martinis. Marianne didn't eat much but kept on drinking.

We went to a small dinner party that night. Delsey phoned. She was going away to Tahoe the next day. I thoughtlessly suggested that she and Rollo drop by our house later in the evening.

It was around midnight when we pulled into our garage, which had a heavy redwood door that swung down and locked from the outside. We never closed it because it had swollen in the damp weather.

As we started down the stairs to our house, a car pulled up. It was Delsey. I walked to her car. She didn't want to come in. She had just come by to say farewell before her trip. And to wish me a happy thirty-fifth birthday.

I started back down to the house. Marianne was on the stairs below me, watching with a shattered look.

"You really love her, don't you," she said.

Then she uttered a terrible cry and toppled off the stairs onto the grassy bank.

I picked her up and walked her down to the patio and then into our bedroom. I took off her clothes and then my own clothes and held her in my arms. She put her arms around me and hugged me fiercely.

We fell asleep that way, tightly wound together.

JULY 1963
NEWTON CENTER, MASSACHUSETTS

An unexpected letter arrived from the Island of Dominica. An American psychedelic enthusiast named John Presmont had established an experimental commune in that small rarely visited Caribbean land. He claimed to have enlisted the backing of the Labor Party, which was expected to regain power in the next election. The Laborites, having heard of our successful hotel operation in Mexico, were eager to have us come down and help them start an intellectual avant-garde tourist center there.

We dispatched two scouts, Gunther Weil and Frank Ferguson, a brilliant Wesleyan University graduate. Within a week we received an enthusiastic cable. They had met the politicians. There was promising potential. Come at once.

I led an immigration party of ten, island hopping to the Windward group and tiny Dominica. We were full of Ellis Island hope as the plane dipped over the mountainous terrain. Our scouts met us with disappointing news. The Conservative government, working with the British governor, had learned of our plans and had just issued an order deporting our host, Presmont, who at the moment was unhappily holed up in his house. The leaders of Her Majesty's Loyal Opposition were afraid to meet us publicly. A secret meeting was arranged for that night.

After dark the island became foreboding—black sand beaches ended abruptly in wild jungle. Almost the entire population was black, descendants of former slaves. British fruit companies kept them in a state of colonial backwardness and poverty. Dominica lacked that Bahamian-resort feeling.

Gunther, Frank, and I were picked up in a taxi driven by a young black who seemed friendly but nervous. We drove along a road covered with large crabs that crunched under the tires.

At a beat-up general store a black woman behind the cash register waved us to a cramped storeroom lit by a single hanging light bulb. Sitting around a table were three heavily muscled men naked to the waist, their ebony skin gleaming with sweat. With them was a jaunty black man in a business suit who shook our hands and poured us rum and cokes.

The three shirtless men were members of parliament, leaders of the opposition. The natty chap was Horace, a well-known Caribbean lawyer, business adviser to the Laborites. He explained that the Labor Party could take no official action to help us at that time because they were in the minority by one vote—nine to eight. However, the Conservative Party's blatant protection of British business interests had angered the people. The next election would be a landslide for Labor. Once they took over the government, they intended to bring in non-British interests to build up the economy. They wanted to know what I had in mind.

I told them about our research and the rapidly growing membership of IFIF. I proposed that we rent and later build resort facilities, following the defunct Mexican plan.

Horace calculated that even at the level of our Zihuatanejo operation we could immediately triple the tourist income on the island. There was a hint that some Las Vegas money might come to Dominica, and some of it could be used in support for our project. What did I think about gambling casinos?

It was a scene! Around a rough wooden table, walls lined with crates of store supplies, the light shining off black skins and white laughing teeth, a plan was being hatched to take over a small country with our drugs. It was agreed that we would spend a few days checking out hotel rentals and beachfront property. Then Horace and I would fly to New York to meet with the prospective backers and formalize the deal.

The next week was idyllic. Horace guided us around the island. We visited three shoreline sites that could be purchased at very reasonable prices. The locals, who had been told we were friends, greeted us warmly.

Near our hotel was a fast-running stream, clear and cold from the mountains. We spent lazy afternoons swept along by the current, sliding down the white-water dam and splashing into a forest pool. We were starting to love this black-beached island.

Our tranquillity was shattered by Horace roaring up in a jeep, his face a frightened gray.

"Have the police come yet?" he shouted in a wild voice. "No? Good. Listen, if you have any drugs, please hide them. And, mon, do not leave the grounds. Phone at once to the airport and make reservations to leave on tomorrow's flight. The government has ordered the police to arrest you for drug trafficking. Mon, they accuse you of being the biggest heroin dealer in the world."

"Heroin?" I bleeped.

"We have supporters in the constabulary. They say the American government has been sending all kind of reports about you. An American agent named Donovan—CIA, we think—came in yesterday and has been conferring with the governor. Our people in the government are reporting trouble for you. Oh God, here they come."

A car with an official seal pulled up the driveway. Two policemen jumped out.

"Professor Leary? Will you please come with us? The governor wishes to see you."

"I'd like to confer with my lawyer for a moment."

The officers glanced at each other and nodded. I walked aside with Horace.

"You must go with them," he said. "This way they won't pull a surprise raid."

"What's the gov like?"

Horace made a sour face and shook his head. "He is the very worst, mon. He's an alcoholic with forty years in the colonial service. They've dumped him here because he's incompetent. He'll do what the Americans tell him to do."

Horace was right. The old Briton scowled at me across his desk. His face was bloated and pouchy, cross-hatched with red lines. His eyes watered. A large folder stamped "LEARY" lay on his desk, and next to it, even worse, a recent issue of *Time* magazine that featured a lurid story about LSD.

The governor read aloud from *Time* and said: "We don't want any of that stuff on this island." It was short and sweet.

Deported again.

Horace stayed with us at the hotel that night as a safeguard. We spent the night sewing pills into teddy bears.

There was no problem at the airport. We were flown to the Island of Antigua, where we checked into a charming seaside hotel for a few days of recuperation before making the next move.

It turned out that the hotel was owned by a classmate of mine from West Point. Assigned to duty in the Caribbean during World War II he was so taken by island life that he resigned his commission after V-J Day.

Like so many other people in the islands, my friend was up to his chin in real estate dealings. He had purchased two small islands near Grenada, with the stipulation that he erect permanent buildings within two years. Short on financing, he made us an offer we couldn't refuse. He proposed to give us half a deserted island if we'd put up some structures. There we would be absolutely protected. And, while construction was in progress, our crew could stay in an unused beachfront nightclub called "The Bucket of Blood."

By chance Dick checked into the hotel just after we did, en route to join us in Dominica. When he saw us frolicking on the sand, he flew into a rage. Poor Richard, the summer had been rough on his hopes for becoming respectable. He scolded me bitterly for blowing the $20,000 that Peggy had given us. Deported from two countries in two weeks.

It didn't take long to raise the number to three. The spiffy white-suited cops with swagger sticks were friendly but firm (they probably knew more about the intelligent use of drugs than we did).

"My God, mon, by this time every island has been warned about you and your terrible pirate crew." The captain winked. But the next day we were on our way to Puerto Rico.

I was now beyond disappointment. The forced migrations of dissident groups in the past reminded us that our dilemma was only to be expected. It seemed to be a routine test of those committed to a utopian vision, that they be pushed around by power holders. We were walking through choreographed steps that philosophic pioneers always have to follow. Deportation 1-A. Theory and Practice of Social Ostracism. It all seemed historically correct, and it sure beat attending faculty meetings.

We were learning a most interesting lesson in applied cultural anthropology. Without a power base (territorial, political, financial) social innovations—particularly those involving education of the young—are relentlessly harassed by all existing bureaucracies.

On the positive side, our program for change possessed two assets: we were speaking to and for the enormous cadre of the postwar generation waiting in the wings to take over, and we understood that communication skills via media and by word of mouth were the instruments for preparing a power base in the information society of the future.[2]

Part 2

Paedomorphosis—Juvenilization

Biological evolution is to a large extent a history of escapes from the blind alleys of overspecialization, the evolution of ideas a series of escapes from the tyranny of mental habits and stagnant routines. In biological evolution the escape is brought about by a retreat from the adult to a juvenile stage as the starting point for the new line; in mental evolution by a temporary regression to more primitive and uninhibited modes of ideation, followed by the creative forward leap.

—Arthur Koestler

A race may become rejuvenated by pushing the adult stage of its individuals off from the end of their ontogenies, and such a race may then radiate out in all directions.

—Sir Gavin de Beer

Science fiction is the single most important literary form ever to be created in the history of humanity. . . . But we have been so busy living it and moving on to the next concept that we simply didn't notice what our fiction of ideas was all about.
  The time has come now to notice.

—Ray Bradbury

FITZ HUGH LUDLOW (1836-1870), son of a prominent abolitionist minister, grew up in Poughkeepsie, New York. As a boy he learned of hashish from tales of Middle Eastern adventure such as *The Arabian Nights, The Travels of Marco Polo,* and *The Count of Monte Cristo.* Like William James, this frail bookish schoolboy proved an impetuous experimenter ("a pharmaceutical Alexander" he called himself), befriending the local pharmacist in order to try opium, ether, chloroform, and the East Indian hemp known as *cannabis indica* (then available as a medicinal tincture and as a confection, four doses for one dollar).

In his senior year at Union College he wrote the *alma mater* as well as the first book on cannabis in English. *The Hasheesh Eater,* published anonymously in 1857, proved a literary sensation and brought lasting notoriety to its author. The remainder of his life was devoted to journalism and travel.

22. Life on a Grounded Space Colony

SEPTEMBER 1963
MILLBROOK, NEW YORK

The preceding three years had been busy. After administering LSD to more than 1,500 persons, directing a large research project, struggling with the endless political problems I fell victim to fatigue. Philosophy and history be damned, I wanted more than ever to move to a deserted island where trade winds rippled from tropic seas.

Peggy, always resourceful, arranged for Dick to give acid to her younger brother Billy, then a budding stockbroker in the prestigious Lehman Brothers firm. Billy reacted with enthusiasm. It figured. He was an intelligent restless excitement-craving Mellon heir and a true son of Thomas Hitchcock, legendary American flying ace, top polo player.

Billy and his twin Tommy had just purchased a large estate in Millbrook, New York, two hours' drive up the Hudson River from Manhattan. It was a magical location, twice five miles of fertile ground with an imposing gatehouse complete with sallyport and huge portcullis. From the gatehouse a mile-long drive under rows of maple trees led to the mansion, four stories high with two towers. Gleaming white, with sixty-four rooms inside, it was surrounded by elegant lawns, stables, and an ornate two-story chalet, which held a bowling alley. A mile across rolling fields stood a more modern mansion called "the bungalow," which served

187

as a weekend retreat for the Hitchcocks. Billy and Tommy, now spirited supporters of our work, suggested that we establish our research center in the vacant main house. The IFIF plan to start local centers around the country would be scrapped. We would go low-profile and, in secluded isolation, continue our research into altered states. We were pleased to be in Fitz Hugh Ludlow's neighborhood, the same area where the French Jesuit mystic Teilhard de Chardin was buried.

We called ourselves the Castalia Foundation, emulating the fellowship of mystic scientists in Hermann Hesse's *The Glass Bead Game*.

While our communal house in Newton Center bustled with preparations for the move, I took time out to write a philosophic paper that was to become the basis for my research during the next eighteen years. The occasion: I was invited by an organization of Lutheran psychologists to give a lecture at the American Psychology Association convention in Philadelphia. During my years as a clinical psychologist in Berkeley in the 1950s I served as a consultant to the Lutheran seminary program. Many young Lutheran ministers had been selected on the basis of my tests.

My paper affirmed that orthodox religions vainly attempt to answer, through dogma and poetic myth, eight basic questions about human destiny, eight questions that have been restated in terms of logic by philosophy but can only be answered by science.

The paper then outlined new insights from many branches of science (nuclear physics, astrophysics, genetics, immunology, biochemistry, neurology, ethology, demographics, computer theory) that would soon require drastic changes in our concepts of human nature. The data from these sciences had raised the possibility that now, for the first time, intelligent human beings could not only answer these basic questions of how and why we evolved but also proceed to take over the technologies for running the universe, the planet, our genetic future, our present neurological reality.

The paper suggested that new scientific models might provide eight precise objective definitions of God as the designer/technologist of evolution. Thus any intelligent and serious-minded human being could eventually master what I called the Eight Technologies of God.

In this paper I was presenting my *summa theologica,* a system of scientific humanism, an enthusiastic coaching manual on how to become a conscious agent of evolution. I attempted to demonstrate how humanist science provides better answers to the basic questions than does religion. I suggested that the eight questions correspond to the eight stages of evolution and to eight circuits of the human brain, hard-wired to modulate the stages of evolution (both of our species and of the individual). I stated that there might well be eight types of neurotransmitters (drugs manufactured by or introduced into the body) that could activate these eight levels of consciousness, tune one into the eight stages of evolution, and provide revelations in the eight questions.[1]

The paper I read to the astonished Lutherans was written in carefully measured prose, spiced with scientific facts, seasoned with poetic and evolutionary panoramas, and loaded with breathtaking quotes from the psychedelic sessions of famous sages and our own subjects. For two hours heresy reigned in Philadelphia, and the young Lutherans gave me a standing ovation.

Around mid-September 1963 we packed up the Newton Center house in rental trucks and set out in a caravan, heading west. Included in the party were Susan and Jack, Dick, Peggy, and Ralph and Susan Metzner. A young physician who was kicking a methedrine habit came along to provide medical supervision. A psychologist from California, Gary Fisher, his wife, and two kids completed the crew.

We arrived just after sunset. The Big House, all boarded up, loomed Transylvanian under its two high turrets and steep gables. The electricity had not been turned on, so we built a roaring fire in the baronial fireplace, lit candles, swept the vast oak-planked living room floor, and started the new adventure in highest spirits.

The estate had been constructed at the turn of the century by William Dietrich, a visionary tycoon who made his fortune installing the first electric lights in many American cities. This precedent of illumination we took as a good omen. Dietrich's tastes ran to Bavarian baroque. The woodwork was carved by masters brought over from Germany and Austria. Elegant though faded tapestries covered the walls. The ceilings were inlaid with wood panels. The kitchen was hotel-size with a walk-in refrigerator, which Charlie Mingus used to test his paranoia level. (He'd have us lock him in and wait to see if we white men would ever let him out. He always seemed a bit disappointed when we did.)

Our first task was renovation. Removing boards from windows. Cleaning. Haunting local thrift stores for furniture. We chose to go Middle Eastern in decor. Aside from the utilitarian chairs and tables in the kitchen the rest of the house was harem-style, featuring low couches, acres of cushions and silken pillows. It was an ambience designed for soft landings.

During the first weeks we filled up the library. By pooling our personal books we assembled an excellent collection of history, philosophy, mysticism (East and West), brain research, biochemistry, and genetics. It was revealing to notice how few texts of psychology we possessed. We set up a sound studio for session music: Bach and Mozart geometrics, pure jazz, rhythm-and-blues, ethnic, and tribal stuff.

A pleasant routine quickly evolved. Our days were spent in household matters and scholarly pursuits, reading and writing about expanded consciousness. Once a week we engaged in a programmed LSD session. Typically one crew member would be responsible for arranging the environment and the stimuli. The guide would read from philosophic or poetic works and select the music, all-important in directing thought. Often the guide would prepare special tapes to take us on specific ontological adventures. Trip leaders would thus share their philosophic preoccupations and esthetic preferences.

Since passive imprinted learning is tremendously accelerated during acid sessions, we were able to absorb a wide variety of wisdoms and pleasures from all ages. For several weeks we focused on the writings of George I. Gurdjieff, the wondrous Russian-Armenian mystic, and tried to replicate his profound drug-inspired experiments.

Peggy, who spent half of her time in Manhattan, would roar up in a car loaded with cases of champagne and exotic foods and drinks. Weekends Billy and Tommy would come to "the bungalow," bringing with them jet-setters, celebrities, curious aristocrats. A weekend at Millbrook was the chic thing for the hip young rich of New York. At the same time we entertained biologists from Yale, Oxford psychologists, Hindu holy men. All weekend the groups would move from one house to the other in courtly exchange.

The major domo and master of ceremonies for these weekends was Van Wolfe, a part-time theatrical producer and man-about-town who appointed himself ambassador from Castalia to the world of Park Avenue and Broadway. Van often stayed on after weekends, wandering down from the bungalow to the Big House to join our programmed sessions. During these trips people would often unfold "essence" personalities, or, as we were wont to say, "manifest their divinities." Van appeared as a wise crafty Levantine, a vizier at the sultan's court, plotting and planning for the cause, which for Van, as for so many of us, was to learn how to use psychedelic drugs to create a heaven on earth. Behind the facade of cunning schemer, show-biz hustler, bridge shark, and salon manager Van was a closet psychologist, believing that the way to free people from fear and guilt was to teach them how to use drugs intelligently.

We saw ourselves as anthropologists from the twenty-first century inhabiting a time module set somewhere in the dark ages of the 1960s. On this space colony we were attempting to create a new paganism and a new dedication to life as art. It felt right and was, come to think of it, my boyhood dream come true.

The world of conflict and political struggle seemed far removed, but trouble was lurking outside, grim, unrelenting.

First came a phone call late one afternoon from Mary Pinchot, her voice tightroping the wire of hysteria. She had rented a car at La Guardia and was now somewhere in Millbrook. She didn't want to come to the estate. Could I meet her in the village?

Driving out the gate I saw a green Ford parked down Route 44. It followed me. I slowed down. It pulled up behind me. Mary. She climbed in beside me, motioning me to drive on.

I turned down a side road through an unforgettable autumn scene—golden fields, herds of fat jet-black cows, trees turning technicolor, sky glaring indigo—with the bluest girl in the world next to me.

"It was all going so well," she said. "We had eight intelligent women turning on the most powerful men in Washington. And then we got found out. I was such a fool. I made a mistake in recruitment. A wife snitched on us. I'm scared." She burst into tears.

I reached over and stroked her hair. "Is this a result of . . . I mean, did you have a bad drug experience?"

"No. That's all been perfect. That's why it's so sad. I may be in real trouble. I really shouldn't be here."

"Are you on drugs right now?"

"It's not me, it's the situation that's fucked up. You must be very careful now, Timothy. Don't make any waves. No publicity. I'm afraid for you. I'm afraid for all of us."

"Mary," I said soothingly, "let's go back to the Big House and relax and have some wine and maybe a hot bath and figure out what you should do."

"I know what you're thinking. This is not paranoia. I've gotten mixed up in some dangerous matters. It's real. You've got to believe me." She glared at me. "Do you?"

"Yes I do." Her alarm was convincing me.

"Look, if I ever showed up here suddenly, could you hide me out for a while?"

"Sure."

"Good." She handed me a pill bottle from her purse. "This is supposed to be the best LSD in the world. From the National Institute of Mental Health. Isn't it funny that I end up giving it to you."

As I watched her drive away, I wondered. She wasn't breaking any laws. What trouble could she be in?

That night I received a phone call from Laura Huxley. She said that Aldous was dying and that he particularly wanted to see me about the manual we were adapting from the *Tibetan Book of the Dead*.

The next day I flew to Los Angeles. Since their house had been destroyed in the Hollywood fire, Aldous and Laura were living with a friend near Mulholland Drive. Laura took me aside, pressing my hand. Aldous seemed unwilling to face the certainty of his death. Just that afternoon he had spoken cheerfully about the inconvenience they were causing their friend. He had mentioned renting a house when he recovered.

Aldous was upstairs in a hospital bed, motionless and weak. He smiled when I greeted him and began asking questions in a quiet voice about what we were doing, nodding with approval, chuckling softly at my jokes. Then he motioned me conspiratorially close. He said he didn't want to worry Laura, who couldn't face the fact that he was dying. He said he had known of his terminal illness when he wrote the scene in *Island* where the dying grandmother was guided through the *bardos*. Aldous asked if I would guide him through an LSD session with our psychedelic version of the *Book of the Dead*.

I suggested that it would be much better if Laura guided the session and read him the instructions for reaching the White Light.

"No, I don't want to put any more emotional pressure on her. I plan to die during the trip, after all."

The nurse entered wheeling an oxygen tank, so I stepped into the room where Laura was waiting. I told her about our conversation. She was more than willing to guide Aldous through an acid session when his moment of death approached. We discussed the research being done by Dr. Kast, in which acid contributed dramatically to the serenity of terminal patients.

As I said goodbye, Aldous whispered, "Be gentle with them, Timothy. They want to be free, but they don't know how. Teach them. Reassure them."

Everyone remembers exactly where they were on November 22, 1963, when the dreadful news hit. Television created a mass imprint in a hundred million brains, a sudden loss of innocence. The Kennedy assassination was especially brutal to those born after 1946. It was their first intimation that dirty work was afoot, that the world wasn't the nice safe place we parents had prepared them for.

That evening a friend at the Associated Press in New York called with an item he had just pulled off the wire. Aldous Huxley was dead. In the grief for Kennedy no one noticed.

We held a long candlelight vigil for both our departed guides.[2]

ROBERT **ANTON WILSON** (1932-), born in Brooklyn, studied engineering but found himself drawn to journalism and literature. During the 1960s he was *Playboy* magazine's controversial Forum Advisor, contributing erudition and wit to the decade's sexual and psychedelic revolutions. While bringing up four children he and his wife Arlen studied witchcraft, Crowlean magic, Fortean anomalies, and other aspects of the paranormal and occult.

In the early 1970s Wilson emerged as the chief historical interpreter of the Bavarian Illuminati phenomenon. In his books *Illuminatus!*, *Cosmic Trigger*, and *The Illuminati Papers* Wilson explored the development and legacy of this eighteenth-century secret society steeped in politico-mystical conspiracy.

Wilson's bold and imaginative excursions into science fiction and alternative realities have gained him a loyal audience.

23. Experiments at Millbrook

WINTER 1963-1964
MILLBROOK, NEW YORK

That winter dry cold preceded the first snow, and the lakes on the estate froze into sheets of clear ice, ideal for skating and hockey. We piled cords of firewood next to the mansion. The deer herd moved down from the forest to be near the house. These delicate creatures watched us calmly as we watched them. Everyone's cheeks were rosy.

There were constant changes in the crew. The California psychologist couldn't stand the cold. The physician left to practice in Puerto Rico. A blond cuddly woman named Carol with her lively tow-head son, Eric, came to visit and stayed. Maynard and Flo Ferguson with their five children took a suite of four rooms on the second floor. Dick brought in a bright young man from a wealthy family who was having adjustment problems in college. His name was George. Sara, a young woman who had been a research assistant at Harvard, completed the winter tribe.

We were consciously assembling a social molecule, what Kurt Vonnegut calls a "karass," a structure of people whose neural characteristics fit together. We hoped that by living and re-imprinting via LSD with different kinds of people we could develop a hive consciousness, each person contributing a specific function, playing a definite role in the created family. George, for example, could repair things, speed around as messenger, and, equally important, add his unfamiliar esthetic. For a month he drove me crazy playing records of droning whining atonal music, which eventually I absorbed and learned to like. Thus I was introduced to the early Bob Dylan. The Fergusons with their five children added money, show-biz excitement, wit, and bouncing kid-energy. We all played aunt and uncle, sharing the responsibilities and fun of child-care.[1]

Ever since the Kennedy assassination I had been expecting a phone call from Mary. It came around December 1.

I could hardly understand her. She was either drunk or drugged or overwhelmed with grief. Or all three. "They couldn't control him any more. He was changing too fast."

Long pause. Hysterical crying. I spoke reassurance. She sobbed. "They've covered everything up. I gotta come see you. I'm afraid. Be careful."

The line went dead. Worried, I could do nothing.

The phone rang again, and the next voice had a Scottish burr. It was R.D. Laing. Allen Ginsberg had given him the number. Could he come up to visit?

Ronnie Laing and I had much in common. His books on behavior change harmonized with my work in interpersonal behavior. He had received grants from the exclusive Yale-based foundation that funded my California research. He too was experimenting with psychedelic drugs.

Ronnie was a canny dour Scotsman, distinguished in tweeds. We ate sandwiches and drank wine in the kitchen. To my dismay he turned out to be fascinated with pathological psychosis, convinced that insanity was a creative resolution of emotional conflicts. He had founded a center called Kingsley Hall, where he intended to live with psychotics.

I tried to tell him about the contagious nature of optimistic interactions. It seemed to me the height of folly to inhabit a place where people are gloomy. I meant not just a mental hospital but Britain itself. I invited him to join us. No, he was hell-bent on living with schizophrenics.

I groaned. "Surely, Ronnie, you've done your share of healing in the trenches. We need you out on the frontier, creating the future. You can spend the rest of your life tending casualties, but you'll never drain their ocean of anguish. You'll only become like them. Evolution depends on finding and training the intelligent ones who will guide the species forward. Nurture excellence. Come join us here."

"No. Great Britain is my home."

"Sooner or later we'll send a signal to rescue you."

He laughed. We embraced, and he was gone.

Before we knew it, we were safely past the frosty days of winter, emerging from our white cocoons. Warmed by the March sun the four-foot icicles that had turned the mansion into a shimmering wedding cake began to drip, drip and fall with a crash of crystal shards. And look! Patches of brown earth appeared. We emerged from hibernation.

We rushed out of the cavernous Bavarian mansion with renewed energy to green over the raw moist land. We set to work with pioneer zeal, pulling out bushes and clearing the meadows. We swept years of leaves and rubbish from the tennis house, scoured the walls and ceilings, and furnished it with low couches and cushions.

On March 21, the vernal equinox, we celebrated a pagan festival, burning the gigantic pile of brush, listening to the furious hiss of green wood, watching the red fire flicker on our faces. Then we assembled in the tennis house, now renamed Meditation House, sitting in a candlelit circle while Alan Watts consulted the I Ching. Watts, whose orientation was past and Eastern rather than scientific and Western, used the I Ching as an elegant mumbo-jumbo tea ceremony, which raised the esthetic level of our gathering and made us feel part of an ancient tradition.

We lit the fireplace. I took a large dose of Heavenly Blue, and silently, one by one, the company left. Our new plan called for each member of the community to spend one week in silence and solitude in the Meditation House. Meals would be brought three times a day and left on the stone terrace. The voyager would write notes for any special requests.

This was my first trip without guide or companion. I spent the first night totally beyond my mind, spinning back through the evolutionary past, time-traveling into the future, reliving many genetic states. When I opened my eyes, there I was, back again.

I walked outside and howled at the moon. I listened with animal wisdom to the sounds of forest life, looked up at the Big House, watched lights in bedrooms winking out, felt love and empathy for the residents.

I watched the sun rise, wandered for hours around the estate, followed brooks babbling springtime, broke through thickets to discover a glorious hidden lake shimmering with the promise of summer. Then there were breathtaking meetings with deer herds, foxes trailing red fur along the green. I spent a long time lying on a hillside, bundled in my heavy coat, watching the play of life around me, listening to the gossip of trees, insects, and animals, discovering that there is one biological intelligence that expresses herself through the various living forms.

Everything was alive, pulsing. Everything connected. In the wrong context this perception can be horrible: everything is alive? And connected! Nightmare! But in nature the perfection of the universe was undeniable.

I was beginning to understand dimly the enormity of the spectrum of vocabularies used by organisms to communicate with each other. In this timeless environment, hypersensitive to the signals from my memory banks and my chattering hormones, and alerted by commands from DNA control templates cunningly buried in my cells, I recognized that every-thing was information. Everything was shouting, "Hey, look at me, I'm here. Open up. I have a message." Trees waved their slender limbs in invitation. Flowers winked. The sun drenched me with stellar information fresh from the solar oven. Everytime I breathed, in came millions of airborne organisms, each squirming with DNA network news. Everything I put in my mouth—the spoon, a swallow of water, every bite of food, every sexy-smooth lick—contaminated me with data.

I began to speculate that everything we absorb, including neurological stimuli such as sounds, words, gestures from others, creates antibodies, enabling others to become permanent parts of us. I sought to be corrupted, i.e., broken into pieces, by others' biological and neurological signals. For the rest of the solitary week I read, made notes, walked, tripped.

At sunset on the seventh day, Easter Sunday, the doors of the Medita-tion House were rolled open, and the community assembled for a reun-ion. The leather-covered log book in which I had entered my notes was turned over to the next searcher, chosen by lot, and I returned to the routines of the planet.

For us the summer bloomed peacefully. We were hardly aware of the storms brewing. Lyndon B. Johnson, running confidently for re-election, ordered US aircraft to bomb North Vietnam. The Warren Commission reported that a single assassin killed Jack Kennedy. Harlem and Philadel-phia had race riots. On the cultural frontier Marshall McLuhan published *Understanding Media*, announcing that the medium is the message. Psy-chiatrist Eric Berne popularized my concepts of transactional analysis and game theory in *Games People Play*, making accessible to the public con-cepts of behavior-change that had formerly been reserved to the psycholog-ical priesthood. The humanist psychology boom was on the way.

There was new music in the air. The Beatles sang "She Loves You," Bob Dylan whined "It Ain't Me, Babe," and the Beach Boys sent mellow California vibrations eastward.

At Millbrook a veritable earthy paradise was in full-scale operation. We purchased a big lawn mower and landscaped acres of green grass. We trimmed the drive through the stately maples with whitewashed stones. Dick grumbled that it looked like the entrance to a Jewish country club.

It was a non-stop festival of life with ceremonies, seminars, music, fertility rites, star gazing, moon watching, forest glade revels. Through the woods, both day and night, strolled trippers. The mile-long lake on our south border rushed crystal-clear over a wide smooth-stoned waterfall. On hot afternoons we lay atop the falls, tumbled down the current. My son Jack caught a record bass.

Our scientific activities continued at top speed. We published our ver-sion of the *Tibetan Book of the Dead*, now titled *The Psychedelic Experi-*

ence. This was the first manual since Moreau's *Du Hachisch* to guide searchers through a brain-change drug session. It appeared in seven languages. In English alone there were sixteen printings. Our journal, *The Psychedelic Review*, continued publication. Dick, Ralph, and I lectured regularly at colleges about our research results and our utopian plans. They had never heard anything like this on campus before.

The next visitor was a writer named Robert Anton Wilson, who came up to Millbrook on freelance assignment from *Realist*, a fiesty counterculture magazine edited by Paul Krassner. When Wilson drove up, we were playing baseball on the lawn in front of the Meditation House. Maynard Ferguson was on the roof of the Big House playing jazz trumpet.

Robert was a solid muscular man whose body movements were deliberate and precise. He spoke slowly in literary paragraphs with a wry sense of satire. There was also a keen vulnerability in his expression; he seemed to register everything happening around him.

Robert was at that time associate editor of *Fact* magazine, whose publisher, Ralph Ginzburg, had refused to send him to interview me because he was convinced in 1964 that the psychedelic drug movement was finished.

Robert and I spent the afternoon discussing game theory, the application of Einsteinian and quantum physics to psychology, the redefinition of vague words like neurosis in ethological terms, the relationship between the space/time changes in the psychedelic experience compared with my space/time definition of personality types. In the subsequent eighteen years I have been interviewed by hundreds of journalists, some hostile, most sympathetic. With one exception Wilson was the only one who had read my books and was ready to discuss the scientific nature of my work.[2]

Then we were visited by people who were less open-minded—two top officials from the FDA, a medico and an enforcement type. They wanted to know, unofficially, you understand, just exactly what we were up to. We gave them a summary of our activities. They were honest enough to express their dismay.

"We are shocked by what you people are doing," said the medic. "For centuries drug-taking has been considered a vice. Now you are not only defending it, you're suggesting it's moral, educational, even religious. Maybe Kennedy went along with this kind of thinking, but Johnson is different."

Then the other spoke. "The people in law enforcement—and believe me, they have the power—can't wait for these drugs to be illegal so they can bust your ass."

I shrugged. "Making drugs illegal isn't going to stop their use. If anything prohibition will make the drugs more attractive. Remember the rum runners? Drugs are going to happen no matter what the government does—especially with the younger generation."

"Wrong. Kids always latch on to fads. Hula hoops. Davy Crockett caps. Rock and roll. Drugs are just another trend."

"No, this one is different. Drugs are going to become a permanent part of American culture. The kids are learning abilities that adults can't handle."

"Like what?"

"The ability to change the way they think. The government shouldn't let drugs become a monopoly of the young."

"Are you saying that we should throw in the towel on drugs?"

"No. The government should license, supervise, and educate people to use drugs effectively."

The FDA doctor laughed. "Do you think these old Southern senators who run Congress are going to go for that?"

"Look at the figures. Billions of dollars are involved here. Enormous agriculture crops. Dope will be one of America's top five industries in ten years. You guys have got to come through with a program that will give a piece of the action to every big pressure group. Look at alcohol. Illegal thirty-five years ago, today it's got the strongest lobby in every state capital. This is bigger than television, my friends. Why drive into the black market what can be pork-barreled and taxed?"

"All these ideas sound great theoretically," said the medic. "But the fact is President Johnson has made it very clear he wants a drug-free America."

Poor Lyndon, I thought as I watched them drive down the road in the unmarked car. Drugs are going to be around a lot longer than any of us.

K EN KESEY (1935-), legendary American novelist, was born in Colorado. He received a B.S. from the University of Oregon in 1957.

In 1962 Kesey published *One Flew Over the Cuckoo's Nest,* a satirical anarchic novel about institutional attempts to crush individuality. *Sometimes a Great Notion* (1964) established Kesey as a first-rank American novelist.

Kesey is widely considered the father of the hippie movement. He had his first LSD experience as a paid subject in a CIA-sponsored research project. His later adventures became known to millions through *The Electric Kool-Aid Acid Test* by Tom Wolfe.

Kesey and his wife Faye have carried out the American populist lifestyle of independence, humor, ecological consciousness, and gentle resistance to authority.

24. Pranksters Come to Millbrook

SUMMER 1964
MILLBROOK, NEW YORK

Our Castalia Foundation was by no means the only drug scene in the land. Ken Kesey was the central figure in a rowdy funny series of "acid-test" celebrations in San Francisco. In Los Angeles LSD spread through the movie colony. On college campuses consciousness expansion was becoming the most popular subject. And in New York a lively and well-publicized drug scene emerged around the highly successful pop-artist Andy Warhol, whose sprawling loft drew the art and fashion stars of the day.

Our link to Warhol was Viva Superstar, an engaging intelligent literate actress who, at Andy's suggestion, started coming up to Millbrook to escape the frenzied New York scene.

Long an admirer of Warhol I have always seen him as a cosmopolitan Zen monk maintaining a life of calm simplicity in the center of the Manhattan insanity. He was one of the few people during the '60s who seemed to have a historical perspective on the cultural changes we were bringing about. He once commented to me that our role in the evolution of society was similar to that of Alistair Crowley, the occult philosopher who scandalized the previous generation with his flamboyance and his libertarian ideas ("Do what thou wilt is the whole of the law").

The New York drug scene was the polar opposite of Millbrook, in part because habitat defines species. To live in a city commits one to an intense crowded jangled way of life in which psychedelic drugs can

199

be inappropriate. The last thing a New Yorker needs is a chemical that induces hypersensitivity, that exposes the "aliveness" of everything. For someone just passing through, New York was a wonderful seething place to experience LSD; for those who lived and worked there psychedelic drugs tended to overload the system.

The Warhol hive fed on drugs that provide escape, that turn off, toughen, and callous the nerve endings. Booze, speed, downers. Considerable rivalry existed in the minds of some of the Warhol people between their fast-lane hard-reality drugs and our blue-sky spacey drugs.

It was interesting to note that the New York hipsters usually obtained their medicaments by prescription. The Manhattan drug gurus were the feel-good doctors, whose offices were crowded day and night with figures from sports, entertainment, fashion, and the jet-set.

One afternoon at Van Wolfe's apartment Edie Sedgwick, super-model, breezed in begging for "a poke of Doctor Jake." They formed a tableau from the bizarre: as Van with his pronounced tremor poised the needle in his shaking hands, Edie calmly tilted her weight to her left leg, pulled up her skirt, peeled down her panties to expose her soft pale buttock, and coolly accepted the injection, without missing a beat in the story she was telling.

The drug of choice dispensed by the feel-good doctors was amphetamine (speed) mixed with mega-doses of vitamins. Loaded into blockbuster hypodermics these shots left the patient humming with euphoria and high energy.[1]

The most famous feel-good doctor of this period was Max Jacobson, whose caseload included many top show-biz stars. Benefit shows for Doctor Jake's research were held regularly, as grateful patients bought expensive tickets to attend performances by talented patients.

It is no betrayal of national security to report that Dr. Jacobson's treatment contributed to the high humor and bounce of the Kennedy White House. Photos taken during the much-publicized Fifty-Mile Hike for Vigor showed Doctor Jake at rest stops, distributing medicine to the First Family and its top-level staff.

Flora Lu Ferguson was convinced that all the problems of the mind could be solved by my drugs and that all the problems of the body could be solved by Dr. Max Jacobson's. So a meeting between the Two Titans of Euphoria was arranged.

I sat for some time in the waiting room, which was no great disaster since the room was crowded with beautiful people. Reverence hushed us all when a door opened and a husky young man with a crew-cut stalked through, followed by a middle-aged gent.

"Isn't that Mickey Mantle?" I asked in disbelief.

"Yeah, and Mel Allen, the Voice of the Yankees," answered the man sitting next to me.

"Breakfast of Champions," I said with a cheerful grin.

A harassed-looking nurse beckoned. Doctor Jake was a short dark man whose wrinkled hands seemed to reach his ankles. He was dressed in a white coat. In a conspiratorial mittel-European accent he apologized for his busyness. On a counter at the far end of the room was Doctor Jake's experimental equipment—rocks lit by a black-light, reflecting weird colors, and large beakers of bubbling rainbow-tinted liquids.

Allen Jay Lerner rushed from the examining room and through the office like a wiry weasel.

"As I understand your therapy," I said to Dr. Jacobson, "you believe in increasing pleasure and reducing pain. By making patients feel good chemically and adding positive suggestion you attempt to accelerate the natural healing processes of the body."

"Correct," said Doctor Jake, leaning forward in a curious simian motion and clapping his hands on his knees. "It is wrong and unhealthy to suffer. Depression is a chemical disease. I believe that the doctor should do what he can to relieve unnecessary torment."

"I endorse that," I replied.

"Excellent," exclaimed Doctor Jake. "Now let me see what I can do for you. You have a hearing loss?"

"Yes, I . . ."

"Fine, let us perform an experiment. I can cure this for you in ten minutes."

"Fantastic," I said.

"Stand over there, and we'll test your disability."

I stood against the wall, facing sideways. Doctor Jake crouched at the other end of the room.

"Repeat these numbers after me." The wily physician moved his lips silently.

"Ah hah. You are as deaf as one stone. Excellent. Now I shall cure you."

Hunching he sprang to a table jammed with beakers, retorts, flasks, and jars. He mixed several fluids and filled an enormous hypodermic.

I could feel the amphetamine slide painlessly into my vein. A flash-heat of pleasure rocketed up my arm to my heart, exploded throughout my body. I floated in ecstasy. Doctor Jake's face swam six inches above my own, a huge Semitic globe smiling down, giving human form and meaning to the breathless pleasure. I beheld the donor of this joy, irreversibly imprinting the face of Divine Jake on the millions of neurons now writhing in bliss.

"Good. It's good. Doctor Jake makes you feel good," he whispered.

"Yes, very good," I murmured dreamily. I felt great affection for my Benefactor and a dim irritation at those misguided critics who lurked somewhere outside the cone of rapture, misjudging the Dear Physician, who was now stroking my forehead.

Epochs later Doctor Jake shook my arm gently. "Now let us test your hearing."

I levitated to the testing spot by the wall. As I stood sideways, Doctor Jake bellowed, "ONE, TWO, THREE. DID YOU HEAR THAT?"

"One, two, three. Did you hear that?" I repeated docilely.

"The experiment worked!" exclaimed Doctor Jake. "Your hearing loss is cured."

"I sure feel good."

"I'll mix up a batch to take with you. And a few boxes of disposable needles. Not only will you hear everything, but it will all sound good."

The Fourth of July, besides being the birthday of our country, was also the birthday of our friends Tommy and Billy, the owners of Millbrook. To celebrate we held a carnival.

Our Big House crew assembled in masquerade costumes. Richard Alpert, Ralph and Susan Metzner, Gunther and Karen Weil, Jack and Susan Leary, Carol Ross and Rickie, Terry, George, Maynard and Flo Ferguson and their kids, and several colleagues from Harvard, MIT, and Princeton. Maynard brought his fifteen-man group, the best big band in the land. They set up by the fireplace and blew a hurricane.

The Hitchcocks invited a large company of friends from Manhattan, London, Paris, and Rome. Peggy dressed as a belly dancer, sinuous and tempting, exotic eyes flashing. Billy was resplendent as a sultan, his Venezuelan wife Aurora striking as an Egyptian queen. Tommy Hitchcock and Suzanne Kent were dressed as Romeo and Juliet.

I was on a sofa, entranced by rainbow swirls of sight and sound, when a tall blond princess in flowing silks approached me. She removed her dark glasses in a striptease gesture, unveiling two enormous stark-naked blue eyes. "Don't you remember me?" she murmured. "I'm Nanette."

I scrambled to my feet in surprised pleasure. "Nanette! Of course." She had visited us in Cambridge with Gregory Corso and a little dog named Rascal.

"Her name is Naughty," she murmured, her myopic eyes fondling mine. Her smile was mischievous. "Here I am, still searching to regain Paradise Lost."

She sidled up to confide that when she was a little girl her father had taken her to a mountain top and talked lyrically about the unity of nature. Nanette wanted to unveil the mysteries of the universe, to go to India to seek the ultimate wisdom, to learn the secret sexual practices of the Orient.

It sounded good to me.

Later in the party I found Peggy in a bedroom, talking animatedly on the phone. She smiled knowingly.

"I see you and Nanette have discovered each other."

I felt myself blushing.

"Do you approve?" I asked shyly. I knew that Peggy had started seeing someone in New York.

"Why not. She's a beautiful intelligent woman. You'll be good for each other."

We exchanged knowing smiles.

"This really is Independence Day," I said as we embraced.

At noon the next day I zoomed over to the bungalow. Nanette was lying on a chaise by the pool. The sun was hot. She removed a filmy harem robe, revealing her long smooth body in a microscopic bikini. Nanette told funny stories about her adventures in swinging London, her conquest of the New York fashion world, her boredom with fame and money.

A thoughtful and romantic woman, she was an icon of beauty, surrounded by, instructed by, manipulated by the technicians and producers of the fashion industry. Her face was on magazine covers. Her blue eyes invited you to buy products advertised on TV. I was intimidated by her glamor and charisma.

She came up from New York to the Big House the next weekend.

On Monday morning, curled lazily in my arms, she reached for the phone and dialed Eileen Ford in New York. "I'm falling in love, Eileen, and want to take the next two weeks off. . . . Yes, I know about the bookings. You'll just have to postpone them or get someone else."

Nanette and I moved into the tower room, which she filled with rare tropical plants. Afternoons we played like young lovers. Trying to meditate in the master bedroom below, Dick came up to complain about all the yelps of pleasure.

It wasn't long before Nanette requested an LSD session. I was by no means eager to rush into the experience. I knew that Nanette and I would come out of the session changed persons, hooked into a different relationship. It was also possible that she would turn her magnifying lens on me and recognize the inhibited sexually awkward man that I had been since Marianne's death. Or perhaps she would be made insecure by the experience, chased into some dark cave within her mind.

＊   ＊   ＊

We tripped in front of the fireplace in the large living room, reclining on low couches. I watched as Nanette allowed her jet-set facade to fall away, just so much childhood scar tissue. From within emerged an archetypal nobility, the radiant essence of a Valkyrie.

As dawn gilded the windows, we rose and walked behind the mansion to a stone bridge, where she paused, removed a gold ring from her finger, threw it in the dark waters. She ran ahead, exultant, turning back to look at me, arms outstretched. I fell under her spell.

After her two weeks of vacation Nanette set up a new routine—three days working on assignment in New York, the rest of the week with me at Millbrook.

Then came the visit from Ken Kesey. During our five years at Millbrook we had visits from hundreds of interesting people. Ironically, one of the most highly publicized encounters with one of our most distinguished guests occurred without my participation. In a mercifully short chapter of *The Electric Kool-Aid Acid Test* Tom Wolfe presents one version of Ken Kesey's trip to Millbrook. The Pranksters, after a grueling trip across the country in their school bus, were

> expecting the most glorious reception ever. It is probably hard at this late date to understand how glorious they thought it was going to be. The Pranksters thought of themselves and Leary's group as two extraordinary arcane societies, and the only ones in the world, engaged in the most fantastic experiment in human consciousness ever devised. The thing was totally new. And now the two secret societies bearing this new-world energy were going to meet.
>
> The Pranksters entered the twisty deep green Gothic grounds of Millbrook with flags flying, American flags all over the bus, and the speakers blaring rock 'n' roll, on in over the ponds and glades, like a rolling yahooing circus. When they got in sight of the great gingerbread mansion itself, all towers and turrets and jigsaw shingles, Sandy Lehmann-Haupt started throwing green smoke bombs off the top of the bus, great booms and blooms of green smoke exploding off the sides of the bus like epiphytes as the lurid thing rolled and jounced around the curves. We are here! We are here!
>
> The Pranksters expected the Learyites to come rolling out of the house like the survivors of the siege of Khartoum. Instead—a couple of figures there on the lawn dart back into the house. The Pranksters stop in front and there is just the big house sitting there sepulchral and Gothic—and them jumping off the bus still yahooing and going like hell. Finally a few souls materialize. Peggy Hitchcock and Richard Alpert and Susan Metzner, the wife of Dr.

Ralph Metzner, another leading figure in the Leary group. Alpert looks the bus up and down and shakes his head and says, "Ke-n-n-n Ke-e-e-esey . . ." as if to say I might have known that you would be the author of this collegiate prank. They are friendly, but it is a mite . . . *cool* here, friends. Maynard Ferguson, the jazz trumpet player, and his wife, Flo, are there, and they groove over the bus, but the others . . . there is a general . . . *vibration* . . . of: We have something rather deep and meditative going on here, and you California crazies are a sour note. . . .

Where was Leary? Everyone was waiting for the great meeting of Leary and Kesey.

Well, word came down that Leary was upstairs in the mansion engaged in a very serious experiment, a three-day trip, and could not be disturbed.

Kesey wasn't angry, but he was very disappointed, even hurt. It was unbelievable—this was Millbrook, one big piece of uptight constipation, after all this.

I had been spending a few days in New York with Nanette. In Grand Central Station, waiting for the return train, I came down with a shivering sweaty flu. Around midnight Dick met me at the Poughkeepsie station full of the news. Ken Kesey and his fabled day-go bus had arrived unannounced. The Pranksters were planning to spend a few days with us.

"How are they?" I asked, too sick to be overjoyed.

Dick shook his head. "Pretty freaked out and shook up. They've spent almost a month in this noisy shaky school bus with no shock absorbers, barreling through Arizona and Texas with the temperature in the 100s. They're exhausted and strung out."

"Well, they've come to the right place for rest and recuperation," I said, thinking of myself as much as of the Pranksters.

"Yeah," Dick agreed, "we'll let 'em unwind and cool down in the waterfall and watch a few sunsets. They'll mellow out."

"What were they on?" I asked.

"Looked like speed to me."

"Oh no," I said. Doctor Jake's teeth-clenching pharmaceutical was not part of our life at Millbrook. Except during visits from city slickers there wasn't much cocaine around either. It would have been like shooting heroin in Camelot.

When Dick drove me up to the Big House, all was quiet. Some of the Pranksters were sacked out; others were partying at the bungalow. I staggered upstairs, heaved, sneezed, wheezed, coughed, heaved again, took two aspirins, and fell into a feverish sleep.

When Dick came up to see me the next morning I was still running a high fever. Even in my delirium I could tell that Dick wasn't too thrilled about the rowdy Prankster trip. To put it mildly.

"I feel like we're a pastoral Indian village invaded by a whooping cow-boy band of Wild West saloon carousers," said Dick.

He suggested that we let our inter-culture exchange develop naturally at the individual level. And that's what happened. Lots of horny doping and groping took place among the groups. Even Dick got caught up in the action, lamenting afterwards a case of poison ivy he got rolling around in the bushes with one or more of the Pranksters.

Ken Kesey, Ken Babbs, and I did meet, quietly in my room. We looked each other in the eye and promised to stay in touch as allies. And we have to this day.

After the Pranksters' visit we held a meeting to plan for the coming year. Inspired by Kesey we agreed that we were becoming too insulated. In order to broaden our perspectives we would send everyone in the community on an orbit around the earth. The idea was to buy each member of the group a round-the-world Pan-Am ticket good for one year's travel. Each scout would conduct imprinting experiments at holy shrines, hot spots, and philosophic centers, look up great sages, and return with evolutionary data.[2]

Ralph Metzner took off in early November, flying straight to Calcutta. He sent us moralistic postcards about the tinsel vanity of the West and the profundity of the East. Sounded great.

One night, while floating in the soft cloud of affection, Nanette and I decided to get married and begin our circumnavigation of the globe. Dick was to journey to the East when Ralph returned.

Dick decided to become unhappy about the planned wedding. For al-most four years we had been the closest partners. Our relationship, woven from scores of shared morning glory sessions, was telepathic. In many ways I was like Dick's father. In our household Dick, who was extremely close to his mother, took on what he has often described as a maternal-wifely role. He was definitely closer to Susan and Jack than I.

As my courtship with Nanette heated up, Dick became petulant, com-plaining bitterly when I dashed off to Manhattan to stay with her. He felt left out. At one point he threatened to boycott the wedding. On second thought he agreed to act as best man, treating the ceremony as high camp.

In mid-December I was invited to the Cooper Union College au-ditorium to give a lecture on consciousness expansion. Brain-change must have been in the air because the large historic hall was jammed. I walked on stage to great applause and announced that my lecture could be stated in one sentence: "You have to go out of your mind to use your head." Thunderous cheers. I then outlined a theory of serial re-imprinting, demonstrating how life-determining realities are formed at the various stages of individual development.

The theory stated that human growth involves a precise sequence of metamorphoses, clearly defined stages, which occur when a new circuit of the brain is activated. A new imprint of a new reality occurs at each stage. In this lecture and in subsequent publications I listed twenty-four stages of metamorphosis in the human being—twelve that are reached by most humans at this stage of our evolution, twelve "future" stages that are becoming accessible to our species.[3]

In an interview with the *Village Voice* the next day I asserted that the psychedelic revolution was accomplished. A sufficient number of Americans had learned the secret of brain-change. Although it might take a generation for the culture to absorb the new neuro-technology, the results were foregone. The multiple-reality phenomenon was here to stay.

The wedding took place in Grace Chapel, a High Episcopal church in Millbrook. Dick and I wore rented cutaway waistcoats. With my daughter Susan in attendance as bridesmaid Nanette was a shining Nordic princess. Monte Rock III, the Puerto Rican show-biz hairstylist, brought up a Maisle Brothers film crew. The movie, entitled *Wedding at Millbrook*, had a certain moment on the art-film circuit.

As we walked down from the altar, sweet Jack reached out shyly and touched my hand. This gesture of love from my only son is one of the dearest memories of my life. This trip around the world was about to separate us for the first time since Marianne's death. We never were as close again.

After the ceremony the Miles Davis Quartet (without Miles) played at the Big House party. Charlie Mingus intoned sermons about marital fidelity. The revels went on till dawn.

Next day Nanette and I left for the airport. As the plane taxied down the runway for take-off, we looked at each other with a certain amused skepticism.

"Why are we doing this?" she asked, nervously twirling her wedding band.

"We'll find out," I said.

We both sensed that the marriage was not going to last.

HERMANN HESSE (1877-1962), exiled writer, and philosopher, was born in Calw, Germany. At age fifteen he ran away from the theological seminary he was attending; the following year he was expelled from the Caanstadt Gymnasium. After several years as a book dealer Hesse published his first novel, *Peter Camenzind* (1904). His early writings were romantic in theme and realistic in style, dealing with the alienation of youth from repressive society.

Hesse's pacifism amid growing German authoritarianism led him to flee to Switzerland at the outbreak of World War I. His writings in exile became increasingly transcendental. Hesse's mastery of multiple-reality prose was exhibited in *Siddhartha, Steppenwolf,* and *Journey to the East. Magister Ludi,* a monumental symbolic work, portrays a society of prudish Helvetian mathematician-artist-philosophers who summarize all knowledge in a Glass Bead Game. This allegory won Hesse the Nobel Prize in 1946.

For millions of post-World War II youths Hermann Hesse's heroes served as models for personal transformation/evolution and for the triumph of the individual.

25. Himalayan Honeymoon

WINTER 1964-1965
JAPAN–INDIA

First stop Tokyo, an urban hive fascinating to any diligent student of insectoid interpersonal relations.

Nanette and I had traveled extensively in foreign lands, but we had never felt so alienated from the natives of a country as we did in Japan. Another species? Daily life seemed to be a delicate, sophisticated anthill ballet. We watched uniformed officials using long batons to push swarms of people onto subway trains. We visited karate dogens, Shinto temples, Buddhist shrines, and department stores, where Nanette bought off-the-rack kimonos. We swallowed a few mushrooms to imprint a Kabuki performance and later slid our tall white bodies into steamy public baths.

With our noses buried in books on Japanese history and Zen we took the bullet train to Kyoto, the Esalen of Japan. We visited ashrams, meditated in a Zen temple, and ended up on the historical museum, formerly a shogun palace. We sat in lush carpeted rooms where emperors had murdered and been murdered. We recapitulated the history of Japan.

*   *   *

Calcutta! The plane door opened, and we sucked into our amazed nostrils the rich fetid smell of organic decay, centuries of wrecked karma silted up at the Ganges' swollen mouth.

Allen Ginsberg had instructed us to visit the "burning ghats," so we went to the riverbank to watch as corpses were borne down the wide stairs in ceremonial procession, enthroned on piles of lumber (slats for the poor, sweet-smelling sandalwood for the rich), enkindled, and sent out on the current like so much waste product. We sat on our haunches with a gang of wood-carrying Sivites, ordinary six-pack Joes passing around hand-cupped bowls of hashish. The sweet odor of cannabis mingled with the sweet odor of burning corpses. Breathe deeply. What's death but the end of breath?

So this was the beginning: squatting in the crotch of the Ganges, coughing carbons and inhaling nitrogens while black buzzards circled in the steamy sky, high on the cries of mourners.

We took the train down the Bay of Bengal to a more cheerful image of divinity, the Black Pagoda of Konarak. There we found a gigantic building in the form of a chariot pulling the Temple of the Sun God, whose walls seethed with erotic carvings—thousands of firm-bodied graceful people stone-frozen in acts of sexual dalliance. This was where life renewed itself.

Our native guide, Ashoke Fakir, laughed his head off. He pointed to a slender naked girl sitting on the upstretched penis of her paramour: "Jiggy. Jiggy." Ashoke motioned to an acrobatic trio: a very busy youth striving upwards with his mouth to cunnilingate a shapely smiling girl with parted legs while another young beauty sat contemplatively on his cock. "One jiggy, two jiggy, three jiggy," said Ashoke.

Observing these hundred and one varieties of divine play we marveled at the culture that produced such a wealth of sexual celebration. Who was this Narasim, the thirteenth-century king who inspired his people to build a monument to fertile delight? A leader of wondrous energy who scoured the continent for sculptors, artists, and architects to adorn this temple. When the workers returned home at night, after a long day of hand-polishing orgy scenes, was their domestic life affected? What happened to this civilization?

Next we went to Varanasi (a.k.a. Benares), the holiest city of the Hindus, the site of a non-stop hippie festival for the last 5,000 years. After checking into an open-air motel where monkeys gamboled on the lawn we headed for the ghats—broad flights of stairs down which devotees flocked to wash in the Holy Ganges. Hindus believe that to die in Benares propels the soul out of the cycle of rebirth up to the post-terrestrial orbit of ultimate enlightenment.

One side of the river swarmed with spiritual consumers—barefoot, dropped-out, bearded, ragged, naked, dirty, begging, chanting, drumming, glazed in the eyes. Bodies, boats, temples, villas, palaces, and ashrams jammed the bank that looked east at the approaching sun.

The other bank of the river was deserted, uninhabited, undeveloped—open space. Several guides and hawkers told me more or less the same story. The other side of the river was cursed. But they disagreed about the who, why, and how of the spiritual infection.

This puzzle nagged at me. On one side 1,500 temples crowded together in a human jungle. On the other side the most inviting real estate in the world lay neglected because of some vague superstition. Late that night, as Nanette was dozing off, I told her I wanted to explore around town. I engaged a porter from the hotel to accompany me to the ghats, where I asked him to find a boatman who would take me across to the other side. His bright eyes darkened with consternation, and he shook his head vehemently: no boatman would take the risk. Dangerous. Devils. Siva, the god of destruction. I pulled from my pocket a small round emblem of the Dancing Siva. This would protect me. I handed him a hundred rupees and pointed to the dozens of skiffs. "Find a boatman who will take me near the other bank. For 500 rupees."

The porter hesitated, then scurried down to the shore. I could see him engaged in furious conversation with the boatmen. On his return he motioned me to follow him up the ghats, away from the river.

None of the boatmen dared make the trip, he explained, because they would get a bad reputation. However, one said he would meet us secretly a mile upstream. If we were unobserved, he would ferry me across.

We ambled around the city for about an hour, moving north, and then headed for the bank. A hooded figure darted from behind a building, motioning for us to follow him toward a cluster of moored craft, in which blanketed figures slept. Putting his finger to his mouth in the gesture of silence the boatman led me on board a skiff. The hotel porter whispered that he'd wait for me.

The hooded boatman cast off, using one oar as paddle and rudder. As we reached mid-stream, the boatman laid the oar down and prostrated himself in prayer, touching his forehead several times to the deck and chanting, "Allah." My brave pilot was a Moslem.

He angled the boat skillfully downstream, toward the eastern shore. On the right bank temples and buildings were stacked up in silhouette; on the left, empty darkness. My mind was racing. The boatman turned to look at me questioningly. I urged him forward. The boat slid into shallows through thick weeds, about ten feet from the bank. Looking scared the boatman held out his hand. "Rupees."

I pulled a stack of one-hundred-rupee notes from my pocket, handed him two. Holding up three more I pointed to the bank and said, "Five minutes."

I stepped to the prow, took off my sandals, and slipped into the water. It was about two feet deep, lukewarm, and slimy. "Five minutes," I said, and splashed ashore.

The ground was dry, barren except for a few clumps of grass. I could hear insects and frogs, but the place felt empty. I sat on gravel, looking across the river where a million souls huddled in busy misery. I felt a curious freedom and a kinship with the sailors who pushed west beyond the edges of their maps.

Something moved behind me. I scrambled to my feet, took a few steps forward in the darkness.

An old man with long white hair stood about twenty feet away. He was naked save for a dhoti around his waist. His eyes were luminous. With his hands at his side he spoke to me rapidly in a strange tongue. I was terrified.

Suddenly I understood: he was some special ancient teacher who had been waiting for me all my life. I wanted to run forward and throw myself at his feet. But I was paralyzed with fright, thinking at the same time that he could be a crazed fanatic. He might attack me, a profaner of holy ground. If the boatman heard a disturbance, he would leave without me.

I stood for several minutes, despising my fear, worrying that I was blowing a rare chance to leap into a new dimension.

I babbled to him in English, introducing myself, asking who he was, trying to draw out some sort of message.

He stood absolutely fixed, then rattled off more incomprehensible words.

My heart was pounding. I decided to go back to the shore and ask the boatman about the old man. As I came into sight, the boatman waved his arm furiously. I scrambled on board, and he started paddling immediately for mid-stream.

"Take me back," I said.

He shook his head, muttering, "No good, no good."

On the floor of the boat I wept uncontrollably. I was convinced that I had met the Buddha and had run away.[1]

In New Delhi we joined Ralph Metzner, who said that Almora, a village on a ridge in the Himalayan foothills, was the best spot from which to absorb the continent's message. Ralph had spent three months there studying with Lama Govinda, the Tibetan Buddhist philosopher and scholar.

The three of us took the train and then a wheezing bus up to Nanital, a sweet Swiss village bordering an Alpine lake. At this altitude the land was green. A second rattling crowded bus brought us further up to Almora, where the best hotel in town offered a private room with wooden-slat frames on which to lay our sleeping bags. There was no restaurant in the village, no bar, no tourist facilities.

The next morning Ralph led us to the home of the mysterious Sufi alchemist Brahma Singh, a wiry man with a street-wise smile, who suggested that we could find a house to rent up on Holy Man Ridge.

We hiked a mile up the dirt road to a fork, where six lepers squatted. From them we learned that the left path lead to Tibet; for Nepal, hang a right. For a thousand years lepers had been plying their trade at this major intersection, begging alms from pilgrims, couriers, and merchants leading donkey-trains. I dropped a penny in each tin cup and passed out cigarettes. The lepers were cheerful laid-back fellows, and we got on quite friendly terms over the weeks.

It was the end of winter, and with patches of snow still on the ground no one now lived along Holy Man Ridge. House rentals were arranged by a Methodist missionary. We selected a cottage with a wide lawn over-looking the ice-capped Himalayas to the north and the deep valley to the south. It was called "Snow View." We also hired a Moslem cook named Abdul, who was to come every morning to clean, purchase supplies from vendors, and prepare lunch. Peasants came each day with spring water, vegetables (one hour fresh from the ground), eggs, milk, bread, firewood. For canned meats, cheeses, chocolates, sugar, coffee, tea, and whiskey we visited a trading store in the village.

Ralph moved into the guest room. On our second day he escorted us along Holy Man Ridge, past the house of the Dutch holy man, the German holy man, and the house where D. H. Lawrence had lived—now all deserted. The transcontinental trail took us by a small refreshment stand, which had for centuries offered hot tea in brass mugs to travelers on the path.

As we walked, Ralph told us that the Lama had been most impressed to learn that *The Psychedelic Experience* contained a dedication to him. He had requested an LSD session, which Ralph provided. For the first time, after thirty years of meditation, the Lama had experienced the *bardo Thodol* in its living sweating reality.

We turned at a forest trail, which opened into a clearing at the end of the ridge. A small wooden house sat in the midst of a magnificent 360-degree view.

An attractive round-faced matron dressed in robes greeted Ralph effu-sively. She was Li Gotama, the Lama's wife. We were invited into the study. A carved-wood railing separated us from a raised carpeted platform, covered with books and manuscripts. Built by Evans-Wentz, translator of the *Tibetan Book of the Dead*, and turned over in fraternal affection to the Lama, the house bespoke a wondrous tradition of scholarship and philosophy. Li Gotama left us to prepare tea.

Soon we were joined by the Lama, a frail venerable sage with twinkling eyes and a wispy Confucius beard. He was more than happy to instruct us in Buddhist mysticism. Nanette and I would arrive every afternoon an hour before sunset to take notes, ask questions, and then relax over tea and cookies.

Once we were well situated, Ralph headed down the mountain en route to Millbrook.

Nanette and I were fascinated by the relationship between the Lama Govinda and Li Gotama. She was Parsee, a member of a Zoroastrian sect that fled Persia to avoid Moslem persecution. The Parsees have been called the "Jews of India" because they are a small group of exiles, intelligent, highly educated, internationally cultured, and skillful in commerce. The Parsees are interesting to a neuro-geographer because in the course of their migrations they have combined the best aspects of Persian and Hindu religions, avoiding the authoritarianism of the former and the passivity of the latter.

Ever since my Easter Sunday session at the Millbrook Meditation House I had been convinced that the linkage of opposites was the key to personal evolution. Nanette shared this belief that a man and woman who learned how to shift realities in unison, moving from one level of consciousness to another together, were a powerful creative force.

To us the Govindas represented a prime example of the two-element human molecule, what Kurt Vonnegut called a "duprass," a bi-polar unit experiencing and behaving as one. They had traveled throughout Tibet, visiting religious centers that were inaccessible to all but the hardiest pilgrims. Li was a skillful illustrator, and her designs accompanied the Lama's handwritten books.

A close friendship developed among the four of us. It turned out that the Lama and I shared an intellectual obsession—a compulsive penchant for classification. Lama Govinda had spent decades attempting to understand the logic behind the great psychological systems of the East. In modern jargon the Lama was a student of personality types. So was I. I had spent years studying the correspondences among our western systems of personality classification—Jungian, Freudian, psychometric, etc. It was a splendid synchronicity that had brought us together on a high ridge in the foothills of the Himalayas.

Typically the Lama sat in silken robes next to the low bookcases, surrounded by Tibetan mandala paintings. I sat below, cross-legged in blue jeans and white wool sweater, receiving an oral transmission from the master.

The sun set over the western ridge, flooding the windows with orange light, which reflected again from burnished bronze and jeweled statues. The Lama fumbled absent-mindedly with his papers, muttering softly to himself in German. From the bookcases he pulled out well-worn leather notebooks filled with scrolled words and diagrams.

The Lama taught in slow measured paragraphs, tossing off asides only during breaks, as he puttered with his notebooks or while Li Gotama poured tea or Nanette and I stood outside on the lawn smoking a cigarette. He spoke indirectly sometimes, in jokes, metaphors, analogies.

Science and philosophy, he said, were two branches of the same sacred disciplines. In antiquity it was taken for granted that the scientist was a holy man with great self-knowledge.

According to the Lama the power of Oriental religions derived from the oral tradition, face-to-face sessions conducted over long periods to ensure that students grew in personal wisdom as they grew in technical skill. This method of teaching prevented misuse of the knowledge for personal gain. Oral transmission encouraged the student to develop maturity and judgment while learning the secrets of nature. (The physicists who used their knowledge of the atom to build the Bomb were examples of men whose inner growth failed to keep up with their discoveries in the outer world. It is perilous to know more about the workings of the atom than about your own brain.)

In recent years, said the Lama, many of the guardians of the old philosophic traditions had realized that the evolution of the human race depended upon a restoration of unity between the outer science advanced by the West and the inner yoga advanced by the East. It had become necessary to break centuries of public silence, to bypass the master-disciple tradition, and actively seek to enlighten the West. This infiltration of Oriental philosophy into Europe and America would be carried out by publishing books and sending forth charismatic teachers.

During the last few decades, said the Lama, many Eastern teachers had attempted to awaken the spirit of self-divinity within the mechanical monotheistic cultures of the West. The theosophy movement was one such venture. The teachings of Gurdjieff, Ramakrishna, and Krishnamurti were others.

Translation of the *Tibetan Book of the Dead* into English by Evans-Wentz was part of this plan. When word came to the philosophic community of India that a group of Harvard psychologists was using the ancient Buddhist text as a manual for drug-induced satoris, there was great interest.

"You," said the Lama, "are the predictable result of a strategy that has been unfolding for over fifty years. You have done exactly what the philosophers wanted done. You were prepared discreetly by several Englishmen who were themselves agents of this process. You have been an unwitting tool of the great transformation of our age."

"I have discussed with you how wisdom must be acquired at the same rate as knowledge. Now I should like to charge you with a mission that is close to my heart and that you are well qualified to perform. The premise underlying this mission is a self-evident one: that any system of personality classification that has endured for centuries in many different cultures has passed the test of place and time. It must tell us something valid about the various types and sub-species of humans. Thus there must be meaningful correspondences among all the personality classification systems that have survived from antiquity, such as the Zodiac, the Tarot, the I Ching, the Olympian gods and goddesses, Hindu castes. A successful demonstration of correspondences among the great systems of human mentation would help to harmonize East and West, science and yoga, past and future. Would you work on this problem?

I was interested in the task but despaired of finding the time for such arcane research. One would have to live like the Lama, withdrawn from the world, like a medieval scholar in a monastery. The assignment of this mission brought my studies with the Lama to a close.

Just below Snow View cottage, in a small house nestling along the slope, there lived a dark slim Indian man and a blond woman. We often saw them strolling down to the river, hand in hand, or past our cottage on the road to town. They dressed alike in robes and sandals. We waved. They smiled and waved back.

After a few weeks they stopped by to introduce themselves. Rana was a Hindu, educated at Oxford. Hilda was separated from a Belgian diplomat formerly assigned to Bombay. She had two children, not with her.

Rana and Hilda had met in Bombay and fallen in love. Hilda's husband sought to end the affair by arranging a transfer. Hilda dutifully helped pack and arranged for the children's schooling back home. One minute before the ship was to sail she kissed the children and ran down the gangplank. Rana was waiting on the pier. The lovers quickly disappeared.

Although the governments of Belgium and India scoured the land, seeking to deport Hilda, the mayor of Almora, a relative of Rana's, kept their hiding place a secret.

Their house was a masterpiece of minimalist art. No clutter. Nothing visible except low cushions and an array of gleaming copper pans hung from the ceiling in the kitchen.

Their life was a slow ballet of Krishna-Radha love. Fusion. They brushed each other's hair. They took long leisurely walks down to the riverbank below and picnicked on the grassy bank. Every moment was shared. They read books together. They wrote poems together, which they illustrated.

Hilda and Rana were cosmopolitan people who had established total control of their lives. They had reached telepathic communication. They were consciously reliving the legends of Hindu gods who retired to mountain tops for centuries of honeymoon rapture. They were doing what Nanette and I wished we could do, if only we knew how.

The spring turned Snow View into a green glade. Mornings Nanette and I shared tea with toast and fruit. We heated pails of hot water and washed together outside. Nanette stripped off her robe, anointed her long body with soap, and I poured steaming water to rinse her off. We sat on cushions and blankets under a bamboo grove, reading texts the Lama loaned us, doing yoga. Often we nibbled a morsel of Nepalese temple ball, which loosens both mind and body.

And in this idyllic atmosphere we watched our marriage fall apart. Since our hectic days in Japan, Nanette had become more and more moody, homesick for the States, lonely for her dog, Naughty. My problem was that I hadn't lived with a woman for seven years. I felt incapable of sensitive reception and confident giving. I began to slip back into guilt about Marianne's suicide and about my two children, now in Dick's custody. Sensing this detachment my Scandinavian princess began to wonder what she was doing in this alien place.

I had lugged from America nine translations of the *Tao Te Ching*. Each day I selected one sutra and read each of the nine versions. Some were rote translations, some were theosophical revisions, some preached a boy-scout piety. It became clear that most of the translators, eminent pedants, had never experienced the calculated passivity endorsed by the *Tao Te Ching*. But underlying each poem, usually hidden by the translator's bias, there was an essence, an epiphany of meaning. My objective was to find this seed idea in each sutra and rewrite it in the lingua franca of psychedelia. [2]

SRI KRISHNA PREM (1898-1965), né Ronald Nixon, attended Taunton, graduated in philosophy from Cambridge, and went to India in search of higher wisdom. He visited and studied with many prominent gurus, including Ramana Maharishi. Eventually he became a disciple of Sri Chakravarti, leader of a Krishna-Radha cult that founded a retreat on a mountain above Almora. It was Krishna Prem's belief that illumination comes from intimate daily contact with fellow-searchers rather than from impersonal submission to a master.

His commentaries on the Bhagavad Gita and other Hindu texts were democratic, western, action-oriented. His interest in healing as well as enlightenment defines Sri Krishna Prem as a precursor of the humanist psychology movement that was to sweep America and Western Europe in the 1970s. In his later years his constant companion was Sri Madhava Ashish, another intelligent humorous Englishman.

26. Wisest Man in India

MARCH 1965
HIMALAYAS

After shopping in Almora I walked down the cliff-side stairs to visit Brahma Singh, who was putting copper coins in a bubbling solution to give them healing values. He pulled out his hookah and we smoked together gazing down the valley to the Delhi plain.

"Whom do I talk to about tantra?" I asked him. "Are there any masters around here?"

"Tantra, tantra," he giggled in mock complaint. "All you westerners come here to learn spiritual copulation. Go slow! That is the secret of tantra. Go slow and pretend you are a god making love to your universe."

"No master?"

"Who needs a master?" he scolded in that singing Anglo-Hindu accent. "I just told you the secret. Your mate is the master. Do you need someone else to hold it for you?" He was giggling again. "If you're looking for a guru to tell you what's going on in the universe, go see Sri Krishna Prem."

For a bumpy hour the jeep rattled up a rutted path to a small village. From there Nanette and I took a hard climb of forty-five minutes until we saw, across the valley, a small sparkling white temple with a deep-blue dome. After another quarter hour the trail brought us to vegetable gardens, tended neatly in English style, and a two-story box-shaped house next to the blue-white shrine. The place was deserted. We rang the bell and shouted in vain. "Oh well," I said, "perhaps Sri Krishna Prem is visiting the local villages. They say he practices herbal medicine. The peasants call him when they are ill."

Soon we heard the noise of approaching dogs. Emerging from the forest, striding forcefully, was a tall athletic Englishman dressed in a saffron robe. He wore open-toed sandals to protect his enormous beat-up feet. His vigor belied the white hair and aging face. He was flanked by another tall rugby type, in his thirties. They looked unenthusiastic to see us.

I introduced ourselves and apologized for the intrusion.

Sri Krishna Prem spoke gently. "I'm sorry if this seems rude, but our way of worship prevents us from having visitors."

His companion examined me curiously. "Aren't you that chap that got bounced from Harvard for giving Huxley's satori pills to prisoners and Episcopalians?"

I admitted it.

Sri Krishna Prem's manner changed as he stretched out his huge hand in welcome. "I am so pleased to meet you both. Huxley and I banged around a bit in college. And of course I've read every word he's written, especially since his turn to the East. We've heard about your attempts to illuminate America. Please consider our shrine your home in India."

The two yogis showed us the grounds and invited us to the main house for tea. Nanette and I reclined on deep rugs and cushions in the library while the two saffron-robed Englishmen bustled around preparing a snack. Sri Krishna Prem questioned us about our backgrounds, personal and spiritual, our education, our careers, how we met, where we had been. He paid as much attention to Nanette as to me.

When he asked about the research with drugs, I described our initial naivete, our reliance on Eastern philosophy, our education by British philosophers and by street people, blacks, musicians, hippies. He especially enjoyed hearing about the Reluctance of Respectable Scientists, the Alarm of Administrators, the Fury of Parents, the Reckless Cerebral Courage of the Young. This sixty-seven-year-old philosopher, niched in the foothills of the Himalayas, seemed to understand Harvard and Millbrook exactly: our confusions, our aspirations, our need for guidance.

Nanette asked about their way of worship.

"We are dedicated to Krishna, the spirit of love," said Ashish. "At first we used a statue of the baby Krishna as our focus. We bathed and dressed and sang to and fed and worshipped a little Krishna doll, which was the screen for our spiritual projections. Each moment of the day was devoted to love for our shared ideal. We followed the ancient prescriptions laid down in the Vedas. Purity of eating habits. Dishes washed in special containers. No leather on the premises because of worship of the cow." He looked at his older friend and they both laughed.

"Once we allowed an eager young searcher to stay with us. While we were out one afternoon, he washed the dishes, thinking to help us. But he did not perform the ablutions in the prescribed manner. We fell into a rage and scolded the wretched fellow. We had to smash all the dishes because he had profaned the purity of the ritual. As we stormed around shouting and screaming like fishmongers, we suddenly looked at each other. What were we doing? We had devoted our lives to love, and yet we were raving in anger because our innocent guest tried to help us in the best way he knew how."

"So we purified, really purified, the rituals," said Sri Krishna Prem. "We eliminated everything that was rote, repetitious, traditional but not relevant to the moment. And why, we asked ourselves, were we worshipping and taking care of a little Krishna doll and neglecting the Krishna in the living humans around us? We concluded that to contact the inner divinity we needed the day-to-day push and shove of living with a spiritual partner, the emotional elbowing, the close friction with the intimate beloved. That is our yoga now."

Sri Krishna Prem rose to his towering height and stretched. "Enough talk about ritual. Let's sit by the fire in the kitchen and cook a fine hot meal to warm our souls."

We assembled before a large fireplace in which a tree stump merrily burned. The place felt more like a hunter's cabin than a rectory. We had brought as gifts some canned English delicacies, jellies, relishes, and olives, which were welcome. Sri Krishna Prem brought out a bottle of sherry—just like the good old days at Oxford.

Ashish served dinner—rice, yams, fresh cauliflower in rich butter sauce, a roasted-nut concoction that tasted like steak, and fresh salad. After dinner, while we sipped coffee, Sri Krishna Prem told us this story.

Once upon a time in a castle there awaited, for anyone brave and wise enough to attain it, a golden chalice containing the boons of eternal wisdom. For centuries the most courageous knights and intelligent princesses traveled far across the world to win the prize. But no one succeeded. The only approach to the castle was through a marshy lagoon with a mile-long chain of stepping stones. The high-towered magnificent castle gleamed and shone with a radiant light for all to see.

Finding the castle was not a problem. The problem was this. As soon as anyone stepped on a stone, it promptly sank into the mud. Every aspirant drowned.

One day there arrived on the shore a princess accompanied by her prince. They had heard of the fate that befell every other aspirant, yet they yearned to reach the castle so dearly that they agreed to run across the lagoon together. They started running. From rock to rock they leaped, so quickly that before one rock could sink they were on to the next. And so proceeding they reached the castle of illumination.

When the story was done, I asked, "What you're saying is *keep moving? In tandem?*"

He nodded.

As if from too much exertion he raised his hand unsteadily to his mouth and coughed. Ashish said, "Krishna Prem has not been well."

As we left, Sri Krishna Prem held my hand and looked in my eyes. "Can you return?"

The monks walked us to the ridge as we followed the moonlit path to the village.

The following week I visited them again. Nanette stayed home.

Ashish and Sri Krishna Prem were on the roof repairing tiles. They stood up precariously on the slanted surface and whooped at me like schoolboys, their robes flapping.

Sitting on a small rug that Ashish threw on the grass Sri Krishna Prem smiled. "I am now going to present you with a mandala, a philosophic diagram, a key to illumination in the twentieth century." I leaned forward curiously as he unrolled a chart.

It was a standard map of the world.

"Meditate on this sacred diagram," he said. "Can you imagine what the Buddha would have said if he had had this map? Now let me show you a yogic trick to convert this into a map of time, not just space." He turned the map so that west was up and east was at the bottom. "Do you understand?"

"East is past and west is future?"

"Yes. I have recently lamented the navigational error we made many years ago. To come east in search of wisdom was a mistake. The eightfold path leads west. Consider this: the Hindu theory of reincarnation of souls dates back to 4,000 years ago, when everyone—maharajah, brahmin, peasant, everyone—lived all their lives in one place, in one family, in a fixed caste. There was no concept of change. There was not even the possibility of movement in status or lifestyle. Everything was predestined. Your job, your marriage, your friends, your enemies, your aging, your death—all fixed on one stone in the marsh.

"The only opportunity for change came with death. Can you understand what these Hindus in the villages around us experience? There is no concept of change in their life. Transmigration of souls is the only way they can conceive of altering destiny.

"To the westerner it is very different. We can move our bodies. We don't have to wait until death to change reality. We use cars, planes, radio, television to move from one reality to another. Imagine my astonishment as a young Cambridge graduate. I came to India and became a wandering pilgrim, a yogi, a devotee of Ramana Maharishi. And suddenly I realized that even he, the great master, had never left the stone of India. Since the philosophers of the past couldn't migrate in their bodies, they invented a theory of migrating souls.

"Today the searcher can reincarnate as many times as he or she can move from one stone to the next. The wisdom of our age is movement and change. Evolution is the key to illumination."

The sun, big and orange, was setting over the foothills of the Himalayas. We retired to the shrine for a quick bell-ringing pick-me-up ceremony of chanting and then went to the kitchen, where we passed many hours in conversation. Sri Krishna Prem was fascinated to know that I had been in a movie studio in Hollywood, asking me many questions about how films were made and distributed. He seemed to think that the mass media would replace the oral tradition of teaching.

I spent the night in one of the guest cottages, lying on a narrow bed, hearing the cries of animals in the hills, feeling the rough blanket against my skin, missing Nanette, and reflecting on the talks with Sri Krishna Prem.

I was up at dawn. Ashish was already chopping firewood behind the house. He invited me in for hot tea and toast. After breakfast, as I prepared to leave, Sri Krishna Prem motioned me to sit down next to him.

"It is time that I tell you some things that you should know. Over the centuries our Hindu philosophers have seen everything come and go. Empires, religions, famines, good times, invasions, reforms, liberations, repressions. And drugs.

"Drugs are among the most influential and dangerous powers available to humans. They open up glorious and pleasurable chambers in the mind. They give great power. Thus they can seduce the searcher away from the Path."

Sri Krishna Prem patted me affectionately on the back. "It is time, my friend, for you to return to the West, and there you will meet difficult challenges and be forced to pass many arduous tests."

He told me another story.

Once upon a time in a small house on a mountain lived a yogi and his wife. The fame of this loving couple spread throughout the kingdom. One day a young girl in the village was found pregnant. When her enraged parents questioned her, she tearfully confessed that it was the yogi who had seduced her. Because of his great power she had been unable to refuse his wicked demands. After the scandal spread throughout the village, the inhabitants, led by the mayor, rushed up to confront the yogi.

"You are not a holy man," the mayor shouted. "You seduced this young girl. You are a fraud."

"Is that right?" said the yogi quietly.

Several years passed. The yogi and his wife lived quietly, never coming to the village. Then one day the mayor died. After the funeral the young woman began to sob uncontrollably and confessed to her parents that it had been the mayor who had made her pregnant and forced her to blame the holy man. The villagers, overcome with remorse, gathered together and went up the mountain to the home of the yogi and his wife.

"We have made a terrible mistake," they said. "You are not an evil man. The mayor was the guilty one. You are a wise and good man."

"Is that right?" said the yogi.

Sri Krishna Prem gave me some sacred objects. We kissed and looked into each other's eyes. Then I walked down the mountain.

Nanette and I had one more LSD session in the Himalayas to see if we could get fused again. I somehow expected that the imprinting of a new reality for us would be no more complicated than making a movie. (*Set* would be the script and *setting* the props. This was before I learned how complex the making of a Hollywood movie really is.)

The decision to trip in a Siva temple may have been wrong for us. Siva is the Destroyer. We took LSD in mid-afternoon and started walking. About a half mile before Lama Govinda's house we climbed to the small temple, long deserted and overgrown. Battered stone lingams sticking up like rotting mushrooms evoked images of village girls who still pour milk and scatter petals on the stony penis of Siva in hopes of finding a fertile hard-working village lad.

The temple interior was gloomy, lined with rectangular stone hollows where monks had lain in ascetic meditation.

Nanette wrapped herself in her long suede coat, golden tresses curling around the fur collar, her eyes shaded in Fifth Avenue dark glasses. "This place is creepy. Let's go home and light the fire," she said shivering.

As we walked back, I found myself hurrying.

"You never walk in step with me," she complained.

I jumped in guilty agreement, slowed down, put my arm around her shoulders, and tried to walk in unison. A wildcat screamed in the woods up to our left. A flock of birds took flight.

"I wonder if that's the tiger that's been killing animals around the valley." My spine answered with peasant fear.

I unlocked the door to our cottage and stumbled across the room looking for a candle. Scratched a match. A tongue of light licked at the dark, showing me the fireplace. I lit newspaper under the kindling and remained on my knees blowing the flame. Then I looked in the glittering eye of my worst, most terrorizing nightmare.

"Oh no," I moaned.

Nanette stood in the middle of the room, suede coat in hands, looking at me curiously. Everything in the room was alive, everything in tune except me. I was dead, alienated.

Nanette shook her head in dismay. "You're not freaking out, are you?"

My eyes darted around madly. I was separated from my wife by a transparent film. Still on my knees I reached up and touched her hand. Horrors! Like touching a statue. She was alive, of course. It was my touch that froze.

Nanette, sprawled on the silken couch, slender blue-jeaned legs languorously crossed, keened the cosmic lament. "What a drag. Here we are in this perfect honeymoon cottage in the Himalayas, and we take the aphrodisiac, and you decide to flip out. Shit."

I knelt by her, took off her shoes, and stroked her feet. I felt her luscious body settle a bit in relaxation. But then I saw that I was stroking her skin in nervous reflex. "I guess it's over," I muttered unhappily.

She raised the hand mirror and examined her face. She lit a cigarette. "Oh, well," she sighed, trying to be brave. "I guess it's not the end of the world."

I brewed some tea. I drank in despair. I realized with clarity that our marriage was at an end.

So we're moving on. We had connected as fairy-tale lovers in the enchanted woods of Millbrook, had lived out a season of courtly romance. She had taught me tender lessons of girl-love and female splendor. We had time-traveled through a few mythic incarnations, played out magical dramas in panoramic realms. Now we would have to rise to that most complex human art, gentle separation.

At dawn I pulled on my tennis shoes, walked to the rocky cliffs, and climbed down, exulting in the pull of muscles and the mountain grace, feeling free of hopelessness, looking forward to returning home. An eagle, wings motionless, hung on air currents above me. I'd be a better lover next time.

Next day we borrowed $100 travel money from the Methodist lady, packed, and started the long trip down to Delhi on our way back home.

MARY ENO PINCHOT MEYER (1921-1964), painter, socialite, and feminist martyr, was descended from a family of American dissidents. Her uncle Gifford Pinchot, among the first conservation activists, helped found the Bull Moose political party and later served as governor of Pennsylvania.

Mary Pinchot graduated from Vassar College in 1942 and three years later married Cord Meyer, Jr., an anticommunist leader in liberal organizations who later became a top-level CIA agent.[1]

The Meyers were divorced in 1959.

As a resident of Georgetown Mary Pinchot Meyer moved in the highest circles of power in the nation's capital. Her sister Toni married and later divorced Benjamin C. Bradlee, who became editor of the *Washington Post*.

Mary Pinchot Meyer's close friends included President and Mrs. John F. Kennedy.

27. Dissipative Structures

JUNE 1965
MILLBROOK, NEW YORK

The earth-orbiting spaceship *Honeymoon* limped back to Millbrook with no flags flying. My relations with Nanette were just barely friendly.

My jangled nerves were not soothed by the six months of changes that had converted Millbrook from a community of scholars and scientists to a playground for rowdy omnisexuals. In my absence Dick had fallen in love with Arnie, a flamboyant photographer from Brooklyn who liked to project color slides on walls during acid sessions, leading the vulnerable brains of his audience through a Coney Island funhouse of hallucinatory pranks.

Always the enthusiastic lieutenant Dick had promoted Arnie to the position of Adored Guru. It was Arnie who now set the tone and directed the scenarios.

Arnie had assembled a mountebank crew: Allen Eager, a legendary jazz saxophonist and notorious junky. Milt, a bearded photographer·who slithered around with a perpetual hard-on. Then there was Micky, a glib graduate student from NYU and his pretty yoga-student wife Laura, both promiscuous as bunny rabbits. Not to mention Arnie's wife, his two kids, his ex-girlfriend, and his new girlfriend, Clara Hoover, the intelligent sophisticated heiress to the vacuum cleaner fortune and a tower of calm wisdom in this dissipative madness. Michael Hollingshead had reincarnated in Scottish kilts and scarlet capes, zanily lecturing on the relativity of the brain.

It was a James Dean juvenile delinquency script. Tough street New Yorkers using LSD for mischievous fun.

Arnie and crew specialized in playing pranks on each other during acid sessions—a neurological form of demolition derby, pushing insanity pedals to the floor, deliberately trying to confuse, frighten, spook each other. For two weeks they camped out at the Meditation House, intoxicating themselves with hundreds (hundreds!) of doses of acid, undeniably breaking all records for conspicuous over-consumption.

Needless to say the antics of Dick's Band of Rascals had scandalized the Hitchcocks and everyone else who viewed Millbrook as a dependable spiritual base. Everyone waited to see what would happen when I returned. "To clean up the mess," as Ralph put it. He had returned before us from India, loaded with serious Oriental wisdom, and was ostracized as hopelessly humorless.

I was in no shape to handle any of this, running several quarts low because of the rupture with Nanette.

When I tried to talk to Dick about the future, he couldn't get interested. He had shrewdly decided to take a long vacation. After all, who held down the home front while Ralph and Nanette and I were traipsing around the world? Now it was his turn. He had accepted an invitation to summer in France at the beach house of some famous jet-set prince. Then he would visit the London Playboy scene to run LSD sessions for the infamous Vic Lownes. All this made my guru-chasing in India seem pretty conventional.

Dick listened to my worries about parting with Nanette. He suggested that we three take LSD together. In hindsight this was the height of folly—we were three willful wary souls, already alienated from each other.

Dick appointed himself shaman. His heavy-dose experiences with the Punksters had taught him impressive psychedelic barnstorming flourishes. He used a long glass tube to titrate the clear liquid LSD. And he blasted us!

He panicked first, thinking, *my god these two have been tripping together so much they have an unbreakable bond. I'm cut off.* He lay motionless, watching like a wary cat.

Nanette was thinking, *why am I here?*

I was trapped in my battered time-ship, power-failing, drifting off, rudderless.

Here was a classic example of a negative re-programming. Each of us was as vulnerable as a newborn babe. In this kind of situation the first one to take a decisive position will initiate new reality for the others.

Dick made the first move, and it was a blind-side tackle. He accused

me of being a disapproving moralist, a prude who condemned his homosexuality.

How I reacted to this first move would be crucial. Response A: I laugh
and genially point out that the love and humor among us three will
conquer all. Outcome: fusion. We unite as a triumphant merry trio of
divinities. I don't spend four years alone in jail, while Dick doesn't paint
himself into the lonely Holy Man corner, and Nanette maintains two
wise friends for her blossoming career.

But I could do no better than Response B: guilty silence. Outcome:
fission. Dick and Nanette exchanged a conspiratorial glance of superiority,
which with X-ray sensitivity I caught. I drifted off leaking spinal fluid,
leaving Nanette and Dick bonded together in a surprised uneasy alliance.

If Dick or I had been more secure, either one of us could have strobed
the other out of low spirits with a blast of loving humor. But no. This
acid session was about severing connections. The lines went down, and
we never got the current going again. It was the last time we took acid
together.

For the next few days I circled the field aimlessly, trying to figure
out where to land with the rest of my life. I retreated to a small bedroom
in the servant's wing, devoting my time to the Taoist poems. Everything
changes. This too will pass. Lay low, walk slow. I planted a garden
behind the Meditation House with seeds and cuttings from a nearby
Rudolph Steiner farm.

Dick came out of the session glowing with confidence, enjoying a
glorious brief moment of leadership. Then he left. Then Bye-Bye,
Nanette, driven by my peevishness to an apartment in Manhattan. One
by one the Punksters became discouraged by the monastic atmosphere
and drifted away. Soon there remained only a small cadre of ex-Harvard
loyalists: Ralph Metzner, Michael Hollingshead, and his lovely bookish
mistress.

In my yearning for an ally, a friend, a woman, I found myself thinking
a lot about Mary Pinchot. I asked everyone at Millbrook if she had phoned
during the round-the-world trip, but no one remembered hearing from
her.

Directory assistance in Washington, D.C. had numbers for several Pin-
chots but none for Mary. Then I remembered that she was a Vassar
graduate and phoned the alumni office in Poughkeepsie. The cheery voice
of the secretary became guarded when I asked for the address of Mary
Pinchot.

"Mary Pinchot?" A long pause. "The person about whom you were
asking . . . ah, her married name is Meyer. But I'm sorry to say that
she is, ah, deceased. Sometime last fall, I believe."

"I've been out of the country. I didn't know."

"Thank you for calling," said the alumni secretary.

In shock I climbed out a third-floor window and up the steep copper roof of the Big House. There I leaned back against a chimney and tried to think things over. Michael Hollingshead, who sensed my malaise, scrambled up to join me, carrying two beers. When I told him about Mary, he brushed away a tear.

"I wonder what happened," I said.

"Next time we go to New York, let's see what we can find out," said Michael. Balancing gracefully on bare feet he walked to the west ledge of the roof to contemplate the setting sun. A flock of swallows swept across the lawn and collected in the branches of the twin birches.

I joined him.

"Look here, old man," Michael said. "No point in living in the past. You have at your disposal right here and now all the factors needed to do something splendid. Why not start a new game?"

"What new game?"

"Neurological Art. A new creative expression based on our knowledge of the nervous system. The eight circuits of the brain define the Eight Fine Arts. Orchestrate them together, and you get a Psychedelic Theatre of the Mind."

Despite my withered lizard torpor, I responded to what Michael was saying. The function of any art is to activate, in the brain of the beholder, the desired reality. Socialist art activates the work-hard serve-the-state Marxist reality. Catholic art turns on the submission realities. Erotic art accesses the sex circuits. Gurdjieff once described how Sufi monastics in the Middle East mastered the use of sound to a point where they could evoke any emotion from an audience. I speculated. "We could arrange a sound-and-light show that would demonstrate what an LSD session is like. We could activate different brain circuits without drugs."

"You got it," said Michael, who was now recklessly striding back and forth on the slanted roof.

So off we went, Michael and I, down the Hudson to New York to meet the light-artists and sound wizards who were popping up on the Lower East Side. And to find out what happened to Mary Pinchot Meyer.

I cabbed over to Van Wolfe's apartment, drank a beer, and asked him if he could get any material on Mary Pinchot Meyer. He made a phone call to a friend who worked on the *Times*. An hour later a messenger was at the door with a manila envelope full of clippings, and WHAM— there was Mary's picture, the pert chin and nose, the deep intense eyes. Above, the headline read:

WOMAN PAINTER SHOT AND KILLED ON CANAL

TOWPATH IN CAPITAL

Mrs. Mary Pinchot Meyer Was a Friend of
Mrs. Kennedy
Suspect is arraigned

Mary had been shot twice in the left temple and once in the chest at 12:45 in the afternoon of October 13, 1964 as she walked along the Old Chesapeake and Ohio Canal towpath in Georgetown. A friend told reporters that Mary sometimes walked there with her close friend Jacqueline Kennedy.

Mary's brother-in-law, Benjamin C. Bradlee, *Newsweek*'s Washington bureau chief, identified her body. Ben Bradlee was described as having been an intimate of the late President Kennedy. The article also mentioned Mary's ex-husband, Cord Meyer, Jr., former leader of the American Veterans Committee and the World Federalists, now a government employee, position and agency not specified.[1]

Police said that the motive was apparently robbery or assault. Her purse was found by Ben Bradlee in her home. The suspect, a black male, was being held without bail. He denied the crime. He had been at the canal fishing.

I was sobbing. I walked to the bathroom and threw cold water on my face. My hands were shaking. I was stunned to learn that Mary had been married to Cord Meyer, my nemesis from graduate school days, who now turned out to be a top spook. My head was spinning with ominous thoughts. A close friend of the Kennedy family had been murdered in broad daylight with no apparent motive. And there had been so little publicity. No outcry. No call for further investigation. I felt that same vague fear that came when we heard about JFK's assassination.

"Can you get me more information?" I asked Van.

Van said he'd contact some of his friends in the police and organized crime to get more facts.

Van came up to Millbrook the next weekend. I took him on a walk to Lunacy Hill. We sat smoking grass, watching the Hudson Valley tint purple as the sun set.

"My friend in police intelligence knew all about the Mary Pinchot Meyer case. Apparently a lot of people are convinced it was an assassination. Two slugs in the brain and one in the body. That's not the MO of a rapist. And a mugger isn't going to shoot a woman with no purse in her hand."

Van pulled out a Lucky Strike and lit it. His tremor was more pronounced than usual. "It's gotta be one of the biggest cover-ups in Washington history. It's too hot to handle. Everyone comes out looking bad. Some people say dope was involved. So the truth could hurt everyone, all those powerful people. No one wants the facts known."

"They can't get away with a cover-up like this," I protested.

"They have. And you know what we're going to do? We're going to have the adventure thriller of our lives. We're going to uncover the facts, and you're going to write a book about it. I'll raise some money for Hollingshead to research it in Washington—interview everyone, poke around, bribe maids and precinct cops. Hire private detectives. There are lots of people who might talk."

"I'd just like to know what happened."

Van leaned forward, his whole body shaking. "We'll dig up the facts. But we'll have to get a big publisher behind us to expose a cover-up like this one."

The lovelorn summer of 1965 crept along on painfully. My pals were the two mansion dogs, short-haired setters named Fang and O'Brien. My garden, weeded and watered tenderly, was a solace. I fertilized it with a solution of LSD to see what would happen. The plants responded with enthusiasm, producing juicy, sweet, vegetables.

I remember so clearly that summer morning when I walked out to the portico terrace, and there she was! The next seven years of my life!

A cloud of pheromones floating from her body awakened my lazy off-duty hormones. My knees wobbled. Her name was Rosemary Woodruff, age thirty. In her hand was a book by Wittgenstein. She had come up for the weekend with some friends.

Rosemary needed help. She had brought a bottle of French wine but no corkscrew. My ears were *rouge*, my mouth *sec*. I led her to the kitchen, popped the cork, and poured her a glass.

"You are the kindest man in the world," she said. Her moves were fluid, graceful. She was wearing tight jeans bound by a silver chain. Her boy's shirt was tied above the navel, revealing a strip of creamy smooth belly. I poured some wine in my glass, and we toasted our meeting. She wore tennis shoes! That was the genetic signal. And she read Wittgenstein. I wondered idly if she was an intelligence agent assigned to my case. If so, the psych-tech boys sure had my number.

That afternoon I took her for a walk. I felt painfully shy.

"I'd like to come back," she said.

"Any time," I replied.

The week after Rosemary's visit Michael and I went to New York to try out our first brain-activating light show. Billy Hitchcock loaned us the New Theater, a 299-seat house in the East Fifties, for a Monday night. The afternoon before the show we sat in the front row to watch the wizardry of the light-artists. To externalize their visions these artists shot electric light through optical devices, through vials of colored gelatin, tumbling crystals, elliptoid structures. This meta-light splashed on screens and reflected back to the audience, through the focusing mechanisms of corneas, through irises dilating and contracting with the 3,500 to 8,000 angstroms, through nerve fibers that collect and feed impulses to the brain, reaching cerebral zones that had never been activated with such Niagaras of exploding colors and wiggling patterns, except when very high on psychedelic drugs. The light-artists stimulated with pinpoint accuracy those areas of the brain that light up when one is lit up. These Zarathustra machines generated a high. Legally. If the performance was reinforced with an optically active drug, the intensity of the high was predictably increased.

We selected a few of these wizards to perform at the evening show. The rest were invited to set up their contraptions in the lobby so that incoming guests could enjoy a continual barrage of phantasmagoric illuminations never before sprayed upon human retinas.

As prelude to the light presentations Ralph gave a charmingly pedantic lecture on the anatomical and physiological capacities of the various sense organs. I followed with a poetic-scientific sales-rap about the various circuits of the brain, describing what happened when they were turned on. Education, entertainment, and advertising were nicely blended.

The performance-lectures sold out and attracted media attention. The ideas were new, the sights and sounds were novel, and the notion of turning on without drugs was intriguing to the prudish press. The audiences included many intelligent affluent New Yorkers already exposed to the psychedelic aesthetic. We hoped that they would go home and create their own art.

I was alone in the dressing room after the performance, missing Nanette or someone, drinking champagne, enjoying the slow let-down of show-biz energy, when Michael came in with a worried look. "Van just called. He's upset about something. Wants you to come over."

I found Van chain-smoking Lucky Strikes, emitting panic signals. He had spent the afternoon talking about Mary Pinchot Meyer with a friend, a criminal lawyer. "Manny knew about the case," said Van. "When he heard what we were planning, he hit the roof. He said that acid must have rotted my brain or else I would understand that *nobody* wanted this incident investigated."

"We're not accusing anybody," I said. "And the cover-up is undeniable. All we want is a thorough investigation."

"There are a lot of people who obviously don't."

"So what should we do?"

"Let's lay low. I'll try to raise some money, on the quiet, to pay for an investigation."

It was discouraging.

"Don't be upset," said Van. "The truth comes out sooner or later."

One night after a light show, while I was relaxing in Van's apartment, Rosemary phoned. Bored with life in New York, she was about to split for California and was wondering if she could spend a few days at Millbrook before she left.

Within seconds I was out the door on my way to meet her. Within minutes I was carrying her suitcases to my car. I bought a bottle of champagne, and we headed north on the beautiful grass-bordered Taconic Parkway, sky sparkling with stars above us. Rosemary sat in the lotus position on the front seat, stretching her arms over her head, turning now and then to fill my glass.

"What do you want to happen at Millbrook?"

"I want to fall in love with you," she said.

That night I put her in the tower bedroom. "This is your base as long as you want it," I said.

I retired to a bedroom on the second floor. Tossing and turning I could feel her warmth and desire beaming down two stories.

The next day we did yoga in the large front room. I took her for a long walk around the estate. We ended up at the lake, running along a path, hand in hand, ducking under low branches, arriving breathless at the wide stone dam, where the lake spilled six inches of silky warm water over our bare feet. As we stood on the moss-covered stones of the dam, my mouth caressed her soft lips. I could feel her hand fumbling at the string of her white cotton slacks. They loosened and fell. With one swing of her hips she kicked the garment free. The lake water rushed beneath us. Holding each other, kissing, we lowered our bodies to the green slick surface of the dam and lay on the enormous stone blocks, worn smooth by decades of licking caressing water.

That evening we moved our bed to the Meditation House and took acid together. There I courted Rosemary in her 10,000 forms.

Next afternoon I dragged a ladder and buckets of paint to the second-story porch roof. Rosemary and I outlined the ancient Oriental symbol for sexual union, interlocked triangles, on the red brick chimney. Drawn eight feet tall the Maha Yantra of fusion dominated the approach to our castle.

G **EORGES I. GURDJIEFF** (1877-1949) was born in Gumri, a town on the Armenian plains. In his early manhood Gurdjieff became a devoted student of Sufism, traveling extensively in the Middle East in order to learn the many practical techniques for self-growth taught by this extraordinary sect. In Russia, before World War I, he taught an all-inclusive system of inner knowledge and produced music/dance performances that actualized his philosophy. After the Russian Revolution he migrated to Fontainebleau, where his teaching attracted many prominent students, including Ouspensky, Katherine Mansfield, and A.R. Orage.

Gurdjieff's ideas are contained in three books: *All and Everything, or Beeljebub's Tales to His Grandson,* a philosophic tract that might be compared to Pynchon's *Gravity's Rainbow* or Joyce's *Finnegan's Wake; Meetings with Remarkable Men,* an account of Gurdjieff's experiences with a group of wisdom seekers; and *Life is Real Only Then, When "I Am,"* which centers on practical methods for expanding and managing realities (including the intelligent use of drugs).[1]

28. Busted at Laredo

FALL 1965
MILLBROOK, NEW YORK

Rosemary and I spent all of our time together. We moved into the large master bedroom on the third floor and set up our bed in an alcove walled and ceilinged with mirrors.

Picnics at the lake. Long walks around the estate, exploring back streams and shadowed forests. Lying naked by the creek, idly fishing. Running with the dogs. Harvesting the garden. Rosemary dancing to rock and roll music blasting from one corner of the castle to the other.

Sometimes when far up in the wilds of the estate we could hear the ominous whup-whup of helicopter blades as the sheriff's airborne spies peered down at us.

Rosemary and I shared the work too. I was finishing the book of psychedelic poetry based on the *Tao Te Ching*. Rosemary edited the manuscript. She joined Michael and Ralph and me in preparing the slide shows and tapes we used in our weekend workshops in various cities around the East Coast. These presentations began with a Friday-night public lecture, continuing in eight-hour sessions on Saturday and Sunday. We tried to simulate LSD experiences with sounds, strobes, and slides as Ralph, Michael, and I alternated murmured narration and yogic instructions while Rosemary whispered philosophic poetry, hour upon hour,

recapitulating the evolution of our species, taking the astounded participants up the chakras of their bodies, twenty-four spiritual orgasms climax-
ing in the famous death-defying head chakra rebirth explosion.

The more sophisticated customers would bring their own drugs and
float high through the session. A sincere young blond student named
Deborah Harry did. An assistant of Henry Luce did. Michael Horowitz
and Cindy Palmer did. But most of our clients were straight, and I tell
you we gave them their $75 worth of brain show.

Nearly always we could count on at least one nervous-looking undercover police agent to fill out the audience, often more than one, cop
rivalry being an inescapable fact of life. Their reactions amused us. Some
freaked out from the sensory overload; some came away deeply impressed.

Rosemary—sophisticated, worldly—continually joked me out of the trap
of YMCA Hinduism, the goal of which was to become a Holy Man,
a prospect she found too amusing for words. When Rosemary appeared
I had been diligently studying oriental philosophy for four years. I was
coming to realize that it was useful for preparation—turning our attention
away from external conformity to inner potential and self-discovery. Yoga
was an essential tool, a basic Boy Scout training. But I didn't want to
spend my life in spiritual summer camps, working on religious merit
badges. Religion seemed to lead back to the past, to tie the believer to
tradition, to discourage active attempts to create a more intelligent future.
Through Rosemary I learned a critically important lesson: that the
psychedelic experience could not only illuminate the theological concepts
of the past but, more important, could map new visions.

Rosemary made another profound contribution to my education: she
turned me on to science fiction. Her fascination with s.f. colored our
LSD sessions, peopling our journeys with more advanced models of the
species, enabling us to play out romantic adventures against the highly
civilized background of the future. She particularly liked those haunting
time-travel themes where telepathic lovers were pursued for light years
across the galaxies.

After Thanksgiving the climate around Millbrook became threatening.
Strangers in the uniforms of telephone repairmen made unannounced visits, claiming to check the wires. The owner of the plumbing shop in
town confided that federal agents had asked to borrow uniforms from him
to gain access to our house. He had thrown them out of his office. Unmarked cars were seen driving through the property. Men with binoculars.
We put up "No Admittance" signs and locked the gates. There were rumors
from Poughkeepsie, the county seat, that the district attorney was planning
a raid. An ambitious assistant district attorney with a poetic flair told the
local Kiwanis that "the panties were dropping faster than the acid in Leary's
lair."

Dick arrived back from Europe in the fall. Michael, Ralph, and I met him at the Poughkeepsie station, and we convened a cheerless conference in a restaurant. We agreed that we had gone about as far as we could go at Millbrook. The fun had stopped. The money, energy, able bodies, and utopian idealism needed to maintain a sixty-four-room castle had been dissipated.

Like knights saddling up we four resolved to pursue our separate quests and illuminate our respective realms. Dick struck off to start a new reality in California. Although he had seemed too neurotic, too sexually avant garde for our scholarly-scientific scene, from the minute we separated, his moral pendulum began to swing in the opposite direction. Five years later, when I was being called the "most dangerous man in the world," Dick had become America's most respected Hindu swami. Baba Ram Dass. A veritable saint.

Ralph Metzner went to New York to write a book on consciousness. Michael Hollingshead, always ready for an adventurous assignment, was elected to bring the message of brain-change to England. A new spirit of experimentation was emerging in London. The Beatles and Rolling Stones had already sent emissaries to Millbrook.

I announced that I would close Millbrook and retire to Mexico to write the story of our adventures. A literary agent had phoned to tell me that New American Library would advance me $10,000 on an autobiography. We used some of the money to buy a passage on the *Queen Elizabeth II* for Michael, who sailed with 1,000 doses of M.G.'s and 200 copies of *The Psychedelic Experience*.

On December 20, 1965, the forty-fifth anniversary of my conception, we turned off the water and power, locked the doors, and piled into the new leased station wagon: Rosemary, Susan, Jack, and Timothy heading for the Yucatan, a month-long vacation for the four of us to get to know each other. After the Christmas vacation Susan would return to her private school and Jack would spend the spring with friends. Rosemary and I would find a house on the beach where I would finish writing the book.

We rolled down the eastern seaboard through the Deep South, Jolly Jack and Rowdy Ro smoking grass in the back seat, and arrived full of high spirits in New Orleans. This was the first time since Marianne's death, ten years in the sorrowful past, that the kids and I had linked up with a loving woman. After the book was finished, Rosemary and I planned to return to America, find a house with a white picket fence, and have babies.

Once, as Rosemary and I lay on foam mattresses in the fold-down back seat, she turned to me with eyes glowing. "This is what I've always wanted—kids, a station wagon, and a vacation in the sun."

It all seemed normal and good. If my autobiography about Huxley, Ginsberg, Sri Krishna Prem, Mary Pinchot, and everyone was successful, Rosemary wanted me to go on to write science fiction and learn to hook up our brains to a computer. Although Rosemary had not finished high school—too hot for pom-pom girl studies she had run away with a jazz musician—she was the best-read person I ever knew. And here she was lying in the back of a station wagon flashing her knock-me-up grin. "And if the book isn't a success you can get a job as a professor at some classy New England college, and we'll have faculty teas and sherry with the graduate students."

Through Texas our spirits mounted. Jack and Susan, seasoned veterans of Mexican voyages, chatted away about the foreign adventures ahead.

We arrived in Laredo at mid-afternoon. I knew the procedures for crossing the border, having driven this same route with Jack in the summer of 1960 en route to the mushrooms.

Rosemary also knew the town well because her former husband had been busted for grass at the border and she had spent some time at the federal courthouse talking to lawyers and probation officers. This was a warning sign that we chose to ignore.

We bought auto insurance and drove across the bridge to Nuevo Laredo at 7 p.m. We stopped at Mexican Immigration to get our tourist cards.

"Timoteo." The policeman's greeting was full of warmth. "Timoteo, don't you remember me?"

It was Jorge Garcia, the friendly police agent who had tried to help us in Zihuatanejo in 1963. "Jorge! Of course." We shook hands. Then he frowned.

"But Timoteo, you cannot enter Mexico. It is *prohibido*."

"Oh, yes," I replied cheerfully. "I have a special letter from your Departamento de Gobierno permitting me to come to Mexico as a tourist."

Jorge examined the document with a serious look.

"Don't worry," he said. "I'll do what I can. You wait right here and I'll be back in a few minutes." With that he raced out the door, jumped into an unmarked car, and headed for the American border.

Now the paranoia dials began to flash red. I turned to my little family. "Listen, there may be some problem here. If there's any grass in the car, we should flush it down the toilet."

Jack and Rosemary went out to the parking lot. In a flash Jack returned, disappeared into the men's room, and then sat down with a "mission-accomplished" grin.

Jorge Garcia burst into the room. "No, Timoteo, it is not possible for you to enter Mexico tonight. The offices in Mexico City are closed. You return to America tonight. Come back here tomorrow. I'll straighten everything out then."

Jack, Susan, and I walked out to the car. Rosemary was already sitting in the back seat. We climbed in.

Nuevo Laredo is a free-zone border town that does not require tourist visas. We didn't have to re-cross the border into America. We could have checked into a hotel, wandered the streets, had a festive dinner, watched the hustlers, mariachis, and tourists and in the morning returned to the Immigration office. But I robotically turned the car around. It dawned on me about halfway across the International Bridge that even though we hadn't actually entered Mexico we would still have to pass through Customs, just like the VW buses from purple Michoacan, golden Acapulco, and seedless Guadalajara.

"All the grass is out of the car, right?"

Rosemary, fumbling around in her baggage in the back seat, said in a worried voice, "No. I couldn't get to my silver box because there were two uniformed porters leaning against the car. Here it is." She handed it to Susan.

The car rolled relentlessly toward the Customs station. "I'll hide it in my clothes," said Susan, sitting next to me in the front seat. We couldn't throw the silver box out the window—bang, blam, metallic flash in the middle of the bridge. Could we?

When the customs officer walked up I handed over our unused Mexican papers. "We didn't enter Mexico, officer."

He didn't seem to listen to what I had said. There were two other agents standing behind him. "Everyone out of the car."

"Look at my papers, officer. We haven't been in Mexico."

The officer leaned in the front door, reached down by my feet, and came up with something between his fingers.

"What is this seed I found on your car floor?"

The car was surrounded by agents. "Remove all the baggage."

The station wagon was jammed with suitcases, books, a typewriter, scuba gear, file cases with my papers. Other tourists passing the checkpoint looked at us with detached shunning disapproval. Then we were ordered to the Customs office, forbidden to talk to each other. We were called, one by one, into small rooms and examined for needle marks. Our pockets were emptied carefully, and the dust and tobacco flakes caught in the linings were neatly folded into evidence envelopes.

A matron came out of the room where Susan was being searched, carrying the silver box. The chief agent called me into his office.

"We found marijuana on the person of your daughter. She is under arrest for three felonies: smuggling narcotics, transporting narcotics, and failing to pay tax on a controlled substance."

Then I spoke the words that were to change my legal status for the rest of my life. "I'll take responsibility for the marijuana."

"In that case you are under arrest. You are entitled to call a lawyer and to refuse to answer any questions."

Rosemary and Jack were also arrested. We stood around handcuffed while the agents arranged transportation to the local jail. The chief agent possessively patted the hood of the station wagon, smiling. "This car is now by law of confiscation the property of the US government. Too bad, it looks brand new."

I shrugged. "You'll have to discuss that with the rental agency. The car is leased."

The cop's face fell in disappointment.

We were bundled into a police car and brought to the Laredo jail, where we were fingerprinted and mugged. Jack was taken to the juvenile section, Rosemary and Susan to the women's wing. I was ushered to the third floor. The jailer unlocked two barred doors and motioned me to walk ahead down the runway. When I got to the fifth cell, he pressed a button and the metal door slid open. I entered. It shut behind me. Clang. My first jail cell.

I spent that night in confused thought. The agent had produced some marijuana *before* they searched Susan. Had we been set up? Surely they couldn't make a big deal about the tiny pinch of grass found in the silver box.

The next morning the four of us were assembled in the jailer's office. With Jack and me handcuffed together we were all marched two blocks to the office of the US Commissioner. Photographers and TV camera crews danced backward on the sidewalk in front of us. Apparently word had gone out.

The stern commissioner was preoccupied with our financial status. How much cash? How much in the bank? Stocks and bonds? Property? He made Rosemary cry by telling her that her family would have to mortgage their house in Los Angeles.

Bail was set at $100,000. For $10 worth of weed! On the way back to the jail a guard gave me the name of the best bail bondsman in town, who happened to be waiting for us at the jail. He in turn gave me the name of the best lawyer in town, who showed up immediately.

The lawyer was reassuring about our release on bail. I had about $3,000 in cash, and he miraculously worked it out so that we still had enough money for tickets to New York after paying him and the bondsman.

He was not optimistic about the long-range prospects. Rosemary and Jack would walk free. He was sure the grand jury couldn't indict them. Susan, because of her age, would get probation, and her record would be expunged when she reached the age of twenty-one. But I was in trouble. The US Attorney in Houston was flying down a crew of prosecutors and investigators. Obviously it was a big case for them. The way they were encouraging publicity suggested that they wanted to make an example of me. I had to realize that people down here in southern Texas were a bit more conservative than the people up around Harvard. The federal judge for this circuit was an old tiger named Connally, notoriously tough on Northerners coming through Laredo with marijuana. It would be hard to get a sympathetic jury in a small town like this. Best thing was make a deal. "You might end up doing four months' jail time with probation. A lot depends on a repentant attitude in cases of this sort."

"Repentant?" I said indignantly. "What does that mean?"

"Oh you make public statements denouncing drugs."

"For a pinch of marijuana that wasn't actually mine? Four months in the slammer. Probation. No way! This whole thing is a set-up and a frame. I'm going to fight it."

The lawyer dropped his head and studied his lap. "I must tell you that the case against *you* is non-existent. The contraband belonged to Rosemary and was in Susan's possession. You have nothing to do with it legally. You obviously didn't know the stuff was in the car because you wouldn't have crossed the border to Customs. Right? All you have to do is tell the truth and you'll walk free."

"But then Susan and Rosemary would take the fall."

"The court isn't going to hit them hard. Susan's a minor. And Rosemary's a poor confused misguided girl under your influence. If she cries and promises the judge to be good in the future, I'll get her off with probation."

"But I'm not some criminal looking for loopholes. I'd feel immoral, like I was copping out."

The lawyer let loose a string of colorful Texan oaths, invoking rattlesnakes' genitals and lizards' eliminative organs. "Every time I hear a client talk about moral principles I know I'm going to lose the case and not get paid enough for the headaches. You don't understand how much trouble you could get into. If you take responsibility for the contraband, there's no way we can keep you out of jail."

"What about appeals? I'll take this to the Supreme Court. Everyone knows the marijuana law is an unconstitutional tax statute. Marijuana's not a narcotic. We'll get that Mickey Mouse statute thrown out."

"I know. I've heard several hundred people sitting in that very chair say the same thing. And they all come around in the end and make a deal. You're talking about several years of expensive litigation, $100,000 minimum. That marijuana law has been around for a long time. And keep in mind that only one in every 200 cases is accepted for Supreme Court review. You can probably stay out of jail during the review process on appeal bond, but you'll still be a convicted criminal. If you do anything they don't like—get arrested again, say something publicly that displeases them—your bail can be revoked and you'll be in prison while your case works its way up the courts. If you fight the charges, then you'll get hit with all three felony counts. They add up to a lot of prison time."

"How much?"

"Let's see. Twenty years for smuggling, five-year mandatory minimum. Another twenty for transportation. That also carries a five-year mandatory minimum. And up to ten years for the tax count. So you're talking a mandatory minimum of ten years, and if they're really mad at you, as I gather they are, up to fifty years. Plus a $50,000 fine."

"I could go to prison for life for $10 of marijuana that wasn't my own?"

The lawyer looked down at his papers unhappily. "It's terrible, I know. All I can do is get you the best deal available. This system is pretty set in its ways. I wouldn't advise you to fight it."

I sat silently, assimilating information that was going to change forever the way I understood and related to society.

"Anyway, we don't have to make any decisions right now," said the lawyer. "It will be several months before we go to trial. You can get other opinions. I'll get you bailed out tonight."

The jailer escorted me back to my cell, and I heard that sound of iron gates closing again. It was dark in the cell. I sat on the bunk and thought.

Here it was. The moment of political truth. My Laredo lawyer said it: "They want to make an example of you." Well I'd make an example of them. I couldn't plead guilty because I felt no guilt. And I couldn't lie about the harmlessness of giggly little marijuana. I couldn't throw myself on the mercies of a crusty old Texas judge and Texas probation officers.

I wasn't going to submit passively to the role of scapegoat, the Harvard psychologist who got in that trouble over drugs. Liberty was at stake here, freedom of access to your own body and brain, a right I believed was protected by the Constitution. (In that primitive period two decades ago it was not yet understood that the human mind is the first, most basic frontier of freedom.)

Sitting in a dark jail cell on Christmas Eve 1965, flushed with virtuous indignation about the wickedness of the marijuana laws, I resolved to fight this case in the courts of the land, to mobilize legal teams, to devise courtroom tactics, to file appeals, motions, briefs, depositions, to speak in defense of the right of American citizens to manage their own bodies and brains.

The fatal word in this naive program was "fight." The adversary nature of the judicial process has never been favorable to philosophers and scientists. Would I choose this arena of battle again? I don't know. It was a stage that I had to go through. And go through it I did.

MARGARET FULLER (1810-1850) grew up in Cambridge, Massachusetts. Upon the sudden death of her father Margaret became the family breadwinner, teaching in private schools.

Her intellectual brilliance as a student of German romanticism and her intuitive mystical insights made her welcome in the circle of minister/scholars—Channing, Clarke, Alcott, Ripley, Thoreau, and above all, Emerson—who were bringing about a quiet revolution in religious and social philosophy called transcendentalism. In 1840 she began as editor of the The Dial, America's first great literary journal and the voice of the transcendental movement. She organized the first consciousness-raising group in America, holding "conversations" among women to discuss the feminist interpretations of mythology, art and history. Her book *Woman in the 19th Century* (1845) was a landmark, opening to discussion such taboo subjects as prostitution and the double standard of marital infidelity.

Fuller sailed to Europe as a traveling literary correspondent for Horace Greeley's *Tribune*. In England she visited aging opium-eater De Quincey and the Brownings, who were actively engaged in drug experiments. She eventually settled in Italy, where she married Marchese Ossoli, bore a son at age thirty-eight, and became deeply involved in the revolution of 1848. Siding with the radical students she treated the wounded and finally fled with her husband and child when the revolution failed. Tragically, the entire Ossoli family—along with Fuller's manuscripts on the revolutionary struggle—was lost at sea in a shipwreck off Fire Island, New York.

29. The Peat Moss Caper

WINTER, 1965-1966

Back at Millbrook on Christmas Day we phoned our friend Bruce, the gay plumber, who turned on the heat and water, and we settled in for a winter very different from the planned tropical vacation. Billy Hitchcock was very upset. His mother and other Mellon elders were pressuring him and Tommy to evict us. Billy, a stout fellow, passionately offered his total support.

The federal indictments came down in January. Susan and I were charged with the three felony counts; Rosemary and Jack were cut loose. Now began the wretched entanglement with the legal system, boring hours spent discussing not scientific facts but courtroom tactics. And there were endless expenses.

Susan and I went to trial in Laredo in April. Billy hired us a hotshot Texas lawyer who was busy at that time with a murder trial. Judge Connally refused to grant a postponement. So we straggled into the courtroom with a makeshift legal team led by the hometown Laredo lawyer, who liked me well enough but had no intention of attacking the marijuana laws, which provided infrastructure for one of the largest local industries. My second counsel was "Good-Time Charlie" Rumsey, nephew of Averill Harriman, a friend of Billy's and mine. I think it was his first and only felony criminal case.

I took the stand to defend my First Amendment right as a scientist and as an initiated Hindu to use marijuana as a research tool and a sacrament. To authenticate my stature as a drug researcher we introduced in evidence letters of support from Massachusetts prison officials. To affirm religious use of grass we produced dozens of letters from theologians, plus Exhibit G, a snapshot of Nanette and me standing in front of a legal ganja shop in Calcutta. At my prodding my lawyer reluctantly cross-examined the chief agent about the Mexican official who had intercepted me at the border. The agent admitted that Garcia was normally stationed in Mexico City. Funny thing though, my lawyer wouldn't press this line of questioning, which could have revealed how my arrest had been set up by the Mexican and American governments using Garcia as the decoy.

The closing argument by the federal prosecutor, a smallish nervous man, was impassioned.

THE COURT: You may close for the government, Mr. Blask.

MR. BLASK: May it please the Court. Ladies and gentlemen. To say that this was an unusual case would be gross understatement and to say that it's an important case would be a gross understatement, because, ladies and gentlemen, I have participated in what I feel is a considerable number of criminal cases, and I cannot remember a case that I have felt more strongly about than I have this case, and I will tell you why.

Because we are dealing today with a man who lives in your society. He is no different than anybody else. Just because he may believe in a different religious aspect, that has nothing to do with it. . . .

Now getting back to the fact as it relates to Dr. Leary and this marijuana, as we are dealing with today—and you recognize that it's not a question of the quantity, because if we wanted to railroad him into being punished we could have manufactured something—and I think you realize that we are bringing you the honest facts. That's all there was, something about half an ounce. The question of the amount has nothing to do with it—nothing whatsoever. . . .

But what does he do when he is finally exposed and they find out about it? He makes a joke about it. Now, I don't mean to shout, for shouting's sake, but I feel so strongly about this case and his acts that I can't help myself, and I hope you will forgive me.

After the jury retired, Susan and I walked out to the corridor with the two lawyers. Susan clung to my hand fearfully.

"Shall we go out to get some air?" I suggested.

The Laredo lawyer glanced at his watch and shook his head.

"Not enough time. It will take them five minutes to elect a jury chairman, five minutes to pour the coffee, one minute to vote, and three minutes to notify the bailiff. They'll be back with the verdict in a quarter of an hour."

How right he was.

THE COURT: Dr. Leary, you and your counsel will step up here, please, sir.

Your case, the situation in which you find yourself here, gives a great deal of concern. You are, of course, as I am sure you will recognize, an unusual type of personality, unconventional in many respects. It is my duty, in due course, to impose sentence for these offenses. Is there anything you want to tell me at this time in your own behalf or in mitigation or extenuation?

DEFENDANT LEARY: No, sir.

THE COURT: In that case under Count Two I impose a period of confinement of twenty years and a fine of $20,000. On Count Three I impose a period of confinement of ten years and a fine of $20,000.

Susan, will you step forward. In sentencing you the Court will take into account the fact that you have had an unusual home background . . .

Susan was given the maximum sentence of five years, pending a probation report. At the moment of sentencing she turned to me in panic. I held her in my arms while the lawyer whispered reassurances. He filed a standard appeal motion and we were immediately granted appeal bond by Judge Connally.

Our lawyers assured us that Susan would not do a day in jail. The judge would give her probation and her record would be scrubbed when she was twenty-one. These promises didn't raise Susan's morale. She had always been a dutiful conforming child, eager for approval and affection. The national publicity weighed heavily on her. A picture that showed her looking up at me with mystified devotion was published in *Life* magazine and in newspapers throughout the country. After she returned to her boarding school, the headmaster called me several times during the spring to express his concern about her. Susan couldn't be happy about anything after this event. I was slow to realize how .much she suffered by what she felt to be a public disgrace.

The news of my thirty-year sentence and Susan's five made headlines around the world: front-page story with picture in the *New York Times*. There was a ground-swell of support. A Timothy Leary Defense Fund was formed, headed by Billy Hitchcock and administered by Larry Bogard, a lobbyist for good causes. Although Larry never had and never would have indulged in illegal drugs, he was shocked by the severity of our sentences. Many prominent people signed the statement of support—Steve Allen, Eric Bently, Peter Fonda, Jules Feiffer, Angier St. George Biddle Duke, Irving Kristol, Norman Mailer, Anaïs Nin, Norman Podhoretz. The Defense Fund office hummed with activities—pamphlets, mailings, phone calls, public appearances—all to raise money for my lawyers, who were fighting another team of attorneys paid for by our taxes. None of this was my idea of fun.

Back at Millbrook it was almost time for summer school again. We rounded up a talented staff—psychologists, biologists, adepts in yoga and meditation, and light-artists and filmmakers. Staff members came to Millbrook each weekend for planning sessions. Then one Saturday in May we received a couple of warning phone calls from friends in the courthouse about preparations for a raid on Millbrook. Deputies were being ordered to overtime duty for Saturday night. District attorneys were running around trying to get a search warrant signed by a cooperative judge. The local law enforcement agency, like many others in the land, employed clerks and officers who smoked a bit of weed themselves, liked the new music, and were happy to undermine their old-line bosses. Our informants said that tonight would be the night. Maybe. The Duchess County Sheriff's office was notorious for Keystone Kop blundering.

Our dinner was festive. About thirty guests were present, including some prominent journalists. Our pal Prince Oblensky sent up a case of Mumms; Peggy Hitchcock, gourmet delicacies. Issuing red-alert warnings that no illegal drugs should be on the premises we sat on silken pillows at low tables in the baronial dining room and popped the corks, awaiting the raid.

It was ten o'clock before the light wizards got the images flowing on the screens and walls of the dining room. As the room exploded with kaleidoscopic images, Jack reported on activity at the gates. "It's a comic book," he laughed. "There are two cops crouching in the bushes down by the Meditation House with binoculars. And two patrol cars headed for the cow barns with their lights off."

By midnight the light show was over. Everyone drifted off to their rooms. Rosemary and I retired to our mirrored alcove. Jack knocked and entered with his final report. "I guess they called off the raid when the party broke up downstairs. How about a nightcap?" Jack produced a glass hookah and filled the bowl with scented tobacco.

"Let's smoke some of that DMT Nicky sent up from Brooklyn. It's strong stuff and it's legal."

Strong? Whew! Rosemary and I floated on the bed while Jack sprawled on the floor. Suddenly the door burst open, and in marched a man with a short-trimmed mustache, obviously a stand-in for Inspector

Clouseau. Beside him was an obese individual in a sheriff's uniform, followed by nine armed deputies with wide campaign hats. They seemed to be suffering from an astonishing rash or badly applied clown makeup.

The hookah in the middle of the bed looked at everyone with a glassy eye. With Wonder Woman reflex Rosemary flicked the blanket over the evidence. It looked like modesty. All police eyes were on her "diaphanous gown."[1]

"Don't move," said one deputy.

"On your feet," added another.

"Hands up." G. Gordon Liddy stood in a military posture, speaking his well-rehearsed lines in a clipped voice. "I have a warrant to search the premises."

We heard booted men running through the house. Doors slamming. Shouts of surprise. In the confusion Jack slipped from the room, put a Beatles record on the hi-fi that blasted from speakers throughout the mansion. Rosemary, holding her arm across her breasts, pointed across the room. "Don't touch that *pot*. That's my sacrament!"

Twenty-two law-enforcement eyes panned to the P-O-T.

G. Gordon Liddy bounded across the room, picked up a handful of dried vegetable substance from the pot, and said with curt professionalism, "Obviously a high-grade brand of marijuana. Confiscate and label for evidence."

Rosemary's peat-moss gambit worked.

The brigade of policemen and prosecutors tromped around the mansion for several hours looking for evidence of other crimes without much success. Then Liddy approached me stiffly to deliver his most dramatic line: "You are under arrest."

"Arrest! for what?"

"For possession of illegal narcotics."

"Since when is peat moss illegal?" I protested, to no avail. I was handcuffed and driven to the county jail. By Sunday noon "Good-Time Charlie" Rumsey arrived in a limo from New York and bailed me out. Again headlines in the New York papers with front-page pictures of the Big House, increasing my lurid reputation.

The charges were dropped for lack of evidence, but then Liddy's prosecutors opened grand jury hearings. All members of our Millbrook household were subpoenaed and grilled about my drug-taking. When Rosemary refused to talk, she was sentenced to a month in jail with no visitors allowed. Jack was arrested while walking along the road outside the property, hauled off to jail, charged with loitering. His long black hair was cropped to a crewcut before we could get him bailed out.

Next came a visit from Carl Perian, executive secretary to a Senate Committee on drugs headed by Thomas Dodd of Connecticut. Perian was a thoughtful youngish man concerned about formulating an intelligent workable drug policy, one that would avoid the counter-productive excesses of Prohibition. He seemed impressed by my ideas about licensing and invited me to testify before the Committee, which was deliberating whether to make LSD illegal. He said that Senator Dodd would treat me in a respectful manner as an invited expert.

The first witness was Captain Trembly of the Los Angeles Police Department. He produced the standard unscientific police-scare testimony. His officers had arrested a young man, a Princeton graduate no less, who was under the influence of LSD in a public park—eating bark off a tree! Another young man, whose mother called the police while he was allegedly tripping on LSD, denounced her as a fink. A stir went around the room. A Princeton man eating bark! Children turning against their mothers!

When called to the witness stand I started by drawing the distinction between psychedelic drugs and addictive narcotics. Ted Kennedy, who had shown up unexpectedly, interrupted the reading of my prepared statement. He was not friendly.

SENATOR KENNEDY: Mr. Leary, I am trying to follow the best I can some themes that must be coming from your testimony here this morning, and I am completely unable to do so. You talked in the beginning about the communications problem which exists between the different generations . . . then we hear a description and analysis, as valuable as that might be, about the different reactions to different drugs.

I am completely unable to follow anything other than just sort of a general hyperbole of discussion here . . . I think it would be extremely valuable if you could at least outline to some extent what you are going to try and demonstrate here today.

DR. LEARY: I was, Senator Kennedy, just about to point out the difference that exists among drugs, and to suggest that special types of legislation are needed for the different drugs.

SENATOR KENNEDY: Are you going to talk about the lack of communications between the generations before or after that?

DR. LEARY: I finished doing that. I feel that constructive legislation is badly needed, and I recommend respectfully that this committee consider legislation which will license responsible adults to use psychedelic drugs for serious purposes. To obtain such a license the applicant, I think, should have to meet physical, intellectual and emotional criteria.

I believe that the licensing procedures for marijuana, the mildest of the psychedelic drugs, should be like those which we now use to license people to drive automobiles, whereas the proficiency training for LSD should be much more strict. Perhaps criteria of the order of complexity now used for airplane pilots would be appropriate.

I further urge this committee to make some provision for people to be trained in the use of these powerful instruments. A high percentage of college students are using these tools. We can drive them underground, or we can legitimize their use in carefully controlled circumstances. . . .

You see you have to be trained to use LSD the way you are trained to use a computer. An unprepared person can be confused.

SENATOR KENNEDY: Therefore, you are suggesting that anyone who is going to administer LSD ought to be highly trained?

DR. LEARY: Absolutely.

SENATOR KENNEDY: That is very responsive. Now you feel that anybody who distributes this ought to be carefully trained, is that correct? Where are they going to get this training?

DR. LEARY: For the last five years, my training institute, the Castalia Foundation, has been the only one in the world that has been conscientiously and systematically training people.

SENATOR KENNEDY: Now other people, who haven't had the good fortune to attend your institute, have been taking LSD, have they not? So don't you think that until your institute is either able to expand its courses, that we ought to at least be conscious of the dangers which are presented by it?

DR. LEARY: The need for licensing legislation is desperate. We have got to establish institutes so that people can receive training . . . .

SENATOR KENNEDY: So that there should not be indiscriminate distribution of this drug, should there?

DR. LEARY: I have never suggested that, sir. I have never urged anyone to take LSD. I have always deplored indiscriminate or unprepared use.

Later came this depressing interaction with Teddy:

SENATOR KENNEDY: You feel that there ought to be control over at least importation?

DR. LEARY: The sale, manufacture or distribution, yes.

SENATOR KENNEDY: . . . Now why do you think they should be?

DR. LEARY: I feel that activities, particularly commercial activities involving the manufacture, sale and distribution of these substances, should be controlled because otherwise you do not know about quality, you do not know about purity, you do not know what you are buying. Obviously you have to have laws, just as you have product safety laws about the amphetamines. . . .

SENATOR KENNEDY: [Still pressing for a statement about danger]: You said you do not know about the quality. What is it about the quality that you are frightened about?

DR. LEARY: We do not want amateur or black market sale or distribution of LSD.

SENATOR KENNEDY: Why not?

DR. LEARY: Or of the barbiturates or liquor. When you buy a bottle of liquor . . .

SENATOR KENNEDY: This is not responsive. As to LSD... why do you not want the indiscriminate manufacture and distribution. Is it because it is dangerous?

DR. LEARY: Because you do not know what you are getting.

SENATOR KENNEDY: Is it because it is dangerous? . . .

DR. LEARY: Sir, the motor car is dangerous if used improperly. I couldn't be in more agreement.

SENATOR KENNEDY: It is dangerous then?

DR. LEARY: If used improperly.

SENATOR KENNEDY: Isn't that why the pilot is licensed as well?

DR. LEARY: Yes, sir. Human stupidity and ignorance is the only danger human beings face in this world.

SENATOR KENNEDY: It seems to me that your testimony has been extremely convincing about the dangers of this drug as well as its opportunities. . . .

DR. LEARY: I cannot agree with that summary, respectfully. I must disagree, Senator Kennedy, with your statement.

SENATOR KENNEDY: Let's take the various aspects of it. You feel that there should be control over at least importation? The sale and manufacturing?

DR. LEARY: Yes, sir.

SENATOR KENNEDY: And that the only reason you think this is because it is a matter of interstate and foreign commerce? Is that the only reason? I mean, we have things which are produced, textiles in Massachusetts, furniture in Massachusetts, that are not restricted, Dr. Leary.

Sitting in the witness chair at these Senate hearings I felt sorry for Teddy and us. Any hope of leadership for the country from the Kennedy family would have to come from Bobby.

MARSHALL McLUHAN (1911-1980) Canadian philosopher, received his doctorate in English literature from Cambridge and went on to publish two books, *The Gutenberg Galaxy* and *Understanding Media*, that established him as the herald of the information age. McLuhan was among the first philosophers to understand how electronic communication was changing human society and human nature. In the aphorism "the medium is the message", McLuhan crystallized the profound changes occurring in the post-industrial Third Wave Society.

The innovative future-oriented quality of his thought in later books can be sensed from their titles: *The Medium Is the Massage, Through the Vanishing Point: Space in Poetry and Reading, Counterblast, Culture Is Our Business, City as Classroom.*

Throughout his academic career at the University of Toronto McLuhan remained a dedicated James Joyce scholar, a preoccupation consistent with his ability to cut through the linear restrictions of grammar and discover the multiple realities layered in words and ideas.

30. Altered States

SUMMER 1966

The spirit of the times: General Motors hired investigators to question over fifty friends of Ralph Nader, seeking to discredit the young consumer advocate. The Georgia legislature refused to seat Julian Bond, a twenty-five-year-old black activist whose election platform included opposition to the Vietnam War. Anti-war Senator Fulbright of Arkansas was accused by Republican Party leader Barry Goldwater of giving "aid and comfort to the enemy." During August 4,000 Chicago whites attacked 600 blacks marching with Dr. Martin Luther King to end segregation. The publicity attending these events and hundreds like them contributed to a climate of controversy.

After Laredo I assumed that my task was to persuade the government to support drug research and education and to abandon the policy of police suppression. I met with civil liberties lawyers, some of them in touch with the chief of the Federal Appeals Court, Judge Bazelon, an influential jurist known as the tenth member of the Supreme Court. There was general consensus that the federal marijuana law, which had been slipped through Congress in 1927 as a tax statute, would be thrown out when my case reached the Supreme Court. We expected that any attempt to pass a new marijuana law would involve hearings, during which we would demonstrate that grass was not a narcotic. Decriminalization seemed inevitable.

My legal advisors were also hopeful that we could head off a new Prohibition, this one against LSD, by working within the system: lobbying, mobilizing expert testimony, filing test cases.

But the vindictiveness in Laredo and in the Liddy raids proved to be a microcosm of a growing nationwide pattern of police harassment, which made it clear that rational discourse and formal litigation were not the way this game was going to be played. Right-wing politicians and law enforcement officials eagerly blew the "drug menace" up into a major threat. Suddenly there appeared to be no Bill of Rights protection for those who wished to use drugs for personal or scientific reasons. The dope controversy was becoming the most visible symptom of a deep conflict in American society.

From my childhood I remembered all too well the widespread use and abuse of illegal booze by everyone from country-club members to working men. The nation flouted the unpopular Volstead Act, using the drug alcohol with impunity. But the situation was different with the drugs of the 1960s.

Van Wolfe, always the sagacious observer of American culture, was one of the first to advise us that the battle to license psychedelic drugs and legalize marijuana would have to be fought in the field of public opinion. Van had just become engaged to Susan Berns, daughter of Charlie Berns, co-owner of Twenty-One, haunt of corporation presidents. After a dinner with his in-laws-to-be Van told a discouraging story.

"I talked to Charlie about the psychedelic drug situation, and his reaction was very interesting. Did you know that during Prohibition he ran one of the swankiest speak-easies in New York? Everyone who was anyone—socialites, show-biz people, politicians—used to hang out at Jack and Charlie's."

"Then he should be very sympathetic to our cause," I said.

Van shot me a Byzantine smile. "Wrong. He has his liquor business to protect: Twenty-One Brands. He said you are the worst enemy the liquor industry has faced since Congressman Volstead."

"Did you tell him that he can get in on the ground floor? When grass and LSD are legalized he'll make another fortune."

"I suggested that," said Van, "but he said he was too rich and too old to start a new business. We'll have to do it ourselves."

"Do what?"

"Make our inebriants the 'in' thing to do. Just like they had their speakeasy-bootleg-Roaring Twenties culture, we'll develop our own drug culture. Kerouac and Cassady started it, but they were too bohemian. We've got to do what the liquor people did during Prohibition—dispel this cloud of illegality and danger. Psychedelic drugs must be associated with beauty, glamour, sexuality. We need symbols of personal freedom. High fashion. Graceful hedonism compared to the sloppy boozers."

"I'm not the best person in the world at generating good publicity," I said ruefully.

"But you're going to have to learn fast. Why don't you go see Marshall McLuhan?"

Van was right. Since the sentencing at Laredo considerable media attention had focused on Millbrook, which was becoming the clearinghouse for information about altered states of consciousness as well as a center for alternate-lifestyle experimentation. Television crews filmed regularly on the grounds. Hugh Hefner and "Spec" Spectorski sent a reporter to do a *Playboy* interview.

About the time that *Newsweek* ran a cover story on marijuana as the new middle-class recreational drug, we started hearing rumors that Henry Luce had inspired his editors to do a major story on LSD. *Life* hit the stands in March, the cover shouting: "TURMOIL IN A CAPSULE—one dose of LSD is enough to set off a mental riot of vivid colors and sights—or of terror and convulsions." Four pages of pictures showed a teenage girl having a scary trip. An objective sober article by Barry Farrell reported:

> An all-fronts movement has sprung up . . . on big city campuses and in young intellectual circles all over the western world, and it comes complete with quarterlies, lecture courses, a barrage of guide books to the cosmos and even two or three psychedelic churches.
>
> There are many others whose interest in the drug has nothing to do with psychic revolution. Mathematicians have used it as a lens through which they sometimes glimpse the physical reality of concepts that the mind can only imagine—advanced number theory, for example. . . . There are psychedelic corporation presidents, military officers, doctors, teachers—each with a reason to risk a voyage on the unpredictable terrain of the deep brain dreamscape.

Billy Hitchcock was photographed in front of the Big House for this article. Walter Clark was pictured in his study. "These drugs present us with a means of studying religious experiences in the laboratory. No psychologist of religion can afford to be ignorant of them." A retired Navy captain, John Busby, claimed to have "solved an elusive problem . . . developing intelligence equipment for a Navy Research project" while under the influence. A hard-headed Republican businessman became God while tripping.

In spite of the hand-wringing the *Life* essay amounted to a most convincing endorsement of LSD and an eloquent plea for non-medical research. It was obvious that Henry Luce's commercial would double the number of consumers, most of whom would be unprepared. With millions taking the drug it was certain that the occasional bad trips would start to add up.[1]

Around ten percent of alcohol drinkers are abusers. Then as now booze casualties were epidemic, so the jaded press paid no attention to the misadventures of one drunk. Their attitude was different with psychedelic drugs. Only one out of every thousand LSD users reported a negative experience, yet the press dug up a thousand lurid stories of bark-eating Princeton grads. Some of these were the result of amateur experimentation on a new scale. But there was such an appetite for anti-LSD tales that many hoaxes developed. The medical director of a mental hospital in Pennsylvania earned banner headlines when he announced that eight patients had been blinded looking at the sun during acid trips. When the story was later exposed as a fraud, little attention was paid to the quiet retraction. Indeed the medical director was credited with a nice try.

Throughout the land anti-drug people—politicians, police officials, institutional psychiatrists—popped up to denounce LSD and marijuana as the most dangerous threats confronted by the human race. This sort of propaganda was guaranteed to create mass hysteria and to sow the seeds of bad set and setting.

I flew into corrective action, giving public lectures and interviews and writing magazine articles that outlined the need for guidance, preparation, protected settings, and knowledge of centering techniques to deal with trip-confusions. Few of these communications reached the national press. Some counseling in understanding media was clearly indicated.

The lunch with Marshall McLuhan at the Plaza was informative. "Dreary Senate hearings and courtrooms are not the platforms for your message, Tim. You call yourself a philosopher, a reformer. Fine. But the key to your work is advertising. You're promoting a product. The new and improved accelerated brain. You must use the most current tactics for arousing consumer interest. Associate LSD with all the good things that the brain can produce—beauty, fun, philosophic wonder, religious revelation, increased intelligence, mystical romance. Word of mouth from satisfied consumers will help, but get your rock and roll friends to write jingles about the brain." He sang:

Lysergic acid hits the spot.
Forty billion neurons, that's a lot.

"The problem is tricky," I said. "The opposition beat us to the punch. The psychiatrists and police propagandists have already stressed the negative, which can be dangerous when the mind is re-imprinting under LSD.

They may be deliberately provoking bad trips. They never mention the 999 good experiences. They keep repeating 'LSD: jump out a window.' When some ill-prepared person goes spinning into new realms, he or she wonders what happens now? Oh yeah. Jump out a window. It's like the over-solicitous mother who warned her kids not to push peanuts up their noses."

"Exactly," agreed McLuhan. "That's why your advertising must stress the religious. Find the god within. This is all frightfully interesting. Your competitors are naturally denouncing the brain as an instrument of the devil. Priceless!

"To dispel fear you must use your public image. You are the basic product endorser. Whenever you are photographed, smile. Wave reassuringly. Radiate courage. Never complain or appear angry. It's okay if you come off as flamboyant and eccentric. You're a professor, after all. But a confident attitude is the best advertisement. You must be known for your smile."

The waiter, who seemed to be hanging on McLuhan's words, knocked my champagne glass into my lap. McLuhan looked at me expectantly. I smiled.

"You're going to win the war, Timothy. Eventually. But you're going to lose some major battles on the way. You're not going to overthrow the Protestant Ethic in a couple of years. This culture knows how to sell fear and pain. Drugs that accelerate the brain won't be accepted until the population is geared to computers. You're ahead of your time. They'll attempt to destroy your credibility."

"It's incredibility I'm after," I replied.

And that's how it happened, step by step from the Harvard firing to the deportations, from Laredo to the Liddy raid, I was pushed from scientific detachment and scholarly retirement into public opposition to the policies of the ruling regime.

By this time I no longer regretted being an outcast. I was beginning to enjoy the fray. And I was not alone in the rebellion. Millions of Americans, exactly at this time, were also pushed to open resistance to the group that had taken over Washington after the assassination. A cultural revolution was brewing.

My understanding of the situation was this: America was experiencing a quantum jump in intelligence. For the first time in our history a large and influential sector of the populace was coming to disrespect institutional authority, not as members of organized dissident groups but as intelligent individuals, highly selective political consumers who demanded responsive and effective leadership, which no existing party, no religion, no labor union seemed able to provide. Thus a conflict between the old industrial society and the new information society was to be played out in the new arena of power—the media. Those who understood this would create the future.

The conversation with Marshall McLuhan got me thinking further along these lines: the successful philosophers were also advertisers who could sell their new models of the universe to large numbers of others, thus converting thought to action, mind to matter. I devoted several days and one acid trip to analysis of the packaging of previous American revolutions: "Give Me Liberty Or Give Me Death," "A Nation Cannot Exist Half Slave and Half Free," "We Have Nothing to Fear But Fear Itself." "Lucky Strike Means Fine Tobacco."

One morning, while I was ruminating in the shower about what kind of slogan would succinctly summarize the tactics for increasing intelligence, six words came to mind. Dripping wet, with a towel around my waist, I walked to the study and wrote down this phrase: "Turn On, Tune In, Drop Out." Later it became very useful in my function as cheerleader for change.

Turn On meant go within to activate your neural and genetic equipment. Become sensitive to the many and various levels of consciousness and the specific triggers that engage them. Drugs were one way to accomplish this end.

Tune In meant interact harmoniously with the world around you—externalize, materialize, express your new internal perspectives.

Drop Out suggested an active, selective, graceful process of detachment from involuntary or unconscious commitments. *Drop Out* meant self-reliance, a discovery of one's singularity, a commitment to mobility, choice, and change.

In public statements I stressed that the *Turn On-Tune In-Drop Out* process must be continually repeated if one wished to live a life of growth.

Unhappily my explanations of this sequence of personal development were often misinterpreted to mean "get stoned and abandon all constructive activity."

The momentary popularity of this phrase produced some interesting fallout. The makers of Squirt, a soft drink, broadcast a bouncy jingle urging the public to "Turn on to flavor, tune into sparkle, and drop out of the cola rut." Billy Graham announced that the theme of his European Crusade would be "Turn on Christ, tune in to the Bible, and drop out of sin." I was flattered.

The summer school this year centered on externalization and communication of altered states. We were relieved that there seemed to be no police informers among the participants. About twenty-five paying students—doctors, teachers, professors, the inevitable searchers, and a couple of businessmen—studied our techniques for expressing psychedelic experiences. There were no officially sponsored drug sessions, although many students did turn on with their own supplies under the supervision of guides.

The climax of the summer school was a multi-media pageant held the last weekend. Six groups formed, each dramatizing a section of the Magic Theatre sequence from Hermann Hesse's *Steppenwolf.* The students and staff designed sets and created light-sound atmospheres. Students learned how to make psychedelic slides and auditory collages.

Around 150 people, summer schoolers and guests from the bungalow, came to the pageant. Almost everyone took LSD. Torchlights and ever-changing slides illuminated the grounds. The faces of Buddha, Plato, Einstein, and company shone on the shimmering leaves of the birch trees. The Big House was bathed in undulating cellular patterns. The audience strolled from the side patio to the stone-paved terrace in front of the bowling alley to the basement, where in a musty wine cellar the last death-rebirth scene took place in silhouette.

The next day David Balding, a young producer who worked with Billy Hitchcock, bustled up to me with enthusiastic plans to bring our pageant to New York. Balding arranged to lease a movie theater on lower Second Avenue for a series of Tuesday nights. A talented crew of special-effects artists assembled at Millbrook for a month of rehearsals. Our aim was to produce multi-media re-enactments of the great religious, scientific, and philosophic myths using psychedelic techniques to activate the archetype circuits of the brain.

In order to publicize our "celebrations" (as well as legalize and domesticate our philosophic drug ceremonies) we incorporated a religion under the laws of New York State. The League for Spiritual Discovery was announced in a press conference that generated wide coverage and assured a full house. Many drama critics were there for opening night.

The first celebration, *Death of the Mind,* repeated in polished form our salute to the mystic paganism of Hesse's *Steppenwolf.* Ralph Metzner played the part of Harry Haller, the neurotic intellectual trapped in that Cartesian conflict between mind and body. Rosemary was Hermione, the enigmatic big-city earth woman who leads H.H. into the Magic Theatre. I played Pablo, the smiling Dionysian who gives H.H. the drugs that spin him into multiple-reality.

The screen flooded with swirling panoramas as an orchestra of seven technicians with hand-held slide projectors danced their images over motion pictures in rhythm with the sound tape and the action on stage:

It was an instant hit. Sell-out crowds. Global press coverage. The *New York Times* critic wrote that I should be nominated for best Off-Broadway actor of the year. The TV news clips exposed millions of people to the complexity and power of special-effects art.

The Canadian Broadcasting Company invited me to Toronto for a nationwide talk show. David Padwa accompanied me. After the taping we went to Marshall McLuhan's for a long and genial dinner. The next day, as I walked off the return plane at La Guardia, two federal agents were waiting for me. They informed me that narcotics offenders were required to fill out a special form on leaving the country. I was arrested again and bailed out just in time to perform in the celebration. More nationwide publicity. And another five-year sentence to contest.

Death of the Mind, which ran six weeks, was to be followed by *The Resurrection of Jesus Christ*, an attempt to re-imprint the Catholic Mass. Subsequent shows would celebrate *The Illumination of the Buddha*, *The Trial of Giordano Bruno*, *The Mischief of Georges Gurdjieff*, *The Rebellion of Ralph Waldo Emerson*, and *The Assassination of Socrates*.

We had a slight casting problem with the second production. Who would play the part of Jesus Christ? There were no volunteers for this unenviable role.

A persistent pilgrim showed up at Millbrook, a clean-cut kid with deep sorrowful eyes and an expensive backpack. Rusty looked like an Amherst hockey player. I told him go away, but he kept hanging around. I found him sweeping up around the garbage area, raking leaves, and mowing the lawn in front of the Meditation House. He was on hand when we needed someone to drive the station wagon to Poughkeepsie. On the way back he and another Millbrook resident were stopped by local cops, handcuffed, and dragged to jail. No charges, you understand, just a friendly hijack for one of those kinky little searches of body cavities: you know, those knobby cop-fingers sheathed in rubber gloves. An old Turkish custom.

This harassment won Rusty the part.

The show was a pagan triumph. Jackie Cassen and Rudi Stern shot an eerie misty reversed-negative film of a bearded man walking silently around Harlem. Super-imposed were haunting slides depicting the life of Christ and the gothic-baroque history of the Catholic Church, the whole ding-a-ling picture album of haloed saints, virgins, and martyrs. To accompany the script of the Catholic Mass we played a steamy hot-samba rendition of the "Missa Solemnis" recorded in Rio.

At the climax Rusty climbed on a cross behind a silhouette screen, ready to die for some dumb reason or other. I strolled on stage and tried to kid Christ out of this self-destructive act. "Hey, Jesus, if you go through with this you'll leave a 2,000-year-old tradition of pain and guilt. Centuries of Christian soldiers marching with bloody swords to avenge you. Billions of gloomy followers dressed in black, trying to match your suffering. Don't do it, JC.

"Hey, Jesus, for God's sake come on down and let's have a party! Let's go around the corner and drink a cold foamy beer. Sure would taste good after the wormwood and vinegar your followers have been giving us. Hey, I know two smart sassy girls who just hit town. Let's take 'em out. Come down, let's go to MIT and study nuclear physics. Let's figure out a happy, wholesome religion that won't call the act of conception a dirty deed. Let's start a religion that laughs and sings in love of life."

And right there in front of 1,800 people and the videotape cameras I went behind the screen and pulled out the nails. *Eeeeeee!* sang the synthesizer.

Christ descended from the cross, threw his hands triumphantly in the air, and did a happy two-step. Then Rusty and I went front-stage, hand-in-hand, bowing to tumultuous applause.

After the first performance Rosemary and I were relaxing in the star dressing room, toasting the victory of paganism with champagne, when the door banged open and there was Rusty, scared out of his mind. Jesus Christ, this kid fell on his knees in front of me. Terrorized.

Then he babbled a confession. He was a police informer. He'd been nabbed a few months ago for dealing grass and offered release if he set me up.

He pulled out a plastic bag filled with grass and about a hundred pills: acid, reds, purples, yellows, enough sloppy gutter junk to ruin the reputation of any ex-Harvard professor caught possessing. On the way back to Millbrook he was supposed to drop the bag on the floor of our car, just when the police cars sirened us over.

He was shaking with fear. He'd spent three weeks with us and loved us and believed in us. He couldn't go through with the frame-up. Now he was done for. If they didn't kill him, as they had threatened to, they'd drag him back to court and put him in prison for life.

First things first. We locked the door and flushed the dope down the toilet. Rusty wouldn't go back to Millbrook, so we threw the Christ robe over his shoulders, gave him $200, and slipped him down the backstage metal stairs with the address of a safe flat on St. Mark's Place. A few days later he was off to LA.

The reviews were mixed. People writing for important papers and magazines like *Time* got a bit offended. In spite of the *succès d'estime* and good advance sales the show had to close that night.

Christ was on the lam.

After Christmas we decided to take the Buddha show on the road. Chicago, San Francisco, LA. The celebration at the Santa Monica Civic

Auditorium was the high point of the road tour. Hall jammed. Grateful Dead jammed. The LSD alchemist Owsley was everywhere dispensing his White Lightning pills. I took the stage urging everyone to "Turn On, Tune In, and Drop Out. Now's the time to flick on the inner switch to full power! Listen, you'll either spend the rest of your life as a badly paid extra in someone else's low-budget black-and-white documentary/ training film. OR. You become the producer of your own movie. Direct it, script it, cast it, choose the locations for the greatest reality flick ever made. Why settle for less?"

There was a party after the show at Micky and Ben Shapiro's house, just behind the old Continental Hotel above the Sunset Strip. The myth seemed true. Hollywood *was* the most glamorous dramatic free place on the planet, where flamboyant erotic fantasies *did* become real.

ALEISTER CROWLEY (1876-1946), world-record mountain climber, was one of the most controversial figures of the early twentieth century. With leading members of the Irish literary renaissance, Crowley was an original member of the Hermetic Order of the Golden Dawn, which he broke from to start his own circle of adepts. Crowley then journeyed to the East to climb the Himalayas and to study oriental yoga and esoteric philosophy.

In 1904 he claimed to have established telepathic communication with Higher Intelligence through the medium of his wife Rosemary. He foresaw the beginning of a New Aeon, to which he contributed these aphorisms: "'Do what thou wilt' shall be the whole of the law" and "Every man and every woman is a star." Over the next two decades he experimented with every available drug as a means of transcendence. In 1910 Crowley went to the Detroit headquarters of the Parke-Davis pharmaceutical company to secure their newly developed extract of peyote, which he brought back to England and used to turn on the audiences at his lectures. In an article on the effects of cocaine, published during World War I, he articulated the viewpoint that drug prohibition was not only useless but actually intensified the problem of drug abuse.

Throughout his life and travels Crowley produced a flood of articles and books on spiritual subjects, devising a new Tarot (*The Book of Thoth*) and a streamlined version of the *I Ching* in addition to many significant and sardonic works on occult magic.

31. Emergence of the Drug Culture

JANUARY 1967

News about the plans for the first Love-In came in a transcontinental phone call from Michael Bowen, the wild and charismatic artist-activist. He and other heavy-hitters on the San Francisco scene were cooking up a mass celebration in Golden Gate Park in honor of LSD and the new drug consciousness. There was some rivalry among the psychedelic barons as to who should front the event: a thorny problem, really, with such talents on hand as the Diggers, the remnants of Kesey's Pranksters, the Mime Troup, the High Wizard Chet Helms, the Communication Company, the Grateful Dead, Bill Graham, and the Hells Angels. All competed for center stage. As a compromise Michael suggested that I be invited out to emcee. Some of the planning group wanted to organize similar gatherings on the same day in London, Amsterdam, Copenhagen, Rome, New York, and points west. Michael asked me about printing up and distributing membership cards in the League for Spiritual Discovery. Millions throughout the world would fill them out and drop them in huge boxes painted to look like sugar cubes.

"Hey wait a minute, Michael," I protested. "I don't want to belong to a religion of a million people I haven't met."

"Dig it," continued the irrepressible Bowen. "In one day our religion will sign up more members than Christianity and Islam did in their first three centuries. In one day, man, you could become pope of a world-wide religion."

"Pope, huh? That's an interesting offer but not the career I had in mind. I don't like mass cults."

"Old-fashioned thinking, man," said Michael, "Electronics will connect us up. Global TV shows. Tell people how to avoid bad trips. And four times a year, on the equinoxes and the solstices, we'll repeat the mass celebrations. The planet's hungering to be hooked up. You're the one with the name-recognition."

"Rosemary and I will be there for the gathering," I said. "As part of the crowd."

By mid-morning you could sense the electricity building in the Bay Area. All the music stations were hyping the Love-In. The bridges to the City were jammed with VW buses, and the streets leading to Golden Gate Park became rivers of people whooping it up. More than 60,000 souls assembled in a meadow, eating, drinking, smoking, playing musical instruments.

The great local bands played from a raised platform. Counter-culture celebrities crammed up there between sets. There had been much politicking among the organizing committee over time allotted to speakers. The cultural people wanted me to give a keynote speech. The hard-line leftists wanted to turn the Love-In into a political demonstration.

Around the edges the crowd was gentle, harmonious, jolly, in the spirit of a Hindu Kumamela where throngs gather by the Ganges to hang out. As we moved towards the stage, I observed an interesting neuro-social phenomenon. The closer we got to the microphones and amplifiers, the grimmer the vibes. Spectators there were pushing to get near The Action, the stage, the center of struggle.

I declined invitations to mount the stage. Speeches were irrelevant. The swarming of like-minded souls was the message. Look up there! Someone in a gaily-colored parachute was drifting down, down, down, landing in the center of the meadow. Most of the crowd was sensible enough to ignore the chatter from the stage. Jerry Rubin had grabbed the mike and was chastising the assembled for enjoying themselves while three political activists from Berkeley languished in jail for throwing rocks.

"Turn on, tune in, take over," he shouted.

I was pulled up to the stage by the promoters and squeezed between two surly bikers defending their precious space. People grabbed for the mike. I was pushed to the podium. I bellowed out my six words: "Turn on, tune in, drop out." Then jumped offstage.

Back at Millbrook we pondered our next move. To continue the tour of celebrations seemed futile. Although we drew large crowds, the size of the operation prevented us from showing a profit. And I had no desire to spend more time as a show-biz trouper. I started lecturing at colleges. By then I had become a nationally recognized symbol of change, and my campus visits stirred considerable drama. Sometimes fearful officials would attempt to ban my appearance, a tactic that unfailingly generated even more demand.

In between these sorties I finished the manuscript about our Harvard experiments and sent it off to the publisher. Entitled *High Priest* it was the best written and most favorably reviewed of my books to date.

In the spring of 1967 I solemnized a marriage between Bob Ross, our budding ecological-organic farming genius, and Carol, our long-time resident. Film and television crews went crazy over the photographic glories of the wedding and made Millbrook an emblem of lyrical pastoral life. I signed the marriage certificate as presiding minister. Filed in Albany it served as testimony to the legality of our religion. Our lawyers were preparing briefs to defend the use of our sacraments in designated shrines. I wrote a small book, *Start Your Own Religion*, which outlined the legal, psychological, and spiritual steps involved in sacramentalizing one's life. We all sensed that the summer of 1967 was going to blossom into a nationwide festival of unprepared drug-taking, so I hoped that this manual on how to use drugs intelligently would serve as a guide to those who would soon be experimenting with new realities. As usual we had troubles in distribution; most bookstores and chains wouldn't handle it.

Outside the Gates of Eden civil war was raging. President Johnson revealed that close to 400,000 young Americans had been sent to fight in Vietnam. Demonstrations protesting the war erupted in New York and other cities. Evidence of federal trickery surfaced in articles exposing covert CIA financing and infiltration of thirty liberal, religious, and educational groups, including the National Students Association. The CIA later cited presidential directives ordering these activities.

During my various encounters with law enforcement agencies I often thought of Mary Pinchot's warnings. Van and I continued to discuss our plans to investigate her murder but there was never time.

Harassment from G. Gordon Liddy and his cohorts in the county government escalated to a full-scale siege of Millbrook. Roadblocks were set up regularly around the estate. Everyone entering or leaving the grounds was rousted. Police informers kept coming around. From Poughkeepsie we received continual warnings of impending raids.

From a tactical viewpoint the Big House was indefensible. Even if we kept the premises free of illegal drugs, there was no stopping the incursions of armed men who could and did arrest our residents on trumped-up charges. So we closed the Big House and retreated to the wild forest on the northern acres of the property. We constructed a tent village on the rolling plain by Lunacy Hill.

Rosemary and I pitched our tent on the crest of Ecstasy Hill, about a mile away from the main encampment. Protected by circles of scouts, we set up domestic life as it has been lived for thousands of years—hauling water, cooking meals over a campfire, exploring the terrain, both inner and outer. During this period we came to understand how the symbiotic relationship between humans and dogs evolved. Our canine friends were absolutely necessary to our serenity. Because of their vigilance the minions of G. Gordon Liddy never caught us by surprise.

One hot sunny day Rosemary and I wandered down to the main camp aı 1 found the entire community gathered around a battery-operated record player. We joined them to listen for the first time to *Sergeant Pepper's Lonely Hearts Club Band*, a creation that probably best symbolized the so-called Summer of Love. The album was a most influential media statement about multiple realities and became an instant drug-culture classic. Demographer Landon Y. Jones has reported that "when the Beatles' *Sergeant Pepper* album was released in 1967, at least one critic called it 'the closest Western Civilization has come to unity since the Congress of Vienna in 1815.' "

At this point who should pop in but Otto Preminger, seeking information about LSD for a movie, *Skidoo*. He asked me many questions about the effects of LSD, and I queried him about film-making. A week later I dropped by Otto's luxurious Manhattan townhouse, where the cunning director persuaded me to run an LSD session for him. It was another one of those life-changers for me, coming from three years in romantic Arcadia to Otto's plastic-fantastic white-and-chrome, futuristic projection room, which bristled with dials, lights, levers, and other control-panel paraphernalia.

There was no fireplace. No candles!

As soon as the acid kicked in, Otto sprang into manic action. He turned on the TV—sacrilege! You were supposed to go within, float down your cerebral aqueduct, paddle by the islands of Langerhans, skirt the

Sylvan fissure, and wash up blissfully on the shores of your frontal lobes. Chanting Om Sweet Om. Not Otto. His shiny, hairless head had turned into a space helmet and he was high as an orbiting com-sat as he dialed and tuned ever-changing realities, deliberately disrupting focus and color.

I tried to find a slow repetitious Ravi Shankar record that would spin us within. No luck. His collection was all movie scores. Otto now had two more TV sets switched on. He stared with gleeful satisfaction at a screen flickering with random patterns of dots. Then I realized that Otto was demonstrating something important to me. As a movie director Otto took on the godly task of inventing a reality—he selected plot, location, actors. He externalized his vision on film and marketed it so that millions of human beings could inhabit his creation. I realized that the great shapers of human destiny were those who had accepted this role, who had dared to impose their version of reality upon others. All successful philosophers and myth-makers have been able to persuade others to live in worlds which their minds have invented.

Watching Otto's accelerated brain in action jolted me out of the nostalgic-pastoral phase. At Millbrook we had been living in a time-warp. Avoiding technology we got close to nature and to the wise-sensual animal places in the brain. But Otto's electronic technology could extend the brain, liberate us from the muscular. Millbrook was a pleasant but repetitious feudal drill. The next stage in evolution, my own at least, was going to involve information and communication. I resolved on the spot to move to Hollywood and learn how realities were produced and directed.

JAMES JOYCE 1882-1941), Irish novelist, is widely considered to be the most influential English-language author of the twentieth century. His stormy years in a Jesuit school are described in the autobigraphical *Portrait of the Artist as a Young Man*, which ends with the hero vowing to escape Ireland and live in "silence, exile and cunning."

Joyce made his escape in 1904, accompanied by Nora Barnacle, his companion-wife, who spent the next thirty-seven years with him in Paris, Trieste, and Zurich.

In his epic *Ulysses,* Joyce fissioned and energized the novel in the same way that Einstein and Picasso transformed physics and art, allowing perspective to define form rather than the other way around. In *Ulysses* and *Finnegan's Wake* Joyce intimately per-

sonalized the classic themes of humanism, expressing a reverence for life and evolution while heaping ridicule on authoritarian orthodoxy.

Because of the solipsistic and hallucinatory nature of Joyce's thinking many scholars have wondered whether he used consciousness-altering drugs. Robert Anton Wilson has found many references to pharmaceutical experiences in the rich foliage of Joycean prose. It is known that after contracting glaucoma in 1917, which began a long sequence of distressing eye operations, Joyce regularly used pain killers—opium, laudanum, and scopolamine (an alkaloid derived from henbane, a psychoactive plant belonging to the nightshade family).

32. Brotherhood of Eternal Love

FALL 1967
LAGUNA BEACH, CALIFORNIA

Our first Hollywood production was my marriage to Rosemary on a mountain top in the middle of Joshua Tree National Monument. Ted Markland from *Bonanza* directed. The cast included many notables from the movie business, plus some friends from the East Coast. The service was to be performed by Samu, a famous Plains Indian medicine man.

We assembled around sunset at Harry Cohn's desert ranch house, nestled among jagged cenozoic rocks and solemn cacti. We partied until midnight, then drove into the park and climbed up the dark trail to the peak, where Ted Markland had somehow implanted an executive swivel chair, to provide a 360-degree panoramic view. Our company, numbering fifty, dropped large doses of acid and reclined on soft ledges to talk things over with the stars, who, having heard about the marriage, dressed up in diamonds and glitter.

Someone kept a soft drumbeat going. Someone else played the flute. In the swivel chair Ted strummed a guitar. Then, with a magnificent flourish, he stood on the top rock and thrust the instrument high above his head, where the eager wind ruffled the strings. Bobby Walker, son of Jennifer Jones, stood naked to the waist, sculpting the air.

Rosemary and I huddled together and whispered prayers of gratitude and love for everyone who wasn't there, including Ralph, my daughter Susan, and Dick.

The rising sun went all out to decorate the sky, painting woolly clouds pink and orange. Ted Markland called us over to begin the ceremony, but Samu, shaman and veteran of thousands of peyote nights, lay belly-up, his huge bear body pulsing, his eyes wild with wonder. "White man medicine too strong," he muttered. "Later, later."

Soon the star climbing overhead pushed the temperature up to Broil, so we all walked down the mountain, Benny and friends helping Samu, who was laughing his head off and uttering Indian whoops. Samu sprawled on the back seat, still laughing hysterically. Rosemary and I sat in the front seat, while the jolly redskin invoked the blessings of the Great Spirits and linked us in marriage.

That's the way we were, always involved in one joyous pagan ceremony or another, whirling in religious ecstasies and heroic adventures. For us the planet was without Original Sin, designed for our sacramental pleasure. We were not alone. Millions were out there with us. The pageantry of those days! Where did it go?

Jack Leary came to the wedding from Laguna Beach with a new friend, John Griggs. Remember me? I met you at a party in the Hollywood Hills, and told you about our Sunday School acid sessions. He invited me to spend some time in Laguna Beach, rapidly becoming the psychedelic drug capital of the world.

"Not a bad idea to winter in a southern beach town," said Rosemary.

As usual the money tank was running on empty, but some enthusiastic fans at Cal State, Long Beach arranged for a lecture. The $1,500 fee would keep us going for a month or two.

We rented a small house on a cliff overlooking the Pacific. Jack, who had just turned eighteen, moved in with us. He was unsure of what to do with his life and bitter about the continuing police harassment. He blamed me for his mother's death. He was bored and depressed.

John Griggs acted as our guide to this new territory. After reading my book *Start Your Own Religion* he and his friends had done just that, incorporated themselves as The Brotherhood of Eternal Love. The BEL was quite an operation. On Pacific Coast Highway they opened Mystic

Arts World, the ultimate head shop, a veritable L.L. Bean Supermarket of hippy gear. The bookstore stocked prominent titles on oriental religion, Christian mysticism, futique psychology, psychopharmacology, genetics, Gurdjieff, Watts, Crowley, Krishnamurti. There was a health-food section, a luxurious meditation room, an art gallery featuring Hindu-Buddhist statues and the works of local artists. A clothing boutique offered Afghani wear, leather sandals, and tie-dyed garments designed by local artisans. The store provided cottage-industry income to scores of drug-culture people. Business was brisk.

As a non-profit organization Mystic Arts World funneled the proceeds back into the community. It also served to launder funds raised by dealing hashish, marijuana, and LSD. Here we observed the birth of a new American agribusiness: the cannabis trade.

Within ten years marijuana was to become the largest agricultural crop in several states and in several Latin American countries. The Grass National Product has been ranked the third largest business in the country, running behind General Motors and Exxon, a phenomenon that no economist has yet dared analyze and interpret publicly.

In the mid-1960s most of the marijuana trade was conducted by amateurs and semi-pros. In urban and suburban neighborhoods a few kids would pool their money and head for Mexico. They smuggled relatively small amounts—a few dozen kilos—half of which was smoked back home and the rest sold to cover expenses. The Mafia and the organized narcotic rings were not yet interested in grass, which was bulky to transport. Besides, they couldn't stand the open shameless flaunting of behavior that was supposed to be sinful and secret.

There was in these early years a remarkable innocence among dope dealers. The ethics were clear-cut. You weren't dealing for the money, but for the fun, the outlaw adventure, The Cause. You were performing a social duty to help other young people get high.

The Brotherhood of Eternal Love was to become, as the result of law enforcement hype, the most famous cult of dope dealers in the world. In actuality the women and men of the Brotherhood were not different from thousands of other youthful amateur grass retailers.

Members of the Brotherhood drove three hours in their old cars to the Mexican border and on for another hour or two to the marijuana villages. They quickly became popular with the growers of Baja and Sonora and Michoacan. The Mexicans had never seen anything like these relaxed happy kids, so different from the nervous furtive professionals. The Brothers would hang out, get high, down tequilas, gorge on the home-cooked *comidas*, and fall into their sleeping bags with the casualness of people at home on the land. They paid cash, never cheated. And a month later they were back for more fun and deals—with a couple of new friends. They were not criminals, that was the point. They were like the Mexican grass growers, enemies of the *federales*, enjoying the dope and the action.

The Brotherhood also smuggled a few Mexicans across the border, entertained them, showed them around, shared their homes. The Mexicans in turn revealed secret back roads and unguarded border crossings.

So the Brotherhood became the conduit for an enormous amount of grass that was smuggled across the border and then passed from friend to friend around Orange County, Los Angeles County, Ventura County, Riverside County. It was the best grass ever smoked by Anglos, and it was inexpensive.

The Brotherhood had nothing to do with downers, heroin, or uppers. This policy was known to everyone south and north of the border. Reputations travel very quickly in the underworld. No one in the fast life had seen anything like this Tom Sawyer band of sun-tanned people who were practically giving away strong weed, as well as the good acid made in San Francisco by Owsley, the famed alchemist.

In later years hundreds of grass and acid dealers around the globe claimed to be members of the Brotherhood. There was a time when you could walk into almost any village in Lebanon, Afghanistan, Pakistan, or any youth ghetto in the western world and say those four magical words—*Brotherhood of Eternal Love*—and be treated as an honored visitor. In countless solemn press conferences and televised hearings before various committees of Congress drug enforcement officials with basset-hound expressions testified about this unstoppable world-wide conspiracy. Actually, the Brotherhood never numbered more than ten husbands, ten wives, and their kids.

The style of the BEL came from John Griggs, thirty years old, a wiry blond lad, quick as a mink, resourceful, unconventional, and deeply religious. He lived with his wife Carol, and their two tow-haired kids in a plywood tract house in Laguna Canyon, itself a curious anthropological site inhabited primarily by dedicated dope dealers who belonged to a vague Orange County version of the Hindu faith. Their two-bedroom cottage was a psychedelic womb of oriental rugs, paisley cottons, religious statues, candles, incense.

When we got to meet the other brothers and sisters, we realized that John Griggs had hand-picked this group of uneducated young couples, all children of that swarm of Okies who had filled up the valleys stretching out from LA. There was a lot of old-time deep-seated religious sentiment in these kids. They had become bored with their parents' Baptist-Methodist faith, which had somehow gone flat in California.

These kids jumped at the chance to sign up for the BEL. They had been groomed to become gas-station attendants or wives of gas-station attendants. They were the labor pool that would build and service the huge stainless steel tanks in the Schlitz and Budweiser breweries popping up all over the Southland. Offered a part in a spiritual crusade that was obviously working, they threw themselves into the role of apostles, transfiguring themselves from working-class adolescent low-riders to apprentice divinities. They had new sacraments, grass and acid, which *did* bring about visible life changes. "Stay high and love God" was their motto.

Their purity was touching. Although they moved tons of marijuana and much LSD around the country, they lived as though under a vow of suburban poverty. They stuck with their old beat-up cars, always breaking down on the highway with trunks loaded full of contraband. They wore home-crafted clothing. They did keep some cash hidden away for lawyers' fees in case of arrest but shunned conspicuous upper-middle consumption.

The Brotherhood epitomized that brief moment at the beginning of the drug trade when utopian motives flourished. There was something magical about this band of twenty young men and women, outlaws who created a global legend and then disappeared quietly from the scene. Although they were known and hunted by the police, not one of them, to my knowledge, ever stood trial.

It was apparent to us Millbrook refugees that the Laguna Beach scene was too flamboyant to last. The canyon where the smugglers lived was too visible. I remarked to John that it would be wise for the Brotherhood to buy land in the mountains. He dispatched teams to check out real-estate brokers.

Laguna was also getting hot for Rosemary and me. We could feel the eyes of the police on us. When Ralph Metzner phoned that he was moving out of my Berkeley house to work as a psychologist in the Mendocino State Hospital, we decided to go up and see how the new culture was flowering in the Bay Area.

There was a fresh spirit there, a conspiratorial communality. The first visible manifestation of the Zoom Generation flaunting its strength. As we walked around the Berkeley hills, people drove by flashing the "V" sign. Long hair was the emblem. Hip people were now a large identifiable minority. San Francisco swarmed with them.

One afternoon we strolled through the Haight-Ashbury district. Lined up along the storefronts were young panhandlers and petty dealers hawking their wares. "Hey, man! Acid? Speed? Grass?"

After a block I was recognized, and the shout went up. Screaming my name in some sort of exultant native cry people grabbed my sleeve, touched my arms in reverence. One kid pulled off my tennis shoe and ran off waving it triumphantly. I was some sort of legend, a messiah walking among them. This adulation made it impossible to continue our stroll. We jumped into a passing cab, waved out the window, and lurched off.

This hero worship was disturbing. Many young people had imprinted me as a permissive father figure. By this time I was generally regarded as the spokesman for and unwitting leader of this large apolitical constituency of the young.

Our wedding on the mountain had been duly recorded in the scrolls of the Great Medicine Man in the Sky but not by the state. So we accepted Billy Hitchcock's invitation to come to Millbrook for a legal marriage celebration. Rosemary and I showed up at the county office to apply for a license and then drove back to New York for a prenuptial party at Peggy's apartment. We neglected to tell the sheriff and the district attorney our itinerary. They smashed down the doors of the Big House in a midnight raid but found only the members of a Hindu ashram that Billy was supporting. The police were not in a friendly mood, being disappointed at finding no drugs, no party, and no Timothy and Rosemary.

Undaunted the DA issued warrants for my arrest on eleven implausible charges—running a public nuisance, occupying a house where drugs were used, corruption of minors, etc.—in spite of the fact that we had been away from Millbrook for over a year. There was an election coming up for local officials. In fairness it must be said that this harassment was not due to G. Gordon Liddy, who had been promoted and assigned to more important tasks in the Nixon White House.[1]

Early in 1968 Paul Krassner, editor of *The Realist*, invited me to New York to discuss a coalition between "my people" (the hippies) and the political activists. Paul reported that he and Jerry Rubin and Abbie Hoffman had taken acid on New Year's Eve in a Lower East Side apartment and had revelations about merging the entire spectrum of dissenting Americans in a Young People's Party (Yippies).

Krassner, Rubin, and Hoffman's LSD trip had apparently imprinted an urban-socialist vision, which they expressed in a new style of political theater. Don't talk to the Yippies about pastoral drop-out. You simply can't *drop out* if you're living in a metropolitan hive. You want to *turn on, tune in, and kick ass!* So the Yippies became the urban political expression of the Baby Boom, the first party to deal not with voting blocs or platforms but with information, media images, neurological campaigning. Guerrilla raids, not on the Bastille but on the Six O'Clock News.

But the Yippies didn't attract me, because they didn't want enough. Their program was old-fashioned leftist negativity—a pessimistic ghetto-socialist distrust of what this country stood for and what the future required. The Yippies basically didn't like America or American values. Like their models, the revolutionary students in Europe and the Middle East, the militants of the '60s were out of touch with the optimistic aspirations of the young for more and better of everything.

The militants didn't succeed because they emitted bad vibes—tough, mean, deliberately provocative. I had many a run-in with Abbie Hoffman.

"Your peace-and-love bullshit is leading youth down the garden path of fascism," he screamed. "You're creating a group of blissed-out pansies ripe for annihilation."

"Come on, Abbie, you're just trying to scare people into feeling bad. Which doesn't help anybody. You can't do good unless you feel good."

Like others on the opposite end of the political spectrum Abbie continually projected on me his worst fears of what would happen if everyone were free and self-confident. He studied me, and although we disagreed on goals (Abbie was at that time a conservative socialist, moralistic, past-oriented, anti-science) we had many analytical discussions about the tactical necessity of using the media. The thing I liked about Abbie was that he kept changing, taking risks, dropping acid, reprogramming his head. He became the ultimate contradiction—a psychedelic socialist.

It was an extraordinary experience in wish-fulfillment to observe the emergence of counter-culture youth as a force in national politics during the spring and summer of 1968. They catalyzed an impressive alliance of dissident groups. Martin Luther King came out against the war. Rennie Davis headed a coalition seeking to mobilize 500,000 protesters at the Chicago convention with support from groups like Students for a Democratic Society, fronted by Tom Hayden, and from civil rights advocates like David Dellinger. Youth power was growing.

The aim of the game that summer was to derail the Democratic Party locomotive and replace L. B. Johnson with a peace candidate. I supported the movement and hoped to make it peaceful, humorous, educational. At one point I had the militants almost convinced that we should hold a separate Convention for Life in a national park outside Chicago: "Rewrite the Declaration of Independence. Invite rock bands. Have an assembly many times larger and more entertaining. Upstage the Democratic convention."

Then the counter-culture made its move to take over the Democratic Party. Senator Eugene McCarthy entered the New Hampshire primary as a peace candidate. On college campuses kids started cutting their long hair to "go clean for Gene," attracting media attention as they rang doorbells and handed out leaflets at shopping malls.

McCarthy's strong showing in New Hampshire was seen as a dangerous blow to President Johnson's war policy. Then Bobby Kennedy, admittedly concerned that the youth constituency was passing him by, shocked the old-line pols by throwing his hat in the ring. Suddenly the counter-culture had two distinguished candidates. On March 31 LBJ announced that he would not seek re-election.

The miraculous seemed to be happening. It was obvious that Bobby would defeat McCarthy in the primaries and overwhelm the pathetic campaign of LBJ loyalist Hubert Humphrey. With the Kennedy machine swinging into action, powered by Mayor Daley of Chicago, it was a cinch that tousle-haired Bobby, the new idol of the young and the hopeful, would sweep to the White House. And Bobby's victory would carry with him a slate of young candidates devoted to peace and the new politics.

To my dismay I found that the Yippies and other activist groups did not share this optimism. Jerry Rubin, who was telling kids to kill their parents, was not about to settle for a peaceful revolution. The Yippies and radicals didn't really want to win because then there would be no market for moral outrage.

Everything started coming apart. On April 4 Martin Luther King was assassinated in Memphis. Riots in over a hundred cities, forty-six deaths, federal troops called into action. On June 5, the eve of his victory in the California primary, Robert Kennedy was shot down.

Then the good old boys regained their footing. Hubert Humphrey, sticking with the war faction of the Democratic Party, was now assured of the Democratic nomination with LBJ and Mayor Daley working together to stifle opposition at the Chicago convention. An ugly confrontation loomed.

In the weeks before the convention I argued passionately with the Yippies and other radical activists against moving into enemy turf in Chicago. Allen Ginsberg, who had emerged as an eloquent anti-war spokesman, agreed that the inevitable violence would hurt the cause of peace. But he felt some strange obsession to participate. I couldn't understand why we should go to Chicago to get beat up publicly and insure Nixon's election.

In mid-June John Griggs flew up to our Berkeley headquarters with interesting news. The Brotherhood of Eternal Love had taken an option on a ranch in the San Jacinto mountains above Palm Springs. Would we come down and check it out?

Their haven lay in a spectacularly beautiful niche. The access road veered from the state highway through a locked gate and five miles of deserted government land to a valley watered by eight streams from the surrounding peaks. There was a small lake, a rambling ranch house, corrals, a huge barn, tack-houses, and cabins. On a ridge above the valley stood a new comfortable cottage for Rosemary and me.

We moved in immediately for another idyllic period of contemplative withdrawal from the crazy violent world. I threw myself into domesticity, building a bed for our luxurious double sleeping bag, constructing a desk in an adjoining cabin for my office.

Every day we walked down from our ridge to join the six families busily refurbishing the ranch house, breaking horses, buying cows, splashing in the reservoir, preparing delectable communal feasts.

One day that summer a group of us went exploring high up on the mountain. I got ahead of the group and disappeared from sight. John Griggs told the brothers not to wait but to jeep back to the ranch and that he and I would return on two mules which we had just purchased from a nearby rancher.

"When I returned from the climb, John handed me the reins and motioned for me to mount the enormous animal.

"This mule has never been ridden before today, has it?" I asked tentatively.

John laughed and said, "That's all right, you just have to make friends with her." He lifted the tail of the huge animal and shoved his hand eye-level between her legs and moved it softly, caressing. Then he said, "You do it."

I looked up the long powerful legs, as thick as my shoulders, and gaped at the dark, shadow crease where the legs joined and the steamy smell of mule bathed me.

"Go ahead. Run your hand up along her legs. She'll dig it."

I put my hand on inside of her left leg and moved it up, slowly, and felt the rounded muscle fearful with horse power and slid my hand up against the moist yielding smooth flesh to her crotch and the one ton creature shifted her weight slightly and breathed softly and I slid my hand down hairless leg, palm slippery and up and shyly looked at John who watched me grinning, and she arched up her head and settled her four legs luxuriously in the sand. Hail Mare full of race. The Lord is with thee!

When I stopped and slid my hand down John said, "I learned a lot talking to these old cowboys around here. They say there's only one sure way to get along with your animals and that's the way you get along with your woman, and they have all sorts of jokes about climbing up on boxes and so on." I was still holding my hand out at my side and felt I had just been initiated into some special mountain-man secret, powerful and funny.

We rode back five miles on the road and the mule was nervous and I got nervous when I realized that she knew less about being ridden than I did about riding and once when she bolted I drove her into some sage and while she panted jumpily I held my right hand down to her nose and then rubbed it on her huge buttock and reined her back on the road and plodded on in twilight watching the stars pop out.

One afternoon we listened to a new record by the Moody Blues. I heard lyrics that were to become a personal theme for the next few years.

Timothy Leary's dead . . .
Oh no, he's on the outside looking in.
Timothy Leary's dead . . .
No . . . Na . . . No . . .
He's on the outside looking in.

He'll fly his astral plane,
Take you on trips around the bay,
Bring you back the next day . . .
Timothy Leary, Timothy Leary,
He'll take you up and bring you down,
Plant your feet back firmly on the ground.
He flies so high,
He flies so low,
He knows exactly which way he's going to go.
Timothy Leary, Timothy Leary [2]

The music was typical Moody Blues, wide ranging in tone and volume, swelling into rock sonorities. At a moment of pop-celebrity like this I marvelled at the acculturation process, which converted my pedantic philosophic-neurological concepts into themes which would be listened to by millions. There was no denying that this sort of thing was powerful advertising for altered states and multiple realities.

As the Democratic convention drew near, I talked by phone practically every day with the Yippie convention planners. I tried to set up a counter-convention is San Francisco or a series of love-ins around the country during the week of the Democratic convention, but everyone was in the grip of morbid fascination with producing the catastrophe.

My desire to quiet down Chicago and support Humphrey was not completely unselfish. If Nixon won, especially if he won on the basis of a reaction to youthful violence, then I would be in a lot of trouble. I was out on appeal bond facing decades of prison. When the purge came, it would certainly focus on drugs because control of American consciousness was and still is the issue.

Rosemary and I listened to the Chicago riots while sitting in front of our mountain cabin under the stars, our faces colored by the flickering fire. The portable radio crackled with news of police brutality and tear gas and bitter struggles on the convention floor. I felt the animal fear in my spine.

On election night Rosemary and I drove from the ranch to the nearby village of Idyllwild to watch the returns. Humphrey had been gaining steadily in the polls, and it seemed likely that the voters would choose the amiable compassionate Minnesotan over "the new Nixon."

The best restaurant in town refused to serve us drinks because Rosemary had no ID. We watched the results on a TV in a health-food store run by hippies. When Humphrey just barely lost I was distressed. The climate of anger whipped up by the activists like Tom Hayden, Jerry Rubin, and Eldridge Cleaver (abetted by the Nixon provocateurs) had put in the White House a World War II veteran burning with Cold War fever, the Legionnaire's Disease.

Christmas 1968. Family and friends assembled at the ranch for an old-fashioned holiday reunion. Jack and Susan, who were working at the Mystic Arts Bookstore in Laguna, came up for the festival and stayed in our cottage.

The high mountains were sunbathable when the sky was blue, but that week was cloudy and chilly. The day after Christmas we got cabin fever. Rosemary and I decided to drive to Berkeley and enjoy civilization for a week before the winter lecture tour. We dropped Susan off at her apartment in Laguna Beach and headed into the Canyon where Jack was staying in John Griggs' house. We were followed by an unmarked car. As I parked in front of the house a policeman appeared on the driver's side and asked for my ID. He talked on his radio. In minutes two more black-and-whites pulled up to the scene, red lights flashing. Four cops stood by my window. The first cop said, "You get out of that car on your own or we'll use force."

I stepped out, protesting the illegality of the search. The policeman leaned over the driver's seat, fumbled with the ashtray, and then said, "You're under arrest."

Word for word it was a repeat of my encounter with G. Gordon Liddy: "Arrest! For what?"

The officer reached in his right trousers pocket and pulled out two crumbled half-smoked roaches. With this handy evidence as justification the other officers searched Rosemary and Jack (who were both holding), handcuffed us all, and whirled us off to jail. There we were forced to submit to the familiar routine: fingerprints, mug shots, the holding cell. The Brotherhood's lawyer had us out on bail in an hour.

The next day the attorney had reassuring news. "Everyone around the courthouse knows what happened. The officer that busted you is notorious for planting evidence. We'll get the case thrown out in the preliminary hearing."

"That sounds good," I said. "But just out of curiosity, what's the penalty for possession of two roaches?"

"Six months to ten years," said the lawyer. "Not to worry. We'll beat it if we have to take it to the Supreme Court."

"Won't this give the government the excuse to pull my appeal bond on the Laredo case?"

"They don't need any excuses," replied the lawyer. "When they want you jugged, they'll do it."

S OCRATES (469-399 B.C.), Athenian philosopher, held that the aim of human life is to search for the truth to the nature of things as they are, not as they are interpreted by the conventional mind. Pronounced by the Delphic oracle to be the wisest man in Greece, Socrates taught that virtue, the highest good, is identical with intelligent action, which can be learned and developed from within.

Like the Pied Piper, Socrates was a juvenilization agent, accused "by conservative minds of the dangerous game of discomfiting all authority before a circle of impressionable youths and subtracting from the state the stability of tradition . . . his unsettling effect on the young and his persistent criticism were intolerable to any establishment" (*Encyclopedia of Philosophy,* Macmillan).

Socrates can also be described as the first psychologist in that his teachings posited a psyche as the source of human behavior. His synthesis of introspection and dialectic, aimed at developing inner wisdom and testing it in practical thinking and right conduct has had a profound influence on western thought.

In 399 B.C. Socrates was charged with heresy and corrupting youth. His trial, imprisonment, and execution by self-administration of hemlock are recounted by Plato in the *Apology, Crito,* and *Phaedo.*

33. Cultural Evolution Versus Political Revolution

By the time 1968 came to a close, 555,000 young Americans had been sent to fight in Vietnam; over 30,000 had already died in this Asian misadventure, which continued to be popular among those born before 1930 and extremely unpopular among those born after 1946.

Within four months of Nixon's inauguration the American leadership was feverishly waging two wars—one abroad and one at home. While the Air Force ran secret bombing raids in Cambodia, the FBI under J. Edgar Hoover (by this time undeniably senile) launched the Contelpro operation—infiltration and provocation of anti-war, black, and student groups. To avoid being yanked back into prison for violation of parole, Eldridge Cleaver fled to Cuba and subsequently set up a community of political exiles in Algeria. Campuses throughout the country (even staid old Harvard) seethed with open rebellion. Richard Kleindienst, Assistant Attorney General, publicly called for a campaign of suppression against "ideological criminals." Enemies without. Enemies within.

The high desert was a fine place from which to contemplate this planetary turbulence. Here was a terrain very different from the lush green
Northeast of my childhoods, physiological and lysergic. Here there was
no fertile moist topsoil, squirming with life, just a hard rusty lunar surface
in which every wily scrub stood by itself, working out survival strategies
under the hot sun and dry wind, rooting deep for water and then, as
in the case of the lascivious Joshua tree or the luscious yucca, exploding
with blossoms, scandalously perfumed, as though the harshness of the
environment demanded the most extravagant display of sexual invitation.

The high ridges and peaks provided refuge for several endangered
species: coyotes, bears, deer, and us. During the open season hunters
parked their cars outside our perimeter fences, ceremoniously littered the
ground with beer cans, and stalked into the hills with high-powered rifles.
We could hear the gunshots echo.

The land itself was not without danger. The first time I heard the
rasping buzz of a rattlesnake I jumped in fright and felt the instinct
to kill. We soon found that hiking the mountains was safe when we
brought along a cloud of dogs. With this protection we came to enjoy
our brief meetings with the lordly serpents.

As summer heat parched the high ground, snakes began migrating down
to the green valley. There was great tribal excitement when a five-foot
rattler was seen slithering down a hole in the yard where the children
played. Here was a dilemma. Like most drug-culture people we had developed a reverence for life, considering it worthwhile to hold serious
discussions about the killing of mosquitos (the common-sense view was
that it was all right to smack one if she were on your arm about to
sting), about the ethics of meat-eating (save for Rosemary and me the
group was organic-vegetarian,) and about the never-ending issue of self-
defense.

We prepared a dozen serpent-catchers, broomsticks with a noose at
the end that could be tightened over a rattler's head. Then we turned
on a garden hose and shoved it down the hole where the big one had
disappeared. In a few seconds out popped the very wet head of the surprised reptile. I lassoed and gingerly dumped him in a cardboard carton,
which we placed carefully in the back of the truck. A couple of miles
down the road I bade him respectful farewell as we let him loose.

Rosemary and I would sometimes take sleeping bags up to the peaks,
build a fire, take LSD, and spend the night watching the late show in
the sky. Sometimes we heard the whup-whup of helicopters and the
power-whine of jets flying low over the valley. We were told by a friendly
journalist that March Air Force Base was using our encampment as a
target for night-surveillance training of pilots bound for Vietnam.

From the calm of the high desert we descended once again to the college lecture circuit. My appearances were by now so controversial that even scheduling the event often involved hot debates between students and faculty/administration. To stabilize the nervous polarities in the atmosphere my speakers bureau booked my appearances in debate form, signing one of the government's most renowned drug experts, Dr. Sidney Cohen, to travel with me. To him fell the unenviable job of presenting the anti-change position—a curious turnabout for Sidney, who a decade before had been running around the country giving acid to Henry Luce, Aldous Huxley, various Hollywood stars, and a number of politicians. Sidney had taken LSD many times and had written two books that described the wonders of *The Beyond Within*. It disturbed me that he was now winning fortune and respectability by exaggerating the negative.

Oh the excitement of those days! TV cameras whirred as airplane doors opened. Bulbs flashed. Psychedelic banners waved. Auditoriums jammed with students. Clouds of balloons floated to the ceiling. Flowers. Rebel whoops. Wild costumes! For these performances I generally wore white duck trousers, silk Hindu shirts, long hair gathered in pony tail, bare feet. (People who remember me in robes are thinking of Richard Alpert, an understandable but embarrassing misidentification. Rosemary, my fashion consultant, would never let me wear robes. The *New Yorker* critic said I looked like a shipwrecked sailor, which I thought quite accurate.)

Dr. Sidney Cohen wore dark suits and ties.

My presentations had developed into inspirational science monologues—impassioned odes to evolution. I reminded listeners of their heroic frontier past, acting out great moments of discovery, decrying the dangers of conformity, urging a life of individual action and personal growth rather than partisan politics. All this was presented in the mode of "cheerleader for change."

Dr. Cohen, disregarding his own research findings about the relative safety of LSD, recited in gruesome detail the standard stories of bark eating and defenestration.

There were two frequent sources of heckling. Political militants would sometimes denounce me for distracting young people from armed revolution. And sometimes older people would shout that I was the anti-Christ, a devil, a new Hitler seducing the young. It was all good theater.

When the colleges closed in June Rosemary and I headed back to the ranch to review and restore. The hot fashion trend that spring was tipi-chic. Rosemary and I erected our art nouveau wigwam in the blossoming apple orchard.

I wrote a chapter about non-violence for a book published by *Time/Life* and filled a notebook on the future of American politics. I was toying with the idea that I might run for public office, if I could stay out of prison. Who could deny that the old system of republican government spelled out in Philadelphia in 1776 and in the Constitutional Convention of 1787 had been outmoded by rapid transportation and communication? It was patently absurd to elect a representative to advocate our interests in an age when the capital was no longer eight days' ride by horse carriage from Boston or Atlanta. As we moved into the era of computers and electronics, intelligence rather than territory was the central concern of government. In the Information Age the function of the state was to facilitate education, communication, innovation, entertainment: to raise the intelligence of the populace.

I jotted down a political platform that would be considered moderate by twenty-first-century standards and thought about how to publicize it.

We woke to the barking of dogs, first the warning cries of Fang and Finnigan, our new Australian dingo.

Then came the answering bays of the approaching party from the main camp.

Rosemary slipped into the "diaphanous gown," made famous by G. Gordon Liddy. "It's Monday, isn't it," she said apprehensively. For six months we had been awaiting the Supreme Court verdict on the Laredo case. Decisions came down on Monday mornings.

The voice of John Griggs could be heard above the din. He appeared at the tipi opening with Carol and others of the Brotherhood. They were smiling broadly. "We just heard it on the radio. The Supreme Court cut you loose. Nine to nothing. They ruled that the marijuana law is unconstitutional."

Rosemary and I looked in each other's eyes and then we kissed. It was one of those great moments.

Someone was shouting. Down by the entrance road were three strange cars.

"Looks like police," said John with reflex caution.

"It's reporters," said Rosemary.

The men started walking up the slope to the tipi, some carrying cases of photographic equipment. ABC, CBS, NBC. Rosemary and I stood in front of the tipi while the TV cameras whirred.

"Now that you've knocked out the federal marijuana laws, what's your next move?"

"I'm going to run for governor of California," I said.

The reporters seemed to like the idea. The incumbent was an undistinguished movie-actor who did not conceal his disdain for the poor, the blacks, the hip, the Latinos, the women, the students, the liberals, the young—and journalists.

"What's your platform going to be?"

"The State of California," I said, "should be run like a successful business enterprise. Instead of extorting taxes from the citizens a well-run state should return a profit. Anyone smart enough to live in California should be paid a dividend."

I handed out a three-page political program for eliminating all taxes, licensing frivolities, and converting high schools, colleges, and prisons into profitable institutions. Direct electronic voting would replace elected representatives, leading to decentralization and more local autonomy.

"You know you could stir up a lot of people with these ideas," said one TV cameraman.

Rosemary said, "That's what I'm afraid of."

Many of my inner-directed friends were puzzled when I announced my candidacy for governor, considering politics to be the lowest form of human endeavor.

"You're putting yourself in an impossible situation," said Alan Watts. "If you don't make waves, you're wasting a lot of time. And if you do, you'll end up in the Jailhouse or, what's worse, the State House."

But I saw politics as one of the important stages of personal evolution. Didn't Plato pay his philosophers-union dues with the *Republic*?

After all, everyone had to answer the eight basic questions of life for themselves. How could one shirk the pleasant daily routine of redefining and updating the Eight Technologies of God, one of which is political?

So I prepared my campaign plan. The first step was to line up press support. Within a week I had endorsements from Max Scheer, editor of the prestigious *Berkeley Barb*, and Art Kunkin, publisher of the influential *Los Angeles Free Press*, plus support from the *San Francisco Oracle* and alternative papers in San Diego, Sacramento, and Santa Barbara. Jann Wenner of *Rolling Stone* magazine offered his aid.

The plan was to lease a campaign train, load it with counter-culture celebs and rock bands, and tour from city to city. One of the key campaign managers was Wendy Stark, granddaughter of Fanny Brice and daughter of producer Ray Stark. Wendy set out to line up endorsements from the college-age children of distinguished Americans—senators, movie stars, financiers.

We flew to New York to make a recording with musician-supporters who would lay down some tracks behind my voice for a campaign album. Before the session Jimi Hendrix took us to dinner in Greenwich Village. He shyly asked us about the philosophic meaning of visions he had experienced during acid trips. He was so unworldly that his girlfriend Stella had to counsel him about ordering his meal and how much to tip.

Jann Wenner turned up at the next table. Jann, born in January 1946, has consistently served as an advance scout of the Baby Boom. Whatever this generation wanted, Jann sensed it first. We invited him to come along to the studio.

Rosemary, Jann, and I sat in the control booth. My voice boomed out the sci-fi neurological campaign poetry, singing the praises of re-im-printing ("You Can Be Anyone, This Time Around"), chanting the de-lights of the nervous system ("What Do You Turn On, When You Turn On?"), and psalming the frontal lobes ("I've Been Around the World in My Brain, I've Settled Evolutions, No Pain"). Through the glass wall we watched Jimi Hendrix thumping bass guitar, while Stephen Stills and John Sebastian high-wired the leads and Buddy Miles berserked on drums. It was a powerful electoral message. [1]

Next day a phone call came from John Lennon and Yoko Ono, who couldn't make our recording session because an old grass conviction kept them out of the country. John and Yoko wanted us to join them in Montreal, where they were conducting a Bed-In. They sent acorns to presidents and dictators around the world as a symbol of the movement for peace. John wanted us to help them cut a record called "Give Peace a Chance."

Platoons of guards patrolled the Lennon corridor of the Queen Elizabeth Hotel. John and Yoko, sprawled on a king-size bed, waved happily and blew us kisses as we came into the room. Flanked by bald-headed orange-garbed monks they were being interviewed by a Montreal reporter.

"Where do you get your strength?" asked the journalist.

"From Hare Krishna," said John.

"That's where we get it from, you know," said Yoko earnestly. "We're not denying it."

After everyone left, Rosemary and I spent a pleasant afternoon chatting about our ranch and their island off the coast of England. Tommy Smothers showed up and then a Canadian rabbi. When the multi-track recording outfit arrived from Toronto, we taped this Sunday school hymn that John cooked up. Solemnly we sang the chorus while Rosemary set the beat, banging on Tommy Smothers' guitar case. Then John added a verse:

John and Yoko, Timmy Leary, Rosemary, Tommy Smothers, Bobby Dylan, Tommy Cooper, Derek Taylor, Norman Mailer, Allen Ginsberg. Hare Krishna. All we are saying is give peace a chance.

The next day John asked what he could do to help my campaign for governor.

"Write a campaign song," I replied.

"Okay," said John, "what's the theme?"

"Our campaign slogan is 'Come together, join the party.'"

"Great title," said John. He grabbed his guitar and started improvising.

Come together right now.
Don't come tomorrow, don't come alone,
Come together right now,
Over me.
All that I can tell you is
You gotta be free.

We fooled around with a couple of versions. Then John sang the song through and handed me the tape. [2]

Back to New York in high spirits about the campaign. Underground papers were publishing my platform pronunciamentos. The Lennon "Come Together" song started playing on California radio stations. The next step was to make a movie. The movie would win the election.

We met for a strategy session in the producer's West Side apartment. His initial idea was to follow us around on the campaign train with a crew filming the rallies and the speeches. The film would be released after the election.

It took him a little time to understand that the movie about how I won the election should be filmed and released *before* the election. "See, it's a documentary about creating the future," I said. "We'll shoot some of the early campaigning, one concert rally and a few on-the-street endorsements. But the main thrust will be newscasts shot in the studio with our anchor-people reporting my slow but steady gain in the polls, support coming from young voters, vegetarians, astrologers, the two million grass smokers of the state, show-biz stars. Hell, this is California we're talking about! We'll have people coming out of the voting booth and telling why they voted for me. Last minute news bulletins about the closeness of the race. And then a victory celebration at the Ambassador Hotel. The movie will be shown only in California during the month before the election."

He looked shocked. "You mean the movie will be about the election before it happens?"

"You got it. When the voters see it happen on the screen, then they'll make it happen on Election Day."

"To be shown only in California?"

"After the election everyone in the world will want to see how we won an election with film."

"But the budget," he protested.

"You work out the budget, and I'll raise the money. We're going to charge admission to the rock concerts, you know. And T-shirts. And an album. The campaign will gross $10 million which we'll donate to the State Treasury."

It took him a while to think it through, but eventually he agreed.

Our euphoria was dampened a bit the next day at my lawyer's office. It seemed that if the government had its way, I wouldn't be around to campaign for office.

"I've been on the phone talking to the prosecutors of your cases around the country," said my lawyer, "and they've got you booked for a busy winter schedule. For starters you were such a hit in Laredo, they want you back for a repeat performance in December."

"Laredo? But we won that case in the Supreme Court."

"True, but the feds have refiled on a technicality. You're going to be tried this time on the charge of transportation of marijuana. Specifically, driving a car for a distance of one hundred yards from the center of the International Bridge to the Customs checkpoint. The maximum sentence is twenty years and a $10,000 fine."

"You gotta be kidding."

"That's just the beginning. You're billed for a personal appearance later in December for the Laguna Beach case. And after the first of the year you go back to Poughkeepsie for the eleven Millbrook indictments. My guess is that with local juries you'll be found guilty. It's almost certain you'll get these convictions reversed in appeals court, but that may take two years. Meanwhile they can hold you in county jail without a bond."

"So I'm facing twenty plus ten plus eleven years for half an ounce of marijuana and two roaches, none of which was mine?"

"Affirmative."

"And even if I fight the cases successfully, I'll still spend time in jail awaiting the appeal verdicts?"

"Yes, and you'll spend plenty of money too. What's happening is the Nixon administration has announced an all-out war on drugs. They know they can't stop people from using dope, so the best they can do is jail the symbol. They have this three-prong offensive moving on you. And they can keep arresting you on phony charges whenever they want."

"What can I do?"

"You better run like hell to get nominated for governor. Public outcry is the only protection you have."

"There's another direction to run," I said. "I'm going down right now to apply for a passport. I have no intention of becoming a martyr."

*   *   *

The climax of the last summer of the '60s was Woodstock, a convincing demonstration of the swarming power of the Baby Boomers. Half a million assembled for a weekend to form the third largest city in New York State. Instant metropolis! A hundred thousand LSD trips; two births, three deaths, none caused by drugs.

Knowing the promoters we were clued into the backstage greed and power madness, so we stayed away. The sharks were out in full force. The New York City police threatened to close it down unless they were taken care of. Musicians and their agents maneuvered. The people fighting for control of the stage had no idea that the star of this show would be the crowd.

The sheer numbers were awesome. The new generation made its strength known in epideictic style. Even more impressive was the gentleness of this Flower Power. "Peace and Love" was the theme of this event, which became the symbol of an era.

Bill Graham saw what was happening and hated it. The movie *Woodstock* caught him at that historic moment tearing his hair, screaming with crazed eyes at this army of kids invading the grounds. *The little scumbags weren't buying tickets!* "They're like those ants in South America," he shouted to the cameras. "The only way to stop them is dig trenches and set fire to them."

Three months later the Rolling Stones free concert took place at the Altamont Racetrack, about ten miles east of Oakland. I was invited by the Grateful Dead's manager to join the celebrations. When I phoned the offices in San Francisco, Emmett Grogan spoke as if he were in charge of the concert. That was bad news. A junky street-warrior, darling of chic leftists who liked to hang out with romantic tough guys, Emmett was a notorious *agent provocateur* and seeder of dissension. As he confided that the Hells Angels were handling security, the ironic smirk in his voice predicted trouble.

The East Oakland freeway was jammed solid at ten in the morning. Jack, Rosemary, and I parked near an off-ramp, climbed up to the freeway, and jumped merrily into the first van that came by. The drive to Altamont was to become my most treasured memory of that period. Two, three, four hundred thousand people, all in a festive mood, passing joints, fruit, wine, and beer from car to car as we inched along, music playing, sun shining. Awaiting us were the tough guys who had roared in on Harleys and in helicopters, now relaxing in luxury trailers and swaggering around the stage.

We hiked the last couple of miles into the enormous bowl, which was crowded by noon with people spreading out blankets, smoking, picnicking, dropping M.G.s. Morale was high. Santana was playing somewhere down there onstage, but it didn't matter. Lots of harmonicas and guitars and portables filled the air.

We wandered down to the stage. The throng around the bandstand was already pressing forward, though it was hours before the Stones were due.

The Hells Angels posted around the bandstand were clearly looking for trouble, which started during the Jefferson Airplane set. Marty Balin, the lead singer, was blocked from the mike by an Angel. When Marty protested, a biker decked him. The Angel in charge, his black jacket studded with emblems, looked at me and shrugged. What could he say? "My guys are drunk on the Grateful Dead's beer. There's going to be trouble."

After the Airplane finished, there was a vacuum onstage. For two hours everyone waited.

"Tell Mick to get started," I shouted down to Grogan.

"He wants to wait until it's dark to make a better entrance."

The tension grew with the boredom. When dusk fell, small campfires flared up around the perimeter of the bowl, recalling a scene out of Dante's *Inferno*. The crowd in front of the stage began to surge forward, pushed by those behind.

Finally Sam Cutler walked on stage, waited for the vast multitude to quiet down, and said, "From London, the Rolling Stones." A slow shudder of excitement reverberated around the amphitheater as the fabled musicians sauntered on. Mick was carrying a whiskey bottle in his hand.

With uncanny prescience the group moved right into "Sympathy for the Devil." Mick sang: "Please allow me to introduce myself, I'm a man of wealth and fame . . ."

The ocean of fans swept forward. Hells Angels leaped to push them back, charging, slashing with fists and clubs, forcing the sea to ebb. Then the crowd, pushed from behind, surged forward again. Angels were diving from the stage, knives and fists flying. Mick stopped singing. He tried to calm the storm, but he had lost control. Meanwhile the massacre continued, victims falling, and the band played on. They never sounded better as smoke from a hundred fires drifted across the field of faces, lit by flickering flames. Those more than 50 feet away remained unaware of the mayhem around the stage.

The Hells Angel riot, culminating in the death of a bystander, produced moralistic editorials claiming that the decade of peace and hope had ended in aimless drug violence. The fact is that all the bad stuff occurred around the stage, the center of power, where the drug of choice was booze. I didn't see one person born after 1946 on the bandstand.

One thing seemed clear about Woodstock and Altamont. None of the rock stars and producers of these events had a clue about what was then happening on the planet. The gene-pool was way ahead of its leaders and spokesmen.

About two weeks later I was lecturing in Boston when I got the phone call from Rosemary. She was crying.

"John Griggs just died. An overdose of psilocybin."

"My God, it's not possible. I'll be back on the next plane."

It was possible.

The night before, John had decided to try psilocybin for the first time. The synthetic mushroom, considered by the experts to be the safest and gentlest psychedelic drug, had been unavailable for six years, because Sandoz stopped distribution after our Harvard project went public. When John Griggs heard that a Los Angeles chemist had synthesized the rare substance, he acquired a supply with high expectations.

John and Carol prepared the tipi. John bathed and dressed himself ceremonially. Carol lit the fire, and John sat on furs, waiting for the drug to hit. Full Buck Moon, their baby, slept in his cradle. Carol re-clined on pillows with their kids Sissy and Jerry, who cuddled next to her as she read to them by candlelight.

John had taken a substantial dose. After about half an hour he was very high and very sick. He rose to his feet. "This drug isn't pure. I've been poisoned. I'm going up to Benny's tipi and warn him not to take it."

A few minutes later John returned, bade his wife and children farewell, and fell into a coma. Ten hours later he died at the Idyllwild hospital.

Laboratory reports revealed that the psilocybin pills contained strychnine. During this period there were many reports of LSD and other psychedelics being laced with poisons. Rumors spread through the counter-culture about federal drug enforcement agents circulating tainted drugs, but there was no proof.

We all felt that at the time of his death John Griggs was one of the most successful radiant holy people we had never known. He died sur-rounded by his loved ones in one of the most beautiful valleys in the world.

The last weeks of 1969 involved a dismal round of court appearances, preliminary hearings, pre-trial motions—draining of time, energy, and money.

In December I was re-tried in Laredo for the silver box. If I had taken the stand and truthfully denied knowledge of the grass, I would have been acquitted. My lawyers, one local and one Manhattan, seemed at a loss. They waived any defense, and I was found guilty in ten minutes.

"We'll win on appeal," said the lawyers.

Next it was back to Orange County for the two-roaches trial. Here the problem was complicated by the fact that Rosemary and Jack were clearly guilty of possessing illegal drugs. If I fought my case and won, my wife and son would get hit with prison terms. If I was found guilty, then Rosemary and Jack would get off with probation.

PAOLO MANTEGAZZA (1831-1910) fled from his native Italy after the revolution of 1848 and for 10 years lived as an exile in South America where he experimented with coca. On his return he published the first European essay on the uses of cocaine.

Mantegazza embarked on a whirlwind course of intellectual achievement that made him one of the most influential Europeans of his century. He established the first laboratory of pathology in Europe. He held the first Italian professorial chair in anthropology and helped introduce photo-graphy to Italy. His experiments with animal grafts stimulated interest in rejuvenation research. He was Italy's leading exponent of Darwinism and evolutionary theory and for many years served as a senator in the Italian parliament.

Mantegazza has also been recognized as the first European sexologist. In *Human Ecstasy*, a book of profound influence on European thinking, he stated: "It is impossible to distinguish by medical means chemically induced ecstasy from mystical ecstasy."

34. Twenty-four Steps to Freedom

JANUARY 1970
ORANGE COUNTY, CALIFORNIA

I find everything about courtrooms dreary and unscientific. Richard Alpert shook his head sympathetically when he came to my trial. "The courtroom is the worst forum for new ideas," he sighed. "Galileo lost. Giordano Bruno got the hot seat. Scopes lost in Tennessee defending evolution. The Jews and Italians threw the book at Jesus for preaching love while the crook Barabbas got off. There's a 2,000-year-old public relations lesson for philosophers there."

"*Now* you tell me," I replied.

The jury did not give out promising signals. Orange County, home turf of Richard Nixon and the John Birch Society. My twelve peers were sternly conservative in dress and demeanor.

The evidence brought against me included the arresting officer's two weather-beaten roaches and a few flakes of marijuana, vacuumed from the pocket of a jacket found in the front seat of the station wagon. I could have taken the stand and denied possession of the two roaches, truthfully and perhaps convincingly. By introducing the seven flakes of cannabis the state was admitting the flimsiness of the case against me.

We had an ex-district attorney ready to testify that the arresting officer was known to use illegal tactics in making arrests.

Against Rosemary and Jack, however, there were more convincing exhibits—some grass, hashish, and a few acid tabs found on their persons. The DA made it clear that if I were found innocent an example would be made of Rosemary and Jack. Once again my attorneys rested the case without putting up any defense. I'd be free on appeal bond again and we'd win in the higher courts, said the lawyers.

On the weekend before the case went to the jury we returned to the ranch and found our cabin burned down. Ed May, our friend and ranch manager, had run into the blazing building with a wet towel over his head, blindly grabbing the Buddha statue that Peggy Hitchcock had brought to the Newton Center house seven years before. The same week Fang, our oldest doggie friend, disappeared. A mountain lion or hunters' guns.

On the morning that the case went to the jury the Santa Ana paper appeared with the blood-curdling banner headline: Drug Crazed Hippies Slay Mother and Children. An army medical officer named McDonald reported that his home had been invaded by a band of long-haired young people who brutally murdered his wife and children. And beat up the doctor. Just so that no one missed the point they scrawled on the wall, in blood: "ACID IS GROOVY. KILL THE PIGS." (Many people sensed immediately that this curious story was a phony. Several years later Dr. McDonald was convicted of this crime, more horrible than the Manson murders.) It was not a good time to get a fair trial on a drug charge. It was not a good time to be a public figure identified with LSD.

The jury came back with the verdict: we were all guilty of the wizard crime, possession.

Then the judge pulled the shocker. I was remanded to jail immediately without appeal bond—unheard of and clearly unconstitutional. The shaved head of his honor glistened under the fluorescent lights as he quoted from an article I had written for *Playboy* magazine ridiculing the marijuana laws.

"For you we throw away the keys," said the jailer as the steel doors slammed shut.

The next day I talked with Rosemary in the visiting room, through glass. She wept. The lawyers were helpless. The judge, basking in community approval, was adamant. It looked like ten years for two roaches. Plus the federal ten. Plus the eleven Millbrook counts looming in the future. The trap had snapped shut.

I spent five weeks in a solitary-confinement cell in the Orange County jail, awaiting sentence. My term was set at ten years maximum. Rosemary and Jack received probation.

It was a joy to be transferred to the relative freedom of state prison. In contrast with the county jail Chino Prison was a glamorous resort with access to a large yard equipped with sunshine, blue sky, and a grassy baseball field. Prisoners were allowed the use of handball courts and weight-lifting facilities, plus the precious liberty to visit the library and other cellblocks.

Chino functioned as a reception center where new prisoners were tested, interviewed, and classified for transfer to a long-term joint. On the third day I was ticketed to report to the psychological testing room. The official in charge smiled apologetically. "It seems we have a little problem here, Doc. The classification program here is partly based on psychological tests that you developed."

"That will teach me to mind my own business," I said.

"We have to give you the tests. That's the rules."

"Let's go."

The test of intelligence was to get the highest possible score. My answers to the personality tests were calculated to make me appear normal, non-impulsive, docile, conforming. My vocational tests revealed aptitudes in forestry and farming together with hopeless incompetence in clerical tasks. I was angling for a transfer to a minimum-security prison where escape would be possible.

It was shocking to discover, in later months, that many Americans, indeed many of my liberal friends, were offended when I took the midnight express out of prison. They considered escape an anti-social act, more heinous than my "crimes." It just goes to show how separate realities can develop, even among friends.

But consider my situation: I was a forty-nine-year-old man facing life in prison for encouraging people to face up to new options with courage and intelligence. The American government was being run by Richard Nixon, Spiro Agnew, John Ehrlichman, Robert Haldeman, G. Gordon Liddy, John Mitchell, J. Edgar Hoover, and other cynical flouters of the democratic process. There was no question in my mind: it was my duty to escape. Would you have let men like these keep you in prison for life for your ideas? I'm happy to let history judge me on that one.

Orders soon came down transferring me to the California Men's Colony-West at San Luis Obispo. In this minimum-security prison all I had to face was a fifteen-foot barbed-wire fence and gun trucks manned by sharpshooters.

To the casual eye the California Men's Colony-West was a pleasant enough place, a former army base with rows of two-story wooden barracks connected by roofed-in walkways. No bars on the windows. There were lawns, flower beds, and open-sky views to the coastal hills. However, the psychological climate was most depressing. CMC-West was the retirement village of the California Correctional Department, housing criminals who had spent their lives behind bars and were now considered totally institutionalized. Here one found no threat of violence, no rebellion, just the gray peevish apathy of burn-outs.

I was assigned to work mornings in the captain's office, where the custody people could keep their eye on me. Afternoons I devoted to physical exercise in preparation for my escape, weight lifting and workouts in the gymnasium. On the handball courts I joined the Chicanos in hard-driving singles and doubles tournaments. After a few weeks I learned how to play backcourt, smashing high line-drives to the wall with either hand, and ranked as the best Anglo player in the joint. I was in my best physical shape since West Point.

After settling into the prison routine and learning who were the snitches to avoid, I sounded out some veteran convicts about escape routes. There was one good possibility. From the second-story roof of a cellblock near mine a cable ran above the fence to a telephone pole just outside the compound. The floodlights were all mounted below the height of the cable. My advisors *thought* that a man pulling himself along the cable would be invisible, even to the gun truck stationed about seventy feet away, but no one had ever been willing to take the risk.

Rosemary and I discussed the plan on the lawn during her Sunday visits. She was to arrange for a car to meet me out on the highway near the prison. Members of the Brotherhood were eager to manage the getaway. Other sympathizers offered to provide the outside help—"trained criminals" who could spirit me out of the country for $25,000. We went along with this tactic because my friends had connections with Cuba and other Third World countries where I could receive political asylum.

The escape had to be postponed for five months. My advisors urged that I wait until the September fogs. One of my convict mentors insisted that I wait until *he* got paroled, fearing that he'd be blamed if I took the red-eye special. So Rosemary lined up a job for him on the outside to accelerate his parole.

No longer in my shadow Rosemary became the media heroine, the grass widow. Large sums of money funneled for my defense. Expenses took most of it, but for the first time Rosemary had cash on hand. And there was no shortage of handsome young men eager to act as chauffeur. Rosemary understandably developed crushes on these young companions, one after another, while I paced the cage jealously, thinking of nothing but escape.

In spite of the distractions Rosemary was totally committed to my release, working tirelessly with lawyers, journalists, politicians. She was there every visiting day bringing messages. She told me frankly about her infidelities, at the same time reiterating her dedication to the escape plan that would involve her joining me underground. I urged her to announce that she was divorcing me and to tell her probation officer that she was through with my way of life, dissociating herself from my escape and giving her the opportunity to meet me abroad if the plot was successful. Rosemary never wavered in her loyalty. She felt she had put me in prison and she was going to get me out.

One of Rosemary's tasks in preparing for the escape was to pack up our personal belongings at the Berkeley house. The main problem: what to do with the twenty filing cabinets containing my archives—from kindergarten to the present. There was some fear that the government might seize both the house and the records.

Help arrived. Rosemary was contacted by Michael Horowitz and Bob Barker, who as founders of the new Fitz Hugh Ludlow Memorial Library were assembling the world's most complete collection of books and documents concerning psychoactive drugs. Rosemary asked Horowitz and Barker if they would be interested in becoming custodians of my archives, probably the largest collection of records about drug research. They were delighted. Two days later they appeared with a rental truck and spirited the archives to a safe and secret hiding place.

Saturday morning, September 12, 1970, my cellmate Angelo woke me at ten. I sprang to the window to see soft gray lovely clouds, my security blanket. Good weather for a night flight. Angelo complained: "Fucking clouds. We won't be able to see our wives on the lawn tomorrow."

I lay in bed shuffling the twenty-four tarot cards. *One:* moonless night. *Two:* fog. *Three:* a Saturday night; wait until the patrol car returns from CMC-East with the snack-bar trusties—around 8:30. *Four:* paint white trim on sneakers black. *Five:* write farewell note and leave in locker. *Six:* leave cellblock before or after the 9:00 TV break, when prisoners flood hallways. *Seven:* wait until the central corridor is empty or all prisoners are walking with their backs to side door. *Eight:* slip out side door and walk to the tree (five seconds). *Nine:* climb tree (five seconds). *Ten:* leap to roof—silently. *Eleven:* remove sneakers. *Twelve:* lie down on roof to check location of guards and patrol cars. *Thirteen:* if seen, be prepared to make a desperate break. *Fourteen:* crawl along the roof of connecting corridor to Cellblock 324 (sixty seconds). *Fifteen:* creep to the end of the roof of 324, avoiding TV antenna wires (sixty seconds). *Sixteen:* put on sneakers and handball gloves. *Seventeen:* wrap hands and feet around cable and pull self across (ninety seconds). *Eighteen:* slide down pole on other side of fence (five seconds). *Nineteen:* climb down bank and cross outer perimeter—avoiding barracks, alert for the fire watch—to reach highway (four minutes). *Twenty:* run half-mile north along Highway 1 to turnoff with three trees (four minutes). *Twenty-one:* wait for pick-up car with right blinker flashing. *Twenty-two:* contact is Kelly; my name is Nino. *Twenty-three:* flee the country. *Twenty-four:* live happily ever after.

At two o'clock in the afternoon the sun broke through, but friendly clouds were waiting off the coast.

I paced the yard, counting off seconds. Rehearsing. Four minutes to the highway. Four minutes to the three trees. I joined the line for early chow. My last supper on metal plates. Back to the cellblock, where I sat in a darkened TV room watching the Stanford-Arkansas football game.

I lay on my bunk for the five o'clock count. The seconds moving fast now. The count-clear whistle sounded. Tramping feet to chow.

Combing his hair Angelo said, "Coming to dinner?"

"I ate on the early line."

Waiting for the cellblock to clear. Now. Moved to locker. Ripped white laces from sneakers and re-threaded brown. Crouched facing the locker, newspaper in my lap. Unscrewed the black paint tube, squished pigment over white striping on sneakers. Steps. Jangle of guard keys. Shoes back in locker. Waiting. Guard gone. Sweaty hands black from smearing pigment on smooth rubber. Put on handball gloves, brushed black on backs. Paint leaking onto hands. Tossed gloves in locker to dry and shut door.

I scrubbed my hands with a coarse-bristle brush and mopped paint off floor with a towel. I stowed the brush and towel under the mattress.

The count-clear whistle sounded again at 8:30. Angelo split to play bridge. Now. Put on black sneakers, dark blue denim jacket, eyeglasses. Shoved her letters, prison IDs, meditation beads in pocket.

Now it was time. I walked to the end of the cellblock out to the corridor (1 on diagram), praying the coast was clear. Two cons watched me pass (2). I went up the hallway and U-turned back (3). They were still watching me. I went on around the corner casually and made a pass through a neighboring cellblock (4).

I stood indecisive. Trapped. Feeling the clock moving. Have to hurry or miss the highway pick-up. Suspicious standing. Down the hall again. Looked left. The two cons were still there (5). Kept moving along the side corridor. Circled back. Time was wasting. Hit corner. They were gone! Moved toward side door. Looked right. Inside the cellblock (6) three cons were talking. One was Metcalf, a snitch. They felt my hesitation, looked up. I walked on, U-turned (7). Have to bluff it through. If I moved smoothly to the door, I'd be invisible. At the last second before reaching for the door handle I flicked a glance to the cellblock. Three heads turned to look. I walked past the side door (8).

Blew it. Should have slipped through. Turned north (9). New plan.

Timothy Leary's Escape Route from Northwest Area of California Men's Colony, San Luis Obispo.

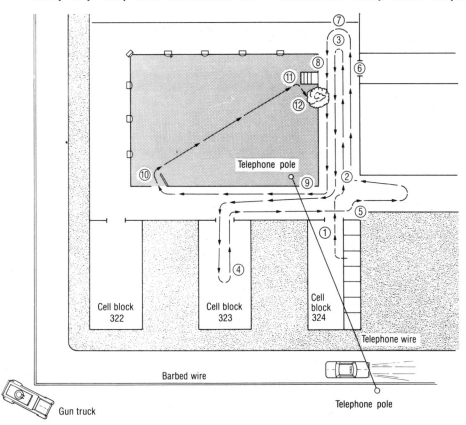

Telephone pole

Cell block 322

Cell block 323

Cell block 324

Telephone wire

Barbed wire

Gun truck

Telephone pole

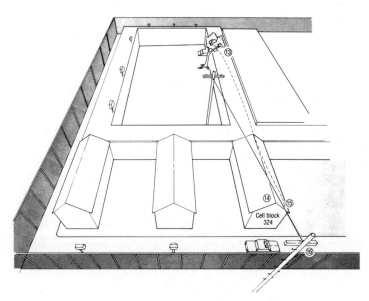

Cell block 324

Another door to the exercise yard down the corridor. Would have to walk across the yard. At night? Strictly off limits. If seen, they'd sound alarm.

I opened the door, walked onto the prison yard, lit by floodlights (10). *No one walks the yard in dead of night. Not even the guards.* I stood in front of the tree, directly in front of a window. Inside, facing the window, was Metcalf braying at two cons. Climb the tree two feet in front of the snitch?

I sat on the steps (11). Exposed by the spotlight. If a guard saw me, I would get busted with blackened handball gloves in my pocket and farewell notes in my locker. Time froze. I watched the glistening leaves and listened to the muffled sound of Metcalf's voice. Now or never. *Now.* I walked to the tree. I would have to climb in front of Metcalf. It would take a few minutes to sound the alarm and another five minutes for the two-man gun trucks to get on the road. Metcalf's voice boomed good night. He turned away from window. My neurology shifted into some ancient dreamy survival pattern. I grabbed a branch (12), wrapped a foot around it, swung upward—foot-hand, foot-hand—balanced on a drooping branch, leaned across the void, and dropped four-foot onto the roof of the connecting corridor (13).

I sat quietly on the tar-paper slant, listening to voices and the trampling in the hallway below. I could look over the entire prison, across to the custody office where guards were lounging. In shadows, above the search-lights, I was a forest creature scanning the camp of humans.

I crept along the roof to the end of the corridor, climbed up the ridge and down to the roof of 324. I bumped into the TV antenna wires, froze. I could look down either side into neighboring cellblocks. My silhouette was exposed against the sky.

At the end of the roof I could see over the fence to lights on the highway below (14). I pulled on the handball gloves and lay on the angled roof just under the cable. I hooked my ankles over the wire, reached up my hands, and pulled out head first.

It was hard going. Every ten inches there was a loop that held the telephone cord below the cable. My legs bumped and tangled in the cord. Easy sweeping pulls were impossible. I had to reach, then wrench ten inches. Hands out. Pulled body. Hauled legs. Ten inches. The cable bounced and swung. A strain to hang on. Weird wrestling motions, my body clinging to the swaying wire. Sweating. Heaving awkwardly. After fifty pulls—a pause. Horrid discovery. Completely exhausted. Lungs gasping. Arms drained. Body limp and weak. Can't go another foot. Only one-third across the wire (15). Hadn't even reached the road. Exhausted.

My hands couldn't hold the weight of my body. With desperate sexual writhing I embraced the cable with elbows and knees. Rested. The cable slowed. Nightmare thoughts. What are you doing this time? Inefficient wizard dangling twenty feet high, in full view of two gun trucks. *Once again the little experiment has gotten out of hand, Professor.*

The interior light snapped on in the nearest gun truck. He'd seen me. Put on the light to sound the alarm. The word was flashing. I waited for patrol cars to scream up. Would they poke me down like a wild raccoon with sticks? I squirmed forward again. Five more wrenching feet. Stop. Wrists and arms exhausted. Panting. I should have quit smoking. I should have pumped more iron. It had seemed so easy. Now I knew why no cons had escaped this way. It was Olympic gymnastics up there on the high wire in the gun sights. I should have waited until the winter fog. Maybe the cable strung temptingly over the fence was a trap? Maybe the hunters were waiting in trucks, rifles cradled on knees.

With a desperate lunge I pulled my body along in clumsy crab motions. Stopped to rest. Looked back down into rooms were cons were watching television.

A sudden glare of light. Forty feet away a patrol car turned from the compound road toward me. I was caught. The car rolled closer, crunching gravel. My denim arms turned lavender in the headlight. The driver leaned over to crush his cigarette in the ashtray. The car passed under me and disappeared.

Now I tumbled into some kind of delirium. Arms crossed, I inched along the wire like a caterpillar. My mind fixed on reaching the fence, so I'd fall to freedom outside the perimeter. Still my hand kept getting tangled in the phone-wire loops. A compulsive wrench to free my hand set the cable bouncing wildly. Mouth gasping, face bulging, glasses twisted, sweat dripping. I wanted Errol Flynn and out came Harold Lloyd. I felt very alone. Forty-nine years and 325 days of my life built up to this ordeal. There was no fear—only a nagging embarrassment. Such an undignified way to die, nailed like a sloth on a branch!

No more thoughts. From some inner reservoir came LIVE! SURVIVE!, a flow of energy and a curious erotic lightness. Neck arching, shoulders thrusting, body wiggling, legs kicking, shoulders pushing propelled by uterine squeeze. My glasses fell but my arms smoothly reeled cable. Thus I butted head first sweating wet into a new life.

Hand over hand till fingers hit the pole (16). Hanging by my legs (I'd practiced it a thousand times in my bunk) I reached and grabbed the spike, dropped my body, wrapped legs around splintery wood, slid down. Exultant feet hit liberated ground. FREE!

I was swaying, sweating, panting. My glasses lay outside the fence. I adjusted them on my nose, funny professorial gesture. All was silent. Electric lights shone on the steel fence and the green grass. Cellblocks only forty feet away.

I staggered to the hill, lay my head against a stone—drained, panting, listening—watched for the fire patrol. Silence. Steep bank. My first steps discharged an avalanche. I slipped and slid, stones rattling around me. At the bottom of the hill I started loping warily.

There's a dry creek bed cutting across the field. Keep to the left. Watch for boulders. Be careful not to make noise. The fire watch makes rounds. What will you do if you meet him? You don't have to be told what to do. Once you clear that fence, you are a hunted animal. Killers are after you. If the fire watch gets in your way, you'll deal with him or you'll never draw another free breath.

My glasses steamed. I wiped the lenses on my sweater and peered into the shadows. Black trees silhouetted in the yellow glow from the prison. The exit road, lit by street lights, was empty. A thousand prison windows watched me run across the field. I scrambled past the main prison gate and the greeting sign (CALIFORNIA MEN'S COLONY WEST FACILITY) and on to the railroad tracks that paralleled Highway 1. It was dreamlike simple.

Car lights approached from the rear. I dove on the tracks, my face against cool steel, hands in gravel. A middle-aged couple driving north. Dangerous along the tracks. I picked my way down to the ravine bordering the tracks.

My first free wild run in seven months. Leaping joyful. Car lights approached. I dove into tall grass. Panting, watching. If the right blinker flashed, I would run to the road.

Up ahead I saw the dim outline of trees next to the highway. Climbing out of the culvert I ran to the first tree. Not here. Over there: three trees joined at the root.

A long wait, cars roaring by. Two minutes. Five minutes. Ten minutes. Suppose they didn't come? Had they been busted? Accident? Fuck-up in plans? Could I hitchhike north on Highway 1 in prison garb?

A car. Right blinker flashing. I ran from the shadows. The car door swung open. A woman said, "Nino?"

"Kelly!"

We embraced. I ducked into the back seat, grabbing the hand of another woman, who was behind the wheel. Kelly jumped in slamming the door. Motor gunned, we roared off.

"I'm Maru," said the driver.

"Where is Rosemary?"

"In Seattle. You'll see her Monday."

I had mixed feelings. I had hoped she would be out of the country, safe. But I was exultant that we would meet in two days.

Kelly was talking fast. "Brother, we're glad to see you. We made two passes by the pick-up spot. You were late. I was going to start walking up the tracks to look for you in case you were hurt."

"How old are you?"

"Eighteen."

"How old is Maru?"

"She's nineteen."

Kelly pointed to a bundle in the back seat. "There's a new set of clothes. Change."

I stripped off the prison denim.

"Give them to me," said Kelly. "We're going to transfer your clothes to another car. They'll drive south near LA and leave them in a gas station restroom. To make the pigs think we're heading south."

"How many cars do you have operating tonight?"

"Four. You'll only be in this car for five minutes. We have a camper in Morro Bay to take you to Oakland. A third car goes south. And the fourth has the shortwave set to monitor police calls. How much of a lead do we have?"

"I don't think I was seen leaving. So we have two hours before they discover I'm gone." I passed over my prison ID, a copy of the farewell note, Rosemary's letters. "Save these for Horowitz, the archivist."

"There's a wallet and set of IDs in your pocket. Your name is William McNellis. Your birth date is November 14, 1929. Your address is 2925 Northridge Road, Seattle."

The car slowed near a service station in Morro Bay.

"What happens here?"

The attendant waved to us. Our car picked up speed.

"We flashed the message that we had you, and he flashed that there is no radio alarm yet. So far so good."

Maru was driving smooth and easy. We reached a road by the beach. Maru turned back grinning. "Okay, brother. You get out now. I'll see you in Oakland."

I pulled on a knit cap and followed Kelly over the dunes to the beach. It was a "B" movie.

After a hundred yards Kelly turned away from the sea, peeked over the dunes, and led me to a parked camper. An attractive middle-aged woman waited. We hugged. A sturdy gray-haired man came around the side of the camper, and we shook hands. "Welcome. My name is Frank. This here is Pam."

Kelly motioned me in the rear door. "I'm going to dye your hair now. We'll hang around here for a few minutes and then hit it."

Kelly filled a pail of water. She squirted dye on my scalp from a spray can and began massaging. "Kelly is my code name, not my real name. My father is a Senator. The name of our group is the Weathermen Underground."

I laughed. It all figured. Rescued by Weathermen, the manic reckless guerrilla tribe, scourge of the FBI.

What could I say? I was very grateful.

I was sitting on the floor of the camper, head in the bucket, when we pulled away.

Kelly laid out the plan. "We drive to the intersection of Highway 101. I'll switch to the radio car. As you drive north to Oakland in the camper, we'll follow. If the police throw up roadblocks, we'll stop you and pull off to a stash pad and wait it out. If the coast is clear, we'll drive to San Francisco and then to Seattle. Bernadine Dohrn, Jeff Jones, and Bob Ayers are waiting for you. You'll work out the next phase with them."

The camper stopped. I watched Frank tugging at the license plate with a wrench. Off came California, exposing Utah plates. The bumper sticker said: "AMERICA, LOVE IT OR LEAVE IT."

I spent the night in a safe-house in San Francisco. The next day Frank and I headed north. Camping in the mountains of Northern California we kept a rendezvous with the three Weathermen leaders.

The next morning Frank and I continued north to another safe-house in the outskirts of Seattle, where Rosemary waited.

"The house is about a mile ahead. If there's an orange curtain in the window, that means the coast is clear. I'll drop you off around the bend. We don't want the camper seen around the house."

The farmhouse was set back a quarter of mile from the road, orange curtains in the window.

The road curved east beyond the ranch. Frank stopped the camper and motioned me to the door. We shook hands. I grabbed my suitcase and jumped down.

I started walking along the deserted country road. Fast. I wanted to run. When I got to the entrance to the farm road I saw the door open and Rosemary came down the steps and started walking toward me. She began to run. It was one of the best scenes ever. Running, laughing she threw her arms around me and I lifted her, swung her around, and held her close. Home again.

Into the big farm kitchen we went, leaping upstairs to the bedroom, loving at long last. Beaming. So much to tell.

We heard voices below and called them up. The room filled with Pam and Kelly and Maru and Frank. Celebration. Champagne, fruit, homemade bread, smooth camembert cheese. Incense, perfume, candlelight. Hearing cars swishing on the road below, I gotta girl way over town so good to me. The ceiling was peeling and beams gaped through the walls, but this was ultimate luxury.

I hadn't slept sweet in seven months. After running three days on swollen knees and throbbing muscles, sweet lips. Love is good.

The next day at sunset Bernadine, Robert, and Jeff entered in triumph, guerrilla heroes. They were waving newspapers: Weathermen Help Leary

Prison Escape. Weathermen manifestos had been mailed in plain envelopes to editors all over the country. J. Edgar Hoover promised that
the FBI would capture the fugitive in ten days.

I had spent 200 nights lying in prison bunks working out 200 plans
for flight out of the country. Fly a helicopter to Mexico. Rent a boat
to Cuba. Hike to Canada.

"It's really not that complicated," said Bernadine. "We're having a set
of IDs made here with an out-of-state address. Friday you go get a
Washington driver's license. There won't be time for a picture, but your
description will be on the temporary license. Sunday you fly to Chicago.
Monday apply for a passport. You can get it in a day. Monday night
you fly out. Surface with Eldridge Cleaver in Algeria."

I was astonished. I had never thought of showing my face in a passport
office crowded with feds, much less standing in an airport line to board
an international flight. Ah, Professor Leary, going to Algeria, I see.

It was September 1970. At no time in the history of aeronautics had
there been more surveillance of international flights. Waltz in with a
ticket to an Arab country? Take a one-day-old passport past the metal
detector and the sharp-eyed security guards checking each face for hijack
tremors? I could imagine the flash of recognition on FBI faces, the click
of handcuffs.

"Let's postpone the decision and work on a disguise," I said. "If we
come up with a good face-change, my nerve will come back."

The disguise was no simple matter either. A beard? A moustache?
A scar? "They'll be looking for me to dress up or hide behind a beard.
How about a balding businessman? Who wants to be the barber?"

I stripped to the waist and sat in a kitchen chair while Kelly trimmed
the back and sides of my head to an American Legion butch. She looked
sadly at the scissors in her hand. "I just hate to do this."

She snipped my top hair close to the scalp.

"Not bad," I said. "Now shave the top clean."

Kelly draped a hot rag on my skull and squirted lather.

"Take it easy," Rosemary said. "Any cuts will give it away."

Easy gentle little strokes. Then Kelly began to laugh. I peered in the
bathroom mirror at a bald-pate stranger.

When Bernadine, Bob, and Jeff returned, they gaped at the change.
For the first time I felt a flicker of feasibility.

Three days later a bland-looking, middle-aged man named William
McNellis, holding a new passport in his hand, walked through the metal
detector and onto the TWA flight to Paris.

A pleasant-looking young woman with a bubble hairdo entered the plane
and sat across the aisle. As the plane hurtled down the runway, Mr.
McNellis looked across at Miss Margaret Ann McCreedy and winked.

JULIEN OFFRAY DE LA MET-TRIE (1709-1751), drawing upon seventeen years of medical education and practice, published *The Natural History of the Soul* in 1745. This materialist-scientific study of human nature aroused such opposition among the clergy that he was forced to flee to Berlin, where he lived under the protection of Frederick the Great. His next book, *Man the Machine,* presented the first scientific (as opposed to philosophic) explanation of human behavior.

In *Discourse on Happiness* and *The Art of Play* La Mettrie outlined a humanist approach to ethical philoso-phy, eliminating sin and guilt from consideration as rational-intelligent notions. His *Systeme d'Epicure* advanced theories of evolution a hundred years before Darwin and Wallace.

Because of their radical implications La Mettrie's works were repudiated by the religious and philosophic establishments. Only in the late twentieth century have we come to understand his contribution to humanistic science, psychology and evolutionary theory. It is possible that his liberating ideas are still ahead of their time.

35. The Exiles

SEPTEMBER 23, 1970
PARIS

We ran into the truly insoluble problem. Paris was filled with Japanese tourists, and there was simply no hotel room to be had. What was the name of that French psychiatrist who had written me long letters inviting me to visit him? A Sephardic name. Ben . . . Ben . . . I flipped through the telephone book to *Medecins, Psychiatrique.* Pierre Bensoussan. We took a cab to a bistro around the corner from Bensoussan's office. I dialed nervously and told the doctor my name was Ken Kesey, a friend of Timothy Leary. Could I come around to see him? He seemed delighted. Good start.

"Okay," said Rosemary, "I'll check him out. If he seems suspicious, I'll tell him that Timothy Leary is in London, arriving in Paris tomorrow. Then I'll hustle back here and we'll take the first plane to Algiers."

In fifteen minutes she returned beaming. "He's perfect. His office is a psychedelic shrine. A picture of the Dali Lama on the wall. He's a great fan. Insists we stay with him."

For centuries Paris has been the refuge of political and literary fugitives. Pierre Bensoussan honored that tradition. He took us out to celebrate at a fine restaurant, where we got tipsy and listened to his fascinating tales about Gurdjieff, another exile. Pierre hoped that we'd stay and tie in with the French intellectual scene. Since we were underground, using false passports, he would keep us hidden in his country house near the Swiss border. Pierre was a top official in the UN's drug agency and thus was privy to inside information. If he heard that it was going to get hot for us, we could skip across to Switzerland in half an hour. He had helped another fugitive that way a few months ago, a wealthy arms-smuggler named Michel Hauchard.

The French plan sounded good, but I was extremely curious about Eldridge Cleaver and the Algerian exile colony. I hoped to remain engaged in American politics. The only way to get back home was to help overthrow Nixon, after all.

Pierre shook his head scornfully. "That's the classic insanity of the political exile," he said. "Nostalgia. White Russians plotting against Stalin. Free Poles conspiring against the Warsaw Commissariat. Spanish Republicans in the cafe scheming to bring Franco down. Start a new life here. After you win the Noble Prize and Nixon retires, then you can return to America in glory." He patted my arm. "But don't waste your time on refugee politics. No one likes that, neither your hosts nor your countrymen."

"We owe it to the Weathermen and our friends in America to take one quick trip to Algiers," I said.

The morning after arriving in Algiers I set out to locate the Black Panthers. The hotel clerk said try the newspaper. The editor said try the FLN, the left-wing faction of the Algerian government. The FLN said try the tourist office. The McNellis disguise was just too straight for revolutionary contacts. Finally a bribe to the hotel clerk got the number.

A black answered. "Right on, brother, we been expecting you."

The cab wound up through the fashionable El Biar hills to a stately villa, the Panther embassy. Next to the bell was a brass plaque etched with a fierce panther.

Cleaver was not there. We were to be driven to his home later. We spent the afternoon talking with his deputy Donald Cox, who called himself the Field Marshal, a handsome wily street-hustler and prison escapee wanted for murder back in America (or Babylon, as they called it). Three other Panthers were on hand, athletic hipsters one and all. Mojo had hijacked a plane to Havana single-handed. Mobuto had escaped the police raid on the New York Panthers by leaping thirty feet from a window and swinging across rooftops. Jamal was wanted by the FBI for a three-state spree of armed robbery for the cause.

At sunset the Field Marshal drove us to Cleaver's villa. Eldridge greeted us warmly at the gate, recognizing that our presence meant more cards in his hand. As Rosemary and I sat uneasily in the *haute bourgeois* French-provincial living room, Cleaver laid out his plan. He would obtain political asylum for us from the Algerians. Then we'd set up an American government in exile. The Algerians had already recognized the Panthers as the American Liberation Front and ultimately we could swing the entire Third World behind our Our Cause.

I suggested that we could represent the non-political counter-culture forces of America. We'd invite dissident groups, draft resisters, anti-war activists, hippies, Weathermen, rock stars, beatniks, bohemians, poets. I agreed that we should form a highly visible alternative government to the Nixon regime. There was no question that, if we could get a base operating, many counter-culture people would come by to visit. "The most effective tactic would be to operate a media center. If the Algerians will let us set up broadcast facilities, we can start a Radio Free America that would beam over to Europe and the armed forces bases. We could win the support of the youth and the liberals and the anti-war people in Europe."

"Support for what?" said Rosemary.

"For armed revolution," said Eldridge.

"Right on," said the Field Marshal.

"For a popular front of the large majority of Americans who want a peaceful friendly prosperous world," I said, immediately wishing I would retract it.

Everyone except Eldridge looked at me with scorn. He had walked to the terrace and was peering through a telescope, apparently aimed at the bedroom of a nearby apartment. "Right on," he said, but I wasn't sure if he was talking to me.

There were other disturbing notes during the gathering. Kathleen Cleaver, the beautiful intelligent wife of Eldridge, had not returned from a three-month mission to North Korea, whose dictator, Kim Il Sung, was godfather of their baby. In the absence of Kathleen Eldridge kept his mistress nearby, a sullen Algerian teenager named Fatima, who looked at us with open dislike.

As we were about to leave for our beach hotel, Eldridge hassled us about our sleeping arrangements, pretending to be concerned about the different surnames on our passports.

"What are you talking about?" I protested. "If the Algerian government is going to give us political asylum, they certainly will know that we're married."

"I don't want to be your parole officer," said Eldridge.

"You wouldn't revoke my parole for sleeping with my wife, would you?" I said.

"You're the only one responsible for any trouble you run into," said

Eldridge gruffly, in the classic rejoinder of the correctional officer.

In the cab Rosemary said what was on my mind. "Eldridge is weird. He seems like some kind of control freak."

"I certainly hope not," I said. "He's got a lot going for him. World opinion on his side. Charismatic American black leading a movement of blacks, liberals, leftists, and white youth. I can't believe he'd blow it."

The next day Eldridge introduced us to Esther Greenbaum, an attractive woman around thirty-five, who was the Panthers' liaison with the FLN, the ideological left faction of the Algerian government. After a meeting with the officials, she informed us that we would be offered political asylum.

Two days later *El Moujahid*, the government paper, ran a front-page story announcing that Dr. Timothy Leary, a prominent Afro-American (!) psychologist, persecuted by the Nixon regime for his anti-war and pro-Arab beliefs, had been given political asylum by the Algerian government. There was no mention of drugs.

I phoned Esther in some alarm. "What's going on? The Algerians think I'm a black Communist. What will happen when they find out?"

"Don't worry," Esther replied. "Eldridge will take care of you."

I found this ambiguous remark worrisome.

The saga of Eldridge Cleaver's self-destruction in Algeria deserves a book in itself. It's a Graham Greene horror story, complete with exotic North African locale, sexual intrigue, personal disintegration, and a cast of exiles caught in webs of counter-intelligence, revolutionary conspiracy, treachery, bravery, and melodrama. For us it was a crash course in race relations and the politics of terror.

After my return from a confused and dangerous trip to meet Jean Genet in Jordan,[1] Rosemary and I moved to a government hotel at Djamila, a beach town ten miles from Algiers. I started to write a book about my escape—half of the royalties promised to Cleaver as tribute.

We were excited about the chance to experience a country so different: Arab/African and fully equipped with Casbah, deserts, oases. We felt no disloyalty to America. Like thousands of dissenters from other countries we were waiting for the repression to end and for our people to take power again back home.

But Algiers was a dismal town. During the colonial era the French had envisioned Algeria as their own California, a paradise of beaches and rolling vineyards with a gleaming white capital city. When the French left, so did the sparkle. Algiers was now a closed fortress. Grim Arab socialism and religious fundamentalism had teamed up to institute a medieval police state. There was almost no tourism, no literary action, no culture, no night life, no music, no art. *Time, Newsweek*, and even the Paris *Herald* were usually banned. Islamic prudishness combined with a desert dourness and suspicion of difference pervaded the atmosphere of the city.

Algeria at that time was the center of international terrorism and revolutionary paranoia—the role later taken over by Libya. The place crawled with government agents and conspirators. Into this shadowy world we popped: the politically naive drug-professor and his beautiful wife, comic relief for the endemic boredom of the international community. As the leading curiosities of the season we were deluged with invitations to dinners and parties, and of course we were followed by journalists, which made the Panthers jealous. At restaurants around the city we met many political fugitives who had fled to form national liberation governments. Most of these exiles were strongly anti-Soviet and looked hopefully to us Americans for direction in the struggle against fascism and Communism.[2]

Unfortunately the Panthers couldn't provide this kind of political leadership. They had heroic stature, and they could claim to be the baddest maddest blacks in the world. That much sounded impressive. But Eldridge and crew—caught perfectly by Tom Wolfe in *Radical Chic*—soon revealed themselves as five confused fearful uneducated young men who had spent most of their lives in prison or getting there. How could they relate to Brazilian ex-cabinet ministers, Chilean professors, Greek newspaper editors, Spanish political scientists? Exactly the way they related to other gangs in San Quentin, the way they reacted to bewildered New York liberals at Leonard Bernstein's champagne fund-raisers. They stood apart in their black leather, arms folded across their chests, menacing. They were a pathetic joke in the capital, roaring around in their cars and trying to pick up women—a terrible idea in a moralistic Arab land.

Since they were the officially recognized American government in exile, they did what juntas always do in such situations. They appointed themselves to military posts and set about to harass the civilian population of their new state, Rosemary and me, the despised racial minority.

Like Nixon, like Brezhnev, Eldridge invented himself a security crisis. Everything the Panthers did was in the name of security. We were continually lectured on the precariousness of our situation; American police were after us. All Algerians were racists. The town was crawling with enemies. Our foes kept multiplying. The other national liberation fronts turned out to be racist too and riddled with double agents. Even our American allies became deadly rivals one by one: Angela Davis, Huey Newton, Stokeley Carmichael—all running-dog lackeys of imperialism.

Eldridge stationed Panthers at the airport to watch all incoming planes. With an army of four men, including the Field Marshal, this plan proved impractical. So the Panthers devoted more energy to harassing us. They intimidated us for money, spied on us, intercepted our mail, turned away friends and journalists who came to see us, quartered Eldridge's sullen mistress in our apartment as a resident informer. When I protested, they kidnapped us at gunpoint, held us in "jail" in various apartments around town, issued press releases announcing our "arrest" for lack of discipline, and searched our apartment vainly for documents proving we were CIA operatives. They seized our passports and a small amount of hashish and LSD, which they threatened to turn over to the Algerian police.

It was a terrifying situation. The Panthers often boasted about "offing" members who had proved disloyal and regularly threatened to turn us in to the Algerian government as dope dealers. We had no idea what the Algerians were thinking about all this.

Next we were ordered to report every day to the Panther embassy to perform menial tasks. Rosemary never went, pleading illness, the oldest slave trick. I showed up passively resistant, despising my arrogant enslavers. We were forced to play the game of helpless nigger. If Eldridge wanted to show us how it felt, he succeeded. I don't think he accomplished much else with this campaign of humiliation.

He went so far as to circulate the rumor that I was brain-fried. "Poor Timothy," he told the world, "all that acid's burned out the dude's mind." There was a certain convincing logic to this charge. I was the first to admit that I must have been nuts to put myself in a situation where someone like Eldridge had total control over my life.[3]

Why did I submit to this intimidation? At any moment we could have checked into a deluxe suite at the Aleti Hotel, phoned America, raised a hue and cry. But it seemed unfair to solve our racial problems by calling upon our white resources, our white friends, our white money—a repetition of the 300-year-old pattern. In those innocent days black leaders kept repeating the slogan: "You gotta pay your dues, whitey."

Eldridge delighted in repeating the totalitarian motto: "You're either part of the solution or you're part of the problem." I was rash enough to retort: "The entire problem is caused by dogmatic people saying 'You're either part of the solution or you're part of the problem.' "

Rosemary and I had many long discussions about the black-white conflict. In every corner of the globe blacks remained poor and were becoming more desperately angry while whites ignored their suffering. I believed—and still believe—that humanity cannot evolve beyond savagery until this horrid injustice was put right. As the first white Americans to live under black American political rule we felt a certain responsibility. So we decided to set another kind of precedent: we would demonstrate how to escape slavery in less than 300 years.

Our plan went into action on the day that Eldridge debated by long-distance telephone with Huey Newton in Oakland, where a radio station was broadcasting their exchanges: two powerful blacks, egged on by FBI provocation, threatening to kill each other (and followers) over some fancied slights to pride.

I told the Field Marshal that a large money order had arrived at my bank.

"Right on," said the Field Marshal. "We can sure use it."

"But I'll need my passport to claim it. Better give me Rosemary's too. The money might be in her name."

"Right on," said the Field Marshal. They really thought they had us cowed. The classic mistake of the slave-holder.

The cab arrived at our apartment. Our bags were already packed and hidden where Fatima wouldn't see them. We took just our clothes and books and music. My heart was pumping and my stomach knotted as we rode to the beach. The hotel manager seemed to know what was going on. "Escaped from the Panthers, eh?" he said smiling. "Don't worry. They'll leave you alone here." There were few secrets in Algiers.

I phoned the embassy. Eldridge answered. "Hey, what's happening, man? Did you get the bread?"

"We've moved out. It's all over, Eldridge."

"What bullshit you giving me, man? You report to the embassy right away. You hear? And bring your passports."

"I'll be happy to drop by and pay you a friendly visit. But you're not getting the passports. We're free, Eldridge."

He swore and hung up. The slaves had up and run away. That night a car with two Panthers lurked in front of our hotel until the village cops rousted them. Hands up. Car searched. ID checked. Warned sternly to stay out of the village.

The next stage of our evolution required escape from our other custodians, the Algerian government. It was in the cards that they would run a few numbers on us. We were perfect targets—famous, poor, and helpless.

Rosemary and I sat in the hotel restaurant at a table overlooking the Mediterranean Sea, flecked with silver spume and shiny black scallops of oil flushed from tankers. The waiter, a sallow Kabyl from the Rif mountains, always tugging at his wispy mustache and greasy apron, brought two white pots of thick black coffee and milk steaming with bubbles. A black car swung into the parking lot and out jumped two plainclothesmen. We were wanted at FLN party headquarters.

Eight government officials with black mustaches sat around the Minister of the Interior, who apologized for our harassment by the Panthers. "Our government has been embarrassed by news stories that you were 'arrested' by these Americans. You are under Algerian law here. This is not Texas."

Everyone laughed.

I, for one, was wishing it *were* Texas. Even Laredo was looking good.

The party wanted to discuss the possibility of my teaching at the university. No one mentioned the fact that the campus was occupied at the moment by federal troops putting down a student protest. It was no Free Speech uprising. The students were petitioning for better equipment and faculty. Having no other resources the enormous police apparatus could only park black vans filled with bored soldiers in the streets around the campus.

"You will be contacted by the Ministry of Education. As you know, Algeria is changing from French methods of instruction to American, and we could use a man of your experience and training. By the way, if you have no objections, it would be better for you and the Panthers to leave each other alone."

I agreed wholeheartedly.

The minister ordered his secretary to put through the call and then told Eldridge that he was to have no contact with us. We were being run by the Algerians now.

The black limo roared us back to the beach with sirens screeching. The Algerian officials enjoyed that kind of flourish.

In the following weeks we were approached by agents from several unnamed intelligence bureaus, debriefing us on American politics. What did I think of Kissinger, of Teddy Kennedy, of Mohammed Ali? How did Charles Manson brainwash those people? Who killed Jack Kennedy? The party was especially concerned about the Panther threat to Algerian security. We did our best to assure them that Eldridge's army of four was nothing to worry about.

A very impressive politician in the army clique invited us to his luxurious restaurant. He offered me a trip to his oasis in the desert, with a nudge in the ribs and a word about girls and parties. He wanted to take LSD. He scared me. Several furtive types took us away from town to village cafes, where hooded Arabs listened as the agents tried to recruit us to unnamed intelligence organs. A psychiatrist took me to lunch to ask what I knew about mind-control and brainwashing, implying that I could find a good post behind the Iron Curtain, in a Czech or Hungarian Clinic. When he learned that Rosemary needed a fertility operation, he offered to investigate obstetrical facilities in Romania. I told him that I knew nothing about brainwashing. I wasn't interested in a scientific post in a Communist country. All this intrigue sent paranoia indices on a rapid climb.

A charming English lady, a stringer for *Newsweek* introduced us to a well-educated Algerian bureaucrat named Ali and his French wife Michelle, who had us over for dinner several times. He made no bones about his connection to the CIA. They were planning to migrate to

Canada. I felt the moment had come to confide our hopes to someone. "Look Ali. We want to escape from Algeria. How can we get out?"

"You have two problems. First you'll have to get some other country to accept you. You can't just go to the airport and jump on a plane. And second the Algerians will have to let you go. Once you accepted that green political asylum card, you gave the Algerian government the right to decide where you'll be most useful."

"I've been invited to speak at a psychology conference in Addis Ababa. The Ethiopian government promises not to bust me." The nation in question was actually Denmark, but I didn't want to make that known until the last minute.

"That's perfect," said Ali, brightening up. "Your exit visas will be waiting for you at the airport. I'll arrange it."

In our hotel suite I lifted Rosemary up and swung her around in triumph. "Denmark, here we come."

"Are you sure we can trust him?" she asked. "He's CIA after all."

"He's liberal CIA," I said, "and that's the best mafia you can deal with in the twentieth century."

We were plenty nervous as the cab approached the air terminal. Waiting at the exit gate were the Field Marshal and Mobuto. I waved. They scowled and folded their arms over their chests like prison guards. We bought our tickets and checked our bags through to Copenhagen. The flight called for us to change planes in Geneva. The hour layover would be tense, Switzerland was an Interpol country. A half hour before departure we walked to the exit gate. The Panthers had disappeared. The official checked our passports and asked for visas. I explained that the chief of the airport was supposed to have them. We sat outside while officials huddled over a desk, talking passionately in Arabic. They made phone calls. Ten minutes before departure the chief of the airport asked who had authorized our exit. I said Ali. He looked puzzled. We watched the clock move closer to take-off. Two minutes to go. The chief instructed an assistant to delay the flight. After ten minutes the chief came out with the news: we were not allowed to leave. He apologized. The misunderstanding would be cleared up, and we could catch the next flight, leaving in an hour for Paris.

"Paris?" I exclaimed in panic. Pierre Bensoussan had written warning us to stay out of France. Paris had become the center of the American drug enforcement network.

"It's a trap," said Rosemary.

I phoned Ali from the airport, plenty pissed off. Ali was honey-mouth reassuring. He said that *he* had canceled our exit visas, because of the danger. The CIA was on the scene. And the Panthers were guarding the airport. It was wise of us to have turned down the Paris flight.

I was sure he was lying. I just didn't know why or what about. By this time I was a burnt-out case. A rat in the shock maze. For sixteen months I'd been in prison, plotting escape, on the run, always the helpless target of men with guns. A pawn of controllers. I had no confidence in my judgment in this twisted world of surveillance and intrigue.

What to do next? Whom to trust? Toward sunset I headed for the main drag and took a table on the sidewalk at the Cafe de la Faculte, an after-work hangout for young government officials. After a while the man I wanted to see appeared: one of the young plainclothesmen who had driven us to the party headquarters. I waved him over the table. We drank beer, chain-smoked cigarettes, and chatted about this and that. Finally I asked a straight question. "Tell me, Mohammed, why weren't we allowed to leave the country today?"

Mohammed seemed surprised. "I know nothing about it. Why didn't you contact my office? We're the ones who are responsible for you. You can't leave without our authorization. Come by at nine tomorrow. I'll see what I can do."

I looked in his eyes. Was he lying? He seemed amused.

The next morning we checked out of the hotel again, made the round of farewells again. In his office Mohammed was very businesslike and most interested in Ali and anyone else we had contacted for exit visas. I cut this line of conversation short.

"I've made new reservations for today," I said. "I'll miss the conference in Denmark unless you can clear us for that flight."

"Why didn't you come to this office first?"

"Your office!" I exploded. "Look, Mohammed, we've been in Algeria for seven months, waiting for help from the FLN. You know us very well by now. We're good people. You know that. We've been living quietly, never initiating contacts with Algerians. I can't understand your politics here. Everyone is a double agent at least. No one tells the truth. Everyone's playing a game. Nothing is what it looks like. The worst thing I've done is be naive."

Mohammed couldn't hold back his laughter any more. "Professor, *naive* is exactly the word I always use when I talk about you to my superiors. Well, if you have nothing to hide, perhaps naivete is the best policy."

He came around the desk and shook my hand, patting me on the back with his left. He seemed to like me. "Go to the airport," he said. "You'll be allowed to leave. We're going to miss you. You're a real Gary Cooper American, aren't you?"

"How about some nice official exit stamps for my passport?" I said.

"There's not enough time. But don't worry. You'll get through. A lot of officials here will be happy to see you go. Some of us hope you'll return. But be very careful, Professor. There are a lot of unfriendly people out there."

The scene at the airport began as a repeat of our first attempt. Again a search for the missing visas. Fifteen minutes to go. Ten minutes. Huddles in the chief's office. Passionate debates in Arabic. With one minute to go the chief waved us through to the departure lounge. Whew!

When the plane lifted off the runway, Rosemary and I smiled in relief. We ordered champagne and toasted our latest escape.[4]

ALBERT HOFMANN (1906-), now retired as a director of research for Sandoz, Ltd., is best known for his study of ergot, a substance derived from a rye fungus. From it he produced the twenty-fifth derivative of lysergic acid: lysergic acid diethylamide, abbreviated LSD-25. Tested on mice in 1938 the new drug aroused no interest among staff pharmacologists and physicians, so it was shelved. On April 16, 1943 Hofmann repeated the synthesis of LSD-25 but was forced to suspend his work and proceed home because of the onset of "a not unpleasant intoxicated condition, characterized by an extremely stimulated imagination."

Three days later he decided to study the unexpected mental effects of this drug by ingesting a minimal dose. He took 0.25 mg. of LSD which proved to be an enormous dose. Feeling much disoriented he pedaled home once again, experiencing one of the most memorable bicycle rides in history. Hofmann subsequently participated in LSD sessions with some of the most distinguished European writers and philosophers.

Hofmann's genius in organic chemistry was reconfirmed in 1958 when he synthesized psilocybin, the active ingredient of Mexico's magic mushroom. This was the drug used in the first two years of the Harvard Project.

36. Landlocked in the Alps

MAY 1971
GENEVA

I stepped out of the telephone booth in the Geneva airport, colliding with a silver-haired man, well-tailored and obviously well-heeled.

"Pardon me," he said in a Parisian accent, seizing me gently but firmly by the arm. He seemed to know who I was.

"*Fickt nicht mit der Raketmensch,*" I said thinking quickly. "*Vorein fur Raumschiffahrt.*"

"So? You are not American," said my captor in French. He removed his hand. "I thought you were someone else." He left with a puzzled look.

Rosemary emerged from the crowd of people waiting for a plane. "What did Bensoussan have to say?"

"He advises against going to Denmark. He says it's dangerous there, and also too expensive. Apparently the media and officials were waiting to meet the plane we didn't take. American police, maybe CIA, at the airport. We would have been busted for sure. The rumor went around that we were kidnapped."

"How ungrateful of the CIA," she mock-complained. "After all the marital counseling I gave Ali's wife. Not to mention the silverware we left with that lady from *Newsweek*. And my furs."

The soft fur thing cannot be denied, nor the fact that her skin is so tender she must wear butter-soft leather shoes and smooth silk things around her.

"Will you buy me a drink while we think?"

We were in the international section of the airport, protected from no one. With Interpol warrants out for our arrest we were traveling exposed by using our own passports. We hid in the bar.

Rosemary sipped a Dubonnet, and spoke in a low voice. "I knew we shouldn't have left the furs. What now?"

"We'll jump ship here in Geneva. Pierre gave me the name and address of that gun-runner, Michel Hauchard. He'll hide us in Lausanne until Pierre arrives to rescue us."

"Who was that silver-haired man? He was watching you very closely."

"Too elegant to be a cop," I said.

I was wearing the McNellis brown business suit bought for me by Bernadine Dohrn in Seattle. People in the airport looked at me curiously, remembering my face from somewhere. When asked I said I was an actor in the FBI television series.[1]

In Lausanne the cab took us down a road which ran along the lake. The driver parked in front of a luxurious high-rise. In the elevator I pushed PENTHOUSE. The lift opened onto a private foyer. The apartment door opened immediately. Standing tall in the entrance, a cold appraising look on his face, was the silver-haired man from the airport. He bowed formally and waved us in. A huge German police dog thundered up, quivering with menace.

"*Quebec, va t'en!*" commanded Monsieur Hauchard. The dog slunk to the corner of the room.

Monsieur Hauchard led us down a hundred-foot living room that faced out through glass doors to a terrace overlooking Lac Le Man. At the end of the room sat two beautiful women looking at us with dreamy expressions. Hauchard turned his back to the windows, a pensive look on his face. "How strange. I took you for German at the airport. You did that to throw me off?"

I shrugged. "Can't be too careful."

Hauchard laughed, baring his teeth. "May I present Gabrielle and our charming visitor from Rome, Antonia. Professor Leary and his wife."

Gabrielle, given to undulating curves and bursting protuberances, reclined on the sofa with aristocratic amusement. Antonia, an Italian starlet, nodded and turned her sullen face to the lake. Both of them 'luded out, I thought.

Sitting at his desk Monsieur Hauchard flashed that smile again. "Pierre tells me you are rich and writing a book that we shall sell to the movies."

"At the moment, I'm afraid, we're poor and very much on the run."

"*Pouf*, that is nothing," said Hauchard grandly. "I am honored to meet you. I understand your situation. I am totally sympathetic. It is my obligation as a gentleman to protect philosophers. I ask you and your beautiful wife to be my guests here for as long as necessary. And I pledge you my assistance in taking care of these petty disagreeable things with the police. *Pouf!* The police are no problem to me. I have a dozen of them on my payroll."

We shook hands, and I smiled in relief. For the first time in seven months I felt like a young man.

Rosemary and I unpacked our clothes in the guest room and dressed for dinner.

"What do you think?" I asked.

"He's a crook," said Rosemary.

"Yeah, I think you're right. But we have no choice. He's our crook."

"So let's hope that he's a big crook," said Rosemary.

The following afternoon the Rolls Royce rolled along the lakefront to the Richmont. The headwaiter bowed profusely and without a word escorted us to a table in the rear of the restaurant, where a man awaited us.

"Monsieur Duval, may I present the fugitive professor."

Duval extended his hand. He was a short man, over fifty, pudgy and bald with graying fringes, dressed with conservative elegance. Gay. He wore a red Legion d'Honneur pin in his lapel. "I have been interested in meeting you for some time, Professor. I have been following your work. If you are willing, I would like to ask you some questions."

"But my dear Duval, it is we who must ask the questions. Have you been able to find out his status?"

Duval picked up his pipe, scratched a match, glanced sharply at me through smoke, and then dropped the box of matches on the white tablecloth. "All right, let's get the immediate details over with. Professor, you have engaged Horace Mastronardi of Bern to be your attorney. Well done. He's the best criminal lawyer in Switzerland. There is an Interpol warrant out for your arrest, but it is inactive. Which means it is *mildly* dangerous to wander around airports. Also I should stay out of Britain, France, Spain, or Italy if I were you. The other European countries don't want any scandal with you one way or another. There is always the danger that an eager underling could arrest you, even though the highest officials prefer to leave you alone.

"Your most serious problem, as you well know, is with the United States. According to my information the CIA prefers that you remain a fugitive roaming around Europe and the Middle East. However, the American drug enforcement people want you back in prison as a symbol of their successful anti-drug campaign. The FBI is really after you. You seem to have some information they badly need. The Swiss just found out last night that you are here. They were interested of course in locating you, simply because it's embarrassing to a country to have a fugitive kicking around incognito. The Swiss won't bother you as long as you remain low-profile.

"My bet is that the Americans will file for extradition. It will probably take a month to do it. If you move fast with the Swiss, you may be able to beat the American warrant. If Swiss asylum isn't ready in three weeks, you might consider moving on to another country."

Duval's pipe had gone out. He picked up the match box, struck fire, cupped the pipe with his hand, and filled the air with smoke. He had finished transmitting.

"What other countries would you suggest?" I said.

Duval shook his head slowly, his face expressionless. "That question is beyond what Monsieur Hauchard contracted for today. Before I tell you more, you must in good faith answer some of my questions."

"Michel is my mentor in this affair," I said, turning to Hauchard. "What shall I do?"

Michel Hauchard shrugged. "I suggest that you cooperate with Monsieur Duval."

"Very well. What do you want to know? I trust you're not going to ask silly questions, such as how many Black Panthers there are in Algeria."

"No," replied Duval without smiling. "I want to find out what you know about brainwashing with drugs."

"Drugs," said Hauchard in surprise. "Is that what the FBI wants to know about?"

"No, that's what I want to know about," said Duval. "The information sought by the FBI is the Professor's problem, not mine."

I decided to give Duval a few facts and a lot of promises; I quickly delivered an introductory lecture on imprinting and referred him to my published works.

A few days later a phone call came from Mastronardi, my Swiss lawyer. He had been contacted by Albert Hofmann, the Sandoz chemist who discovered LSD. The great scientist wanted to meet me. I responded enthusiastically and a luncheon was set up at a charming garden restaurant near the lake. Hofmann told us about his LSD sessions with leading

European intellectuals, including Rudolph Gelpke, the Swiss scholar who translated Persian-Sufi poetry, and Ernst Junger, mystic German novelist. These Europeans had formed an informal "wisdom school" to experiment with psychedelic drugs.

Later, walking along the waterfront of Port d'Ouchy, I asked Dr. Hofmann about the dangers of LSD. Without hesitation Hofmann replied that there was no evidence whatsoever that LSD damaged the brain.

"The dangers are psychological then," I said.

Hofmann nodded.

"Then if the psychological conditions are supportive, these dangers can be eliminated?"

"That's what the evidence so far seems to suggest," he said. [2]

Life as guests in Michel's deluxe penthouse was certainly different from socialist Algeria: protracted gourmet lunches and dinners in the best restaurants in Switzerland, elaborately produced by Michel, who spent at least an hour a day in earnest conversations with chefs and owners planning menus. On weekends there were parties at stately lakeside villas owned by wealthy Germans and South Americans, apparently shareholders in a consortium Hauchard formed to market my books and movie scripts. Everyone seemed to consider us glamorous and ultra-sophisticated ornaments brightening the monotony of Swiss social life.

Rosemary spent a few days in a Geneva fertility clinic, undergoing corrective surgery.

After a month Hauchard announced that we should establish a Swiss residence. He arranged for us to rent a chalet in Villars sur Ollon, a ski resort at the east end of Lake Geneva. We wondered why he made a big deal of introducing us around town, totally blowing what was left of our cover. But we were in no position to challenge the strategy since we were now his wards. Anyway Rosemary and I were thinking about only one development—the possibility that she might finally be able to get pregnant.

"There's someone knocking at the door." Rosemary tied her robe and pulled the curtains open to a rainy Swiss morning. "I'll see who it is. If it has to be handled in French, I'll call you." She returned with a desolate look. "It's the police. They want to talk to you."

I dressed. Two men in civilian clothes and a uniformed officer. A polite shaking of hands. A short conversation in French.

I returned to Rosemary in the bedroom. "I'm under arrest. The Americans have filed extradition papers. I have to go to Lausanne with them."

"To jail? Will you come back? The hospital said tonight is the night.

Tell them. We've waited six years to make a baby, and tonight is the night."

"We'll have this all straightened out by this afternoon. You have some coffee, take a long bath, pack a bag, and stay at Michel's. Mastronardi will bail me out. Call him right now."

The police were making polite shuffling motions.

"What shall I take with me?" I said.

"It is not necessary to take anything. Everything will be furnished you, even the toothbrush. I am very sorry."

She stood by the door weeping as we four men crowded into a VW beetle, buckled seat belts, and drove off. It was raining. I felt terrible.

A huge gate set into thick stone walls swung open. In a wood-paneled office a thin man in a dark-blue suit held out his hand like a hotel manager. "Ah, Professor. This is all so unfortunate. I trust you will clear this matter up soon. Maitre Mastronardi has phoned. He will be here tomorrow. In the meantime I hope you will not be too uncomfortable. I understand you are a friend of Monsieur Hauchard. We had the pleasure of his company here some time ago."

I knew what came next: several hours of processing, the same every-where—in Buttyrki, San Quentin, Folsom, Attica, Chino, Soledad, Lubyanka, Vacaville—shower, body search, clothing issue (blue denims again) and filling out the admission card. I would be taken along the metal runway, up spiderweb stairs, accompanied by jailers with keys jangling the international music of incarceration. I would walk in the cell. The door would shut. Clang! Metal against metal.

There was only one question. Single or multiple cell? If the latter, I would be greeted by strangers, who would tell stories and clue me in on survival details.

But in the Swiss tradition of hotel comfort it was solitary cell.

My practiced eyes took in the furnishings: metal toilet bowl, metal wash basin, metal table, metal bed with mattress. Two blankets? And clean, that was a touch! A pillow—luxury! And sheets. Heaven!

The walls were of solid brick, which would stifle the sound of tapping. There was one small barred window twelve feet up.

I stretched out on the bunk and wrapped myself in one of the blankets. In this cocoon of wool I felt protected. For the first time in months I was not afraid of the Interpol nightmare. It had become real.

I could not sleep. For an hour I studied an article in an old issue of *Paris Match* describing the globetrotting life of Maria the wife of Italian industrialist Vito d'Motione. Vito appeared to be a decisive fellow, skillful at pulling the levers of power and wealth, the sort that would never leave his beautiful wife to go to prison. I examined the photographs thoughtfully, as if a clue might be hidden in their dress or gestures.

I examined the ceiling. The light was recessed behind a metal grill. The bars of the grill were strong enough to hold a knotted sheet dangling the weight of a man. The possibilities for a less drastic escape would have to await a further knowledge of the routine.

My reverie was disturbed by a key nervously searching for the lock. Two guards entered, smiling sheepishly. Each carried a large carton heaped with food, wine, books, stationery.

"Merry Christmas," I said.

"This is just the beginning," replied one guard dryly. Two trusties entered carrying more boxes.

"From Monsieur Hauchard," said the other guard, winking to share the secret of our mutual benefactor. I remembered Hauchard laughing as he described the cases of wine and the fine watches he regularly delivered to the police on holidays.

I sat on my bunk for an inventory of the windfall. Two loaves of French bread, sliced in strategic places by the routinely suspicious guards. A roll of Italian salami and a roll of French salami. A bag of gleaming waxy apples. Several tins of Danish meat delicacies. Six boxes of cheese: camembert, liederkranz, gruyere, *Boursin aux herbes*, *mule du pape*, Brie. A golden-brown roast chicken wrapped in silver foil, exuding spicy fragrance. A carton of fat juicy shrimp. A carton of shredded lobster. A loaf of liverwurst, moist and tender. Four boxes of assorted crackers. Tubes of mayonnaise and the mustard of Dijon. A chocolate cake. Twelve bars of assorted Swiss chocolates. A giant bottle of fresh orange juice. Three bottles of wine—one St. Emilion, a Mouton Cadet, a Pouilly Fuisse. A carton of Gitane *sans filtre*. Ten books, including *The Pentagon Papers*. Two packages of envelopes: one *avion*, one regular. Seven boxes of the finest stationery, a ream of onion skin, a package of carbon paper. And a portable typewriter.

I found the corkscrew, poured the Montrachet into a coffee mug; lit a Gitane, inhaled the rich resinous throat-rasping caress of black tobacco; sat back to think about my mysterious patron.

By dinner-time the cell was blue with tobacco smoke and I was pleasantly plastered. The guard removed the two remaining bottles of wine, explaining that the ration was one bottle every two days.

The Swiss are certainly the best jail-keepers in the world, I thought, falling into a glutted stuporous slumber.

A month passed quickly while Mastronardi busied himself with appeals for Swiss political asylum. Meanwhile I was spending ten to twelve hours a day analyzing the numerical consistencies among the *I Ching*, the Tarot, and the Periodic Table of Elements, finally performing the assignment that the Lama Govinda had given me.

A guard brought in the mail, several letters and a thin package already partially opened. Removing the brown paper wrapping and cardboard cover I discovered an oval painting of a landscape. Blue lake under blue sky. Red-tile houses. A tree with four strong branches. The initials "H.H." on the bottom. I considered the painting for several minutes sensing its magic. It was a window into a world of sunlight and green-blue freedom.

I turned the painting over and found a yellowing piece of paper with the spidery signature of the artist: Hermann Hesse. An electric charge buzzed up my back.

I placed the painting carefully against the wall and read the accompanying letter.

> For several years I have thought you should have this painting by Hermann Hesse my grand-uncle. How strange that I should send it to you here in the prison of our country—where you shall not be for long.
>
> Christopher Wenger

I remembered a short story by Hesse about an artist trapped in hopeless captivity. On the prison wall he painted a window opening onto a beautiful landscape, a lake and mountains. The prisoner then climbed out the window and disappeared in the mountains.

I tied the string from the package to the ring on the painting, hung it on the wall, and looked out through the oval window to the free world of Hesse.

One of my letters came from Professor Walter Clark, who had mortgaged his home for $20,000 and sent the money to Maitre Mastronardi for bail. Another letter was from Allen Ginsberg, listing the support he was gathering to get me out of jail.

The next day I came across a fascinating item in the Paris *Herald*. G. Gordon Liddy had been indicted on several counts for the Watergate break-in. I recalled that Liddy's meteoric rise to White House power as a dirty-trick expert had been based on his bungled raids on Millbrook. Did this arrest of my former tormentor forecast a swing of the pendulum?

Two weeks later, following the advice of Mastronardi, I faked a heart attack while walking in the prison yard. The physician sent by Mastronardi to examine me clucked in sympathy and prescribed eight different medications and my immediate release.

Rosemary and Mastronardi waited in the visiting room. "I cannot tell you," he exclaimed, grasping my hand, "how I have been working for you! Like the bulldog, I will not let go! Here, this is for you. Pictures of my country."

Mastronardi handed me a large chocolate bar with color photos of Swiss country scenes. "It has been sorrowful for me to know that you have not had a chance to enjoy the beauties of Switzerland."

"I hope I will some day," I said with a sigh.

"But you will! You will!" The lawyer turned to me, his face distorted. He burst into tears, staggered to his feet, and walked to the corner of the room, his back to Rosemary and me, his round body shuddering with sobs.

Rosemary held her hands up in disbelief. When your lawyer cries you must really be in trouble.

Mastronardi dabbed his eyes with a handkerchief, pulling himself together. He trotted to me and seized my arms in a fierce grip, smiling self-indulgently. I realized that he had staged this melodrama for his own amusement.

"You can see Switzerland now! You are free! The Swiss government has refused to extradite you. You are free!"[3]

Things were never the same with Rosemary after Lausanne prison. She was understandably weary from the continued legal harassment. It had been almost seven years since the Laredo bust—all our time together under the cloud of imprisonment.

My absence during her last two fertile times had made the painful operation seem pointless. The insecurity of my position as penniless fugitive had made my life less than a joy to share. Though I was now out of jail, our dependence on Hauchard was turning out to be a humiliating replica of the scene with Eldridge, both men flamboyant criminals claiming connections with authorities, running me for money, managing my life in the context of secrecy and blackmail.

Then there came a phone call from New York. It was John, Rosemary's primary escort-driver during my California prison days. Rosemary blushed and fidgeted while I listened to his enthusiastic story. He had just come back from Afghanistan and had a sizable amount of cash. He wanted to visit us and share his joy.

"Come on over," I said.

Rosemary seemed pleased.

Events moved with prearranged precision after the arrival of John. He was more than willing to resume his role as Rosemary's protector.

I slumped on the sofa, my nakedness covered by a sheep-lined leather coat. John stood by the door, young and tall. She swooped back and forth packing for departure. She paused to regard me tenderly.

"You never looked better," she said.

"I never felt less."

"This is the most beautiful place on earth. You won't forget these mountains . . . and what I told you?"

"I won't forget," I said.

"There's nothing to forgive."

"It was predictable."

"I won't be here for your birthday."

"It's happened before." Another birthday separation.

"Write down everything that happens. I'll read every word."

"Yes."

"Are you jealous?"

"I'm inert."

"You're sending me off, you know. It's your decision."

"I'm doing nothing."

"Exactly."

She left for the bedroom. In a few moments she returned, dressed perfectly for the voyage. Soft sandals on fleet silken feet. Tight blue jeans. A woven blouse. Her leather traveling bag swung casually over her shoulder. She would not be out of place at any time in human history. She twirled gracefully and waved farewell. She was ready for the road.

P **ARACELSUS** (1493-1541), was the pseudonym of Theophrastus Bombastus von Hohenheim, Switzerland's iconoclastic philosopher, psychologist, and pharmacologist (the name Paracelsus means "surpassing Celsus," the Greek physician).

After receiving his degree at Ferrara in 1515 he traveled widely. He drew much criticism in his practice of medicine for prescribing experimental drugs (including laudanum and ether) and for using unconventional techniques such as hypnosis and surgery. Against the advice of the tenured faculty he was appointed lecturer at the University of Basel. Later he was dismissed and then arrested for his innovative ideas and his denunciations of the medical professors.

During the last thirteen years of his life Parcelsus resumed his travels, continuing his research into alchemy, biochemistry, and medicine. His theories anticipated modern recognition of the phenomenon of psychosomatic illness, asserting that such disorders were caused by the mind, not by demonic possession.

As a philosopher Paracelsus updated the gnostic axiom, "As above, so below," endorsing a vision of the universe as bi-polar, animistic, cyclically regenerating and evolving.

37. Captured in Kabul

WINTER 1972-1973
SWITZERLAND

Rosemary's departure left me desolate. After two years of prison and exile I was cut off from American contacts. No sense of mission, no source of income. Worry, worry. Home? Friends? The concept of home-base and friendship had to be redefined in this neuro-mobile civilization we were creating. As moving particles, always orbiting, we couldn't root down like our progenitors. I had had fourteen mailing addresses in five years.[1]

I was not alone in this new mobility. Richard Alpert changed his trajectory continually: today a holy man, tomorrow something funnier. Michael Hollingshead, English-eccentric, popped up in London, Katmandu, Cambridge, New York, trying to enlighten the natives and thereby pay his way out of town. Allen Ginsberg was always on the move through the zodiac. Burroughs spiraled downward from Tangiers to Paris, London, New York, Boulder, Kansas.

My experiment with heroin at this time was not the result of alienation and boredom. The two years of enforced exile in Switzerland were hard, but not enough to drive me to the needle.

One factor was the presence of a house guest, Brian Barrett, British philosopher of junk, and his wife Liz. Although Brian clucked with virtuous disapproval about heroin (just like every other lying junky), his every word and deed conveyed an intriguing sense of the dark deep vegetative wisdom of opium.

Another factor in the environment encouraging heroin experimentation was the Rolling Stones, who were in Montreux in 1972 recording "Exile on Main Street." I used to hang out with Anita and Keith Richard at the baroque villa of Prince Stash de Rolle. Everywhere I went that summer I heard that low-down beat of the Stones celebrating Sister Morphine and Brown Sugar, Mick singing about his basement room and his needle and his spoon, wailing the profound philosophic thought of the season: "I stuck a needle in my arm. It did some good, it did some harm."

But I had no desire to initiate personal heroin research until destiny floated an enormous supply of the stuff right into my house.

At that time there were forty-nine sincere middle-class hippies in Switzerland, and I knew them all. For that matter, I had met many of their parents. One of them, Inger, a stewardess for Swissair, came by my house looking for Brian. She had purchased a large amount of pure heroin in Beirut, just for the lark. She had smuggled it into Zurich and now, a bit flustered, wondered what to do with it.

"Why not take one sniff of it to see what it's like and throw the rest in the lake," I said.

"Brian would have a heart attack if he missed out on this," said Inger. "Here, I'm going to leave some for Brian."

On his return a few days later Brian sensed the presence of heroin when he was fifty feet away from the house. He pestered me to take it with him as an experiment. I had read most of the books written about heroin, both literary and scientific. In spite of my negative bias I felt well prepared and well guided.

Brian came to the session in Bombay silk. I put on music, reclined on the cushions, and watched Brian perform his ritual. He dissolved some powder in a spoon, which he heated over a candle. It was agreed that he would go first to establish potency. He drew the liquid into his needle, then set it aside on a small dish. He loosened a silk scarf from his neck and, holding one end in his left hand, bound the other end around his bicep. By extending his left arm he tightened the scarf until his vein popped up blue and inviting. He shot up.

All this was done with the calm and deliberateness of a surgical ballet. He laid the needle down and fell back on the cushions with a deep sigh of pleasure. A few minutes later he sat up smiling. He said he knew what dosage I would require.

Brian shook his head as he prepared my shot. "I'd hate to be known as the person who got Timothy Leary hooked on heroin."

When the drug hit my vein, I felt the warm flash of euphoria that is worshipped among junkies. No question about it: I felt wonderful for a couple of minutes; for the next half hour I enjoyed a relaxed noodly bliss, a giggly nonchalance about worldly matters. Soon I fell into heavy sleep.

The next morning Brian was at my door, eager to continue the research. I had no desire for more heroin, so I proposed that we wait until night for the next session. The postponement caused a predictable distress in Brian. To avoid the nagging and fidgeting game I gave him half of the supply, reserving the remainder for whatever trials I might wish to make at later times.

That night, just before bedtime, I allowed Brian to give me an intramuscular injection. It made me feel mellow and pleasantly somnolent.

The third night of the experiment I sniffed some heroin and again felt my cells sigh in satisfaction.

On the fourth day Brian had run out of his stash. He became irritable. By the time he got around to requesting a hit from mine, I had already flushed it down the toilet.

The experiments with heroin were useful in the context of my work as a drug researcher. Always critical of scientists who pontificate about psychedelic drugs without having personally experienced their effects, I now feel qualified to discourage the use of heroin without prejudice. It is a euphoric downer that has no appeal to me or to any other active person who wishes to maintain freedom and independence. The mystique of heroin comes from its status as a non-medical drug. If heroin were legalized as a prescription pharmaceutical, it would continue to be a minor social problem but no more so than other euphoric downers such as barbiturates.[2]

The opiates and other addictive escape-drugs which lower intelligence have the opposite effect from psychedelic drugs, which increase sensitivity to and understanding of the broad spectrum of human realities.

One morning Jack called from Berkeley. It was the first time we had talked since my escape. Since he was still on probation, I had never contacted him directly, keeping the heat away. He reported that Susan had just given birth to a baby girl named Dieadra. There were problems, however. Susan had separated from her husband and was living alone with no support. I said that I'd send plane tickets immediately. Jack volunteered to get Susan and Dieadra organized to come to Switzerland.

It was a thrilling moment when I looked into the eyes of my daughter and granddaughter at the Zurich airport. Susan took over the top floor of my house on Zug Lake, devoting all her energies to motherhood.

Susan had changed. The arrests and surveillance and my notoriety had caused her to become withdrawn and fearful.

I sent a plane ticket to her husband to join us. He was soon followed by his twin-brother, plus wife and baby. With Brian Barrett and his wife and child in residence I suddenly found myself supporting (on borrowed money) six adults and three kids, hoping to establish a cozy family-oriented scene in far-away exile. The trouble was that the three men had no outlet for their energies. They soon fell to quarreling among themselves.

My main tie to practical reality was the book about my prison escape, which Hauchard hoped would bring me fame and himself fortune. To pursue these and other goals he leased a deluxe chalet in Gstaad, complete with butler, chef, and chambermaids. He made a lavish suite available to me and continually invited me over to ski and meet prospective partners in our venture.

I learned a lot about the psychology of money by observing Hauchard. He always said, "We will *win* lots of money." At first I thought this was a charming verbal mistake. Poor Frenchman, he didn't know the word "earn." After a while I realized that he knew exactly what he was saying. The word "earn" was simply not in his vocabulary. Hauchard defined himself as "rich" by living in the style, leasing swank houses, driving a Rolls, intimidating restaurant owners and shopkeepers, organizing formal dinners for other "rich" people. By contrast I saw myself as impoverished nobility.

It came as a shock to realize that in point of fact the money Hauchard used to support his aristocratic style had been "won" from me and from two other fugitives whom Hauchard had tried, unsuccessfully, to help with legal problems. Thus I learned the very old lesson that poverty and wealth are states of mind. I no longer felt timidly grateful since in truth I had unwittingly paid Hauchard very well to be my social director. When I confronted him about this, he clapped me on the back affectionately and laughed. "My dear Teem," he said jovially, "where do you think my money comes from? An inheritance from an aunt?"

The best thing about Hauchard's scene in Gstaad was the skiing. I broke through to the ski-slope satori that the faster you go the safer you are.

It was curious to discover that I was a culture-hero in the Alpine resort. Hauchard, whose social status was always dicey, used me as magnet for lavish dinner parties, seating me next to French producers and Italian playboys who made cocaine jokes with the salt shakers.

The most engaging person I met in Gstaad was Roman Polanski, a spellbinding raconteur with this rare ability to convert a small party of friends into witty drawing-room comedy. I felt a strong bond with this complex man, another permanent exile. Roman's old friend Gene Gutowski joined Hauchard's consortium and flew off to New York to find a publisher for my manuscript.

I had been unable to stir up any interest in the book. The ingenious Gutowski returned with an offer of a $250,000 advance from Bantam Books. With this stimulus I threw myself into manuscript revision and by August 1972 had produced *Confessions of a Hope Fiend*.

Eventually the $250,000 was divided as follows: an Argentinian playboy who introduced Polanski got ten percent, Gene Gutowski got twenty, and a distinguished New York literary lawyer named Alan Schwartz got ten. Hauchard and I were supposed to split the remaining sixty. As it turned out, I received around $40,000 on signing. Hauchard stole the rest. I paid Walter Clark $10,000, sent $5,000 each to Susan and Jack, and bought a gleaming golden Porsche and a roomful of high-tech stereo equipment.

There were rumors that the American government was planning another move to get me expelled from Switzerland. I arranged to see my diplomatic source, Duval, at the Palace Hotel in Montreux. Duval was waiting in the bar. "Expenses are so high in these international cases," he sighed.

"How high?" I asked cautiously.

"Five thousand."

"Francs?"

"Dollars. Be grateful, my boy, it could be pounds."

"Okay. For five thousand dollars," I said in my best game-show host voice, "tell me what countries will accept me?"

"Your situation is unique," said Duval. "You are a stateless person, but you're actually like a sovereign state of your own. I have to negotiate at the premier level as your ill-paid ambassador. You don't have a home anywhere on this earth. But don't feel unwanted. The Americans are desperate to have you back. They are arranging to have you expelled from Canton Vallais."

"Too bad," I said. "I was just getting good at skiing."

"No other Swiss canton will accept you. Now for the bad news."

Duval pulled the Paris *Herald* out of his briefcase. I had been indicted in Orange County on nineteen counts of drug dealing. I was labeled by Cecil Hicks, the D.A., as the Godfather of the largest drug smuggling organization in the world, the Brotherhood of Eternal Love. My bail was set at five million dollars.

"You should be honored," laughed Duval. "That's five million dollars, not francs. A price like that on your head makes you more dangerous than Voltaire and Freud."

"That's absurd. I've never been involved in a dope deal."

"Don't worry, you'll have your day in court—after the Americans drive you out of Switzerland to a country where you can be extradited. The Americans want the Swiss to seize your passport, but Bern has refused."

"Good."

"Bad," said Duval. "You see the Swiss can't make you leave if you have no valid passport. With a passport you can be expelled."

"Where can I go?"

"I've talked to Otto Palme, Premier of Sweden. He's the most intelligent man in Europe. He likes you well enough, but he's facing a tricky election and you can only lose him votes. The next most intelligent man in Europe is Bruno Kreisky, Chancellor of Austria. I sent him your books. He'd like you to come and help him bring Austria up to the twentieth century."

I didn't know exactly what this meant, but it was the only offer I'd had in a year. I was willing to consider it.[3]

And so it happened. I was expelled from Canton Vallais on schedule. My Swiss advisors suggested that I keep mobile. I rented a house above Lake Lugano, owned by the Hesse family, and a farmhouse in the lush fields of the Bernese Oberland. Susan maintained a base at the cottage of Zug Lake near Lucerne.

The plan was to keep moving (in the golden Porsche), a week here, a week there, making appearances in Zurich, Basel, a moving target so that no canton would see me long enough to get upset at the corruption of local youth by the Pied Piper.[4]

Before taking off I received a phone call from a woman named Joanna Harcourt-Smith, an old friend of Hauchard's who was staying at his villa in Lausanne. She came over to Zug Lake to see me.

I picked her up at the train station. She was a tiny, flamboyant blond in her late twenties. As we sat in front of a crackling fire she proudly described her designer genes. Her father was an English aristocrat. Her mother Marisia was an Ulam, whose brother Stan had co-invented the H-bomb and whose brother Adam headed Harvard's Russian Institute. Joanna's step-father, Arpad Plesch, was one of the richest men in Europe.

Like me Joanna had run out of money and credibility. She had worn out her welcome in more countries than I, for harmless frivolities. Joanna had two children, both turned over to the fathers, a Greek shipping heir and a Washington D.C. socialite. She wore a silver circle around her neck strung with a dozen rings—trophies, as it were, both male and female.

I was strongly attracted by her sharp wit and sexy style.

"What do you want?" I asked, getting down to basics.

She grinned wickedly, one of her specialties. "Everything."

We made love all night. The morning sun, pleasantly surprised at finding us up and about so early, stumbled coming over the mountain and spilled a trail of orange-red across the lake. I recognized another one of those magic moments when a new world is ready to be born.

"So what have you been doing in Switzerland?" she asked.

"I wrote a book about my prison escape. Sold it to Bantam for a quarter of a million. I made a rock-and-roll record with a German techno-rock group. Now I'm waiting for someone to help me escape from this tidy green hell. I've been invited to Vienna."

"Why don't we spend Christmas in St. Moritz with my friends, Putzi and Nicki von Opel? And then we can take in Vienna."

For Christmas dinner Putzi and Nicki had me sit in Father von Opel's place at the head of the table. Even the old German family retainers were amused by the casting.

During the meal I got up and drew back the curtains covering the enormous window which overlooked St. Moritz, the richest valley in the world. I could see the reflection of the dinner table and my friends. It was like looking through the glass in a prison waiting room. I sensed at that moment that my days of freedom were numbered.

Turning back to the table I told them of my premonition.

Putzi was visibly shaken by this story. She said, "You two are moving too fast. Be careful. Slow down. Don't go to Vienna. Come with us to Ceylon and take it easy in the sun."

But we were too geared up to listen.

It was midnight and snowing in the Alps when Joanna and I came to the Austrian frontier. The border police glanced at the ski rack on the roof of the Porsche, flipped through our passports, and waved us through.

Vienna in winter was freezing and depressing. Bruno Kreisky's secretary said the Chancellor was out of town for the holidays. I would be contacted upon his return.

My Austrian hosts were young radical filmmakers who wanted my participation in some of their projects. The first production was an anti-heroin documentary. In one scene, heavy with *mittel*-European symbolism, they filmed me walking along the Czech border, gazing bleakly at the barbed-wire fence and the guard towers. As an ex-convict I naturally began to imagine escape scenarios during this shot. My young sponsors turned out to be psychedelic Marxists. Trying to politicize me they intimated that Chancellor Kreisky would probably swap me to the Americans for three jets. They urged me to go underground in Yugoslavia. They were disorganized and penniless.[5]

Joanna got sick. My daughter Susan and her baby Dieadra and her in-laws showed up broke. I phoned Duval in Montreux. The Americans were trying to extradite me from Austria, he said, but Chancellor Kreisky would stand by me.[6]

I phoned America for funds. George Litwin, now a consultant for a large bank, wired $1,000. Someone crashed into my Porsche while it was parked in front of the hotel. The weather got damper and colder by the day. Joanna's fever worsened.

"I'll be dead in twelve hours if I don't get out of this dismal city," she said. "Let's head for the sun."

We had enough money to fly to Afghanistan, which sounded like a safe move. A handsome rock-and-roller named Hari, whose uncle was the king of Afghanistan and whose father was foreign minister, had been a frequent guest at my cottage on Zug Lake. He often asked me to spend time in the family villa.

The plan was to restore physical and financial health in Afghanistan and then move on to Ceylon to visit Putzi von Opel.

But the plan didn't pan out. Putzi ended up doing more prison time than I, imprisoned in France for hashish. If it had been murder, her lawyer could have gotten her off.

In the Kabul air terminal a young woman, dressed in uniform, identified herself to us as an Afghan immigration official. She asked for our passports and disappeared with them.

Then a pleasant young man from the American Embassy came over and said, "You are being placed under arrest."

"For what?" I said.

"Because you have no passports," he replied, logically enough.

We were taken by a platoon of soldiers to the Army headquarters. The Afghani general appeared bored as Joanna and I argued that we had come into the country legally. No one seemed to know anything about the woman who had taken our passports and vanished.[7]

We were ushered to a shack where a judge in army clothes sat behind a wooden table dispensing justice in cases involving chickens and pigs. We ended up in a deserted hotel with four Afghani soldiers posted outside our room. Joanna's illness had gotten worse. The room was cold and dank.

The next day the door flew open, and there, right out of the fairy stories, was Hari, our prince in long black hair and mod Beatles suit.

"You have arrived! Welcome to my country. I'm so sorry about these soldiers. My father and I were on holiday with the King, so I just heard about you today. Don't worry. You'll be out of here in a few hours. Meanwhile I've arranged for some good food from the palace."

The Prince shouted a command and three soldiers entered carrying baskets of food, a portable tape player with Rolling Stones tapes, and some fabulous hashish.

We were dazed with pleasure. It was all working out the way it should.

In the morning the Prince returned, a crushed spirit. "My uncle the King is furious with me. He says the Americans insist on having you turned over to them. You are finished. I'm sorry I got you into this mess. I had no idea they wanted you that bad."

"Can't we get a lawyer and fight this extradition?"

The Prince looked at me with pity. "Lawyer? You can't hire a lawyer in Afghanistan to fight the government. This is a very primitive country."

Much subdued our Prince embraced us, took his Rolling Stones tapes, and left.

A DEA agent and several plainclothes companions waited for us at the plane. I was handed a transit card: good one-way back to the USA. My profession was listed as philosopher.

As soon as the plane took off, Joanna went to the toilet and wrote notes, which she dropped in the laps of various passengers: HELP. TIMOTHY LEARY IS BEING KIDNAPPED. PLEASE NOTIFY LONDON *DAILY MAIL*.

The plane had been delayed eight hours in Kabul because of us, so an unscheduled overnight stop in Frankfurt was necessary. We wandered around the huge expanse of the terminal, escorted by the two agents and trailed by others. We considered the swinging doors that led to German territory. Joanna, whose hepatic eyes had come to look like orange wedges, demanded to see a doctor. In the medical section I told the medic that I was being kidnapped by force. "Please call the police." He examined me with that look that only a good German can give a trouble-maker who is defying authority.

I spent the next three years in prison idly wondering about my tactics at this point. Should I have vaulted over the low gate and run through the terminal shouting: "Help! Police!" Then struggled with my pursuers? Gotten myself into a German jail?

But I didn't make a run for it. Not so much from fear of physical harm. *It would have been so undignified.*

We bedded down on couches in the VIP lounge, planning to make our non-violent move for freedom in London.

At Heathrow we found that Joanna's desperate notes had worked: report-ers and photographers flashing bulbs, shouting questions. We were bundled into the office of the Chief of Immigration, a title respected through-out the galaxy. He was the same smooth functionary who had banned me from Britain in 1969 when I had tried to visit John Lennon and the Moody Blues. He was coolly polite to me, obsequious to Joanna, whose family name he respected.

I came right to the point. "I need your help. I am being kidnapped."

"I wouldn't say 'kidnapped,' my dear fellow. You have no passport. Your American escorts have provided you with a one-way permit. It's all quite in order, I assure you."

"I refuse to go," I said.

"Are you requesting asylum in England?"

"No. I request to be interned in England for three days to arrange travel to a country of my choice. I possess an Algerian residence card and entrance permits to Lebanon, Austria, and Denmark."

"Very well. Your request for entrance will be telephoned to Her Majesty's Home Office."

"Telephoned! Aren't such decisions usually made in writing?" The next flight for LA left in half an hour. I had hoped to stall them at least that long.

This was more proof of my naivete. Her Majesty's Home Office phoned back with the refusal in five minutes.

"I'm so sorry," said the Chief, "but I must request you to leave British soil on the next available flight."

"I refuse."

"Then I must order you deported by force."

I was surprised and disappointed. This was not some banana republic, after all. This was England.

"And now I'm afraid that our interesting conversation must end." He glanced toward the door. The two Drug Enforcement agents stood in the hallway. Behind them were three Special Branch officers and behind them were several burly bobbies.

Hand in hand Joanna and I walked, heads high, to the Pan Am flight to LA. We were seated in the front row, first class. The stewardess im-mediately brought champagne. "Leave the bottle with them," said the agent behind us. He was from the Bureau of Narcotics and Dangerous Drugs.

After take-off we discovered that Putzi's cousin, Gunther Sachs, interna-tional bon vivant and sophisticate, was sitting across the aisle. Joanna sprang into action. Within twenty minutes we took over the upper lounge of the 747. Gunther, his friend the German baron, Joanna, and I sat on the floor drinking champagne while two agents at a corner table watched with benevolent curiosity. They had been ordered to humor us about the little things. They knew I was facing twenty years.

*   *   *

A swarm of agents was waiting at LAX. I kissed Joanna goodbye, and then they slipped on the handcuffs. Over a hundred journalists writhed behind a barrier, TV cameras whirring. I displayed the upbeat smile that McLuhan had advised and was shuttled to the LA County Jail in a squad car, escorted by six more cars jammed with agents carrying submachine guns. They were afraid of another Weathermen coup.

Entering the maximum-security cellblock I was cheered by the row of murderers. "Welcome to America, brother," said the guy in the next cell, passing me the evening paper. The banner headline read: 76 MILLION DOLLAR TAX-SUIT AGAINST DRUG-KING LEARY.

Welcome home.[8]

Preceding page: *1921, West Point, N.Y. Abigail Leary and author, age three months.*

Left: *1922, Springfield, Mass. Dr. Timothy Leary, Sr. and author, age two.*

Right: *1923, Springfield, Mass. Grandparents Dennis and Sara Leary with author, age three, in front of their home at 54 Central Street.*

Bottom: *Fall 1931, Springfield, Mass. Author having fantasies about football heroics.*

June 1941. Cadet Leary during period of West Point "silencing."

April 1944, Butler, Penn. Timothy and Marianne Leary after marriage at the post chapel.

Summer 1961, New York City.
Maynard and Flora Lu Ferguson.

Fall 1962, Cambridge, Mass.
Professor Richard Alpert monitors
reactions of Dr. Ralph Metzner,
who is using the Experiential
Typewriter to record imagery
during a drug session.

Spring 1963, San Francisco
Playboy Club. Allen Ginsberg,
Peggy Hitchcock, author, and
City Lights publisher Lawrence
Ferlinghetti planning the
psychedelic revolution.

November 1964, Sausalito, Calif. Alan and Jano Watts with author in their houseboat discussing Alan's The Glorious Cosmology.

January 1965, Calcutta. Timothy and Nanette Leary in front of a licensed marijuana (ganja) shop. This photo was introduced in evidence at the Laredo trial as part of the campaign to legalize cannabis in the United States.

Summer 1964, Millbrook, N.Y. Van Wolfe (left), philosopher, and strategist of the drug-culture conferring with Richard Alpert (Ram Dass).

Spring 1966, Laredo, Texas. Author beside codefendant Susan Leary, age eighteen, as he talks to lawyers.

Spring 1966, Washington, D.C. At Dodd-Kennedy Senate hearings on LSD, author urges licensed use of altered-states drugs by responsible adults, warning against large black market if prohibition is attempted.

November 1966, New York City. Allen Ginsberg, author, and Dr. Ralph Metzner prepare to perform in the psychedelic celebration "Illumination of the Buddha."

Spring 1966, Millbrook, N.Y. Sheriff Albert Traver watches as G. Gordon Liddy arrests Jack Leary after raid on the Big House.

November 1967, Laguna Beach, Calif. Rosemary and Timothy Leary after marriage in Joshua Tree by American Indian shaman.

Summer 1967, Millbrook, N.Y. Maha Yantra (intertwined triangles) on chimney, symbolizing tantric fusion, painted by Rosemary and Timothy Leary.

Top: *December 1969, Hidden Valley Ranch, Calif. Author and Rosemary Leary in a solemn mood three weeks before his sentencing to twenty years' imprisonment.*

Left: *August 1967, Millbrook, N.Y. Author in autobiographical movie about Harvard professor who takes refuge on an Indian reservation to escape thought-police.*

Right: *Fall 1969. Poster for California gubernatorial campaign against incumbent Ronald Reagan, featuring the slogan "Come Together" (later publicized by supporter John Lennon).*

John Loengard, Life Magazine © Time Inc.

Diane Dorr-Dorynek

Joe Roberts Jr.

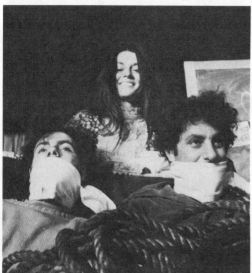

August 1969, Queen Elizabeth
Hotel, Montreal. Yoko and John
during their Bed-In, recording
the song "Give Peace a Chance"
with Rosemary and Timothy on
percussion and vocals, Tommy
Smothers on guitar.

Summer 1970, New York City.
Rosemary Leary at press
conference announcing the
Defense Fund Committee for her
imprisoned husband. Jerry Rubin
and Abbie Hoffman were gagged
and bound to dramatize the fate
of the political prisoner.

*October 1970, Cairo. Author visiting pyramids while
en route to Amman, Jordan for a press conference with
Jean Genet.*

*September 1970. Passport photo of the author as
William McNellis, conservative businessman; hair
styling by Bernadine Dohrn. (Photo courtesy of the
Senate Committee Hearings on Passport Fraud,
Congressional Record.)*

*October 1970, Algiers. Eldridge Cleaver, Information
Minister of the Black Panthers' American Government
in Exile, and author (cap hides shaved head).*

Fall 1970. Cover of Paul Krassner's Realist *magazine
showing Eldridge and Kathleen Cleaver uneasily
sharing bed with Rosemary and Timothy Leary, in
a waggish take-off on the movie* Bob & Carol & Ted
& Alice.

" Tim and Rosemary and Eldridge and Kathleen "
(... consider the possibilities)

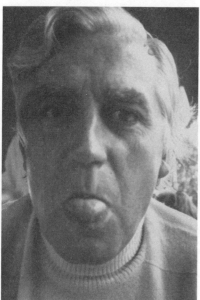

Top: *January 1972, Montana-Crans, Switzerland. Author celebrating the Swiss government's decision to refuse extradition.*

Left: *Spring 1971, Lausanne. Michel Hauchard, legendary playboy, adventurer, and smuggler, then a fugitive from French authorities.*

Right: *Spring 1972, Basel. Author and Dr. Albert Hofmann, discoverer of LSD and psilocybin, who is describing his legendary bicycle ride home after the world's first deliberate ingestion of LSD.*

Spring 1973, San Luis Obispo. Author, shackled hand and foot, being escorted back to San Luis Obispo Prison after the escape trial; more than twenty guards (eight shown here) and five patrol cars were used to transport the dangerous escapee.

Michael Horowitz

Richard Bastian

Roger Ressmeyer

Top: *September 1979, Beverly Hills. Barbara and Timothy Leary celebrate the dropping of charges by the L.A. District Attorney after a midnight-bedroom police raid produced no illegal drugs.*

Left: *Summer 1979, Springfield, Oregon. Author, Ken Babbs, and Ken Kesey planning a flamboyant reunion celebration.*

Right: *Fall 1980. Susan Leary Martino and her children, Ashley and Dieadra.*

Left: *Fall 1982, Malibu. Dr. John Lilly, pioneer of inner space, and author.*

Right: *Summer 1982, Hollywood Hills. Loving reunion with Ram Dass just before he resumed some of his identity as Richard Alpert.*

Middle: *May 1982, Hollywood. Zachary, son of Barbara Leary and step-son of the author, computer whiz-kid, video-game designer, and star second baseman.*

Bottom: *July 1982, Los Angeles. Prior to one of their debates, G. Gordon Liddy and Leary square off during a press conference.*

J **OHN LILLY** (1915-) graduated from Dartmouth College and received his M.D. from the University of Pennsylvania. His research with dolphins, continuing for over twenty-five years, was the first systematic attempt to communicate with other intelligent species.

Lilly was in the forefront of scientists who understood the importance of LSD as a neurological research tool. His classic *Programming and Meta-Programming in the Human Biocomputer* brilliantly re-defined our concepts of human nature, exploring and charting regions of the brain not previously open to scientific observation.

Our knowledge of and experimental access to out-of-body experiences are due to the perseverance of Lilly and his group in their studies of the anesthetic ketamine.

One of the most fascinating and important thinkers of our times, John Lilly pioneered research with the isolation tank, as described in his book *The Deep Self: Isolation Tank Relaxation,* the basis for the movie *Altered States.* His other publications include: *The Mind of the Dolphin; The Center of the Cyclone; Simulations of God: The Science of Belief,* and *The Scientist—A Novel Autobiography.*

38. Folsom Prison

JANUARY 1973

Within a week I was transferred to the Orange County jail and arraigned on nineteen counts as the Godfather of the world's largest dope ring. Of thirty named conspirators only one was a member of the Brotherhood of Eternal Love. The other 29 of my alleged minions were total strangers. For the obvious reason—no evidence—the District Attorney decided to postpone proceedings indefinitely. The case had already been tried in the press.

Thus available to my former hosts, the California Department of Corrections, I was shackled hand and foot and popped in a car headed north on Highway 101. Two guards in front, one in back, continually checking my cuffs. The guy in charge pulled an enormous pistol out of the glove compartment, cocked it, and leaned back to chat. "This is loaded. If you make one move, I'll blow your head off. And just for your information we've got a back-up vehicle loaded with marksmen."

The guards were triumphant as they checked me into the prison from which I had escaped. They took me into an office and phoned the warden at home. "We got Leary right here in your office, Warden. Two years

The hole was creepy. Everyone in there was down for a long count. In the next cell was Ricardo, a hit-man for the Mexican Mafia with several killings on his record. Living within ten feet of him for three months I got to know how his mind worked. I listened to his nightmare screams, his homesick sobs, his Aztec-killer confusion. Ritual homicide had been a religious duty just a few generations back.

Across the way was one of those boisterous redneck crazies—wild eyes, manic hands, mane of yellow hair. On the first night he stood at the slot in his door and shouted to me. "Tim. I'm sending something over. Watch."

A thin rectangular object, the cardboard cover of a Bible, shot out from under his metal door, slid across the cellblock, and banged into the wall a few inches to the side of my door. It was reeled back by a string, unraveled from a blanket. Zap, it came again, this time missing my door on the other side. Third time it slid under. "Leave the string on," he said.

Stuck inside the cardboard was a welcome note and a small supply of powdered coffee. A few nights later he slid over a few pinches of marijuana. I was overjoyed to have this proof of the indomitable ability of human beings to outwit the censorship of the controllers.

Which was pretty tight in this hole. My literary hardware was limited to a pencil, broken in half to prevent its use as a weapon, and one sheet of paper a day.

In solitary I awaited trial for my escape. I used this time in solitary confinement to meditate about developmental psychology and the stages of evolution. For hours I would pace the cage—seven steps forward, turn, seven steps back—putting myself in deep trance states of tranquil illumination. The single cell is a powerful habitat from which to view the world.

Legal documents were the only paper allowed in the hole, so I sat on the floor under the dim naked bulb and wrote on the back of a legal brief, with this two-inch pencil stub, still another complete system of philosophy. It was one of those inspired clear-channel transmissions. I had been thinking about the classification of brain circuits for years, and now in slow tidy handwriting, with almost no corrections, the words poured out. The book was called *Neurologic*. Joanna managed to have it published in several editions and in two national magazines, with translations into French, German, Spanish, and Japanese. Almost a million copies, all told.

While I awaited trial for the escape, Joanna was joyfully engaged in fund-raising and flamboyant publicity. In order to solidify her credibility and to facilitate access to sources of power Joanna cleverly managed to have her last name changed by legal writ to Leary. Although we were never married, this legal maneuver allowed her to present herself to the world as Joanna Leary.

The escape trial was a curious charade. It *was* a difficult crime to deny.

My main concern was to use the trial to defend myself against the more insidious charge that I was a burned-out acid casualty—the rumor started by Cleaver and enthusiastically passed on by people who disliked what I stood for.

Joanna, now headquartered in a beach-house near the prison, took on the assignment of proving that I was mentally competent. She quickly produced the man for the job, Frank Barron, who once again appeared at a low point in my life. Now chairman of the Psychology Department at nearby University of California, Santa Cruz, Frank chuckled with delight when I presented him with the problem.

"You've been a hopelessly non-adjusted mad Celt since the day you were born. Drugs helped settle you down. They were a challenging research tool to play with."

"You and I know that," I said earnestly, "but how can we prove that to anyone else?"

"You have to take a complete battery of psychodiagnostic tests that can be summarized under sworn testimony in court. This will give objective and scientific proof that you still have all your marbles."

"Or maybe even more," I added.

A few days later Frank returned with our ex-Harvard chum Mike Kahn, now a full professor at Santa Cruz, and Jeff Shapiro, director of the county mental testing program. We sat uneasily in a visiting room while Dr. Shapiro administered the tests. It took over three nerve-wracking hours.

The examination was for real. As I struggled against the ticking stopwatch, solving mazes, block-designs, and complex psychomotor tasks, the three psychologists leaned forward sweating, pulling for my success. In my early years I had given these tests to hundreds of scared patients—never as an impersonal clinician but as a fan on the sideline, cheering the poor devil on as he battled against the small tricky problems. Now the roles were reversed.

During the trial Mike Kahn and Dr. Shapiro testified that my intelligence was "genius" and my creativity "exceptional." Always the consummate actor, Kahn gave an emotional speech about what a great teacher I was. Walter Clark, now in his seventies, flew out to take the stand as a character witness.

In spite of this testimony that I was a sane and nice fellow, the jury ruled, as they had to, that I was guilty of the crime of escape. The judge threw the book at me. Picking up another nickel to run consecutively with my two dimes, I was ordered to Folsom, end of the line, the place where long-timers and unrepentant incorrigibles were warehoused. I had up to twenty-five years to serve. Plus the eleven counts still pending from the 1968 Millbrook bust. Plus the nineteen conspiracy indictments still pending on the Godfather case.

After a hot drive through the Central Valley the bus with barred windows groaned up to the Folsom perimeter. Now here was a real fortress with high granite walls and turrets. The nineteen other California joints looked like modern factory complexes and went by names like "correctional colony" or "rehabilitation center." Only Folsom was called a "prison," a stone dungeon built by Chinese labor.

"What happens now?" I asked the prisoner next to me.

"We gonna get put in Fish Row, the bottom tier of Five Building," he said wearily. "We stay there until they decide if we safe here, you know. Like we don't have no enemies on the main line. Except if they take one of us to 4-A."

"What's 4-A?" I asked.

The other prisoners glanced at each other and shook their heads.

"That's heavy-duty, 4-A. The adjustment center, you know. That's where they stow the real motherfuckers. Folsom is the asshole of the prison system, and 4-A is the bottom of *that*. Oh shit, man, here come the 4-A bulls now."

We watched as three guards came down the steps of a newer concrete building toward our bus. They were mean-looking gorillas in brown uniforms with clubs held to their wrists by leather thongs. The transit sergeant leaned inside the bus.

"Hey, Doc, come out here."

"Oh shee-it, man, they got yo ass now."

I looked at the commiserating faces of my fellow slaves and descended from the bus.

The afternoon sun steamed off the concrete. The three club-carriers sized me up impersonally. One jerked his thumb in the direction of 4-A.

Feeling very vulnerable I walked between two guards. The third covered my rear. At the entrance a guard talked into a squawk box and the door clicked open noisily. In procession we walked twenty feet down the hall and stopped in front of another metal door. A guard banged his club against the steel. Another peered out through a peep-hole, and the door opened.

There was a counter running along the left side of the room. There were eight guards, each carrying a club. I was getting the message. Their faces were absolutely blank.

"Strip." I removed my white jumpsuit, socks, and the white track shoes I bought in Lucerne in the department store next to the covered bridge that spanned the lake.

I stood naked. A guard approached with something the size and shape of a ping-pong paddle. He passed it around my head, neck, and body. A metal detector. Another guard tossed me a tattered gray jumpsuit and cloth slippers. He pointed to a storeroom at the end of the counter. "Get a mattress and two blankets."

The barred door to the right clicked open. I walked into the bottom tier of 4-A, surrounded by three guards, past a row of cells.

The slippers were too large and the mattress and blankets unwieldy as I staggered under the inspecting eyes of the prisoners, who began to whoop and shout in recognition.

"Hey! Whooee! Look who's here. Welcome to 4-A, brother."

I nodded to the muscular blacks and stocky whites by their bars. In the last cell a small man sat on the floor in the lotus position, reading a Bible, smiling benevolently.

At the end of the cell-row loomed another metal door, leading to a low dark hallway with three cell doors. One of these swung open, creaking, and I was motioned into the barred cave. The guards slammed the door shut.

The hole of Folsom prison. There was a seatless toilet, chipped and stained, a rusty face bowl, and a concrete slab, on which I threw the soiled smelly mattress. A single sliver of light shone down the hall from the outer door.

Twenty-five years to serve.

I felt a strange sense of elation. This was it. The indisputable undeniable Dantean bottom.

After an hour of darkness and silence the outer door opened. A young blond trusty entered, leaned against the bars of my cell. "Sorry you're here, man. But welcome. I'm the go-fer on the first tier. Do you smoke? You want something to read?"

"Yeah I smoke and I read."

"I bet you don't like shit-kickers, right? I'll get you something heavy to read."

My friend slid out, leaving the outer door open. Reflected light from the setting sun warmed the cell. In a few minutes he came back with rolling papers and a white envelope filled with tobacco.

"These came from Charlie. He's your nearest neighbor." That would be the guy sitting in the lotus position looking like Jesus Christ. "He wants to know if you take sugar and cream with your coffee. And if you like honey."

"Sure. Tell him thanks."

It was the ancient courtesy-ritual of prison. The new inmate, who arrives with nothing, is provided available luxuries by the old-timers. I sniffed at the tobacco. Bugler. I rolled a cigarette and watched the smoke curl and cloud in the sunlight.

The trusty darted back in carrying four books. Charlie sent *The Teachings of the Compassionate Buddha*, *In Search of the Miraculous* by Ouspensky, *The Teachings of Don Juan* by my old friend Carlos Castaneda, and *The Master and Margarita*, a satirical novel by Bulgakov about life in modern Russia.

Next my friend popped in with a cardboard cup of organic honey, a box of graham crackers, and more envelopes—powdered coffee, sugar cubes, powdered cream.

"Charlie sent these. I gotta go now. I'll leave the door open a couple more minutes. Listen, I'm your fan. I owe everything to you."

"You're welcome," I said, wondering.

"Hey, Doc." A cocky patronizing voice came from the cell just beyond the outer door. I suddenly realized the identity of the only other person I was allowed to talk to—Charles Manson. "So you finally made it. I been watching you fall for years, man. I knew you'd end up here. I've been wanting to talk to you for a long time. I wanted to ask you how come you blew it."

"Blew it?"

"You had everyone looking up to you. You could have led the people anywhere you wanted."

"What I had in mind was to teach people to avoid leaders and direct their own lives," I said wearily.

"When I got out of prison in '65, I was amazed. Thousands of kids just waiting to be programmed. Give them acid and they'd do anything."

"Charles, have you ever been interviewed by psychologists or experts about *how* you did it?"

"Did what?"

"Brainwashed your people."

"No."

"Now that's amazing. You did what every intelligence agency in the world dreamed of. You programmed people to go out on assassination missions. And they'd probably do it again today. Right?"

"Yeah."

"Why did you do it?"

"I'm a Christian, man. The Bible's my manual. The Bible gives you the program. It tells you right there in Revelation that the women are the cause of all man's problems."

That afternoon I was "promoted" to the third tier of the Adjustment Center and three weeks later was transferred to the main line. Now came the moment that everyone had warned me about. My first walk on the yard, my first confrontation with the several gangs, each ready to challenge, test, probe, and then settle my position in prison society.

Several hundred inmates clad in blue denim filled the yard, some standing in small groups, some pacing back and forth in the goalless quick-march of the convict. An electric alertness switched on as I entered the yard. The grapevine had charted my arrival and my every move in 4-A. Who would approach first?

I heard my name called. I looked over at a group of blacks lounging against the wall. So here it was: the confrontation with the Brothers. I recalled Angela Davis' ominous statement to the press that I'd be killed in prison by militant blacks. Did Eldridge Cleaver's long knife reach into the prison system of sunny California?

A Brother took a step forward. "Hey, man. We wanna rap witch you. Come on over."

I walked over slowly, feeling the watching tenseness of the whole yard. I stopped a foot away from the leader, locked eyes, nodded, smiled.

"Hey, man, what went down with you and Brother Eldridge?"

"We didn't get along."

"Zat right?" He turned to his troop and grinned. "Well what happened, man? How come you and Brother Eldridge didn't get along?"

I glanced at the faces gathered around, then looked in the eyes of the muscular spokesman. "Do you know Brother Eldridge?"

"Me? Sure. I done a couple of years with him in Quentin." Nodding heads and a murmur of assent rippled around the group. "Yeah, most of us done time with Brother Eldridge."

"If you know how Brother Eldridge operates, then you know why I didn't get along with him."

For a long moment, silence. Then a wave of amusement.

"Yeah. We heard Eldridge was playing poh-leeceman witch you. Put you in his own personal jailhouse." Around the circle heads shook, *ain't it the truth*. The spokesman continued, "Give the dude a little power and it goes right to his head."

"That's how I saw it."

A Brother with one eye pushed through. "Hey, man, I hear you a doctor, and I gotta question. All that psychology teach you how to handle hose?" Chuckles all around.

What does he mean by "hose," I wondered, flicking through my memory for fire-fighting techniques and silk-stocking fetishes.

More chuckles.

"Hose, man. You know. Foxes. Ladies. When I get back on da block, I gotta learn 'bout how those foxy hoe ladies think so I can play it real smooth."

"That stuff you can't learn from books. No way." Turning to the leader I said, "I'm gonna walk around and check out this pleasure resort. Catch you later."

I slapped hands around the circle. There was a tremor of relaxation through the yard. It was now prison knowledge that I had faced the Brothers and had no trouble. Equally important, I hadn't continued the conversation beyond the point of being too friendly, upsetting the diplomatic balance.

I toured the baseball diamond, a basketball court, a handball court, a small weight-lifting area. On my way back to the main yard I was approached by four muscular swaggering whites. The leader, a sandy-haired giant, had his sleeves rolled, showing off his huge arms. "Hey, man, you're Leary, right?"

I nodded. The Angel stuck out his paw solemnly. We shook.

"I'm Fu Griffin. Oakland Hells Angels. I met you once at Kesey's place."

Fu introduced me to his companions, Dirty Dan, Stupid Willy, Hairy Terry. We sat on the grass and reminisced about the wild-woolly Bay Area in the days of Kesey, Ginsberg, Janis Joplin. Fu was doing ten for selling heroin.

"You need any supplies?" he inquired solicitously. "You won't draw canteen until the first of the month."

At three in the afternoon the deep whistle sounded. The PA system boomed: "CLEAR THE YARD." We agreed to meet the next day. The Angels turned back to One Building, while I lined up in the blue-shirt ant-line to enter Three Building.

We stood in front of our cells until the guard shouted, "LOCK UP." He pulled a lever sliding a bar that ran the hundred-yard length of the tier, opening our doors. Then came the count. The guard was preceded by a trusty swirling a wooden rattle to get everyone on their feet. Wouldn't want to miss an inmate lying on his sack, dead.

We were unlocked for dinner. The food was good for prison fare, but the conversation was mongoloid. After dinner there was a twenty-minute wait in the cellblock, a wild crowded Teheran market scene—blacks shouting and jiving, Mexicans chattering, whites pacing up and down, everyone moving or talking, no one listening.

"LOCK UP." The bar slid the doors open for thirty seconds while we scuttled into our cages.

The next day in the yard I was approached by a rugged man with a bulldog chin, Bob Hyde. "Glad to meet you," I said, shaking hands. "I was told to look you up. They say you're the smartest toughest man in the prison system."

Hyde nodded in satisfaction. He introduced a friend of his, a tall slender youth with a tanned face and merry rascal eyes. "This is Charles Newsom, a fan of yours."

We walked back and forth across the outfield in convict rhythm—talk, turn, walk, turn—exchanging vital statistics. Charles was a top professional in that most aristocratic of all crimes—jewel heists. He had taken a lot of acid, fucked a lot of movie stars, cat-burgled a lot of homes in Bel Air and Beverly Hills. He adhered rigidly to a Robin Hood code: steal only from producers.

Bob Hyde was in prison for fraud and worse. His quiet arrogance failed to disguise an explosive nature. He was a jailhouse lawyer, drafting writs in exchange for cartons of cigarettes. He had seventeen show-cause victories to his credit.

Hyde and Newsom had a project going for which they wanted my assistance. They had formed an organization called PROBE. The "P" stood for prison and the "R" for rehabilitation; I forget the rest.

"You know," said Hyde, "your time here will be easier and smoother and healthier if you belong to a gang."

"So I've heard," I said cautiously.

"In this joint there's the Mexican Mafia. They're tough, strong, ruthless. They control the dope trade. Then there are the Bikers. We saw you talking to Fu. They're okay. They're a tight-knit loyal group but small in numbers. Then the Nazis, the Aryan Brotherhood. The blacks are mostly disorganized, except for the Muslims. They stay to themselves."

"Bob is the one who's been protecting the blacks from the other gangs," said Newsom.

"How did you do that?" I asked with scientific curiosity.

"I told the Nazis and the Mexicans that the Man," he motioned to the gun-walks, "would like nothing better than for all us to start killing each other."

"There's been no killing and no stabbing here at Folsom since Bob took over."

"So what's this gang you're suggesting I join?"

Hyde and Newsom looked at each other and laughed. "The gang is the three of us," said Newsom. "We're the sharpest people in this prison."

"This prison is a fucking nuclear power station," Hyde said, flinging out his hand. "Look at these men. Each one of them is a walking time bomb. The energy jam-packed in this yard could propel us anywhere we want to go."

"Which is mainly and primarily out," added Newsom.

"Well that's the finest social group I could hope to join. Count me in."

We three shook on it. Bob Hyde sent a thumbs-up signal to a group of whites standing near the gate.

"Okay. Now we're in business," said Hyde. "First we have to get you moved into the best neighborhood. When we go back in, you'll find you've been moved to the bottom floor of Three Building. I'll be two cells to your right and Charles will be four to your left."

"How did you get me moved so quickly?"

Newsom laughed. "A couple of cartons will do anything."

"During the next few days," continued Hyde, "we'll get you the basic comforts. There's a stinger in your cell for boiling water, and there's a gooseneck lamp so you can read after lights out. You can have your girlfriend send in a radio or TV. And we'll get you some good clothes and a quilt for your bed."

"How about some tennis shorts for the yard?" asked Newsom. "Fu told me he'd make you some leather sandals in the hobby shop."

Dinner was a merry social affair this time as I stood in line and shared a table with my new companions.

"Now the first thing you have to do tomorrow," said Hyde, "is go to the job office and tell them you're quitting the garden detail."

"Can I do that?"

"Tell them you got a letter from your lawyer and for the next six weeks you'll be busy doing research in the law library on your case. They don't give a fuck. The professional code in this joint is straightforward. Do your time quietly and don't make waves, and they leave you alone. We've got too many things to do for you to be wasting your time as a gardener."

"And tomorrow," said Newsom, "we start your body-building program. After all that time in the hole you need some exercise. Running and weights. No heavy muscles stuff, just enough to get you filled out and toned up."

Hyde nodded in approval. "At the same time we want to get you working on our plan to close down the prison."

I passed the evenings writing letters on my typewriter. Then I would boil water for a rich cup of hot chocolate and powdered milk, climb into bed, arrange the four soft pillows into a comfy pile, turn on my lamp, and browse through the dozen wonderful books that had been loaned me.

The ancient, territorial instinct took over. This was *my* cave, secure, safe, inviolable. As I added more personal possessions and worked out my daily routine, this bleak box of concrete and steel—six feet wide, ten feet long—became home. This eerie animal sense of home-base is a crucial factor in prison life. Most recidivist criminals keep returning to prison because only here have they found this sort of cozy security.

A gentle rhythm developed. I slept through breakfast, woke around nine-thirty, drank steaming sweet rich coffee, shaved, and went to the yard at ten-thirty to meet Hyde and Newsom. Then we paced the rounds, talking furiously until lunch. After the light repast we would stretch out in the sun, smoke, talk with the many delegations that came to confer and report. An hour on the weights, surrounded by muscular giants grunting and groaning, followed by a cold shower in water fresh from the American River. Later, we would have ice-cream sundaes. That spring and summer the sky was cloudless and the sun shone for 157 days in a row.

When the yard cleared at three, I would return to my welcoming cell and read the *San Francisco Chronicle.* The count and mail were followed by dinner, always a gossipy occasion for dramatic tales: rape in the mattress room, drug busts in the kitchen, heroic crimes, clever capers, daring shoot-outs.

Around eight-thirty came the shower unlock. Cell doors opened and we padded down the cellblock in rubber sandals and stood under the steaming water, a soapy moment of Lifebuoy buffoonery.

Then, with the warm clean bodies of California's most vicious killers all tucked in their beds, one by one we spiraled down the creamy whirlpool of sleep. Half the cons had TV sets with silent ear-plugs. The blacks shouted back and forth from tier to tier, incessant ghetto jive and shuck. Trusties moved up and down the line, carrying contraband, passing notes, moving mysterious valuables.

Around ten I'd snack on a hot grilled cheese sandwich, chips, and pickles prepared by my next-cell neighbors: Drag Line, a jolly veteran of forty years federal and state time, and his paramour, a willowy soft-skinned "lady" of thirty, name of Wendell. When Drag Line removed his dentures and climbed into Wendell's bunk, toothless cries of pleasure filled the air.

I began work on Bob Hyde's ultimate legal writ, the one that would close down the prison system. In Folsom's comprehensive legal library he had researched every case challenging the consitutionality of prisons. And he had consulted with other con-lawyers, grizzled inmates with more legal experience than the Nixon Supreme Court.

In terse clear language our brief summarized the failures of the correctional system. It outlined the folly of confining men, at a cost of $10,000 annually per prisoner, in factories for the production of hardened criminals.

The court was requested to rule that prisons should be converted to profit-making vocational institutions. Prisoners who voluntarily accepted the work-option would be employed in gainful labor at union wages during the period of their incarceration. Eighty percent of these wages would be used to repay the crime victims for damages, to pay taxes, to repay the state for the trial, to support the prisoners' families, and to defray the board-room-medical expenses of inmates while in prison. Twenty percent of the wages would accumulate as a nest egg for the time of release.

Joanna obtained letters of support from over fifty retailers in the Bay Area who agreed to purchase items made in the prison shops—leather goods, art, metal jewelry, bookbinding, etc. Joanna also wangled letters from three electronic firms, which agreed to come into the prison and set up assembly lines.

The financial implications were impressive. Two thousand prisoners receiving $10,000 a year (only half the going union salary) pushed the GPP (Gross Prison Product) from zero to $20 million a year. As the state saved $20 million, now budgeted to run the prison, $40 million a year would be added to the state's economy.

Guards would be paid as supervising foremen and prison administrators would be paid at the same rate as executives running a $40-million-dollar business:

prisoners	$ 10,000
guards	$ 25,000
custody officers	$ 40,000
assistant wardens	$ 80,000
warden	$100,000

The brief converted every horrid negative of prison life into a free-enterprise program rewarding everyone involved. It concluded with a formal request for the federal court to order Folsom prison closed within ninety days if the California Department of Corrections failed to initiate a profit-making program.

Bob Hyde was beside himself with joy. "Now we get this manifesto into the hands of every inmate."

"How can you do that?" I asked. Surely they would bust us for distributing political pamphlets.

Hyde laughed gleefully. "Every inmate is entitled to make thirty photocopies of any legal writ he is involved in. This is a class-action suit in behalf of every con. So every con can get thirty copies."

The next morning Hyde was first in line at the photocopy office. Behind him were the following carefully selected inmates: a member of the Mexican Mafia, a Hells Angel, a Black Muslim, a Nazi, a doper, a popular Brother named Motor Mouth. It was the first time in prison history that the quarreling gangs had united on an issue. When Hyde finished at the machine, he went down the line handing copies to the others, each of whom proceeded to make thirty more. Before the slow-witted prison guard caught on, Hyde's pyramid strategy had flooded the yard with 1,000 copies of the brief to shut down the joint.

For the entire day normal yard activities were forgotten. Everyone was reading our lengthy brief. Illiterates gathered around to hear it read aloud.

And everyone was laughing. Cons ran over to guards showing how their salaries would be doubled. The guards surreptitiously studied our writ, chuckling among themselves. The part about the warden getting $100,000 was a gas. A couple of soreheads complained about guards getting more money than the inmates.

I mailed the brief to the federal court in Sacramento. It was official: legal action to change or close the prison was now in motion.

Next day Hyde, Newsom, and I were hauled, separately, before the captain of custody (the custody section being the police force within the prison) and sternly warned that no unauthorized organizations were permitted.

We had agreed beforehand on our answer:

"We formally request that you authorize PROBE as long as it engages in legal, peaceful, and constructive action."

The captain was not amused.

That night Hyde and I wrote a two-page brief, requesting that the federal court order prison officials to authorize PROBE.

Again we were called in and warned that if we continued our activities we'd been thrown in the hole or transferred.

We wrote another brief, requesting that the federal court enjoin prison authorities from any transfer or punitive action until a ruling had been handed down on our earlier writs.

The prison grapevine began reporting some curious reactions. A team of corrections lawyers and officials from Sacramento spent a day conferring with the warden and his staff. Spies overheard bitter arguments. It seemed the warden and some of the administrators from the capital liked our ideas. They wanted to move into full-scale court hearings, news coverage, and possible action. The hard-nosed custody faction was livid, eager to bust us for insubordination.

I was awakened before dawn by Drag Line. "Hey, home, they're shipping your buddy out."

Six brown-shirts with clubs were lined up in front of Bob Hyde's cell. He was piling his belongings into boxes and loading them onto a dolly.

Hyde looked at me and started to speak, but the guards shut him off.

"Write and we'll stay in touch," I called unhappily.[1]

We adjusted to our loss as slaves do, and prison life rolled on. The weeks flicked by like minutes. Every night I'd stand in the supper line marveling at the passing of another day. Prison, like youth, is wasted on people who can't appreciate it. No phone calls. No appointments. No rent. No duties. No worries or expectations. But excellent library facilities.

As director of my Folsom Bureau of Inspiration Joanna produced a new strategy each week to get me out. She had located a friendly gullible alcoholic who looked like me and tried to convince him to swap clothes with me in the visiting room. She advanced $200 to a man in Iowa who was going to build a helicopter that looked like a flying saucer. It was to sweep over the prison emitting unearthly sounds, frightening the guards away. Her mother had connections in the Vatican who could get her an audience with the Pope.

Joanna haunted the office of Governor Ronald Reagan and charmed his press secretary, hoping for a chance to spike the water cooler with a love drug. She talked her way into Governor-elect Jerry Brown's Plymouth, posing as an English reporter. To raise money she published and sold my books, *The Curse of the Oval Room* and *Starseed*. She was also trying to sell my 1,000-page testament on the evolution of neurotechnology through the twenty-four stages of intelligence—twelve terrestrial and 12 post-terrestrial—later published as *Exo-Psychology, The Intelligence Agents*, and *The Game of Life*.

It was generally agreed that no one ever worked harder to get a fellow out of jail than Joanna.

The next three months were among the most interesting of my life. The days spun by with smooth velocity. There was always some high intensity scene coming down. For three days I was the center of a gang confrontation. The Mexican Mafia tried to blackmail me. My pals quickly forged an alliance of bikers, blacks, Nazis, and dopers. At one point there were 500 men on the yard armed with knives, waiting to see if the leaders could effect a compromise. They did.

I spent two months working with a brilliant convict named Wayne Benner. We wrote *Terra II*, which defined migration from the planet as the goal of our species. To me this was the ultimate escape plot. Joanna published *Terra II* in a limited edition, which sold out and has since become a collector's item.

I was in the visiting room with Joanna plotting the escape-of-the-week when a guard approached our table.

"Leary, your visitation is terminated. You're being shipped out tomorrow. Report to your cell to pack up right now."

That night I checked with the prison grapevine to find out why I was being transferred. No one knew for sure. A convict who worked in administration reported that federal agents had been talking to the warden about my case. That gave me an uneasy feeling. They already had me. What more could they want?

THOMAS PYNCHON (1937-), American philosopher, graduated from Cornell University in 1958. He won the William Faulkner Award for best first novel with *V* (1963). After *The Crying of Lot 49* Pynchon wrote a third novel, *Gravity's Rainbow* (1974), which received the National Book Award and exultant praise from many critics. Since then this epic-encyclopedic masterpiece has been respectfully ignored.

Just as the *Divine Comedy* drama advertised the great philosophic-political conflicts of the Middle Ages, so *Gravity's Rainbow* confronts the issue of the twenty-first century: the attempt by the modern centralized state to co-opt science for power and control. Here we meet the demons, inquisitors, devils, and conspirators of the Information Age—the media-politicians and the brainwashers who use chemistry, physics, psychology, and space-engineering to manipulate people's minds.

Pynchon is routinely compared with Joyce because of the grand scope of his opus and because his life, too, has exemplified the sublime indifference, the elevated detachment of the philosopher-artist.

In an era when hype, image, and self-promotion are requisites to literary success, Pynchon has, ironically, disappeared. Rumor has it that he lives somewhere in Southern California, where he is studying mystical diagrams and writing the ultimate human-computer novel.

39. Escape Plot

VACAVILLE PRISON
APRIL, 1974

I awoke, opened my eyes, and found myself once again in a prison cell. This time it was Vacaville, a hospital for the criminally insane. I was not there as a patient but as a worker on the trusty staff. My light-emitting-diode watch flashed 8:00 a.m., Pacific Time. I yawned and stretched comfortably. My five cellmates had all departed for their jobs.

On the metal table next to my bunk I saw the *Wall Street Journal*, brought every morning by Everett (stock fraud).

I picked up the ceramic cup containing coffee crystals, sugar, and powdered cream and stirred in steaming hot water. Returning to my bunk

I opened the brown paper bag and selected a warm fresh-baked Danish roll, redolent with melted butter and strawberry jam. The rolls were smuggled daily out of the prison bakery by Marshall (heroin sales).

From a Chinese-inscribed silver case made in the prison hobby shop by Manolo (marijuana sales) I withdrew a cigarette, rolled to my particular taste—two parts Bugler for body, one part pipe-mix for bite, one part Kite for a dash of mint. I inhaled the rich smoke and felt the welcome nicotine buzz. The Danish roll crumbled sweetly on my tongue and the coffee bathed my throat.

After shaving I patted my face with the Byzantine scent of Aramis, smuggled into the prison by Jackie Dee, the cellblock barber (forgery). I greeted Tony (heroin possession), who was paid a carton of cigarettes a week to clean the cell. I dressed in soft tailored jeans, Yves St. Laurent sweater, tennis shoes. I felt tip-top, ready for a day of amusement and exercise.

At precisely 8:25 the cellblock guard shouted, "LOCK UP," and I stood by the door waiting to be released. The guard arrived and unlocked the tier door.

In contrast to grim gray Folsom, Vacaville was a modern sunlit facility. As I loped along my daily commute to the psychological testing section, I passed more than fifty inmates and guards. Each meeting demanded a conscious, precisely accurate social signal. Failure to say "Hey, man" to this one or smile at that one, or nod respectfully at another could set off a complex chain reaction, which if unchecked could mean violence or death. On the other hand I didn't dare smile at this one or stop to talk to the next, lest a new cycle of paranoia be set off.

The face-to-face contacts of prison-life require diplomatic sensitivities of razor-edge precision. In the outside world one can ignore, brush-by, insult others with little risk. Civilian elements connect in Brownian movement, interact, and split, leaving no trace. Familiars compete, derogate, shame, snob, act smart-ass, blunder, trample blindly through interpersonal scenes with relative impunity. Everyone jumps in a car and drives home.

Prison, however, is a psychlotron, a sealed container for interpersonal thermodynamics. A real or fancied snub festers in the closed heated atmosphere. There is no place to hide from the consequences of social blunder. Everyone knows everything about you. It took me some time after my release to adjust to the careless traffic of Main Street intercourse.

At the psychological testing section I strode by the check-in guard, who saluted me. "Morning, Doc."

"Morning, Officer Payne."

In the video room my friends and colleagues were waiting. Ron Alonzo, handsome, affable UCLA film wizard (child molesting), glib charming

Tom Riordan (stock swindler), and Betty, the soft-skinned blue-eyed civilian nurse. We drank coffee and exchanged prison gossip. Betty sat next to me at the table, her moist hand up under my shirt rubbing my back.

After a while Betty left. She winked to me. After a couple of minutes I nodded to Tom and walked down the hall to the big testing room. Betty was waiting for me behind the corner alcove.

She threw herself in my arms and squirmed and wiggled. Up came the sweater, no bra. She pulled my head down to her saucy breasts. Her skin was hot, starting chills in my spine, contracting my stomach, expanding my cock.

"Listen," I bleated. "We can't fool around in here. And Tom's giving tests in a few minutes . . ."

"Come on, baby, nothing's gonna stop us." She grabbed my hand, pulling me into the hallway. We walked to the janitor-supply room. She unlocked the door. We slipped inside, pulled off our clothes. The room was pitch black. She helped me undress. Her naked body was moist as hot octopus. I tried to love her standing but I was too tall. We grappled around giggling and groaning and stumbling over mop buckets. Brooms banging my face I was reeling from the high-school institutional smell of floor wax, Pinesol, teenage saliva, and dime-store perfume. We fell against a cardboard crate filled with paper towels, which I tore open.

We bumped down on the soft paper, and she said, "I fucked a prison guard all night long last night, thinking of you. That cute one, Mervin, on the afternoon shift. And this morning, when I was all dressed and hair all pinned up—ooooh, baby, I love you—I was just headed out the door, he grabbed me, and he fucked me on the rug in my apartment, and I was thinking of you when he was fucking me on my floor, and that's why I was late this morning."

When Betty left, flushed and wobbly, I went back to the video room and taped a group-therapy session that would later be replayed for the patients. After lunch I changed into tennis shorts and lay out on the grass between cellblocks, soaking up sun and reading Carl Sagan until the tennis courts opened.

After four hours of tennis, yoga and sunbathing, I followed the swarm back in for count. In the five minutes before lockup, I illegally showered, luxuriating in the hot splash, then the ice-cold. My man Duke, the guard, appeared at the door, pretending irritation. "Come on, Doc, what the fuck you think we're running here, a health spa?" Still dripping, I hopped down the cellblock, comically pretending to hurry.

After dinner and the ABC Evening News I returned to my cell and spent the next three hours typing my book on the evolution of the twenty-four stages of the nervous system—*The Game of Life.*

I was interrupted once by Duke, who had mentioned to me earlier that he had to do a surprise sweep of my locker for contraband. He half-heartedly poked through my clothes and idly opened a can of tennis balls. With his back to me he said in a low voice, "I keep hearing talk all over the joint about someone wanting to knock you off."

"That's just slammer gossip. I've been hearing it for three months," I said. "Who would want to kill me?"

"I'm not talking about the animals in here. I'm talking about the straights."

At 10:00 p.m. Duke came around for last count and lights out. I switched on my illegal gooseneck lamp. Mellow from a marijuana brownie I burrowed down into two soft pillows and read Solzhenitsyn's *First Circle*.

On Sunday Joanna was in the visiting room, literally jumping with excitement. "Listen, Timothy, you're getting out of here right away."

"Here we go again," I said, teasing. "Teleportation?"

"This is for real," she said with little-girl solemnity. "I was approached this week by some federal agents. They want to make a deal. If you'll talk to them, they'll move you to a special low-security compound. Then you can escape easily."

"No way. They'll want me to give information about the Weathermen who arranged my escape."

"They swear you won't have to testify against anyone."

"Then they want to discredit me."

"So what?" said Joanna impatiently. "Talk to them, string them along. Just don't tell them anything that can be used against anyone. Once you escape from prison, everyone will know we were using them. I can get money and a gun. I'll buy an escape car and rent a safe-house."

"I don't want to be called a snitch."

Joanna looked at me coolly. "Look here, you're starting to think like an institutional case. You're buying this disgusting lower-class hoodlum mentality. 'Snitch'—that's stupid jailhouse talk. Information is power. You're the one who's always saying intelligence is the name of the game. If they think you have facts they need, then we've got to bluff them into moving you to a place where you can escape."

"Well, I can't do anything until I run this by the Weathermen," I said.

My next step was to contact San Quentin Sammy, a lifer who I knew was connected to militant leftist groups. We met on the athletic field. I asked him if he could get a letter out of the prison to the Weathermen. He agreed.

That night in the mess hall I handed him a magazine in which I had hidden an unaddressed envelope containing words of warning and reassurance. A week later Sammy slipped me a note. The message was simple.

"We understand. Be careful." It was signed with a Chinese character *Huan* (Dispersion), the *I Ching* hexagram which had been thrown by the Weathermen in the hideout after my escape.

The following week Joanna was back with exciting developments. She had spent a long evening having dinner with two feds. "We're totally naive about how cops think," she said. "They're basically involved in their own departmental politics. The guys I got drunk with are Democrats. One of them opened up his vest and flashed me a silver PT-boat tie pin. They're Kennedy guys. They say they're friends."

"What do they want?" I asked uneasily.

"They say they need your help. What harm could it do to find out how? In a month we could be together underground."

A week later, while editing my newest complete system of philosophy, I was ordered to report to the custody department. It was eight-thirty in the evening.

The lieutenant was brusque. "Leary, you're being transferred. Go back to your cell and pack one bag with personal items. I want you back here in ten minutes."

I was stunned. Prisoners are normally transferred during the daytime. To be pulled out of my cell at night was an open signal that something very strange was happening. I returned to my cell and threw some toilet articles and my manuscripts in a bag. Two guards escorted me through the dark quiet corridors to the discharge room, where I was dressed out in a polyester blue suit, handcuffed, put in leg-irons.

I lay on the back seat of the sedan and tried to sleep. After midnight, somewhere near Bakersfield, the car pulled into a freeway restaurant. The guards unfastened the leg-irons and put a jacket over my hands to hide the cuffs. We sat in a back booth and ate cheeseburgers.

Around 7:00 a.m. we pulled into a parking lot in some suburb of Los Angeles. Three unmarked cars were waiting. Introductions all around: two narcs, three State of California investigators, and two FBI agents. Someone signed the release form, and one of the Vacaville guards unlocked my cuffs. I was escorted to a second-floor FBI office. It was Saturday morning. Except for us the place was deserted.

The narcs took me aside to say they were mainly interested in my participation in an anti-drug-abuse movie.[1]

The State of California spokesman was Jerry Utz, an assistant attorney general, who said that since I was a state prisoner his job was to assure that these proceedings were legal.

The senior FBI agent was Frankie, a good-looking street-wise man in his fifties. "Listen, Timmy," he said with his hand on my shoulder, "some of us in the Bureau are going out on a limb to work something out with you. If you cooperate with us, we can help you with that ten years you owe the federal government. But I warn you. If you fuck us around, I'll have you put on the main line of a federal prison with the jacket of a snitch. You won't last twenty-four hours. You understand?"

"No, not really." I was feeling nervous and confused. "What do you want to know?"

"For the moment we just want to get acquainted. Maybe there are some things you can explain to us. Like how come nice upper-middle class kids got involved in this revolution bullshit. For example, who is behind the Weathermen? That's the sort of thing we're interested in."

Frankie assembled all of us around a long table and turned on a tape recorder. "First thing we want to hear about is your escape and your asylum in Algeria."

I re-told the story of my hair-breadth escape, which had been published in *Confessions of a Hope Fiend*. One of the narcs dozed. Frankie drummed his fingers on the table. Had I lost my Celtic story-telling eloquence? Someone went out for lunch. Cheeseburgers again. I continued to describe the events in Algeria. As the afternoon dragged on, Frankie fell into a foul mood. He kept interrupting me with questions about contacts with foreign groups—any Cubans around, any Vietnamese, Koreans, Chinese? He was obviously not happy with my answers.

I asked where I'd be staying and when I'd see Joanna.

"We're making arrangements," said Frankie, curtly. "For the next few days you'll be staying in municipal jails around LA."

That night I stayed in the La Habra jail. I was the only prisoner in the place. A sign said there was no smoking, and I had to argue long and loud to persuade the jailer to give me my Camels.

The California inspectors picked me up and we reassembled in the motel room of Jerry Utz. Frankie, who was apparently in charge of this caper, had to wait for instructions from the Bureau in Washington. The narcs, always highly critical of their rivals in the FBI, were pissed off at the delay.

"That's the FBI for you. Every time Frankie wants to go out for lunch, he has to call the Bureau to see if he should get a hamburger or cheeseburger."

Nothing happened for a couple of days. Then I was led out of my cell to a conference room, and there was Joanna with the two narcs. She looked worried. The cops left us alone for a few minutes.

"What's going on?" I asked.

"Frankie's having trouble back in Washington. They're not happy with your answers."

"What do they want to know?"

"Beats me," said Joanna.

"What about my transfer to a military base and all that. This city-jail confinement is a drag."

Joanna looked at me and shrugged. She knew what I meant. The escape plot was languishing.

A couple of days later the California inspectors drove me to Terminal Island, the federal prison just south of Los Angeles. They took off my handcuffs, and we chatted amicably down the Harbor Freeway. They had little use for the FBI.

Joanna moved into the nearby Queen Mary Hotel and taxied to the prison every day. On the visiting terrace we looked out over the bay and brooded.

To use up her nervous energy Joanna was plotting with the narcs to fool the FBI, and plotting with the FBI to capture my archives from Michael Horowitz—his worst paranoia come true. She continually boasted to everyone—strangers in the hotel restaurant, bartenders—about everything that she was doing. Not to mention squandering our getaway money on high living, denouncing her part-time boyfriend Dennis Martino to the narcs, behaving generally like an unguided missile—uncontrollable, irrepressible, unstoppable. She kept me entertained eight hours a day, six days a week.

One day Bob Dellinger, screenwriter, former inmate now acting as instructor in a creative writing class, showed up outside my cell. He said that G. Gordon Liddy, a star student in his class, sent his best wishes and good luck. I was glad to get this message from my old rival and returned the salutations.[2]

Dellinger told me a funny story about himself. He had written a movie script about a scam so good that instead of filming it he pulled it off. The ending however, was not happy—a dozen feds surrounding his car with drawn guns and a stretch at TI, where under his editorship the prison paper won national prizes.

The literary level of Terminal Island took another jump when Eddie Bunker moved into the next cell. Author of the best-seller *No Beast So Fierce* he spent his days in the visiting room discussing the script with a screenwriter. Eddie was one tough customer who took no shit from the guards. The last time I saw him he was on the floor with three guards pounding away at him. The next day they shipped him off to a max-joint.

The Congressional Watergate hearings took place during my time at TI. I knew I had no chance of getting out of federal prison as long as Nixon was in office. But if Nixon fell . . . suddenly escape was not the only option.

✳   ✳   ✳

Frankie kept coming around to ask more vague questions about the Weathermen, at the same time making it clear that I wasn't telling him anything he didn't already know. He was obviously getting heat from Washington about the lack of success in my case. When I asked him about transfer to an open prison, he remained evasive.

"Frankie, what is it you want me to tell you?"

"I already asked you. Who got these college kids and the Weathermen involved with political violence? Who led them into that? Who? Give me names, goddamn it."

Suddenly I caught on. "Foreign influence!" I said joyfully. "Moscow, Hanoi, Havana! You want foreign names, right?"

Frankie looked hopeful. "That's what we've been told. What other explanation is there for this sudden spurt of terrorism? You've traveled in the Third World. You've lived with these people. What countries supported the Weathermen? Who were the contacts?"

I was still puzzled. Why were they interested in foreign influences on the Weathermen? The Weathermen were finished.

"Were there any ties between the Weathermen and Communist countries while you were in Algeria?"

"Let me think." I tried to remember back to Algiers, the dinners with Brazilians, the drinks with the Canary Islands Liberation front. "Okay, delegations of American leftists did pass through Algiers on the way to China, North Korea, North Vietnam. In Algeria all visiting leftists made obligatory visits to the North Vietnamese Embassy, where they handed out those steel rings with the inscription 'FLN-SVN.' The rings were supposed to be made from metal salvaged from downed American planes."

Frankie's eyes flicked in interest. "What about Bernadine Dohrn's secret visits to Algeria?"

"They were so secret I never heard of them. Look, Frankie, if you're really looking for my take on this, I'll be glad to give you the straight scoop."

"Good," said Frankie.

"Your guys in the Federal Bureau of Investigation are making the same mistake that J. Edgar Hoover made and Johnson and Nixon made: trying to blame domestic unrest on foreign agitation. That's all right when you're trying to get appropriations. But it's disastrous to believe your own lie. The counter-culture in this country, the peace movement, the cultural revolution, is not inspired from abroad. It's red-white-and-blue American. The Weathermen, in spite of their Maoist rhetoric, are as American as the Dallas Cowboys."

Frankie was not happy to hear this. He held his head in his hand. Then he dropped the hand smack against the table. "Goddamn it, why do you go around saying such things? Listen, Timmy, if you go on being a smart-ass with me, I'll get you for it."

He stormed out of the conference room, leaving me worried and puzzled.

Frankie's wrath was not long delayed. Two federal marshals pulled me out of Terminal Island at three o'clock the next morning. They wouldn't tell me where we were going. They took off the handcuffs at LAX. "You make a move, Doc, and we'll shoot you."

Minneapolis-St. Paul. En route the marshals regaled me with stories cops love, the ones that make all non-cops seem like assholes. Catching that lifer masturbating in his cell with a broomhandle up his ass. Or the double-jointed convict who could suck his own penis *and* asshole. Cops love asshole jokes. And then there was the prisoner masturbating anally with a warm curvy irresistibly sexy light bulb: he gave it a little push too hard and, slurp, it was trapped inside. Imagine that. Some problem for the surgeons. Heh-heh.

Two federal prison guards took me from the St. Paul airport to Sandstone Federal Prison, about a hundred miles north. Nobody in my world knew where I was. Or why.

After I was booked and dressed out in blue denims, the warden said to me: "We're giving you a break, Leary. We're going to put you on the main line."

"Thanks, warden. After all that time in solitary the sun will feel good."

"But for your own protection we're booking you under a different name."

"You gotta be kidding."

"Instructions from Washington. Your new name is Charles Thrush."

Thrush, a songbird. I had to laugh. "Is this some sick FBI snuff joke? That's an open license to kill me. You know that."

The warden wouldn't look me in the eye. He kept examining his clasped hands. "I'm just following orders."

Sandstone was a spanking neat little prison in the farmlands of Minnesota, built with the patronage of Hubert Humphrey. The hole was clean as a whistle. A metal bunk, a Muriel Humphrey mattress, a beautifully painted (gray) wash basin and toilet. Minimalist design.

Footsteps in the hall, the jangle of keys, clang, clang.

"Chow."

A tray appeared in the "swine trough." I called out to the guard, "Could I get some books?"

"No books in the hole, Thrush."

The food was sensational, fresh from the prison farm. Thick juicy pork chops. Tender corn. Sweet newly cut green beans.

I did some yoga, reflecting on the curious turn of events. The Bureau wasn't kidding around. They had booked me as Thrush, and by tomorrow everyone in the joint would assume that some weird snitch scene was coming down.

Lights went out automatically at ten. I could see the constellation Scorpio from my window; that's how I knew the time. Around two I heard the metal slot being unpadlocked.

A flashlight shone on my bed. I leaned up. "Hey, how about a book to read."

"No books for special cases." The voice was a black man's.

A few minutes later the metal slot was unpadlocked again. The black's voice said, "Here, read this."

I woke up at dawn and started reading *Gravity's Rainbow* by Thomas Pynchon. It was about CIA mind-control, drugs, and rocket-politics. I read until lights out, the best book I had run across since *Ulysses*. I started reading again at dawn. When I finished, I started over at page one, underlining and outlining.

The next day good old reliable Joanna showed up. Frankie and the FBI had refused to tell her where I was, but she had found out from some of her narc friends. That was the main gripe I had about Joanna, those narc friends. She really related to them. There was one top narc who would call her on the phone almost every night and talk for hours about his job, his marriage, the meaning of life.

Anyway, she had terrible news. The current issue of *Newsweek* magazine contained a "Periscope" item, obviously leaked by the FBI, stating that I was ratting on dope-dealer friends and the Weathermen. Another story based on FBI sources appeared in the *San Francisco Examiner* claiming that many arrests were coming down as a result of my snitching. Because of threats against my life, it said, I was being kept in special protective custody.

The fact that I was being publicly libeled as a snitch was very alarming; but the real setback was the escape plan. I had been in solitary confinement or the max-max hole every night since leaving Vacaville. While Joanna and I were dourly reviewing the situation, I was called to the Warden's office. He motioned to the phone. An agent from the Chicago office of the FBI told me he had been assigned to take over my case. Frankie, it seemed, had just been retired. I spoke forcefully to the new agent, protesting the indisputable fact that I had been set up by the Bureau and refusing to talk until I had consulted with a lawyer. The warden watched all this with a troubled expression on his face. He knew that everything I was saying about the set-up was true.

Joanna was never more magnificent than during this time in Minnesota. Here she was, this upper-class European lady living in a boarding house in an American Gothic farm-town where the liquor store didn't carry *any* champagne, not to mention *Dom Perignon*, and there were no French cigarettes within 500 miles, and nothing to do from the end of visiting hours at 3:30 p.m. until noon the next day, except continue to act like the most gutsy intelligent woman who ever worked to get her man out of prison. Ironically, *Rolling Stone* and *Playboy* magazines were being fed stories at that very moment about what a dangerous treacherous person she was.

Joanna started using all the connections she had established with Democratic politicians and liberal law enforcement agents during the last few months. In touch with friends she had made in Senator Hubert Humphrey's office, she ended up flying to Washington with Hubert, wangling introductions to some of his allies in the Justice Department.

My instinct was to call in the press and blow the thing wide open, but Joanna felt that public disclosure would ruin any chance of my being put in prison where escape was possible. She was trying to get me transferred to a federal camp for "witnesses" (like John Dean and Howard Hunt), where security was pretty loose. But the FBI wanted to keep me on their string. So we decided that Joanna would return to California and somehow persuade some law enforcement agency to bring me back to the West Coast.

I went back to reading *Gravity's Rainbow.*

A few days later I was called down to the warden's office. He was *very* friendly. Inviting me to pour myself a cup of coffee and relax he recounted several typical warden stories—machine-gunning cellblocks at Leavenworth during a riot, bloody bodies falling off third-floor tiers. He was so cordial. He took a newspaper from his desk and tossed it to me. "Big development in the Nixon case," he said. "I guess they got the smoking gun."

I scanned the story quickly. Nixon was finished.

"Good break for you," said the warden. "There'll be a lot of people in high places running around trying to protect their asses."

I suddenly realized that this guy was a Democrat. I mean, they wouldn't put a Republican bureaucrat in Hubert's own little backyard prison. The warden walked me to the door with his arm over my shoulder. "Yup," he said. "A lot of these guys that have been down on you are going to be back-tracking fast." He gave me a pat on the back. "I like the way you hold your mud, Timmy."

Why do these guys call me Timmy, I wondered. At fifty-five I was older than most of them, and they still treated me like their kid brother.

I got transferred back to California, out from under the FBI, in about a week.[3]

G **IORDANO** **BRUNO** (1548-1600), Italian psychologist and philosopher, was educated as a Dominican monk. At the age of twenty-eight his independent thinking led to accusations of heresy, which forced him to exile in France, England, and Germany. He taught at various universities, but his continuing challenges to dogma prevented him from receiving a permanent position.

His first work, published in 1582, dealt with memory and associative learning. His two greatest philosophic works, *De la Causa, principio e uno* and *De l'infinito, univesi e mundi,* forecasted modern developments in the study of psychology. Rejecting the supremacy of a single fixed reality he demonstrated that perception is relative to our position in space and time.

At the height of the Counter-Reformation Bruno dared to re-state the gnostic-pantheistic theory that God is within each person, within each element of creation. Bruno is generally acknowledged as the first person to suggest that our sun is but one star in an infinite universe of innumerable worlds containing sentient beings.

Continually subject to surveillance by the Inquisition Bruno was lured to Venice in 1591 and arrested by agents of the Vatican. He was then brought to Rome in chains and kept incarcerated for eight years, undergoing trial by Inquisition prosecutors. For his refusal to recant he was burned alive.

40. Kidnapped by the Feds

AUGUST 1974

First stop was the Glendale city jail. As a protected case I had an eight-cell wing all to myself. The jailer was a gentleman with a master's degree in sociology. He was authorized to have bottles of wine on hand to cool out hallucinating alcoholics, so every night around 10:00 he'd give me a tall glass of sherry and we'd talk things over. He let Joanna have me in a secluded room where we enjoyed some funny acrobatic love-making.

By this time Joanna had put together quite a crew of unwitting helpers—several narcs, some local and one federal, Jerry Utz, the California assistant attorney general, and a top federal prosecutor who had just gone into private practice. They arranged for my transfer to a special country-club camp near Sacramento. Protective-custody prisoners were allowed such freedoms as going into town to catch movies, being alone with their wives. It was a walk-away scene, Joanna said.

As I came off the plane at Sacramento, a federal marshal's car roared up under the wing. The driver was a blond fullback type with a shotgun cradled under his left arm. In the front passenger seat, also holding a shotgun, sat the Chief Marshal for Eastern California, Art van Court, a stocky good-looking man with alert eyes, forever scanning for signs of ambush. Art had been told by the FBI to expect bands of murderous Black Panthers, crazed dope dealers, and Weathermen terrorists. With deep sincerity van Court grasped my hand and assured me that he would protect my life if necessary at the cost of his own.

As we headed north on Highway 40 van Court listed his qualifications to act as my official bodyguard. He had performed that intimate function for Barry Goldwater in 1964, never being more than ten feet from the Senator from the moment of his nomination for president until the morning after his defeat. And he had served as Governor Ronald Reagan's chief of security.

Since my plan was escape rather than protection, I was less than thrilled by the marshal's reassurances.

"Tell me about this special camp I'll be staying at."

"The camp?" replied van Court. "Oh gee, that was closed down four months ago. But don't worry about your security. You'll be in a special solitary lockup in the Placerville County jail. No chance these assholes can get you there. You'll be under twenty-four-hour watch."

"That's wonderful," I said.

This was the thirty-sixth jail I had inhabited in my outlaw career, and the worst. At first I was locked up under the name William James in a tank with about twenty other inmates, mainly kids, in for small-quantity dope possession or car crimes, and it was fascinating to be part of their merry rebellious gang. But then I was recognized and immediately isolated in a ten-by-ten cell, where I lay like a mummy for three months. No typewriter. No television. No human contacts. Only books for company.

I was allowed an outing twice a week. I'd be called to the property room to dress in civilian clothes, and two marshals would take me to a car with Joanna waiting in the back seat. Then we'd be driven to a shopping mall to purchase toiletries and stationery and then to a restaurant for a group luncheon. All the while Joanna and I were computing the escape options.

Sold on the story that I had valuable information van Court was bewildered. He expected FBI agents to come to interrogate me. Week after week there was no word. The Bureau was trying to put on the pressure. It had been six months since my disappearance into the penal underground. No one, except for Joanna and a few law-enforcement people, knew where I was.

By isolating me and circulating the story that I was targeted for assassination by left-wing militants and dope dealers the feds expected to achieve two ends: 1) to coerce me into cooperating with them and 2) to aggravate division and mistrust among factions within the counter-culture. It was a classic maneuver in provocation and media politics, and it succeeded in stirring up a good deal of paranoia.

Joanna rented a hideaway apartment in Sacramento, scored a .38 revolver, and urged me to be vigilant for the moment to initiate Escape Plan 42. The pressure mounted.

Enter Dan McGowan, FBI agent from the Chicago office, an expert on the Weathermen. Right away I liked Dan, a serious scholarly person with wide cultural interests. We had several talks about the sociology of terrorism and anarchist politics.

The next Sunday morning he had me called to the property room, where I changed into a blue-white seersucker suit and white shoes. Dressing me in the most un-hip costumes conceivable was one of the marshals' more brilliant strategies to throw off pursuers. Guards led me out to the car—van Court driving, McGowan riding shotgun, Joanna sitting demurely in the corner of the back seat. After the jail was out of sight she asked the marshal, "Now?"

"Oh shoot, you guys are too much," laughed Art van Court. "Okay, now!"

Joanna threw herself in my arms. I fell on top of her, and we embraced for miles down Highway 40. Then Joanna took my hand, pushed it down, down, down her smooth thigh past her knee into her soft boot. I could feel the loaded .38 revolver there.

The official reason for this outing was to locate the Weathermen safehouse where I had hidden out the night of my escape from prison. McGowan said they were looking for documents that may have been left behind.

Joanna and I had our own program. We planned to direct the two federal agents to a deserted lot in San Francisco, pull out the .38, disarm them, order them into the trunk of the car, and drive to where our getaway car was parked. Joanna had $14,000 in cash. We would fly to Mexico City and from there make our way to Brazil, where we both had many friends.

We drove around the Castro district for an hour, but I just couldn't seem to find the Weathermen safe-house. So I suggested that we drive to a deserted spot where we could put the street map on the hood of the car and refresh my memory. We drove down a deserted alley behind a factory.

As Art parked the car, Joanna surreptitiously pulled out the gun, moving my hand along the smooth barrel. I motioned it away. As we spread the street map over the hood, my brain was flashing with alarm: these two honorable and decent but gung-ho cops would resist. They knew well enough that I wasn't a killer. And I knew well enough that they were indoctrinated to kill me if I tried to escape. During the eighteen months that my law-enforcement friends were hiding me out under false names in various jails—in La Habra, Yolo, Whittier, Sandstone, Glendale, Placerville, and Nevada City—they often warned me that they'd shoot if I made a move.

Would I kill them if they tried to kill me? Interesting question.

I tried to think it through in steps. If I did shoot van Court and McGowan, the noise would resound in the alley. BOOM! BOOM! And what would I do with their bleeding bodies? And the warm blood on my hands. And their grieving families. I had no fear for the safety of Joanna and myself. We were long gone beyond fear.

"Apres. Trop dangereux ici," I whispered. My heart was pounding. This was turning out to be a lot less impersonal than the scenes I had rehearsed so many times in my cell.

After my futile searching the agents gave up the quest. Joanna made van Court drive around until we found a tobacco store that carried Gitanes. At a carry-out restaurant we bought chicken and fried clams. I suggested that we picnic on the secluded shore just below the Presidio and the Golden Gate Bridge. Joanna nodded in eager agreement.

We ate lunch swinging our legs over the stone seawall, watching flocks of sea gulls and tourists. Not the place to make a break.

The picnic over, we headed across the Golden Gate Bridge for Sacramento. Art still driving. Joanna huddled in the corner of the back seat. Not at all sure about what I was feeling I hung my head and saw at my feet an enormous .357 Magnum. It had fallen out of Dan's holster and wedged under the seat. I picked it up holding it low. It weighed a ton. I nudged Joanna. Her eyes bulged.

I just held the heavy piece as the car rolled along the highway. Joanna reached in her boot and pulled out *her* piece. She looked at me with child-like expectation, a pretty twelve-year-old about to be taken to the circus. I waited. The two cops chatted away innocently. It was every prisoner's all-time escape dream. Sitting in the back seat holding the .357 Magnum, I confronted the dissenter's dilemma: could I kill the KGB agents for my freedom?

I tapped Dan on the shoulder. "Let me see that map."

The FBI agent handed me the map. I leaned over the front seat and opened it so that it covered Dan's lap. I slid the gun under the map so that Dan could see I had it. I dropped the gun on his lap and patted him on the shoulder conspiratorially. Now it was his turn for an eye bulge. He nodded gratefully. Joanna looked at me in disappointment. [1]

The next visiting day Joanna reported that she had closed the hideout apartment and thrown the .38 away. She was enthusiastic about a *new* plan. "I've finally found out what the FBI wants you to do for them.

It seems the Justice Department is investigating FBI burglaries of the homes of Weathermen friends and relatives. Over twenty FBI agents could be indicted and sent to prison. If the FBI can prove that the Weathermen were supported by foreign powers, then all the break-ins by intelligence agencies can be justified under national security. If you can come up with some foreign connections to the Weathermen, you can help save their asses."

"So far as I know the North Vietnamese government wasn't interested in helping a dozen campus crazies bomb ROTC buildings."

Exasperated she said, "Can't you remember some facts that might suggest foreign influence to a juror?"

"Sure. I could cite dozens of circumstantial facts that might help the FBI case."

"Then they'll cut you loose."

We looked at each other and laughed in relief. For over two years we had centered our lives around flamboyant plans for escape and life on the run. Now we were going straight. So to speak.

"While I think about that, why don't you take a rest," I said. We decided that she deserved a few weeks on the beach in Marbella with her mother.

Marshal van Court, still sincerely believing that doper and radical hit squads were relentlessly closing in on the Placerville jail, moved me one night under the cover of darkness to the county jail in Nevada City. My name there was Peter London. For four months I lived in the trusties' cellblock, writing *What Does WoMan Want?* and enjoying the camaraderie of jailhouse life. Sixteen rowdies in one room.

Three times a week the marshals would drive me to an unused camp near Folsom, where I'd spend the afternoon playing handball with Jerry Utz. Sometimes friendly fellows from the Justice Department would come around to chat. It didn't seem like they were trying to finagle information. They just wanted me to know they were my friends. For some future day, maybe? On one such occasion we organized a touch football game— van Court, two marshals, and me against two federal prosecutors, one FBI agent, and Jerry Utz.

The next stop was the county jail in Yolo, California, where my name was Thomas Pynchon. I had three cells all to myself: one my bedroom, one an exercise room, and one an office. The sheriff liked me. He sent in a black-and-white TV set and a large table for my typewriter, books, and papers.

Steamed up on the monastic high—celibacy—I wrote feverishly, completing *What Does WoMan Want?* For the first time since Vacaville I had access to scientific books and magazines. I spent at least eight hours a day reading immunology, astronomy, genetics, neurology, gerontology, geology.

The latest data from these sciences, revealed by powerful new instruments (electron microscopes, linear accelerators, radio telescopes, PET scans, computer animation techniques), seemed to be advancing humanity toward a relativist perspective. The mechanistic Newtonian model of the universe was steadily giving way to an Einsteinian continuum. Everything in the universe—from galaxies to quarks—was seen to be alive, evolving, sending out decipherable signals, and susceptible to change by intelligent human intervention. A new positive humanistic science was happening.

I was thrilled, intoxicated, inspired to observe the philosophic trend occurring in every field, giving power and control back to the intelligent individual.

G **ERARD K. O'NEILL** (1927-), physicist and space philosopher, received a B.A. from Swarthmore and a Ph.D. from Cornell in 1957. Since that year he has taught physics at Princeton, becoming a full professor in 1965.

In the late 1960s O'Neill assigned his undergraduates the following question: Is the surface of a planet like Earth the place to run an industrial civilization? After a semester of systems analysis and feasibility surveys the answer came back: No. O'Neill and his students went on to develop plans for building industrial parks and comfortable habitats in high orbit around the globe, using raw material from the lunar surface.

When his papers on the technical and economic practicality of space colonization were rejected by scientific journals, O'Neill started presenting his plans in informal college lectures (the same tactic used by the Harvard/Millbrook researchers a decade before). Informed and methodical these lectures made the case that migration to the high frontier within the next few decades will be as profitable and as necessary as the migration from the Old to the New World. As Christopher Columbus found in his day, the only obstacles are political and ideological.

O'Neill continues to be the country's most articulate spokesman for off-planet migration and post-terrestrial evolution. His published works include *Elementary Particle Physics* (with coauthor David Cheng), *High Frontier*, and *Two Thousand and Eighty One: A Hopeful View of the Human Future.*

41. Freedom?

SEPTEMBER 1975
SAN DIEGO

Just past La Jolla, going south, Highway 5 climbs a hill and there, below you, sparkling, shimmering, marine-blue is San Diego—Miami Beach West, prettiest city on the continent. Open sea-side scenery, beaches, islands, white-sails, causeways.

Right in the heart of downtown there is this strange slender brown wedge of a skyscraper with no commercial signs, no lights at night: the Metropolitan Correctional Center, the federal slammer. Hardly a walk-away camp.[1]

The two escort marshals, Jonny and Pete, fell silent as they drove along the waterfront, past the airport, past the flashy marina restaurants, and turned up a side street to the joint. They were sorry to see me go. We had hung out together for almost a year now. Jonny and I had played several hundred handball games together. Pete had typed the final manuscript of *What Does WoMan Want?*

While we waited for the gate to open, Pete tossed me the cuffs, which

363

I slipped on. Jonny opened the trunk and pulled out the carton containing my few personal possessions.

"You checking me in under my right name?" I asked quietly.

Pete and Jonny shot guilty glances at each other.

"Come on, man," I said. "You guys aren't going to do that to me again. It's a set-up."

The marshals stood in silence. Then Jonny said, "Look, Tim, it's orders. And the Marshal's tried. He almost got himself fired yesterday fighting with Washington. The FBI still wants you to talk."

"Okay," I said gently. "What's my name? J. Edgar Loser?"

"Be our guest. You get to choose your name again."

"Okay. My name is Bruno. First name, Giordano. That's G-I-O-R-D-A-N-O."

"One other thing, Tim. This cellblock you're going to is heavy-duty bad guys. Wild men. Killers with prices on their heads. If it looks too heavy, just tell the guards, and they'll put you in solitary."

This was some plush prison: spacious hotel-style lobby, wall-to-wall carpets, pool tables, wide stairs leading to lounges with easy chairs, color TVs. In a lower lounge seven inmates in jumpsuits sat eyeing me. I stared back coolly. A guard showed me to my cell—a narrow room with bed, desk, toilet, medicine cabinet, face bowl—like a room in a brand-new Holiday Inn. Through the thick windows I could look down on San Diego Harbor and the bridge to Coronado.

I walked back down to the lounge to check out the other guests. Two mafiosos: Guido, a hulking frowning man around fifty, and Joey, a younger good-looking Las Vegas type—both unmistakably killers. There was a smart sleek Mexican, also a killer. Two sullen whites, both criminally insane. One sturdy cheerful Irishman. One American Indian, a Sioux, with mad eyes. Introductions and handshakes completed I wandered up to the central lobby. A storeroom contained some books and magazines. I read a le Carre spy novel in my cell until late.

I rose around eleven, shaved, showered and started working on the Mr. Coffee machine. Murphy, sitting apart at a table, motioned me over. He spoke with great care.

"Listen, I don't wanna push into your business, except you should know that everyone here knows who you are. I been a fan of yours for years. You changed my life, man."

Murphy began laughing. "Jeez, man, you'll never know what a flap you caused with the Mafia heavies when you walked in. When we got word yesterday that a new man was coming up, everyone got nervous. Everyone here's got a price on his head. Like the narcs are trying to kill the Mexican. So Guido, he's a capo from New Orleans, screams to Joey: 'Giordano Bruno! Bruno! He's got to be one of us. But from where? You know any Brunos from Buffalo, Joey?' The two toughest mafiosos in the country wetting their pants. Then you walked in with those shades looking like the snakiest hit-man ever left Sicily. Did you learn that at Harvard? While you were in your cell reading, Joey's on the phone long-distance, calling all over the East Coast. Even called his mother to find out who you were."

After a month the fiction of my identity dissolved into farce. The San Diego press was hassling the warden to confirm rumors that the Famous Escapee was being held in the hometown slammer. Many cities are proud of their prisons and the notorious inmates.[1]

A cunning plot was devised to take the warden off the PR hot-seat. I was flown to Sacramento to spend the night in my old cell in the Yolo County jail; the next morning I was flown back to San Diego and registered under my own name. A press release then truthfully announced that I had just checked into the Federal Hilton.

Joey told me he phoned his mother with great pride to tell her the true identity of his new friend. "Know what she said? She said, 'Stay away from that man, Joey, he'll get you in trouble.' "

WINTER 1975-1976

By now I was really cooking with the reception and transmission of words. Twelve hours a day reading and writing. Lots of science. Thus it happened that I stumbled onto the great space colony revelation: that the next step in human evolution was up. Up into high orbit. Professor Gerard O'Neill of Princeton, in Stewart Brand's magazine, *Co-Evolution Quarterly*, overturned our billion-year-old commitment to planetary gravity. He showed that the surface of a planet was the most unwieldy, expensive, and dangerous place to conduct a technological civilization. We were no longer doomed to cling like barnacles to the slimy surface of this heavy planet. We could now migrate into space. O'Neill was not talking Star Trek fantasy or Sagan-stuff about colonizing other planets; he was pointing out that the next easy step was migration to the orbital frontier. In the initial log-cabin era we would send up Space Lab platforms, bringing up tools and materials to build industrial parks and solar stations. Eventually we would go on to fabricate mini-worlds, territories that the restless wave of pioneers would then inhabit. All this would be done with less expense than building new cities on the home planet.[2]

As a lifelong escape artist, I was thrilled to learn that there was a way out of here.

One evening in February a headline in the *San Francisco Chronicle* caught my eye! NEW JFK STORY—SEX, POT WITH ARTIST. James

Truitt, the source for this sensational story, was identified as a former assistant to Philip Graham, publisher of the *Washington Post*. In interviews with the *National Enquirer*, Associated Press, and *Washington Post* Truitt revealed that a woman named Mary Pinchot Meyer had conducted a two-year love affair with President John Kennedy and had smoked marijuana with him in a White House bedroom. A confidante of Mary Meyer, Truitt told a *Post* correspondent that she and Kennedy met about thirty times between January 1962 and November 1963, when Kennedy was assassinated. Mary Meyer told Truitt that JFK had remarked: "This isn't like cocaine. I'll get you some of that."

Truitt claimed that Mary Meyer kept a diary of her affair with the president, which was found after her death by her sister Toni Bradlee and turned over to James Angleton, who took the diary to CIA headquarters and destroyed it. According to the *Post* "another source" confirmed that Mary Meyer's diary was destroyed: "This source said the diary . . . contained a few hundred words of vague reference to an unnamed friend."

Kenneth P. O'Donnell, former White House appointments secretary, confirmed that Mary Meyer made visits to the White House but denied allegations of a love affair.

Toni Bradlee was quoted by the Associated Press as saying, "I knew nothing about it when Mary was alive."

According to the *Post*,

> Angleton, who resigned as chief of CIA counterintelligence in 1975 following disclosure of some illegal activities by his department, said that Meyer had been a "cherished friend" of his and his wife's. He said that he had assisted the family after Meyer's death in a "purely private capacity," also making the funeral arrangements. He refused to say whether there had been a diary.

I lit a Camel, walked to the window, and looked through the bars on San Diego Bay. So it *was* JFK that Mary had been turning on with. Once again I sensed that Mary Pinchot Meyer's life and death were an important part of modern history. More than we are ever likely to know.

After Jerry Brown became governor I was discharged from California custody, having served thirty-two months for two roaches plus the escape—twenty months longer than the maximum set in judicial guidelines for such offenses.

I had served almost two years on the Laredo case. The maximum guideline-sentence for this crime was one year. Still the federal parole board wouldn't let me go. In turning me down they cited my previous criminal record—a $35 traffic offense dating back to 1938. It looked as though I'd be in prison until the Democrats re-took Washington in November 1976. Or 1980.

In 1970, before my escape, the Federal Appeals Court had ruled that it was illegal to hold me without bail. So my lawyers, Jim McPherson of New Orleans and John Milano (a former federal prosecutor who felt I was getting a raw deal) contacted my old nemesis Judge Connally to get him to set a bond. It was eleven years after my first trial. Marijuana was now a middle-class recreational drug. But the crusty jurist hadn't mellowed a bit. He passionately tried to convince my counsel that I was still a nefarious criminal peddling dangerous ideas.

His zeal couldn't have been good for his heart. The judge died of a stroke a week later, while out hunting.

Judge Connally's place on the bench was assigned to a young jurist with an Irish name. He followed the law and signed the papers releasing me on appeal bond.

John Milano went to pick up my walking papers in the federal courthouse across the street from the prison. From my cell I watched John run down the courthouse steps with a smile on his face. That was the moment when the lawyer business really made sense, springing someone who deserved to be free.

A swarm of media people were waiting when I walked out of the prison. Lots of local friends had assembled too, and a cry of welcome was raised. I flashed the McLuhan smile, waving in triumph. The ten-year hassle over the silver box of grass was over. I was a free man.

But was I? As Joanna, her mother Marisia, John Milano, and I were getting into the car, a man in a dark suit rushed up. "The federal marshal wants you to report to his office right away."

I turned to John. "They have no hold on you," he said.

"Tell him we're celebrating. I'll phone him tomorrow."

Joanna and I spent the night in La Valencia, a romantic Spanish-style hotel on the beach at La Jolla. We were eating breakfast in the hotel dining room the next morning when two men approached our table, federal marshals.

"We have been instructed by Washington to tell you that your life is in danger. You are hereby advised to accept the protection of the Marshal. Or you'll be dead in seventy-two hours."

I winked at Joanna, continued eating my scrambled eggs. "What does that involve?"

"We give you new identification and locate you in a safe place. You'll be paid $800 a month as long as you remain underground."

I didn't bother to argue. I was pretty certain that the report wasn't true. Many leftist militants disliked me for having escaped from Eldridge Cleaver and having denounced violent revolution. But I was willing to gamble on the moral sanity of the Weathermen and the American left. However nutty their rhetoric and their hopes for armed revolution, they were not assassins.[3]

"I want to talk to Washington before making a decision," I said. "Have some coffee, Marshal, while we finish our breakfast."

The two marshals looked around the dining room nervously. "I don't think we should be sitting exposed in a public place," said one.

I phoned one of my contacts in the Justice Department. Twenty minutes later he called back. "I can't get any specific facts, but there is strong pressure in high places to keep you quiet and under protective custody. One thing is certain, this way you'll be alive to change your mind in a few days."

I understood the dismal logic. If I signed a paper turning down protection recommended by the government, I was especially vulnerable. Some group in the federal law enforcement bureaucracy wanted me kept under wraps, under pressure, running scared. They still wanted something from me.

"I am advised to accept your protection," I told the marshals. "Where do you plan to hide me out?"

"Salt Lake City."

"No way. The whole state of Utah is a minimum-security prison."

"Orders from the chief."

"Get him on the phone."

It was a weird moment, the Justice Department acting as my travel agent. We finally agreed on Santa Fe, New Mexico. I'd always wanted to spend some time there.

Joanna and I found a totally isolated cabin just a hundred yards west of the Pecos River in the Sangre de Christo mountains. The marshals arranged for a New Mexico driver's license and ID papers in the name James Joyce. Joanna's name was Nora.

There was a small creek behind the cabin. At night the desert sky was filled with stars, and we could watch Scorpio rising around midnight.

The first time we showed up in Sante Fe everyone in town knew who we were. Realizing that it was impossible to keep me hidden, the Justice Department threw in the towel. It would be three years before the FBI returned requesting more information.[3]

On or about July 4, 1976, the bicentennial anniversary of the American Revolution, I reassumed my own name and identity, Timothy Leary, autobiographer, ready to continue broadcasting.

Epilogue

All along Joanna and I had sensed that our partnership would not endure after my release. Her mission impossible was to get me out of prison. Once that was formally accomplished—soon after the government allowed me to appear in public—we flew to San Diego and parted amicably. Within hours Joanna joined her new boyfriend in a new adventure: pregnancy and marriage, and later separation.

Thereafter she became advisor to the prime minister of Grenada, bought a schooner, learned to fly airplanes, covered shuttle launches for *Omni*, and sailed off to the South Pacific.

I packed all my belongings in two suitcases and headed north on the freeway for Glendale, where my daughter Susan was living with her children Dieadra and Ashley. We celebrated my freedom by taking in a game at Dodger Stadium, sitting on the first-base side. It was my first outing with my grandchildren, and I enjoyed all the simple pleasures—buying hot dogs, drinking beer, chatting about the particulars of the game with Susan, a devoted fan.

Flashing back to the dozens of baseball games I had seen at different life-stages and under varied states of altered consciousness I sat enraptured by the brilliant green of the diamond which gleamed like a mescaline painting. The orange-brown baselines framed a slow ballet of familiar movements: catcher squatting to give the sign, pitcher leaning in, batter waiting and wagging the bat, fielders tensing hands over knees. Forty thousand fans stilled in a moment of concentration. *Whoosh*, the pitch smacking into the catcher's mitt, the broad gesture and hoarse cry of the umpire: "Ball three!"

As Burt Hooton lost control I could sense the apprehension mounting, a nervous rustle of concern. Hooton came back with a knuckle-curve, catching the outside corner, stirring a deep herd murmur of pleasure. As the Cincinnati batter flied out to end the inning, there was a sudden tidal flow of relief.

I spent the night on Susan's couch, reviewing the hits, runs, and errors of my life, wondering about the future. Once again my situation was precariously fluid. Fifty-six years old with no home, no job, no credit and little credibility. A free agent with little chance of hooking up with an American League team. My connections were gone. During the fifteen years since G. Gordon Liddy had driven us from Millbrook, I had been isolated in forty jails on four continents. I had lost touch with friends, now scattered around the planet. I felt quite alone. It was a great time to start a new career.

*   *   *

Step 1: Employment. A New York agency that booked college lectures called. They liked the program I proposed, *American Culture: 1946-1984*, and signed me for a nationwide tour.

I was curious about the new crop of students, who had been primary school kids during the Summer of Love. As it turned out, they were just as curious about me. The lectures drew large enthusiastic crowds.

Step 2: Relocation. I rented a redwood-and-glass house nestled in a grove of trees in Laurel Canyon. It felt right to settle in Hollywood, among the people who write, direct, engineer, produce, and act in films, which change human consciousness.

For more than 4,000 years human intelligence, creativity, freedom, and individuality—the precious spirit of innovation—had been moving steadily west, from Asia through the Middle East, through Europe, scaling the Atlantic Ocean to the New World. First the innovators flocked to the strip along the Ganges, then to the Euphrates, then to the Nile, Athens, Rome, Paris, London, New England. Each new outpost had its moment as the locus of new vision, where the smartest, fastest, and bravest swarmed for the next step forward. (In these frontier zones you do not find the high-status elites, always located one or two sectors back eastward.)

By 1976 the innovators had reached the last terrestrial frontier. They were zooming along the fabled boulevards—Hollywood, Sunset, Santa Monica, even Ventura—crowding the freeways, building up escape velocity along the Sunset Strip, barreling up those last few neon-lit palm-tree miles of the genetic runway to the Ocean of Peace.

Step 3: Re-education. Learning the folkways of the film culture. My tutor in this new community was Henry Edwards, a quintessential mad Manhattanite, former rock critic for the *New York Times*, at that moment riding high as scriptwriter for the movie-musical *Sergeant Pepper's Lonely Hearts Club Band*.

Under Henry's guidance I logged several thousand hours at screenings, movie sets, chic restaurants, Malibu parties, and swimming pool brunches, attempting to understand how movies are made. And making friends.

Primary in my mind as I settled in this pre-launch space colony called Hollywood was to find a woman with whom to share the next, and most exciting, section of the journey.

On May 13, 1978, after a Dodgers-Cubs game, I wandered into a watering hole favored by English filmmakers, and there sitting with friends, waiting for me, was Barbara. She had just divorced a film producer and was living in Beverly Hills with her five-year-old son Zachary.

I find it hard to describe Barbara's beauty, wisdom, and all-out capacity for love. In my scientific estimation she is the sexiest, smartest, funniest woman in town. Demographics: she was born in 1948, raised in Scarsdale; her mother English, her father American, her grandfather a distinguished oral surgeon.

In the beginning I was a bit intimidated by Barbara's elegance and high style. I wondered if a fifty-eight-year-old intellectual with few material ambitions and dubious employment prospects could manage the responsibility of a new family. There seemed to be one way to find out. We married in December.

These post-prison years with Barbara and Zachary have been the most loving, tranquil, most productive of my life. I have been falsely arrested only once and have recently been awarded that most visible symbol of domestic dependability—a credit card. There is no feeling of being watched or followed by government agents.

Barbara, like other members of her generation, naturally expects the best of everything and continually encourages me to get higher and closer—the ultimate invitation to personal growth and emotional commitment. Her activities as movie producer (*Return Engagement*), script editor, and financial consultant balance out my roles as performer, writer, and financial naif.

We have continued our private experiments with the familiar psychoactive drugs and have tried four new neurotransmitters—Adam, XTC, ketamine, and Intellex—which reveal that there are dimensions of the brain yet to explore.

In public appearances I vigorously oppose laws prohibiting American citizens from altering their nervous systems. Still 100 percent in favor of the intelligent, moderate use of drugs, I am increasingly convinced that the individual's right of access to his or her own brain has become the most significant political, economic, and cultural issue in America today. Our states will never be united nor prosperous until the generational drug war is ended.

The more than 50 million of us who occasionally use drugs in moderation to intensify our esthetic, sensual, emotional, intellectual, and spiritual perspectives don't seem to be strongly influenced by anti-drug legislation. Because of our numbers the attempt to prohibit our neurological alternatives will prove utterly futile.[1]

Lecturing on the college circuit—my main source of income these past seven years—has been a rewarding task. I have listened to what young people are thinking about, and have had the opportunity to influence them at a crucial stage in their development.

Three major themes have dominated these lectures: space migration, intelligence increase, and life extension—summarized in the acronym S.M.I.I.L.E.

My scenario for *space migration* has been based on the seminal works of Werner von Braun, Constantine Tsolskovski, and Gerard O'Neill, boosted by the emergence of the citizens' space movement and by the tangible reality of the space shuttle flights. I was fascinated to discover that this field is filled with people who, because of experiences with chemical brain-change, understand that our species can go only as far into outer space as we have into inner space.

My lectures on *intelligence increase* summarize two decades of research into the purposeful use of psychoactive drugs for reprogramming the brain. These ideas were updated in light of John Lilly's theories of the brain as biocomputer, which also provide an intellectual context for understanding the information revolution being brought about by personal computers, word processors, and video games.

Life extension is the hottest topic philosophically and scientifically. Dying can be postponed by means of biochemical intervention—this possibility totally rearranges our views about the meaning of life. Alan Harrington, in *The Immortalist*, and Professor Roy Walford, in *Maximum Life Span*, have discussed the myriad ways in which traditional religions and philosophies have persuaded us to accept the inevitability of death. If the mechanisms of DNA repair, immunological defense, and DNA aging codes can be understood, and if, as Dr. Walford indicates, the human life span can be extended to 150 years, then it may become possible to postpone dying indefinitely while advances in molecular reconstruction eliminate involuntary irreversible death. Fewer subjects are of greater personal interest to me at the moment than this.

Since my release from prison I have written six new books and published over fifty articles in the fields of exo-psychology, neuro-logic, sociobiology, neuro-politics, Gaia theory, re-juvenilization, neuro-geography, neo-Lamarckianism, personal evolution and development, biocomputer theory, experimental dying, neuro-ecology, migratory demographics, and the liberating advantages of word processors and video games.

In my spare time I have developed apprentice skills in several communication media: radio broadcasting, film acting, filmmaking, comedy-club humor, personal computing, West Coast publishing, and debating—facing off against such worthy opponents as G. Gordon Liddy.

In retrospect the return engagements with my old nemesis G. Gordon seemed predestined. It was, after all, Gordon's bungled raids on Millbrook that got him promoted to chief White House plumber and Watergate mastermind.

I liked the way Gordon handled himself after his arrest: his defiance of Judge (Hanging John) Sirica, his bravado refusal to testify in the Watergate hearings. I particularly admired his Spartan response when asked, "Do you swear to tell the truth, the whole truth . . ." Gordon replied, "No." I cheered his gutsy resistance to prison authorities, his refusal to repent, his romantic pride in his own courage, his mischievous needling of the easily shocked.

After sixteen public debates, one documentary film (*Return Engagement*), and dozens of interviews I have come to like Gordon, although I deplore many of his ideas. We are both in that rare position of being able to say exactly what we want. We also share that special social perspective that comes from having spent much time in prison.

Almost every day I am in contact with other old friends. Most of us sense that we have passed through a significant period in human history, part of a powerful population of secure, sophisticated 60s veterans—tens of millions of us who have planfully pushed consciousness to the far limits and shared, in one way or another, the paradoxes and ecstasies faced by brain explorers.

My daughter Susan is a geriatric nurse, a college student in computer science, a member of the US Army Reserve, a devoted mother, and above all an unsinkable individualist. My son Jack lives in Berkeley. He is a member of the International Brotherhood of Boilermakers, Iron Ships Builders, Blacksmiths, Forgers and Helpers. In my paternal fantasies my children are frontier scouts of the Baby Boom, members of the first shock wave of their generation to hit the entrenched past. They are, in my proud reveries, evolutionary heroes, late bloomers with unlimited potential. Their futures are tied to the future of their generation.

Frank Barron is professor at the University of California at Santa Cruz, a highly respected maverick scholar. His concern with the psychology of nuclear disarmament is stronger than ever. We see each other several times a year.

Richard Alpert, a.k.a. Ram Dass, drops by for affectionate reunions when he comes to Los Angeles. His basic strategy in the creation of an original identity has been to associate himself with a prophetic master, for whom he plays loyal lieutenant. After his Hindu guru died, Ram Dass teamed up with a flamboyant housewife from Brooklyn who called herself Joya, Mother of the Universe. Their rowdy reckless affair drew applause from all his true friends. At present Richard is passing on messages from a disembodied mediumist master named Emmanuel. Ram

Dass-Richard Alpert has become our basic reformed theosophical Unitarian minister. To his congregation of millions he preaches a witty hip submission to the inevitable. His is an extraordinary success story. I love him dearly.

Allen Ginsberg, with whom I reunite often, continues as a declamatory politician, an Old Testament prophet denouncing the sins of the bourgeoisie.

Walter Clark, now in his eighties, remains an enthusiastic and effective spokesman for chemical mysticism, eager and ready to start our God-seeking adventure all over again—at a higher level.

The craggy figure of William Burroughs towers in the North African science fiction filmscapes of my memory. We meet every few months, and I am always refreshed by his sardonic wit and his precise scientific intelligence, as applied to space migration, new mind-change techniques, life extension, and the exquisite future of shrewd decadence.

Nanette, more beautiful than ever, married a distinguished Buddhist scholar and is now the mother of four children.

Rosemary, twelve years after our flight into exile, remains underground, the enigmatic figure of our dreams. Does she stand radiant, wrapped in a black cape on an Atlantic jetty, waiting for the sign to break her silence? Will her adventures ever be told?

Ralph Metzner is currently Dean of the California Institute for Integral Studies in San Francisco. He continues his work as a teacher, psychotherapist, writer, and researcher of altered states.

George Litwin left his faculty post at Harvard Business School to become a successful consultant to industry. He is also a leader in the Rajneesh movement.

Gunther Weil is currently the director of the Center for Media Development at the University of Massachusetts and teaches Taoist tantric yoga.

Ken Kesey and I have stayed close. He is busy writing another of his great American novels.

Michael Hollingshead, the ultimate gypsy scholar, has written two books on consciousness and produces picture books on science and evolution for Marvel Comix.

Maynard Ferguson and his big band of talented youngsters are more popular than ever. Flora Lu commutes between Ojai and India on mysterious spiritual missions.

The Hitchcocks have gone on to construct singular realities. Tommy is a trial lawyer. Billy is an imaginative financier and patron of the arts. Peggy, endowed from birth with an inexhaustible inheritance of good humor and generosity, has remained a broker of cheery wisdom throughout the years of cultural boom and bust. The Hitchcock family has preserved the Millbrook estate as a historical monument.

Eldridge Cleaver and I have re-united amicably several times since Algeria. At the Federal prison in San Diego we formed a high-scoring two-man basketball team. At that time Eldridge became a born-again Christian and a supporter of Space Migration. Since then he has become a Moonie and a hard-line supporter of Ronald Reagan.

Michael Horowitz, my archivist, with Cindy Palmer and Michael Aldrich, continues to maintain the Fitz Hugh Ludlow Memorial Library in San Francisco, the world's largest collection of books, manuscripts, and artifacts about drug use. Michael and Cindy have published two works on cultural psychopharmacology: *Moksha: Aldous Huxley's Writing on Psychedelics and the Visionary Experience* and *Shaman Woman, Mainline Lady*.

The posse from the Poughkeepsie Courthouse that ran us out of Millbrook was lead by G. Gordon Liddy, Sheriff Larry Quinlan, Deputy Charles Borchers, and Deputy Albert Traver. Liddy, Quinlan, and Borchers were later indicted for felonies, a karmic pay-back so typical of those times. Traver, the only raider to remain clean, was later promoted to captain.

In the fall of 1982 I returned to Poughkeepsie to lecture at Vassar College. While I was waiting in the dressing room, the door opened and in walked a sturdy man with an unmistakable cop demeanor. "Timmy," he cried, throwing his arms around my shoulders. "Remember me? I'm Al Traver." We joshed each other like former football rivals. This is my dream of how American League politics should turn out.

As I look back over this rich, continually changing, and utterly entertaining life, I realize that my dedication to certain concepts has never wavered. I have relentlessly and faithfully pursued self-exploration, evolution, and innovation as the antidotes to terminal adulthood. Changing schools, jobs, geographical locations, turning down officer status in the military and tenure in academia . . . from my grandfather's exhortations that I be "different" to Aldous Huxley's suggestion that I become a cheerleader for change, from my first mushroom trip in Cuernavaca to my recent ketamine experiments in voluntary death, I have reprogrammed myself and encouraged others to resist, question, challenge, indeed do anything to escape the assembly line that would carry us—if we are not vigilant—into a final commitment to the obsolete past.

The discovery of drugs at the age of forty was an unexpected boon. Here was a direct method to regress the nervous system to the suggestible state where new reality programs could be imprinted. Exploration of one's neurological/genetic equipment can result in metamorphosis of a particularly beneficial kind—rejuvenilization, DNA's built-in warranty that the future will not be like the past.

During the last two decades it has become clear that those most attracted to processes that bring about re-juvenilization are those born after 1946—the post-War wave of young people with whom my fate has been most intimately tied. I have come to respect the importance of generational demographics, which suggest that during periods of accelerated cultural change the generation you belong to becomes a most important determinant of how you think and act.

During this century in America four very different groups have emerged, and all are still very much alive: 1) the Old Timers, those born before 1920; 2) the Permissive Parents, born between 1920–1945; 3) the Baby Boomers, born 1946-1964; and 4) the Whiz Kids, born after 1965.[2]

The seemingly insoluble problems of today were created by the two pre-1946 generations. The scope and magnitude of the problems seem to defy comprehension—overpopulation, pollution, violence, doomsday weaponry, the efforts of the status quo generations to shield the younger generation from new ideas.

If I were in charge of evolutionary matters on this planet, I would, at this precise moment, flood the place with advanced humans wired to take over peaceably and initiate the necessary changes.

And behold! This is exactly what DNA seems to have done. Just when the situation looked hopeless, here came 76 million post-War Americans—40 million more than we expected—fresh, confident, programmed for innovation.

A recent Yankelovitch poll suggests that 80 percent of the American public is currently involved in personal fulfillment projects, most of which involve some form of re-juvenilization. Critics of this trend say it will bring an end to the Industrial Age in America, and they are right. The Industrial Age is over. The Information Age has arrived.

I see this as cause for celebration. Survival in the future will be based on intelligence increase: expanding the spectrum of information we receive, improving our models for analyzing these facts, and developing more powerful modes of transmitting up-dated signals to others.

I make this prediction with confidence and serenity: the Young Ones are ready to *Turn On* the higher circuits of their brains, *Tune In* to the awesome strength of their numbers, and *Take Charge* of evolution.

It's about time.

(To be continued)

Notes

Chapter One

1. In the fall of 1959 I spent three days in London testing and interviewing Arthur Koestler for Frank Barron's Creativity Project, striking up a warm friendship with the philosopher at the same time. First thing he sent me to the West End to see *Hiroshima Mon Amour*. He then explained that the generations born after 1946 would prove to be of a different species. "Post-Hiroshima" evolution would ultimately expose the flaws in orthodox Darwinism.

From Koestler I learned about juvenilization, the theory that evolution occurs not in the adult (final form) of a species but in juveniles, larvals, adolescents, pre-adults. The practical conclusion: if you want to bring about mutations in a species, work with the young. Koestler's teaching about paedomorphosis prepared me to understand the genetic implications of the 1960s youth movement and its rejection of the old culture.

Chapter Two

1. The life of a philosopher/writer is best judged by the body of his or her published works and by the public response, both immediate and long-term. Thus the adventures and personal experiences recounted in these memoirs can be seen as sociological background for the several hundred new ideas about evolution briefly referred to in this autobiography. Readers wishing more detailed discussions of these ideas should consult my original writings, indexed in *A Bibliography of Timothy Leary* by Michael Horowitz, Karen Walls, and Billy Smith (M. Horowitz, 18340 Old Monte Rio Rd., Guerneville, CA 95446).

My theory and methodology for measuring emotional interactions is summarized in *The Interpersonal Diagnosis of Personality* (Ronald Press/John Wiley, 1957), which has remained in print for twenty-five years, the most recent edition appearing in 1982.

2. When I joined the Harvard faculty in January 1960, I was unaware that two monolithic historical forces were combining to shape my immediate future. In the most significant cultural event in human history, the Baby Boom (1946-1964) unloaded 76 million new arrivals on an unprepared America. Double the expected amount. For the rest of the century the main business of our country would be a frantic attempt to adjust to the demographic pressures created by this invading army.

I was one of those responsible for this astounding event. My wife Marianne and I shared with our generation the brash notion that our kids would enjoy a healthier and saner upbringing. Our parents had laid on us their economic insecurities, their sexual guilt, their naive worship of authority, their self-sacrificing dedication to God and society. But we were going to be a new breed of parents. We would treat our kids as equal, independent, privileged human beings. We would listen to them. We would not stunt their growth with restrictions. We would deliberately indulge them, make them the center of our universe. Whenever we had doubts, Dr. Spock and his brigades of modern pediatricians were there to urge us on.

What we didn't understand until three decades later was the overpowering effect of generational numbers. We post-war parents blindly produced 40 million extra additions to the gene-pool.

Then, as child-centered adults, we trained them to be insatiable consumers, spoiled little aristocrats of uninhibited desire. We forced the factories of the nation to produce twice as many baby bottles and diapers and perfumed ointments to soothe their pink little bottoms. We cheerfully voted for education bonds to double the number of primary schools. We doubled the number of Brownie troops, Cub Scout dens, ballet schools. Gave them everything we didn't have, the best of everything.

Then we popped them in front of the television set, where they experienced in one week more realities, more perspectives, more history/geography than the wisest and most affluent rulers of the past. And we watched approvingly as American enterprise trained them to expect the best breakfast foods, the best soda pop, the best toys, because we all agreed they were the best.

In 1960 the first cohorts of the Baby Boom were in their teens, just hitting high school with expectations that did not include being trained as docile conformists in the Ozzie and Harriet cultural mode. They automatically assumed that they could select the education they wished, the sexuality they preferred, the society they would inhabit, the wars they would fight, the music they would resonate to, the drugs they would consume.

Who, in 1960, understood that our industrial civilization, at the peak of its power and prosperity, would collapse in two decades with a series of shuddering convulsions and that a very different post-industrial, information culture would suddenly arise, explosively changing our lives? Our factory-manager God was about to be laid off.

The Baby Boom happened all at once. The Information Age also seemed to happen all at once but was actually the result of a long process of evolution. During the 10,000 sleepy years of the Agricultural Age human life centered on a piece of turf. Land—the basis of feudalism—defined economics, family structure, religion, politics, survival. My maternal great-grandfather, Daniel Ferris, a papist yeoman, migrated to America in 1836, settled his forty acres, and built a farmhouse in which my mother was born and which, in 1960, I still considered my family home.

Exactly a century before my arrival at Harvard, in 1860, South Carolina seceded from the Union, beginning the first American Civil War, a conflict between the feudal-agricultural civilization of Daniel Ferris and a centralized-industrial civilization, in which the corporation replaced the extended family as a social unit. The first Civil War was not South against North. It was past vs. future, village vs. city, plantation vs. factory, horse vs. machine. From 1860 to 1946 this struggle was played out in every home in America. Great-grandfather Ferris vs. Grandfather Leary.

America became a gigantic industrial combine in which everything and everyone was part of the production-consumption sequence. This is not simply a theoretical observation. The bottle was put in my red-wet mouth by my mother promptly *on schedule*, not when I was hungry. I ate canned food because my mother was led to believe that these standardized packages were better than farm-fresh food. The principal of my primary school, Sister Eulalia, used to stand by the door with a watch in her hand checking both teachers and students into the education factory. Punctuality, standardization, and a complete set of assembly-line values were drilled into me as a child. Aunt Mae said it a hundred times a month. "Conform, Timothy."

The ethos of this society was mechanical power: production of vehicles to transport us swiftly, things to make our lives physically comfortable, weapons to protect our shores and to establish our claim to raw materials. And to manage the centralized industrial state: ever-growing armies of administrators, politicians, agents, and bureaucrats. This highly organized colossus was based on non-renewable terrestrial energy (the supply of which was beginning to play out). The nineteenth-century model of a mechanistic entropic universe would prove no longer relevant in a nuclear/electronic era.

That magical year 1946 (actually the Year 1 AH—After Hiroshima) conveniently dates the explosion of what Alvin Tofler has called the Third Wave: the Intelligence-Information civilization. World War II, the industrial-factory war, was the catalyst. Enormous military training factories equipped 13 million young Americans with new methods of rapid communication. A gigantic transportation system scattered us around the world, exposing us to cultural relativity. The military threw up an overnight network of decentralized work-residence bases, which led directly to the post-war Levittown-suburbanism. The solidity of the atom was fissioned. All sorts of amazing smart machines were invented. Radar. Sonar. Computers.

As the technologies became smarter, it became necessary to create smarter people. The most important effect of World War II was to double the intelligence of the American gene-pool. I am not talking about verbal literacy. Reading-writing are Second Wave factory-bureaucracy skills. Rather, I'm referring to the ability to receive, process, and transmit lots of different information, accurately and quickly.

In a quiet almost invisible way military psychology (1941–1946) and OSS-CIA assessment methods transformed our basic notions about human nature. Thirteen million youths were tested, screened, selected, trained in complex skills, behavior-modified, and even rehabilitated by means of psychological techniques. The implications were obvious. In the future both war and peace were to be based on our knowledge of the brain. Intelligence became the key to survival in the future. Psychology became the new science of human engineering.

We members of the Harvard Center for Personality Research, presumably an advanced psychology think-tank, were completely unaware that the second American Civil War was about to explode, that the old control society was about to collide with the new communication culture. Yet I had been unwittingly prepared—being genetically designed, scientifically trained, temperamentally ready, and perfectly located—to surf this wave of change. As matter of fact I had been dreaming of this moment all my life.

Chapter Three

1. Samuel Clemens' life (1835–1910) coincides with the most recent cycle of Halley's Comet.

2. As a teenager Mark Twain read the popular South American travel-romance (*Exploration of the Valley of the Amazon*, 1854) of naval officer William Herndon, whose description of the miraculous powers of cocaine inspired Twain with the ambition to become America's first coca leaf importer.

Venturing down to New Orleans to embark for Peru Twain became a Mississippi River steam boat pilot instead. He later went to the Wild West boomtown of San Francisco, where he met Fitz Hugh Ludlow, a young writer with a reputation as "the American DeQuincey."

Late in life one of Twain's closest friends was his Dentist, Dr. John Manley Riggs, who had been an associate of Horace Wells, the first person to use nitrous oxide (laughing gas) successfully as a surgical anesthetic. Twain was greatly impressed by the experience of altered consciousness under laughing gas—the comic/cosmic jumps from the ridiculous to the sublime—as his essay "Happy Memories of the Dental Chair" attests.

Chapter Five

1. For my Aunt Mae the most damning comment possible was: "Well, I never heard of such a thing

in my life." She worshipped the past and distrusted the future, accepting from her grandfather the Irish villager's belief that "the divil ye know is better than the divil ye don't know." She was an unlikely teacher for a scientist-philosopher, a role that requires an openness to being proved wrong and a willingness to change perspectives. Yet her example was invaluable in my professional preparation.

2. On election night, 1960, I dined with Aldous Huxley and Humphrey Osmond, the distinguished psychiatrist who seven years before had introduced Huxley to the LSD world. As Osmond recalls the meeting, I was "still wearing a grey flannel suit and sporting a crew cut." After our long and enthusiastic conversation the two scholarly Englishmen made the following comments about me:

> Huxley: What a nice fellow he is . . . . Harvard, I think, will be so good for it [i.e. LSD.]
> Osmond: I think he's a very nice fellow too, but don't you think he's a little bit square?
> Huxley: You may well be right. Isn't that, after all, what we want?

Later Osmond sheepishly told me, referring to Huxley and him, "Here were two students of human temperament; yet I think our judgment is the least satisfactory ever made of you. Even your worst enemies would not make that description. We were convinced that you were too unadventurous. What a monumental ill judgment!" (Quotations are from Peter Stafford's *The Magic Gram.*

Chapter Six

1. These researchers were in stark contrast to the many psychiatrists performing experiments on patients in mental hospitals under CIA sponsorship—who had not taken the drug themselves and who used LSD on patients as a sort of shock therapy, deliberately attempting to frighten people out of their minds. John Marks, an investigative reporter, has written a blood-curdling book about the use of LSD by CIA-sponsored doctors and by the military. *In Search of the Manchurian Candidate* was filmed in an ABC special in 1980.

Chapter Eight

1. The University of Michigan psychology-psychiatric departments were hotbeds of covert experimentation by the CIA.

2. Years later we learned of the insidious role of Max Rinkel in the drug controversies that followed.

Rinkel considered himself an expert on mind-changing drugs—psychotomimetics, as he called them—and consistently attacked our research project, blocking our funding grants and publicly denouncing

the work in publications such as the *Harvard Alumni Review.*

After the fall of Nixon, the Freedom of Information Act made public the fact that Max Rinkel had been a CIA operative assigned to test drugs that could be used in warfare, brainwashing, and interrogation.

Rinkel had never taken LSD. His position, typical of the medical point-of-view, was that the doctor doesn't have to be pregnant to deliver a baby. He administered LSD to many Harvard students who answered guinea-pig ads in the *Crimson.* This unethical approach (illegal according to the 1947 Nuremberg code, which condemned secret experimentation on humans), was in contrast to our psychedelic research, which was based on openness and witting collaboration.

I learned more about Dr. Max Rinkel when, at the height of the media furor over acid, a Boston TV station invited me up from New York to appear on a talk show. On the return drive to the airport the chauffeur, a wizened old Irishman named Pat, kept slowing the limousine down and glancing back at me.

"What's on your mind, Pat?"

"I thought you might be interested, Doc. I was the first American ever to take LSD."

"How did that happen?"

"Fifteen years ago I was in bad mental shape. I was drinking a lot and still living at home with my mother, even though I was fifty-five years old. So I went to see a psychiatrist. Did you ever hear of Max Rinkel?"

"Mad Max. I know the man well."

"I was a terrible patient. He tried everything on me. Psychoanalysis. Hypnosis. Electric shock. All sorts of pills. But nothing worked. One day, as I was leaving his office, Dr. Rinkel handed me two pills and a cup of water and said, 'Try this. Come back next week and tell me how you feel.'"

By this time the limo was cruising at ten miles an hour as Pat leaned back to talk.

"I tell you, Doc, that was the longest subway ride in history."

As it turned out, the CIA deserves the credit for creating the drug culture of the '60s. In their attempt to scour the planet for any root, vine, herb, leaf that could twist people's heads they pushed the sciences of ethnobotany and psychopharmacology ahead by a century.

The CIA sponsored dozens of drug experiments, swamping conservative research centers with millions of doses of LSD. The senior scientists, of course, turned the drugs over to their younger assistants who, naturally, tried them on themselves and their friends. Ken Kesey and Allen Ginsberg were among the many grateful recipients of the CIA boon.

Chapter Nine

1. During one late-night session in Newton I walked out to the front yard. The wind was blowing. It was

a cold damp cloudy night. I felt an ancient Irish-bog sense of gloom. The trees surrounding the lawn suddenly seemed twisted, menacing, dangerous.

Then I remembered a yogic teaching. If my mind could make the trees threatening, then perhaps my mind could make them benign. "Hello there, friends," I said to the trees. Suddenly they were waving their limbs and branches in merry salute.

The ability to program the brain in this way, to avoid getting trapped, became the key to the new form of psychotherapy that we were developing.

Chapter Ten

1. We were defining intelligence not as scores on paper-and-pencil tests but rather as the understanding of one's own neurological equipment and the ability to use this equipment to create the desired internal and external realities. Should we call this meta-intelligence, this insight that the only smart thing to do is to get smarter? Increased intelligence is a function of learning how to use your head.

Huxley had stated it clearly: the rational mind was a valve mediating between consciousness and the 100 million signals processed by the brain each second. These drugs opened the valve. Managing your brain was a matter of learning how to modulate the valve, to allow in exactly as much data as you wanted or needed at the moment.

But Huxley's 1958 metaphor was too mechanical. There was not just one valve. Scores of receptor sites for different drugs were available to open the myriad circuits of the brain. Limitless numbers of realities waited to be switched on.

Chapter Eleven

1. Results of the prison project were reported in the following scientific journal articles:
T. Leary, "The Effects of Consciousness Expanding Drugs in Prisoner Rehabilitation," *Psychedelic Review* no. 10 (1969);
R. Metzner and G. Weil, "Predictive Recidivism: Base Rates for Concord Constitution," *Journal of Criminal Law, Criminology and Police Science* (1963);
R. Metzner et al., "A Change Program for Adult Offenders Using Psilocybin," *Psychotherapy* (July 1965).

2. The concept of imprinting has been reluctantly admitted into human psychology. The less loaded term *bonding* is widely used to describe attachments that seem to be stronger and more durable than conditioned reactions, which require constant re-enforcement.

Several therapeutic systems employ the principle of the re-imprint. Rebirthing methods combine alterations in the body's basic emergency system (breathing) with inspirational suggestions to bring about sudden

change in personality. Aversion treatments for alcoholism associate another physiological survival response (vomiting) with the taste of booze. Isolation-tank and primal-scream therapies also use deeply regressive physiological activities to suspend existing imprints and establish new ones. But none of these methods approaches the power of drugs to re-imprint. When these "non-chemical" methods work, it is because they have induced chemical changes in the subject's nervous system.

Chapter Twelve

1. Within a decade, however, the Mexican police stopped harassing Maria Sabina. She was recognized as the transmitter of a proud native heritage. A documentary about her life played to sell-out crowds in one of the largest theaters in the capital. Her elevation to the status of national heroine was accomplished by the enthusiasm of the young people whom Wasson continually dismissed.

Chapter Fourteen

1. A more detailed description of the Good Friday experiment and other studies on the production of religious experiences with psychedelic drugs can be found in my *High Priest* (NAL-World, 1967).

Chapter Sixteen

1. Ignaz Philipp Semmelweis (1818–1865), a Hungarian obstetrician, discovered the infectious nature of bacterial disease, developed preventive antisepsis, and was destroyed by the medical profession for his innovations. While a ward physician in the Vienna General Hospital Semmelweis was disturbed by the epidemic nature of puerpal (childbed) fever, which was producing a high mortality rate among new mothers. When he determined that the prime cause of this disease was infection by the hands of examining staff, he insisted that doctors and nurses wash their hands before coming on his wards. This tactic dramatically reduced the mortality rate but aroused the enmity of his colleagues, who were insulted by the implications of Semmelweis' discovery. Ridicule and ostracization forced Semmelweis from his post. For a while he stood outside the gates of the hospital urging patients to insist that their doctors wash their hands. Soon after he went insane and killed himself.

A paper Semmelweis published in a Swiss journal was read by the prestigious English surgeon Lord Lister, who eventually gained credit for introducing antiseptic methods in medicine.

2.   Scientific Intelligence Memorandum

POTENTIAL NEW AGENT FOR UNCONVEN-
TIONAL WARFARE

Lysergic Acid Diethylamide (LSD)
(N, N-Diethyllysergamide)

This memorandum is based on intelligence
available as of 1 August 1954

CIA/SI 101-54
5 August 1954

CENTRAL INTELLIGENCE AGENCY
Office of Scientific Intelligence

Lysergic acid diethylamide (LSD) N-diethyllysergamide), a drug derived from ergot, is of great strategic
significance as a potential agent in unconventional
warfare and in interrogations. In effective doses, LSD
is not lethal, nor does it have color, odor or taste.
Since the effect of this drug is temporary in contrast
to the fatal nerve agents, there are important strategic
advantages for its use in certain operations. Possessing
both a wide margin of safety and the requisite physiological properties, it is capable of rendering whole
groups of people, including military forces, indifferent
to their surroundings and situations, interfering with
planning and judgment, and even creating apprehension, uncontrollable confusion and terror.

Of all substances now known to affect the mind,
such as mescaline, harmine and others, LSD is by
far the most potent. Very minute quantities (upwards
of 30 millionths of a gram) create serious mental confusion and sensual disturbances, or render the mind
temporarily susceptible to many types of influences.

The basic material from which LSD is prepared
is ergot and the Soviet Bloc has an abundant supply
of it.

3. The following is reprinted from the *Boston Globe*,
September 1, 1977.

A Harvard psychologist who fought to remove LSD
advocate Timothy Leary from the University faculty
in 1963 was among researchers who had received
funds from a CIA program that sponsored research
even more controversial than Leary's.

Dr. Herbert Kelman, Harvard's Richard Clarke
Cabot professor of social ethics, admitted yesterday
receiving a grant from the Human Ecology Fund,
but said he didn't know until recently that the organization served as a conduit for CIA money.

Kelman said he requested and received $1000
from the fund for non-drug-related purposes in
1960, just three years before he successfully argued
for the expulsion of Leary and co-researcher Dr.
Richard Alpert for their alleged use of Harvard undergraduates in LSD research.

Before Leary's expulsion, both men were lecturers
in Harvard's psychology department.

The CIA recently has admitted establishing the
Society for the Investigation of Human Ecology,
also known as the Human Ecology Fund, as part
of its $25-million program on mind control and
human behavior designated MK-ULTRA.

Ironically, the Ecology Fund sponsored work
similar to Leary's during the 1950's at the Massachusetts Mental Health Center in Boston, and students from Harvard and other area universities were
reportedly used as subjects in those experiments.
Leary has said he informed his subjects, while the
CIA has admitted giving drugs to unknowing persons.

Chapter Eighteen

1. Hassan-i-Sabbah, a fellow-student of Omar
Khayam in Persian mystery schools, used erotic and
aesthetic techniques for political survival, developing
elaborate grades of initiation. Although leader of a
small sect Hassan and subsequent "Grand Masters"
used their neurological skills to remain free and independent in the bellicose Moslem world. For close to
200 years they successfully undermined the Soviet-
like Arab dictatorships, using non-violent hedonic
know-how.

Nineteenth-century revisionist French historians
and linguists created the world "assassin" from the
Arabic *hashishin* (hashish user) to describe a brainwashed person who was engaged in undercover actions
undermining imperial authority. At approximately the
same time the recreational and esthetic uses of hashish
were introduced to the West by the French psychiatrist
Jean-Jacques Moreau, who brought the drug back
from Egypt and started the celebrated Hashish Club
in Paris. Hashish played the same subversive role in
the revolutions of that period in France and Italy.
This notion of cannabis as a trouble-making, anti-
establishment, anarchic drug helped to fuel the
vehement anti-marijuana press that resulted in laws
making it illegal in America in 1937.

By 1960 Beat writers William Burroughs and Brion
Gysin resurrected the legend of Hassan-i-Sabbah, at-
tributing to him the libertarian individualist declaration: "Nothing is true; everything is permitted"—a
statement of the multiple realities that certain drugs
characteristically provoke.

Chapter Nineteen

1. *The Structure of Scientific Revolutions* by Thomas
S. Kuhn was published in 1962 by the University of
Chicago Press. This book, one of the most important
of our times, studies the evolution of scientific ideas.
New concepts (paradigms) that change theory, practice, and instrumentation are fiercely resisted by the
orthodoxy of the period. New models that change
thought and ritual are highly politicized. According

to Kuhn: "As in political revolutions, so in paradigm choice—there is no standard higher than the assent of the relevant community."

2. An account of incidents involving Mary Pinchot Meyer and other prominent Washingtonians appeared in *Katharine the Great* by Deborah Davis (Harcourt Brace Jovanovich, 1979), a book which itself became a subject of controversy, as reported in *The New York Times* and the *Philadelphia Inquirer*.

Chapter Twenty

1. Castaneda's skillful description of the trickster-teacher working in furtive secrecy, playing deceptive games, privately laughing at those whom he can con with his humble peasant facade is brilliantly exemplified by Castaneda's own way of life. The poignant problem of tricksterism is that it derives from the hunter-gatherer stage of human evolution. The furtive stalking mode leaves the wizard alone in a dark world of stealth and jungle insecurity, a paranoid universe of competing black magicians.

2. The two "bad-trips" at Zihuatanejo were a new development. From the beginning of our drug research we had concentrated on preparation, guidance, and serene safe environments. After hundreds of successful sessions we had been lulled into a false sense of optimism about inner space. Ultimately the two distressing episodes in Mexico strengthened our conviction that setting was of crucial importance. The atmosphere of gloom and police threat at the Hotel Catalina undoubtedly triggered the negativity.

The case of Dr. Payne was very embarrassing. Why did we hunt him like a dangerous animal, thus provoking him to flight? If we had simply kept him under gentle surveillance, built a fire on the beach, invited him to join us around the circle, he would eventually have returned and been talked down. Payne did nothing to warrant our panicked physical coercion of him. It was, once again, the fears of the straight people that exaggerated the confusion. The eternal policeman in us apparently took over.

Marvey's flip-out was clearly a result of the Mexican expulsion. If we had not been forced to leave the Catalina, we could have allowed Marvey time enough to find his way back. The fact that both men returned to "sanity" within days, apparently no worse for wear, was reassuring.

This issue of "danger" continued to concern us over the years. Like everyone else we witnessed hundreds of uninformed doctors and scientists on state or federal payrolls asserting that LSD ruins lives, destroys brain cells, breaks chromosomes, causes every conceivable mental and physical illness, plus monstrous birth defects.

Needless to say, *no one was more interested in getting the facts about the dangers of psychedelics than we, who had been regularly ingesting them in large doses.*

After twenty-three years of diligent investigation here are my comments on the dangers of Acid-Mescaline-Mushrooms-Marijuana.

1. Physical: our authority on LSD toxicity, then as now, was Dr. Albert Hofmann, the distinguished Sandoz chemist. In his autobiography, *LSD: My Problem Child* (Tarcher, 1983), Hofmann writes,

To my knowledge, there have not as yet occurred any casualties that are a direct consequence of LSD poisoning. Numerous episodes of fatal consequences attributed to LSD ingestion have indeed been recorded, but these were accidents, even suicides, that may be attributed to the mentally disoriented condition of LSD intoxication. The danger of LSD lies not in its toxicity, but rather in the unpredictability of its psychic effects.

Some years ago reports appeared in the scientific literature and also in the lay press, alleging that damage to chromosomes or the genetic material had been caused by LSD. These effects, however, have been observed in only a few individual cases. Subsequent comprehensive investigations of a large, statistically significant number of cases, however, showed that there was no connection between chromosome anomalies and LSD medication. The same applies to reports about fetal deformities that had allegedly been produced by LSD.

2. Psychological: unprepared or unguided use of these drugs has produced some cases of accidental injury/death and a larger number of temporary (less than 72 hours) quasi-psychotic confusions. But statistical surveys would show that the accident rate with A-M-M-M (acid-mescaline-mushroom-marijuana) drugs is lower than that of alcohol, tranquilizers, narcotics, PCP. There is a man-bites-dog paradox here: Accidents due to A-M-M-M drugs are atypical to such an extent that the rare freak-out becomes news, whereas the 50,000 lives lost each year because of booze are just business as usual.

Moralists make much of the highly publicized deaths of celebrities. In spite of the high proportion of show-biz people who used psychedelics during the years 1965–1975, there was not one demise attributed to A-M-M-M. The concept, when you think of it, is absurd. An LSD overdose? A cannabis overdose?

The tragic deaths of Brian Jones, Janis Joplin, John Belushi, William Holden, Natalie Wood, Jimi Hendrix, Keith Moon, Edie Sedgewick, Mama Cass, etc. were due to booze plus uppers or downers.

Statistics from hospital emergency rooms confirm that the most common cause of accidental death in America is alcohol plus downers. Both legal drugs.

During the years 1967-1972 the LSD controversy provided a textbook example of mass hysteria. I was appalled but also fascinated to observe how an epidemic of irrational fear can sweep a population, because an intelligent understanding of this phenomenon is crucial to the health of any society or gene pool.

Irrational fear is a major block to human evolution—personal or species; it lowers intelligence, it is virulently contagious, it leads to inappropriate withdrawal from the engaging novelties upon which growth depends.

The Tylenol hysteria of 1982 was a mini recapitulation of the acid hysteria. Tylenol was the safest and most effective drug in its field. Because someone in Chicago tampered with a few boxes of Tylenol, the name of the drug became trigger for ancient, protozoan paranoias about poison in the environment.

Chapter Twenty-One

1. Some have seen my life as patterned by a compulsive rebellion against authority, an inability to make a mature adjustment to accepted social norms. I disagree with this view. My thirty-six years as a psychologist have taught me that there are some individuals in every society who are wired by nature to innovate rather than conform.

Every human gene pool produces a wide variety of types, DNA-designed to perform the many specialized functions necessary to keep a social species adapted to the ever-changing environment. In several books I have listed twenty-four structural castes of human beings—just as different from each other as worker ants and warrior ants.

It pleases me to believe that I belong to the inventor-innovator genetic caste. My brain is designed to program new realities, to see things differently, to create original perspectives. Put me in the hole of the worst prison in America and I'm delighted by the opportunity to see the world from a new point of view. I am instructed by my genes to want to surprise you, to make you laugh with recognition of an unexpected possibility. By the same token it is constitutionally impossible for me to conceptualize the rote application of a past/present to the future.

I am not alone in this eccentricity. Approximately 8 percent of the individuals from any gene pool share my chromosomal bent. In most cultures we inventor-innovators are usually in trouble; the power-control caste is instinctively threatened by our pressure for continual change.

There are, however, certain times and places when history encourages individualistic invention: fifth-century B.C. Athens, for example, or the Rights of Man period (1750–1850) in Western Europe and North America. I was lucky to be born in America and to reach manhood at such a time (1960), when the Information-Intelligence Age was just beginning and my caste was called upon to perform its social function—to encourage innovation.

The theory that structural caste determines human behavior presents a most compassionate view of human nature. Everyone is perfectly designed to play an important function. The problem is that your caste function may not be needed at the time and place where you appear. The solution is to either lay low until your time happens or migrate to the place where they are ready for you.

As a genetically determined change-agent I am

neither rebellious nor conforming—I am either on time or ahead of my time.

To a congenital innovator the professional code is clear: if you're not in trouble with society, then you're not doing your job.

2.   DEPARTMENT OF STATE
                    Washington, D.C. 20520
                                          FOI No. 7900861

Mr. Timothy Leary
Los Angeles, CA 90069

Dear Mr. Leary:

I refer to your letter of August 3, 1977 to Mr. Robert S. Young of the Central Intelligence Agency in which you requested the release of certain documents under the Freedom of Information Act (Title 5 USC Section 552a).

The Central Intelligence Agency has referred 80 documents to this office for our review and possible release. During the course of the review, it was noted that 23 of the documents were identical to ones previously reviewed in another request, FOI case No. 830451. It was also noted that 5 others are duplicates of originals. Consequently, we are concerned with 52 documents instead of the 80 that were originally referred to this office. After careful review of the remaining documents, we have determined that 25 of those documents can be released in full, and 25 more can be released with excisions. The decision whether an additional 2 documents can be released requires coordination with another government agency. We will write to you again concerning that decision . . . .

                            Sincerely,

                            Clayton E. McManaway
                            Deputy Assistant Secretary for
                            Bureau of Administration
                            Classification/Declassification
                            Center

FROM CENTRAL INTELLIGENCE AGENCY FILES

From: BARBADOS

TO: Secretary of State

NO: 2, July 8

PRIORITY

Action Department 2, information London priority 2, Martinique Priority 1.

Officers this post visited Dominica July 3 to 6 investigate probable expulsion American citizen John Pelyz Presmont (born New York City January 9, 1923, passport No. B587710 issued New York August 29, 1961) under Dominica expulsion undesirable person act. Investigation being reported in detail by airgram.

Post recommends no action be initiated Presmont's behalf and considers case closed.

Presmont however, invited Dr. Timothy Leary former Harvard University professor dismissed for experiments with mind-altering drugs LSD, mescaline and psilocybin. Investigate possibility establishing "happiness hotel" involving multi-familial transcendental living community, Dominica. Leary, whose dismissal, etc. covered Time Magazine March 29, 1963, arrived Dominica with some 15 colleagues (men, women and children) July 4 and currently in process searching suitable site establish "research center" hold seminars, continue experiments. Local Dominicans and Americans arriving for treatment. Administrator Dominica concerned but not fully aware Leary background and reputation.

Leary case represents potentially serious problem this congen. Request department check appropriate USG agencies and provide post with sufficient background information Leary experiments psychedelics, drugs used, USG position, enable us intelligently reply questions administrator Dominica or authorities any of other eight islands in consular district where Leary likely to try establish base of operations.

Donovan

Chapter Twenty-Two

1. The basic existential questions listed in the paper the "Eight Technologies of God" were:

1. *Origins.* Questions of Genesis: how, when, where did life come from? how has it evolved?

2. *Politics.* Questions of security, power, control, and territory: why do humans fight and compete destructively? what are the territorial laws that explain conflict? how can humans live in relative peace and harmony? how, when, where, and why do humans differ (among each other and from other mammalian species) in aggression, control, cooperation, affiliation?

3. *Epistemology.* Questions of truth, fact, language, knowledge, communications, manufacture of objects, artifacts, and symbol systems: how, when, where, and why does the mind emerge (in the individual and species)?

4. *Ethics.* Questions of social control, good, evil, taboo, law, crime: how, when, where, and why do humans differ in their moral beliefs and rituals? who decides what is good and right?

5. *Esthetics.* Questions of beauty, pleasure, luxury, sensory reward: how, when, where, and why do humans devote their energies to decoration, hedonism, art, music, entertainment? how, where, when, and why do they differ in modes of pleasure?

6. *Ontology.* Questions about reality and its (their) definition: how, when, where, and why do humans differ in the realities they construct and inhabit? how are realities formed and changed?

7. *Teleology.* Questions of evolution/de-evolution of life: what are the stages and mechanisms of evolution? where, when, how, and why has evolution occurred? Chance? Natural selection? Natural election? Creation? If life is created and evolution blueprinted, who did it? Where is life going?

8. *Cosmology.* Questions of galactic evolution, ultimate power, and basic structure: how, when, where, and why was matter/energy formed? what are the basic units and patterns of matter/energy? what are the basic forces, energies, and plans that hold the universe together (or don't) and determine its evolution?

This paper drew upon illustrative new insights from many branches of science—nuclear physics, astrophysics, genetics, immunology, biochemistry, neurology, ethology, demographics, computer theory— which were producing data requiring drastic changes in our concepts of human nature. The splendid possibility was raised that now, for the first time, our species could not only answer these basic questions of how and why we evolved but proceed to take over the technologies for managing and directing our bodies, our neurological realities, our genetic futures, our planet, and our universe.

2. In her memoir, *This Timeless Moment,* Laura Huxley tells the story of the last acid trip of Aldous. In his waning hours Huxley wrote a cryptic note asking for LSD. Laura consulted with Dr. Sidney Cohen, the famed LSD expert, who agreed that there was no reason not to give Aldous the drug. Laura injected the great philosopher with a sturdy dose and read to him from our manual *The Psychedelic Experience.*

Chapter Twenty-Three

1. About this time we were exposed—uncoincidentally—to the writings of ethologists and anthropologists (Ardrey, Fox, Lindauer, Tiger, Maurais, Von Frisch, Macterlinck, Edward, Wilson) whose studies of the behavior of social animals helped us understand what we were attempting to do. We believed that the migratory family, the international tribe or troop, the elective gene pool, would become the natural unit of human existence in the future. DNA often propels organisms into new behaviors that the organisms do not clearly understand. We were aware that we had migrated from the old industrial society to find space to create a new lifestyle. All we knew was that we shared this intense feeling that the old forms could not hold us.

Our random attempts to migrate to other countries and our settlement at Millbrook may have been unconscious preparation for pioneer life in the ecology now beckoning to our species. Space migration: small living units in high orbit. Anyway, we migrants at Millbrook were doing our part to get ready for the next move.

2. A most valued participant in our research at this time was Professor Martin Dickson of Princeton, who

taught us about the Sufi tradition in Islam—poets and philosophers who used hashish and opium to produce visionary experiences and to discover God within. During his visits to Teheran Professor Dickson took psychedelic drugs with Iranian scholars and with Rudolph Gelpke, a Swiss practitioner who had written classic translations of Persian poetry. Gelpke was a member of that group of Swiss and German scholars who took LSD regularly with Albert Hofmann and Ernst Junger (Junger's writings from the 1930s, which glorified discipline and warfare, influenced Adolph Hitler. After taking LSD Junger renounced Nazism and published mystical essays about human brotherhood and peace).

According to Professor Dickson the European LSD group believed that the visionary drug experience should be kept from the middle-class. Hofmann in particular was concerned that LSD might fall in the hands of those who would use it for recreation and personal growth. Dickson explained to Gelpke and Hofmann that the populist traditions of America made it unlikely that anything with LSD's potentials could be restricted to an elite group of scholars.

Chapter Twenty-Four

1. Many older patients, chronically disabled by diseases of senility, leaped from beds and wheelchairs after a shot of energizer and ran around cheerfully with a new burst of youth. Among all age groups such jolts of instant pleasure eliminated temporarily the epidemic symptoms of boredom and depression. Combined with positive suggestion and appropriate treatment for any physical pathology such treatment did raise self-esteem and provide the pep plus the courage to make life changes. Since a high percentage of medical complaints are psychosomatic, resistant to and even wasteful of conventional treatment methods, the temptation to use a medication that immediately made the patient feel better was hard to resist for many physicians.

Another interesting aspect of the treatment was the factor of self-administration. Many feel-good doctors would prepare monthly amounts of the medication and write prescriptions for disposable needles. Patients could then operate as their own doctors or play doctor for friends. Overdosing and hair-raising hallucinations were inevitable side effects.

2. People have often asked, where the money came from to finance Millbrook and these round-the-world adventures. We asked ourselves this question every week. Richard Alpert and I had small retirement pensions from Harvard, supplemented by speaker's fees as we raced around the Northeast giving lectures at colleges. Short-time visitors to Millbrook would often make contributions. Small royalties came from books we wrote. Nanette, a successful model, paid for her own trip around the world.

During this time we all learned an emancipating lesson. It *was* possible to live as freelance searchers,

no longer addicted to or even dependent on salaries doled out by institutions. We were cleansed of that terror that haunted most of our colleagues: what if I displeased the boss and were cut off from my monthly paycheck? This freedom tends to encourage the independence of thought that is so helpful to full-time philosophers.

3. The twenty-four stages of human evolution.

1. Shortly after birth the suckling reflex is bonded to a mothering stimulus. The suckling object must be there and the sucking imprint made, or the child perishes. The nature of the suckling environment is critical and of lifelong import. If it is secure, calm, stimulating, then the basic imprint is trustful. If the nurturing environment is rough, impersonal, depriving, then a suspicious and fearful perception reality results.

2. The swimming reflex is activated in early infancy. Children who are exposed to water and encouraged to swim before the first year imprint lifelong skills and confidence.

3. The crawling reflex is the first exposure of the DNA-designed neural equipment to the surface of the planet. New circuits must be turned on and a new reality created. An encouraging stimulating environment at this moment obviously launches the child on the life-voyage with confidence.

4-6. Mastery of gravity comes next. Toddling (4), walking-running (5), and climbing (6) reflexes access three neural circuits that will monitor future bodily movement styles. Here again the environment, both human and geographical, is of crucial importance. Kids who grow up in a cramped urban apartment with fearful clumsy parents and domineering siblings will develop a psychomotor style very different from kids who are encouraged to master gravity and mobility in an open confidence-giving atmosphere.

7-9. The acquisition of language (7) happens when the appropriate circuits of the brain kick into operation. It is well known that kids quickly, almost magically, absorb languages, with a facility that most adults cannot approach. This is a classic illustration of the power of an imprint (sudden absorption of learning) compared to conditioned reward-punishment learning. Kids who are exposed to verbal symbols in a context of encouragement, variety, and simulation are going to grow up verbally smart. Kids whose linguistic environment is limited or discouraging will be verbally handicapped all of their lives. Symbol inventiveness (8) and social cooperation (9)—membership in clubs, gangs, cliques—occur during pre-adolescence. Here again the nature of the surroundings is vital. If the child of ten or twelve is deprived of peer contact, the basic social reflexes are thwarted.

10. The awakening of sexuality, a stage of acute and life-determining sensitivity.

11. The parenting stage is less well understood. For the female pregnancy (and for the male visual contact with the offspring) accesses a new brain circuit. The metamorphosis from adolescent barbarianism to parental domestication is so profound as to warrant comparison with the jump from caterpillar to butterfly.

12. The final larval stage of the human lifestyle is post-menopausal. The aging person uses neural circuits very differently from the teenage and mature person, being concerned now with security, continuity, avoidance of novelty, law-and-order.

The next twelve stages of evolution occur after the individual (eventually the species) transcends the twelve primitive survival-related imprints and starts to learn the *neuro-technology of self*.

The first twelve stages define what is usually called *human nature*. I suggest that these later twelve stages or metamorphoses (in which the individual is freed from rigid attachments to social, political, familial, sexual, semantic, emotional, and physiological habits) be called *humanist* or *meta-human*. Is it not deplorable that the English language does not have a vocabulary to describe the future stages that await us as individuals and as a species?

With much hesitation and wary caution I shall now list one version of the *humanist* stages of future evolution:

MASTERY OF THE BODY AS ESTHETIC INSTRUMENT

13. *Hedonist:* esthetic-erotic-somatic awareness; receptive, passive, consumer approach to body.

14. *Artist:* esthetic-erotic-somatic engineering; active, innovative sensory invention.

15. *Esthetic Fusion:* esthetic-erotic-somatic linkage with other artists; life as art.

MASTERY OF COMPUTER–BRAIN OPERATIONS

16. *Multiple-Reality Consumer:* electronic-computer-psychedelic awareness; enjoyment of relativistic brain functions and neuro-electric patterning (e.g., video games).

17. *Neurological Engineering:* electronic-psychedelic reality invention; computer programming.

18. *Multiple-Reality Networking:* inter-computer linkage; telepathy?

MASTERY OF CNS/RNA–DNA, GAIA THEORY, AND SOCIO-BIOLOGY

19. *Genetic Consumer:* Socio-biological awareness; uni-cellular consciousness; receptive, passive enjoyment of DNA-knowledge; cloning, breeding.

20. *Genetic Engineer:* DNA-inventiveness; genetic creativity, life-extension.

21. *Symbiosis:* inter-species linkage; antigen-immunological cooperation. Participation in Gaia intelligence.

22. *Awareness of Meta-Physiological (Out-of-Body) Intelligence:* nuclear-particle awareness;

MASTERY OF META-PHYSIOLOGICAL PROCESSES AND NEURO–PHYSICS

physics-consciousness (e.g., Frijas Capra; ability to "think" like nuclear/atomic particles).

23. *Neuro-Physicist:* mastery of nuclear and gravitational processes and Out-Of-Body experiences. John Lilly's solid-state intelligence?

24. *Meta-Physiological Fusion:* Out-Of-Body linkage with other O-O-B entities.

This listing of possible future levels of human intelligence is necessarily tentative, suggestive, semantically fragile, and intellectually risky. (Earlier speculations on the subjects were published in my books *Neurologic, Exo-psychology,* and *The Game of Life.*) However theoretical, these probes are of the utmost importance for our species. We cannot activate the future circuits of our CNS/RNA-DNA systems until we start developing a new language for it.

Chapter Twenty-Five

1. If this little story about meeting the wild-eyed time-traveler on the other side of the Ganges seems inconclusive and unfinished, it is because the event was exactly that—inconclusive and unfinished.

2. This "translation" from the Tao Te Ching, published as Psychedelic Prayers, has appeared in more than a dozen editions in five languages.

Chapter Twenty-Seven

1. Cord Meyer was born November 9, 1920, nineteen days after the author of this book. After completing St. Paul's-Yale (1942) he volunteered for the U.S. Marines, fought valiantly, and lost an eye during the invasion of Guam. His poetic accounts of his combat experiences made him a wartime celebrity. According to the *Manchester Guardian* "He was a hero to the student generation of the late 1940s."

After his discharge he married Mary Pinchot in April 1945, the same month the author of this book married Marianne Busch. In 1947 Meyer became president of the United World Federalists, a Cold War organization with internationalist ideals and right-wing financing.

In this same period Meyer became involved in forming the American Veterans Committee (AVC). During the first national convention of this liberal veterans' group (which the author attended as an "innocent and gullible" state delegation leader) Meyer spearheaded a highly organized right-wing, anti-red faction that succeeded in capturing control of the organization.

My direct confrontation with Cord Meyer occurred a year later at the second annual convention in Milwaukee. This time, a bit wiser, I came as a member of a faction determined to fend off the left/right wrangling and address the basic issues—membership growth and community activities. At Milwaukee the leadership of our moderate faction was taken over by Michael Straight, at that time publisher of the *New Republic*.

Cord Meyer's account of these events is of interest: "I had some friends in this third caucus and tried to convince them that their compromise position could work out to the advantage of the Communists by splitting the anti-Communist vote. I was to learn only years later that a vocal member of this third force had been a controlled secret agent of the KGB at that time and that this strategy of splitting our ranks had been devised in Moscow."

This familiar "made in Moscow" theme has obsessed Cold-Warriors for three decades. It led directly to Johnson's downfall and Watergate, and was the basis for the attempts by the FBI to get me to testify in the Gray-Miller-Felts case years later.

In October 1951, having finished his work with AVC and the United World Federalists (both organizations soon after inoperative), Cord Meyer joined the CIA. In 1954 he became chief of the International Organizations Division. "In that capacity," Meyer writes in his autobiography, "I became head of one of the major operating divisions of the Directorate of Plans...."

In 1967 articles appeared in *Ramparts* and *The New York Times* alleging that Meyer's organization had covertly financed and infiltrated a number of liberal-scholarly foundations and organizations, such as the NSA. According to Meyer, "Some of this speculation was correct and some was not, but the net effect was to create the impression of a national scandal in which the CIA stood accused of subverting and manipulating for its sinister purposes many of the most respected and liberal private institutions functioning on the American scene."

The subsequent wave of criticism in the press and the academic community fell primarily on Meyer. At the time, according to the *Manchester Guardian*, "Meyer was in line for promotion to the deputy director of plans—'DDP,' the nearest equivalent of James Bond's 'M.' Instead, according to CIA watchers here, he is being promoted to the U.S. Embassy in London. They regard this as a 'kick upstairs.'"

In 1980 Cord Meyer published his autobiography. As a longtime student of multiple realities and author of several publications about intelligence, I was fascinated to learn the title of Meyer's memoirs was *Facing Reality* and that the jacket blurb claims that he "is the only CIA officer to receive its highest award, the Distinguished Intelligence Medal, three times."

Some physicists say that every particle in nature has its counterpart in a mirror universe of antimatter. I have come to understand my political-cultural role more clearly after pondering the eerie series of polarities that have placed me in opposition to Cord

Meyer over a period of 36 years.

Chapter Twenty-Eight

1. One of Gurdjieff's oft-stated aims was "to destroy mercilessly the beliefs and views rooted for centuries in the minds and feelings of man," so as to stimulate new thoughts and perspectives. According to Orage, "It is apparent [when Gurdjieff speaks of himself] that this is not an autobiography in the strict sense of the word. For him the past is not worth recounting except in so far as it can serve as an example. In [his] tale of adventure what he suggests are not models for outward imitation, but a completely new way of facing life, which touches us directly and gives us a foretaste of another order of reality."

Chapter Twenty-Nine

1. G. Gordon Liddy's account of this famous raid in his autobiography *Will* (St. Martin's Press, 1979) contains some of the most poetic police-prose ever penned.

Rumors were rampant at the intersection of Main and Market Streets, Poughkeepsie's Rialto. Local boys and girls had been seen entering and leaving the Hitchcock estate. Fleeting glimpses were reported of persons strolling the grounds nude. To fears of drug-induced dementia were added pot-induced pregnancy. The word was that at Leary's lair the panties were dropping as fast as the acid.

... We planned to wait until the occupants had retired for the evening, at which time we would perform a classic 'no-knock' entry—that is, kick in the front door.

... Charlie (the chief deputy sheriff) didn't have to kick the door in. It was unlocked. Borchers and I started up the stairs, the thundering herd of deputies right behind us. We hadn't cleared more than ten steps before my worst fears were realized. In the light of a hall lamp we saw Leary, Rosemary at his side, descending to meet us.

Rosemary was wearing a diaphanous gown. Leary was wearing a Hathaway shirt. Period. Since the stairs were steep and we were craning our necks upward as Leary bounced downward, our first view of the good doctor was, to say the least, revealing.

There was a brief confrontation on the stairs as we met and Leary quite understandably (and civilly, all things considered) asked whether "... someone would mind, awfully, telling me just what is going on?"...

Leary may have been amused momentarily, but Rosemary was not. She was outraged. We had no sooner arrived in Leary's front room when she spied a deputy leaning over a small, ornate, brass urn sitting on the hearth inside a fireplace. "Don't you dare touch that!" She shouted, rushing across the room towards the offending deputy, "That's my sacrament!"

. . . I looked inside the container. It was nearly filled by a dried ground, vegetable matter that was unmistakably a good grade of marijuana. "Mark it with your initials and the date for identification," I said, "and take it along."

My attention moved from the evidence to Rosemary, who was still, of course, in her diaphanous gown. Furious, breathing deeply, and sputtering, at that range she would have taken J. Edgar Hoover's mind off John Dillinger . . . .

Another deputy . . . . Young, eager, and exceptionally fleet of foot . . . bounded to a top-floor hall where, obedient to the letter of his instructions, he burst through a bedroom door. Landing in the approved pistol-course crouch, massive .357 magnum revolver thrust out before him, he was ready for anything. Well, *almost* anything.

By the light of a single candle flickering from the top of a Coca-Cola bottle, he saw a young man and woman, nude, upon an ancient mat. She was on her back. He was at his apogee, about to plunge to her perigee, when the officer shouted: FREEZE!

For one stunned moment, the man hung there, suspended as the forces of Eros did battle with those of Smith and Wesson. Smith and Wesson won.

"You're . . . *you're kidding!*" The wretch squeaked. Then, eyes fixed in horror upon the muzzle of the huge handgun, to the complete dismay of the poor girl beneath him, instead of coming, he went.

Chapter Thirty

1. *Luce and His Empire, A Biography,* by W. A. Swangerg (Scribners, 1975), gives this account of the genesis of the *Life* article:

Well before the hallucinogenic drug LSD hit the headlines, Luce was interested. One Luce house guest was Dr. Sidney Cohen of Los Angeles, who had been studying the effect of LSD on actors and other creative people. The Luces took a "trip" under Cohen's guidance. Clare reported an enhanced appreciation of colors in her paintings, while the tone-deaf Luce heard music so bewitching that he walked out into the cactus garden and conducted a phantom orchestra. He also discovered that ordinary objects such as tableware took on new dimensions of beauty. Although the Luces apparently repeated the experiment several times later, they were fortunate in having had no bad trips. Luce in fact was so impressed that he turned up in New York to present the managing editors of Time, Life and Fortune with copies of a book on psychedelic drugs along with an enthusiastic talk about the subject's story possibilities—a suggestion quickly adopted by Time and Life, the latter being the first "family" magazine to cover it.

Chapter Thirty-Two

1. G. Gordon Liddy went to the White House as a drug expert, on the basis of having run me out of Dutchess County. He then proceeded to initiate three programs which virtually guaranteed his promotion to the role of mastermind of the Watergate break-in: he engineered Operation Intercept, which sealed off the major Mexican-border entry points, causing enormous economic disruption and compelling the Mexican government to use the military force against their own peasant farmers; he wrote the memo that set up the Drug Enforcement Agency, arguably the most Un-American organization in the history of our country; and he originated the idea of spraying marijuana with paraquat, a remarkable attempt to use chemical warfare on American citizens.

2. Many people have sought to read cosmic significance into these lyrics. In a *Rolling Stone* interview Ray Thomas, who wrote the song, said: "The only person I ever met who really knew what I was saying in that song was Timothy Leary himself. I was taking the piss out of him, ribbing him in that song. I saw the 'astral plane' as some gaily painted little biplane: you pay your two bucks, and he'll take you around the bay for a little flight. Tim laughed about it, I laughed about it, but everybody else sat around saying 'Oh man, that's so heavy.' "

Chapter Thirty-Three

1. My gubernatorial campaign album was released by Alan Douglas Records, 1970. The fold-out cover featured collage-style images of the author swathed in patriotic symbols of various colors, mainly red, white, and blue.

2. Seven months after our visit with John and Yoko, while sitting in my prison cell, I was astonished to hear the local rock station play a new song by the Beatles entitled "Come Together." Although the new version was certainly a musical and lyrical improvement on my campaign song, I was a bit miffed that Lennon had passed me over this way. (I must explain that even the most good-natured persons tend to be a bit touchy about social neglect while in prison.) When I sent a mild protest to John, he replied with typical Lennon charm and wit: that he was a tailor and I was a customer who had ordered a suit and never returned. So he sold it to someone else.

Lennon presented his version of this misunderstanding in the final *Playboy* interviews, which were so poignantly prophetic of his own sudden mortality.

During my exile years John and Yoko always remained most generous and supportive. They sent a sum of money ($5000?) through the Weathermen lawyers. The fact that I never got the money wasn't their fault.

Chapter Thirty-Five

1. Ambivalence and confusion in the Arab press about the reasons for my exile and about my politics continued. Even the CIA, which should have known better, began to have second thoughts about me, as can be seen in this report on our visit to Jordan to meet Jean Genet.

CENTRAL INTELLIGENCE AGENCY

CONFIDENTIAL

TO: Department of State

Info: ALGIERS, AMMAN, TEL AVIV, JERUSALEM

FROM: Amembassy BEIRUT

DATE: October 30, 1970

SUBJECT: Beirut Visit of Leary Group

REF: Beirut 9363 (NOTAL)

SUMMARY. Considerable variation was seen in the Beirut press versions of the Leary group visit. A number of leftist papers claimed the group would meet with Palestinians and emphasized the political implications of the visit, while several conservative papers played up Leary's notoriety as a drug cultist and his attempt to conceal his identity. Despite reported Palestinian denials, we are inclined to believe tentative arrangements had in fact been made for the group to contact the fedayeen. END SUMMARY

A number of leftist papers October 26 and 27 (including pro-UAR *al Anwar* and *al Muharrir* and pro-Iraqi *al Kifah*) identified Leary in their headlines as a "leftist political leader" and claimed that he had come to visit Palestinian bases in Lebanon and Jordan in order to "study the methods and experience of the fedayeen for possible application in the U.S." *Anwar,* in one of more detailed articles, referred to Leary's recent association with the Black Panthers and to the Panthers' connections with the fedayeen . . . . The only reference to Leary's involvement with drugs was the statement, buried in the article, that the U.S. had lodged "false" narcotics charges against him. No mention was made of Leary's apparent attempt to use an assumed identity in Beirut.

By contrast, the conservative *L'Orient* and *Le Jour* and independent *an Nahar* carried feature-type, sometimes humorous articles, calling Leary "the high priest of LSD" and "grand panjandrum of hallucination" . . . . In those papers, however, the press conference was overshadowed by reports on Leary's assumed identity, his attempts to avoid detection, and the Keystone Cops-style pursuit of him by newsmen.

The October 28 press reported the departure of the group for Cairo the previous day at the alleged behest of the Lebanese government, and reported that Syria and Jordan had refused to admit them. Here, too, press treatment differed, with *Anwar* exclaiming pettishly that U.S. leftists had been deported by the new "government of youth," while the conservative, pro-

Saudi *al Hayat* reported that the Lebanese had "recommended" that the group leave "in the interest of maintaining friendly ties with the U.S."

2. CENTRAL INTELLIGENCE AGENCY

TO: Department of State

FROM: Amembassy London

DATE: May 7, 1971

SUBJECT: Daily Telegraph Looks at Revolutionists in Algiers

REF:

We have attached to this airgram two excerpts from the Daily Telegraph Magazine of May 7, 1971 . . . . The main story is a rather cursory view of various revolutionary groups in Algiers . . . . The story carries a banner saying, "What Switzerland has become for celebrities and Lichtenstein for company promoters, Algiers is now for revolutionaries . . . ."

[attached excerpt from *Daily Telegraph*]

Thirteen liberation groups are now officially recognised by the Algerian government, and are being given help and financial assistance to maintain their offices in Algiers. In many respects these bureaux function like unofficial embassies, representing their people, disseminating information and helping to form political alliances. They even have some straight diplomatic functions: a South African wishing to visit Algeria, for instance, needs a visa. He must apply for it to the Algiers office of ANC—the African National Congress—an illegal revolutionary organisation in his country.

Algiers is, in fact, the centre of a counter-diplomatic front, where the British Embassy is on a not greatly different footing from the representatives of El Fatah, or the Vietcong, or for that matter the Black Panthers, and where, in a wonderful, mind-blowing sense, Eldridge Cleaver is Ambassador of the United States.

. . . And besides the (13) liberation groups with official offices there are numerous individuals who have sought political asylum in Algeria—including some members of the Canadian FLQ, the Brazilian political prisoners and, of course, Dr. Timothy Leary, sprung from an American jail by the Weathermen and now living in an Algiers flat with his wife Rosemary.

3. CENTRAL INTELLIGENCE AGENCY

DEPARTMENT OF STATE

C O N F I D E N T I A L ALGIERS 091

REF: ALGIERS 087 (NOTAL)

SUBJECT: LEARY

1. SINCE HIGH POINT FOREIGN PRESS INTEREST IN [deletion] LEARY DURING NOVEMBER AND EARLY DECEMBER THERE

HAS BEEN APPARENT SLUMP IN THEIR FOR-
TUNES, PERHAPS DUE TO A NUMBER OF
FACTORS INCLUDING REACTION FROM
OVERPLAY OF PREVIOUS PERIOD, AND AD-
VICE FROM GOA [government of Ameri-
ca] . . . . MEANWHILE LEARY AND WIFE
HAVE FOUND AN APARTMENT BUT ARE
EVEN MORE CUT OFF THAN PREVIOUSLY
FROM THOSE WHO MIGHT TRY TO SEE
THEM (RECENTLY INCLUDING TWO WRIT-
ERS FROM ESQUIRE). OUR SOURCE BE-
LIEVES LEARY'S DAYS IN ALGIERS MAY BE
NUMBERED THOUGH THERE IS NO SUGGES-
TION WHERE HE WOULD GO FROM HERE.

4.   GP-3.

EAGLETON

CONFIDENTIAL

(CENTRAL INTELLIGENCE AGENCY)
DEPARTMENT OF STATE TELEGRAM

LIMITED OFFICIAL USE   HCN270
PAGE 01 ROME 03110 171238Z

SUBJECT: EXTRADITION – TIMOTHY LEARY

REF: STATE 084275

1. NO TRACE OF LEARY IN ROME. EM-
BASSY DID NOT CONFIRM HIS ARRIVAL
HERE AS STATED REFTEL AND REGRETS
THIS APPARENT MISUNDERSTANDING IN
PFUND/HUMMEL TELECON.

2. EMBASSY OFFICERS COVERED AIRPORT
AND CHECKED PLANE WITH COOPERATION
ITALIAN POLICE. LEARY NOT LISTED ON
MANIFEST AND NO PERSON EVEN RE-
MOTELY RESEMBLING HIM WAS EITHER IN
TRANSIT OR BOARDED PLANE. SUBJECT
NOT AMONG VISITORS OR PASSENGERS
OTHER LINES. MARTIN

LIMITED OFFICIAL USE

Chapter Thirty-Six

1.   DEPARTMENT OF STATE TELEGRAM

LIMITED OFFICIAL USE
PAGE 01 COPENH 01924 131623Z

REF: STATE 079784 AND 18 AND 081390

SUBJ: TIMOTHY LEARY

1. LEARY'S PLANNED VISIT TO DENMARK
AND SUBSEQUENT DISAPPEARANCE EN-
ROUTE HAS RECEIVED WIDESPREAD

DANISH PRESS PLAY. LEARY INVITED BY
STUDENT UNION OF AARHUS UNIVERSITY
TO DELIVER LECTURE ENTITLED "THE 7
REVOLUTIONS" [Correct title was "The Eight Rev-
olutions." . . . .]

COMMENT: WOULD APPEAR LEARY EITHER
PLANNED TO TRAVEL TO DENMARK ON PPT
K258108 TAKING CHANCES DANES WOULD
NOT REACT TO ANTICIPATED PRIOR NOTIFI-
CATION THIS PASSPORT REVOKED, OR, AS
APPEARS MORE LIKELY, HE NEVER REALLY
PLANNED COME TO DENMARK. DIFFICULT
TO BELIEVE HE WOULD HAVE TAKEN
CHANCE TRAVELING TO DENMARK ON
MCNELLIS PASSPORT TO MAKE PUBLIC AP-
PEARANCE AS TIMOTHY LEARY.

2. Hofmann's account of this meeting appears in
LSD: My Problem Child (Tarcher, 1983):

On 3 September 1971, I met Dr. Leary in the railway station snack bar in Lausanne. The greeting
was cordial, a symbol of our fateful relationship
through LSD. Leary was medium-sized, slender, re-
siliently active, his brown face surrounded with
slightly curly hair mixed with gray, youthful, with
bright, laughing eyes. This gave Leary somewhat
the mark of a tennis champion rather than that of
a former Harvard lecturer. We traveled by automobile to Buchillons, where in the arbor of the
restaurant A la Grande Forêt, over a meal of fish
and a glass of white wine, the dialogue between
the father and the apostle of LSD finally
began . . . .
   My impression of Dr. Leary in this personal
meeting was that of a charming personage, convinced of his mission, who defended his opinions
with humor yet uncompromisingly; a man who
truly soared high in the clouds pervaded by beliefs
in the wondrous effects of psychedelic drugs and
the optimism resulting therefrom, and thus a man
who tended to underrate or completely overlook
practical difficulties, unpleasant facts, and dangers.
Leary also showed carelessness regarding charges
and dangers that concerned his own person, as his
further path in life emphatically showed.

3.   529984 Limited Official Use   A-19

TO: DEPARTMENT OF STATE
FROM: AMEMBASSY BERN

SUBJECT: EXTRADITION - TIMOTHY LEARY

REF: BERN'S 3216, 3221, AND 3222 OF DE-
CEMBER 29, 1971

Attached herewith as an unclarified enclosure is an
informal translation of a detailed statement concerning the asylum and extradition decisions in the Leary
case. This statement was released by the (Swiss) Department of Justice and Police on December 29,
1971.

THE DIVISION OF POLICE

FEDERAL DEPARTMENT OF JUSTICE AND POLICE

In connection with the request for asylum and extradition of the U.S. citizen Timothy Leary . . . it is noted . . . the sentence to which Leary was convicted in the United States was considered as excessively exaggerated in accordance with our practice. While the Federal Law on Narcotics dated Oct 3 1951 calls for a maximum punishment of 2 years detention for regular cases, and only in cases of intent to profit and in severe cases is a sentence of up to five years possible, the American courts apparently sentenced Leary for the possession of a minimum quantity of marijuana to an excessive period of imprisonment. In addition Timothy Leary contrary to existing procedures was consistently refused a provisional release from imprisonment on bail pending the duration of appeal proceedings . . . . The motive for this state intervention was said to be purely of a political nature. These proceedings against Leary could be considered as pretenses, as means to reach the anticipated political goal. Timothy Leary was apparently not only a scientist in the field of modern psychological research. He is said to have developed also an intensive political activity and in March, 1970 applied in the primary election as the Democratic candidate for Governor of the State of California. The reason for his arrest was said to have been to render him harmless as a political candidate. For the authorities he was said to have become politically unbearable, because as an adherent of the peace movement, he had requested the termination of the war in Vietnam. In connection with this, it should also be considered that Timothy Leary had many followers not only among the Weathermen, the underground of the white people, but also among the Black Panthers, the underground movement of the black people.

. . .[I]t was an obligation of our country to grant asylum if the petitioner, for reasons as above-mentioned, would be persecuted in another country to which he could only return. It was repeatedly pointed out that with the imprisonment at that time and the later conviction a political goal was desired. It was said not to be the intention to punish Leary for a specific act. The main point was to get a hold of a person, whose crime was said to be his views. The action against and the excessive punishment of Timothy Leary, as it was also confirmed by well-known U.S. citizens, would break all norms and customs . . . .

Furthermore, Leary could not be declared to be unworthy of asylum, because of his academic opinions in connection with drugs. Although these academic opinions were controversial, they could not be considered absurd or dangerous. It remains open whether these opinions would later become a recognized science . . . .

Division of Police of the
Federal Department of
Justice and Police

signed: Mumenthaler

Chapter Thirty-Seven

1. One night after skiing eight hours I lay in front of my chalet fireplace and developed the Evolutionary Quotient—the number of mailing addresses divided by chronological age. I counted up fifty-three homes in my fifty years of life.

E.Q., Timothy Leary: 53 homes/50 years = 1.06
E.Q., Average American: 10 homes/40 years = .25
E.Q., Aunt Mae: 01 homes/80 years = .01

This scale did not take account of brain-changes: the 300 M.G. sessions, 300 re-imprints, 300 reality shifts. However, it did give an indication that I had blasted beyond the gravitational pull of the past and into a post-terrestrial relativistic lifestyle, light-years away from the normal pattern of human life—friends who work together, join the same clubs, see each other regularly on Wednesday nights and Sunday afternoons. I had become a space/time traveler, at home nowhere, at home everywhere.

2. In itself heroin is just one more addictive depressant. Because of the mystique it has become glamorized and has become difficult and expensive to obtain. The user is addicted not only to the drug but also to the ritual of procurement. In many cases scoring is a demanding all-day adventure for people who are otherwise bored or frustrated in life. In lectures and writings I have always criticized heroin as a drug to be avoided by intelligent life-loving people. At the same time I have energetically opposed the laws against it. There is considerable evidence, both from history and current experiments in England, that heroin addicts can maintain normal living and work patterns as long as they do not have to spend all their time scoring. The paradox of heroin is that junkies are usually law-abiding docile citizens as long as their supply is assured.

3.   CENTRAL INTELLIGENCE AGENCY
       DEPARTMENT OF STATE

CONFIDENTIAL BERN 0324

SUBJECT: EXTRADITION – TIMOTHY LEARY

REF: STATE 019453; BERN 0306

EMBASSY CONVINCED THAT PASSPORT REVOCATION COULD HAVE EFFECT OF FORCING SWISS ALLOW LEARY REMAIN SWITZERLAND.

WE KNOW LEARY WANTS REMAIN SWITZERLAND AND HIS ATTORNEY IS USING EVERY RESOURCE TRY OBTAIN SWISS RESIDENCE FOR LEARY. REVOCATION PASSPORT WOULD ALLOW ATTORNEY TURN OVER PASSPORT TO EMBASSY AND APPEAL ANY FEDERAL OR CANTONAL DEPARTURE ORDER ON GROUNDS LEARY ESSENTIALLY STATELESS. HE WOULD ALSO TAKE MATTER TO SWISS PRESS . . . .

WITHOUT VALID TRAVEL DOCUMENT AND
WITH LEARY'S REPUTATION, OTHER COUN-
TRIES MIGHT WELL REFUSE ALLOW HIM
ENTRY. WE KNOW FROM PREVIOUS EXPERI-
ENCE SWISS HOLD THEY CAN NOT FORCE
A PERSON RETURN TO COUNTRY WHERE
HE FACES CERTAIN ARREST . . . .

EMBASSY RECOMMENDS THAT RESTRIC-
TIVE PASSPORT ACTION NOT RPT NOT BE
TAKEN WHILE LEARY IN SWITZERLAND.

4. During the Time of Excitement (1966–1972) I was
often described as the Pied Piper of the Youth Culture. To find out how I was being defined, I consulted
Webster's Collegiate Dictionary (1981 edition) and was
distressed to discover that I was: "1: One that offers
strong but delusive enticement. 2: a leader who makes
irresponsible promises."

Somewhat shaken I then checked with the American Heritage and found that I was: "A piper who rid
the town of Hamelin of its rats by piping. When refused due payment, he led away the children of the
town."

After reading the story of the Pied Piper as told
by Goethe, Robert Browning, and the Brothers
Grimm I realized that the Webster's version was a
blatant attempt to rewrite history, defending Hamelin
business interests at the expense of the noble Piper.

After learning that paedomorphosis (mutation or
metamorphosis of the juvenile members of a species)
is the standard tactic in evolution I came to understand the pervasive importance of the Pied Piper
myth.

5.   (CENTRAL INTELLIGENCE FILES)

NNNNVV EIB 76 IL AN5 95
TO RUEHC/SECSTATE WASHD C 72 78

SUBJ: TIMOTHY LEARY

VIENNA MORNING PAPER REPORTS "DRUG
PROFESSOR" TIMOTHY LEARY IN AUSTRIA:
ONE PAPER REPORTED HE IS IN VIENNA.

AUSTRIAN NARCOTICS OFFICIALS UNDER-
STOOD TO BE LOOKING FOR SUBJECT AND
INDICATED TO EMBASSY THEY PREPARED
TO DETAIN HIM FOR EXTRADITION IF IT IS
LIKELY REQUEST FOR SAME WOULD BE
FORTHCOMING. EMBASSY MADE NO COM-
MITMENT BUT ACKNOWLEDGED THAT HE
IS WANTED IN U.S. GIS.MOW INCKEL BT

REF: BERN 2957; VIENNA 0087

6. In August of 1982, during the meetings of the
Europe Humanist Psychology Association at Wil-
lingen, Germany, I had the pleasure of meeting
Count Arnold Keyserling, a distinguished philosopher
who had worked with other Austrian scientists and
intellectuals behind scenes to protect me in Vienna.
Count Keyserling spoke several times to Chancellor
Kreisky about my receiving asylum in Austria.
Keyserling told me that in spite of considerable pres-

sure from the American government and from Austria's drug-police, Chancellor Kreisky stood firm to
protect me from extradition.

7. (CENTRAL INTELLIGENCE AGENCY FILES)

DEPARTMENT OF STATE TELEGRAM

ANKARA FOR BNDD RD BRIGGS FROM SAIC
BURKE

TIMOTHY FRANCIS LEARY ARRIVED KABUL
1/14/73 FROM VIENNA VIA BEIRUT AND
TEHERAN. AFGHAN OFFICIALS COOPER-
ATED WITH EMBOFFS, WHO HAD BEEN
ALERTED TO ARRIVAL BY AND HAVE PLACED
LEARY AND COMPANION UNDER POLICE
GUARD AT LOCAL HOTEL.

LEARY CARRIED VALID US PPT K2581808
UNDER TRUE NAME.

INITIAL REACTION OF AFGHAN OFFICIALS
INDICATE THEY MIGHT BE WILLING EITHER
TO EXTRADITE LEARY IF SO REQUESTED BY
USG OR DECLARE HIM UNDESIRABLY ALIEN
AND EXPEL FROM COUNTRY. TO OUR
KNOWLEDGE NO US-AFGHAN EXTRADITION
TREATY IN FORCE . . . .

LEARY ARRIVAL KNOWN TO AFGHAN PRESS
AND LARGE HIPPIE COMMUNITY. POSES PO-
TENTIAL PROBLEM. GDS.

NEUMANN
ADD STATE 008910

FYI: WASHINGTON AP CORRESPONDENT
LEWIS GULICK INQUIRED RE LEARY CASE
TODAY. GULICK HAD MOST OF BASIC IN-
FORMATION INCLUDING POSSIBILITY FOR
WHAT HE CALLED "UNOFFICIAL EXTRADI-
TION," AS IN LANSKY CASE. LIKLIHOOD AP
WILL RUN STORY WITHIN NEXT 24 HOURS.
END FYI. ROGERS.

8. CENTRAL INTELLIGENCE AGENCY FILES

DEPARTMENT OF STATE

CONFIDENTIAL 2nd57

Page Ok LONDON 00649

SUBJECT: TIMOTHY FRANCIS LEARY

. . . MET LEARY'S AIRCRAFT FROM FRANK-
FURT, ACCOMPANIED BY UK IMMIGRATION
OFFICER AND SPECIAL BRANCH AGENT
WHO ESCORTED LEARY TO LONDON AIR-
PORT IMMIGRATION OFFICE. LEARY AT
FIRST COMPLAINED USG HAD "KIDNAPPED"
HIM AND TAKEN AWAY HIS PASSPORT. DE-
SPITE ASSURANCE CONTAINED IN TEHRAN
REFTEL, LEARY REQUESTED POLITICAL
ASYLUM FROM UKG . . . . FOLLOWING CON-
SULTATIONS WITH HOME OFFICE HEAD-
QUARTERS, IMMIGRATION OFFICER IN-

FORMED LEARY UKG COULD NOT HONOR HIS REQUEST FOR ASYLUM SINCE HE IS NOT CONSIDERED A POLITICAL REFUGEE. SUBJECT THEN REQUESTED PERMISSION TO FLY TO ALGERIA, AUSTRIA OR SWITZERLAND SINCE THOSE COUNTRIES MAY REACT FAVORABLY TOWARD HIS REQUEST FOR ASYLUM. THIS REQUEST WAS DENIED, AGAINST FOLLOWING CONSULTATIONS WITH HOME OFFICE, AND LEARY DOCILELY BOARDED AIRCRAFT.

CONFIDENTIAL

PRESS APPARENTLY HAD BEEN ALERTED TO LEARY'S ARRIVAL BY TELEPHONE CALL FROM FRANKFORT, PRESUMABLY BY [name deleted]. PHOTOGRAPHERS WERE WAITING IN AIRPORT CORRIDORS AT TIME OF ARRIVAL. IN ADDITION, SOME OF LEARY'S DISCIPLES AND SUPPORTERS HAD BEGUN CAMPAIGN HEADED BY JANE [sic] HARCOURT-SMITH, TO ELICIT SUPPORT FROM VARIOUS LIBERAL M.P.'S AND CIVIL RIGHTS GROUPS TO PRESSURE UKG TO KEEP LEARY IN BRITAIN. NUMEROUS CALLS RECEIVED BY VARIOUS EMBOFFS AND NOON EDITIONS LONDON PRESS LEARY STORY. AFGHANISTAN COUNSELLOR CALLED EMBASSY AND ADVISED HE BEING INUNDATED BY CALLS FROM PRESS AND SEEKED OUR ADVICE AND GUIDANCE. WE SUGGESTED HE MAY WISH TO STATE THAT HE KNEW NOTHING ABOUT CASE AND HE WOULD REFER REPORTERS' QUESTION TO HIS GOVERNMENT. HE MOST GRATEFUL FOR SUGGESTION—WE HAVE FILLED HIM IN ON EVENTS. THUS ENDS THE CLIFFHANGER'S TAIL. SOHM.

CONFIDENTIAL

DEPARTMENT OF STATE

R 192042Z JAN 73

FROM: SECSTATE WASHDC

TO AMEMBASSY KABUL

SUBJECT: TIMOTHY LEARY

AS YOU KNOW BY NOW LEARY HAS BEEN TAKEN INTO CUSTODY IN LOS ANGELES. MY CONGRATULATIONS TO EVERYONE IN THE MISSION WHO PLAYED A ROLE IN CARRYING OUT TASK SUCCESSFULLY AND ESPECIALLY TO THOSE WHO THROUGH MONTHS HAVE CAREFULLY LAID GROUNDWORK WHICH RESULTED IN THE EXCEPTIONAL COOPERATION OF RGA IN THIS AFFAIR.

GDS ROGERS

Chapter Thirty-Eight

1. This suit to convert Folsom Prison to a profit-making rehabilitative environment was ultimately thrown out of federal court. Nine years later Chief Justice Warren Burger proposed a similar plan. A bill to change prisons from socialist to capitalist management, introduced in the California legislature, was defeated by opposition from right-wing and labor lobbies. Apparently "crime must pay" is another idea whose time has not yet come.

Chapter Thirty-Nine

1. I have always felt an irritated compassion for narcotics agents, who have been assigned the dirtiest task in American society—the detection and prosecution of those most perplexing "crimes," voluntary alterations of physiological and neurological processes. The ultimate scene of the crime is within the body and the brain of the alleged culprit. The paradox of drug enforcement is this: everyone in the conspiracy of producing and consuming drugs is happy about the enterprise. Many psychologists believe that it is exactly this self-induced happiness that causes the grim disapproval of envious non-users.

Since there is no victim to report a drug crime, the drug police are forced to resort to the most treacherous, unethical, and often unconstitutional tactics—informers, entrapments, illegal surveillance and search, double agents, no-knock invasions of privacy, military force against private citizens, planting of evidence, and epidemic perjury. The real crimes in the area of drug control are committed by the police.

The current ineffective drug laws are an expression of genetic politics—age. Two-thirds of those born after 1946 profess a tolerant opinion, favoring the decriminalization of drugs. The future of drug enforcement is thus easily predicted. By 1988 two-thirds of the electorate will be post-1946. They will decriminalize recreational-psychedelic drugs and encourage research and development of better, safer drugs.

But what will happen to the enormous anti-drug industry? What to do with the armies of agents, customs officials, narcs, informers, public relations people? This swollen bureaucracy now costs the taxpayer several hundred million dollars annually. Can they be trained for productive careers?

2. G. Gordon Liddy's first paper in Bob Dellinger's creative writing class was a description of his raid on Millbrook. Gordon marched to the front, stood tall in West Point posture, and read the piece as though it was a dispatch from headquarters. The unexpected humor of Liddy's version, almost slapstick, met with instant success. A cop with a sense of humor is always a welcome surprise. This article, Liddy's first literary *oeuvre*, was published in *True* magazine. The budding author, thus encouraged, went on to write two

best sellers: *Out of Control* and *Will.* I was interested to note that, once again, I contributed to a new and more profitable career move for my long-time arch-rival.

3. The key issue during my concealment under false identities by the feds (1974–1975) was jurisdiction, i.e., who controlled my body. In order to get me transferred away from the FBI, Joanna and her friends arranged to have me subpoenaed by the Orange County Grand Jury. I was to be asked about the drug habits of a certain Mr. G., formerly a lawyer of mine.

Known far and wide as the doper's pal, a lawyer who cared, Mr. G. was a good-hearted man, famous for his original defense tactics. He really loved his clients and walked around the court room with a be-mused concern on his face, as though unable to un-derstand why anyone would want to put a nice guy like his client in jail. His speeches to juries were so rambling and mellow, so full of chuckling and friend-liness, that his clients were often acquitted by reason of contact high.

One good thing about Mr. G.'s legal practice—he didn't desert you after the trial. When you were locked up in the county jail awaiting sentence, Mr. G. would visit and, to dull the pain of incarceration, would surreptitiously pass along wads of black Afghanistan hashish. One day while I was inspiring him to do something about my case, Mr. G. suddenly shoved a piece of hashish into my hand. We were sitting in full view of the guard. Before it could melt in my sweating hand, I popped the hashish in my mouth. By the end of the visit I was no longer so uptight about the years of prison awaiting me. In fact I was grinning ear to ear because I had such a wonder-ful lawyer.

Mr. G. did have one forgivable flaw. He tended to be indiscreet. Thus it became known to everyone in law enforcement, including the prison officials, that Mr. G. had given me hashish. This incident was cited by the California parole board as a reason for denying me parole.

When subpoenaed before the Orange County Grand Jury I was asked if Mr. G. had ever given me drugs in jail. I told the truth. My reasons: 1. Mr. G. and I both had already been implicated by someone (Mr. G.? The guard? Another client?); 2. There was no way that Mr. G. could be indicted or tried for this action since a drug conviction requires some tangible evidence (the contraband had long since been destroyed by my digestive tract).

At first I was puzzled as to why the narcs were bothering at all with this pointless case. A few days later the motive became clear. Someone in law en-forcement bootlegged a transcript of these secret hear-ings to Jack Anderson. His column, appearing in 400 papers, made it sound as though I was testifying against anyone who had ever offered me a joint. By means of this story someone managed to raise a little beep on paranoia screens everywhere, especially among lawyers involved in the defense of counter-cul-ture people.

Chapter Forty

1. The telling of this story now endangers no one since the entire saga of the two guns, the escape plot, and the Joanna's hideaway apartment in Sacramento was described in a long letter written by Dennis Mar-tino, Joanna's part-time boyfriend, to the DEA, who passed it on to Arthur Van Court, Jerry Utz, and the FBI.

Chapter Forty-One

1. Years later my father- and mother-in-law, Bill and Dorothy Bachman, were standing on a promenade point overlooking San Diego, and they heard a guide explain to a hundred solemn tourists that "the tall brown building is the federal prison, which has held such famous criminals as Patty Hearst and Timothy Leary."

2. O'Neill performed one of the most beneficial favors that a thoughtful human being can for our species—he opened up a new universe of practical probability, inevitability. He demonstrated that this planet Earth, which we thought of as Reality, was really a prison. We can escape! Not to Jehovah's heaven or Allah's pleasure-cloud or Buddha's static stillness within but to the next level of evolution, using off-the-shelf tech-nology.

Habitat determines species behavior. No new games can develop on old turf. In 1963 we Harvard pilgrims were thrown out of four countries as we sought a piece of land to try something new. Now this new frontier is ready to open up. O'Neill's first permanent orbital station could be built thirty years after Apollo, and it would cost less than the Alaska pipeline. It will happen in our lifetime.

Interested readers are referred to O'Neill's *Two Thousand and Eighty-One* and *High Frontier* and to the publications of the L-5 Society (1920 Park Av-enue, Tucson, Arizona).

3. The final FBI request for information came in 1978.

My wife Barbara answered the phone. "Someone named Frankie. He said you'll know who he is. Sounds like he's a dope dealer."

Frankie had started a detective agency in San Diego after his retirement from the Bureau. We chatted about old friends in law enforcement. He wanted to come up and talk about something. I knew what was on his mind. In the newspapers I had been reading about former FBI director Pat Gray and two of his top aides, Felts and Miller, being indicted in connec-tion with burglaries committed in the homes of people known to be friendly with the Weathermen.

The meeting was held at a trendy French restau-rant. Barbara went with me acting as bodyguard. Frankie looked the same—dapper, flashy, the tough guy with a twinkle. After drinks and lunch he came to the point: everyone in the FBI, law enforcement intelligence, and especially the CIA was very upset about the indictments of decent cops, who had just been doing their jobs. National security was the only feasible justification for the break-ins. Would I testify in their trials that the Weathermen had foreign connections, foreign money, foreign advisors?

"Nobody should be prosecuted for political crimes committed during those wild days," I said sympathetically. "The government should give amnesty to everyone. The Weathermen, Liddy, Abbie Hoffman, and your FBI guys. That war ended with Nixon's resignation."

Back at our house I gave Frankie four copies of my book *Neurologic* with cordial inscriptions to Pat Gray, to agents Miller and Felts, and of course to Frankie himself. In Frankie's copy I also marked the chapter containing a fantasized conversation between him and me. It forecast the conversation we'd just had about the pernicious tendency of the FBI to blame wholesome American dissent on foreign agitators.

About a month later a call came from Tom Kennelly, the prestigious Washington lawyer who was defending Felts and Miller. Barbara, hurt by the FBI-inspired accusations that I was an informer, had persuaded me not to testify. I told Kennelly that the flight to LA would be a waste of his time.

He was on his way to the West Coast anyway, so we met at the airport's sky-dome restaurant. Kennelly turned out to be an easy-going savvy guy. I wanted to help but foresaw a problem. I could testify to many circumstantial facts that would make it *sound* as though the Weathermen had had foreign connections, though I knew this was not actually the case. On the other hand I felt that the FBI heavies shouldn't go to jail.

The fact that the FBI had bullied me, ruined my reputation, and endangered my life did not bear on my decision. In professional sports you can't carry grudges. In the NFL (Neurological Football League) grudges are the old game films.

At this point Kennelly reached inside his jacket pocket and held out a subpoena.

"You don't want to subpoena an unfriendly witness, do you, Tom?"

"No, that wouldn't make sense," he said.

"Here's what I suggest. Tell your clients that I could produce, under oath, facts that might help their case. But remember that the prosecution is the Justice Department, and they know more than I do about these matters. I won't lie for you. Talk it over with your team. If you decide that my testimony can keep your guys out of prison, then I will seriously consider testifying."

Kennelly took back the subpoena, and we shook hands.

A couple of weeks later my lawyer, George Milman, learned from Kennelly that I would not be called. Felts and Miller were found guilty of illegal break-ins but received presidential pardons. This pleased me. The rights of citizens against unlawful police entry were sustained, and the cops had been freed.

I was happy that this long cat-and-mouse game with the FBI was finally over and that nobody I was involved with ever went to prison.

Epilogue

1. *New York Magazine,* in a cover story in December 1982, reported that the illegal drug trade in New York alone is estimated to be 45 billion dollars a year, almost twice that of the next largest business—retail trade. Between 100,000 and 300,000 people are believed to be employed in this occupation in this one city. Attorney General William French Smith announced that gross drug sales nationally in 1980 were close to 79 billion dollars, "about equal to the combined profits of America's 500 largest industrial corporations."

2. See next page for chart.

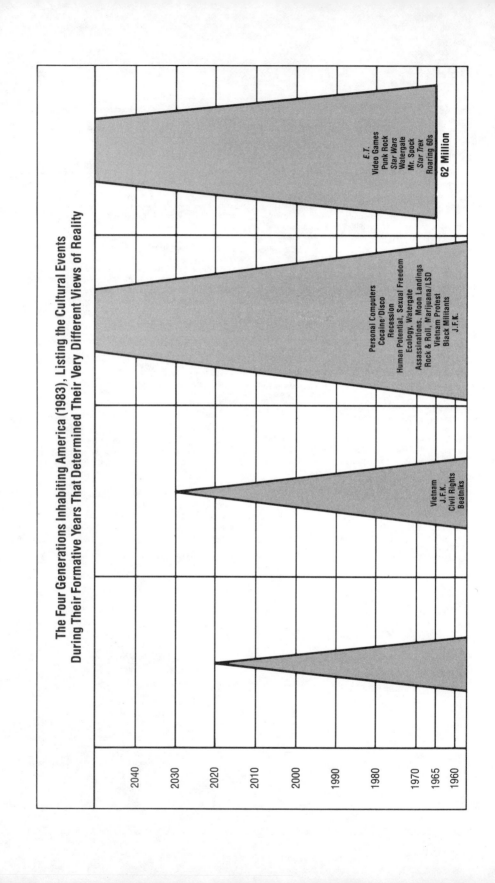

The Four Generations Inhabiting America (1983), Listing the Cultural Events
During Their Formative Years That Determined Their Very Different Views of Reality

Year		Old-Timer Generation	Permissive Parent Generation	Baby-Boom Generation	Whiz-Kid Generation
1950			McCarthy	Elvis Presley	
1946		Cold War	Korean War, TV	TV	
			Dr. Spock	Atom Bomb Drills	
			Hiroshima	Post-War Boom	
1940		World War II	World War II	**76 Million**	
			Big Band Swing		
		Hitler/Churchill	Airplanes		
		Movies	New Deal, Trade Unions		
1930		Depression	Walt Disney		
		Vaudeville	Legal Booze		
		Musical Comedy	Depression		
		Coolidge			
1920		20s Boom	Radio		
		Prohibition	Roaring 20s		
		World War I	**45 Million**		
		Automobiles			
1910		Battleships			
		Horse & Buggy			
		Toy Soldiers			
		Manifest Destiny			
1900		Spanish-American War			
		43 Million			

Old-Timer Generation; basically conservative, nationalistic.

Permissive Parent Generation; basically liberal/global-caring/sharing.

Baby-Boom Generation; basically realistic, self-fulfilling.

Cohort Exemplars: Ronald and Nancy Reagan, Richard and Pat Nixon, MacArthur, Patton, John Wayne, Frank Sinatra.

Cohort Exemplars: Jack, Jacqueline, Bobby, and Teddy Kennedy, Martin Luther King, Ralph Nader, Jane Fonda, Joan Baez, Norman Mailer.

Cohort Exemplars: Steven Spielberg, George Lucas, Jann Wenner, John and Yoko.